THE BIG BOOK OF BIBLE SKITS

104 SERIOUSLY FUNNY BIBLE TEACHING SKITS
BY TOM BOAL

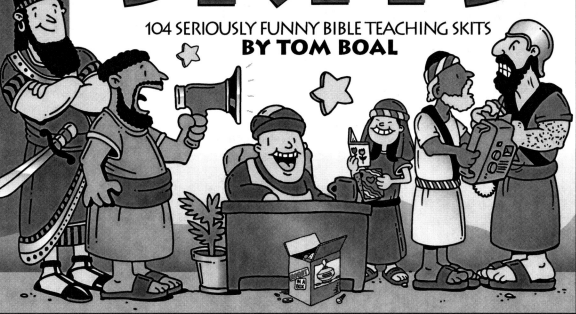

Gospel Light

YOU MAY MAKE COPIES OF THE SKITS IN THIS BOOK IF:

▲ you (or someone in your organization) are the original purchaser;

▲ you are using the copies you make for a noncommercial purpose (such as teaching or promoting a ministry) within your church or organization;

▲ you follow the instructions provided in this book.

HOWEVER, IT IS ILLEGAL FOR YOU TO MAKE COPIES IF:

▲ you are using the material to promote, advertise or sell a product or service other than for ministry fund-raising;

▲ you are using the material in or on a product for sale;

▲ you or your organization are **not** the original purchaser of this book.

By following these guidelines you help us keep our products affordable.

Thank you,

Gospel Light

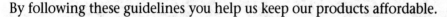

Gospel Light

CONTENTS

INDEXES

ABOUT THE AUTHOR

Tom Boal lives in Leduc, Alberta with his wife, Marilyn, and their two teenage children, Christian and Kelly. Tom writes skits for his fifth and sixth grade Sunday School class as a diversion from his profession of accounting.

EDITORIAL STAFF

Publisher, William T. Greig • **Senior Consulting Publisher,** Dr. Elmer L. Towns • **Publisher, Research, Planning and Development,** Billie Baptiste • **Senior Editor,** Lynnette Pennings, M.A. • **Senior Consulting Editors,** Dr. Gary S. Greig, Wesley Haystead, M.S.Ed. • **Editor, Theological and Biblical Issues,** Bayard Taylor, M.Div. • **Contributing Editors,** Mary Gross, Sheryl Haystead, Linda Mattia, A. Michele Sveiven • **Designer,** Curtis Dawson

Using This Book

BRING BIBLE STORIES TO LIFE!

Drama activities in a classroom are valuable learning opportunities because of the *process* group members experience, not because of the quality of the final performance. Bible stories come alive when acted out, and Bible truth is seen to be relevant when applied to contemporary situations. In addition:

▲ Acting out a situation will push group members to think about the application of Bible truth to a real-life circumstance.

▲ Dramatic activities provide a unique opportunity to briefly step into another person's shoes and experience some of his or her attitudes and feelings.

COPIES OF THE SKITS

Purchase of this book includes the right to make copies of the skits for those who will be involved in putting on the skits.

SKIT FEATURES

The skits contain the following features to help you prepare: **Scripture, suggested topics, Bible background, performance tips, discussion questions, characters list** and a **pronunciation guide** for those tough biblical names. Optional props are often suggested, but any real prop can be replaced by an imaginary one simply by miming accordingly.

CHOOSING A SKIT

The skits may be used in a variety of ways:

▲ to **summarize** a Bible story;

▲ to **illustrate** a concept or topic;

▲ to **introduce** a Bible character;

▲ to **reinforce** a Bible story or life application.

The skits will be enjoyed in a variety of settings by students from **ages 10 through adult**:

▲ Sunday School, churchtime or midweek programs;

▲ large or small groups;

▲ special events.

To help you find a skit that matches a topic or Bible story you will be studying, indexes list:

▲ **Bible characters** (p. 434);

▲ **Scripture references** (p. 440);

▲ **Topics** (p. 444).

GETTING READY

After you've chosen and reproduced copies of the skit for the participants, here are some tips for preparing to lead the group:

▲ Read the Scripture passage. Familiarize yourself with the corresponding Bible story, if applicable.

▲ Read the skit, noting any vocabulary or pronunciation help you will need to give your group.

▲ Adapt the script if needed by reducing or increasing the number of characters, adding a scene, etc.

▲ Take note of the discussion questions. Decide which questions will be most appropriate for your group.

▲ Collect props.

PRACTICAL TIPS

One of the nicest things about skits is that they are easy to prepare. Skits are not big Broadway-type productions. They can be informal and spontaneous. They can be primped and polished to the hilt when the mood strikes. A lot or a little—it all depends on how you want to do it. Here are the basics to go on:

▲ Good acting is a plus, but it's not essential in order to have a positive experience. What is essential is that the lines are heard by the audience. The performers need to speak slowly and clearly—with their mouths directed at the audience.

▲ It is not necessary for performers to memorize the script. Reading works just as well. Provide several highlighter pens for performers to mark their parts. You may give out the script ahead of time for the performer to practice. However, if you hand out the scripts ahead of time, bring extra copies on performance day, because someone will undoubtedly forget his or her copy.

▲ Practicing the skits ahead of time will be most important for younger groups and groups for whom English is a second language.

Using Skits with Poor Readers

If your group includes students with poor reading skills or learning disabilities, or those for whom English is a second language, don't lose heart! With a little planning and some TLC, you can help poor readers gain badly needed confidence and self-esteem and liven up your classroom with Bible skits.

The following list of ideas can be adapted for use in any setting. Choose the techniques that best suit your group and resources.

FOR INFORMAL PRESENTATIONS AND READ-THROUGHS:

▲ Highlight each character's lines on a separate copy of the script and add pronunciation pointers as needed.

▲ Have the entire group read through the skit in pairs or small groups before presenting the skit to the whole group.

▲ Give everyone in the group a script to follow as selected readers read aloud. Receiving information through more than one sense makes the drama more accessible. This technique also assists students who are better visual than aural learners. It can also ease performers' nerves a bit by providing something other than the readers on which to focus.

▲ Use lots of visual aids and props.

▲ If a skit is particularly long or has long speeches, the teacher or leader can summarize a portion of the skit. Never feel obligated to perform a skit in its entirety; use only as much as your group can handle.

Use a "jump-in" technique that gives readers control over how much they want to read: When a volunteer has read as much as he or she wants, another volunteer jumps in and continues reading. Or let each reader choose a helper to consult whenever necessary.

On an overhead projector or chalkboard, post a word bank or key with pronunciations and/or definitions to words the group might have trouble with. Before the group reading, review the words and locate them in the script with the group.

FOR MORE FORMAL PRESENTATIONS AND PERFORMANCES:

▲ Assign a "drama coach" to each reader to provide one-on-one help in interpreting and learning lines. Coaches may be other students or an adult.

▲ The leader may read aloud all character parts before they're assigned. The leader should also discuss the tone of the skit, pronunciation and meaning of difficult words, and make suggestions for changes and word substitutions.

▲ Students practice reading their parts into a cassette recorder. To provide extra help, the leader may record each character part on a separate cassette to distribute to readers. Record each part twice, the first time speaking slowly and distinctly with no dramatic flair, the second time with dramatic flair so students hear how the lines should be delivered.

▲ For struggling readers, write out each sentence on a separate index card; this technique makes the job look smaller, and each line is an accomplishment.

▲ Hand out the script well in advance of the performance date; call and have the student read his or her part to you over the phone to practice.

▲ Give permission to improvise. Students who understand the sense of a speech, and whose verbal skills exceed their reading skills, may communicate better if allowed to paraphrase.

THE SAVIOR

SCRIPTURE: Genesis 3; Isaiah 9:6,7; 53:3-6; Jeremiah 23:5,6; Micah 5:2-4; Romans 5:12,17-19

SUGGESTED TOPICS: The Savior; prophecies about Christ; witnessing; God's plan of salvation

BIBLE BACKGROUND

The history of humanity tells of people living their lives according to their own wisdom and desires, rather than obeying and loving God. As a result, they drove a wedge between themselves and God. Throughout those years, God repeatedly chose men and women to call people back to Himself. Also, He repeatedly promised to send a Savior to reconcile people to Himself.

Who is this Savior? Many expected a political or military leader. Others were sure God would send someone who was part of the established religious order. However, careful study of the prophetic messages clearly shows both the character and the mission of the Savior: He is God in human flesh, God who loves us so much that He willingly took our sin on Himself.

PERFORMANCE TIPS

1. Suggested props: two telephones for Tony and Kelly to use in their conversation. (Adjust opening lines accordingly.)
2. Introduce the skit by asking, "How would you summarize God's plan for the world?" After group responds say, "Compare your answers to those in this skit."

DISCUSSION QUESTIONS

1. What is sin? What has happened in the world because of sin?
2. What sins do you think are most common?
3. People often rate sins: this one isn't too bad, this one is much worse. Do you think God rates different sins? Why or why not?
4. Because of sin, what did God do?
5. Are you a member of God's family? What would you like to know about Jesus, the Savior?

THE SAVIOR

CHARACTERS

KELLY

TONY

KELLY: Hi, Tony. Where are you going?

TONY: Sunday School. Wanna come?

KELLY: No way! I go to school all week. Why would I want to go on Sunday, too?

TONY: Sunday School isn't like regular school, Kelly. We have lots of fun.

KELLY: I doubt it. My mom made me go for years. I hated it.

TONY: Bummer! We do all kinds of interesting stuff and learn fascinating things from the Bible.

KELLY: Oh yeah? Like what?

TONY: Right now we're studying about Jesus.

KELLY: Well then, I sure don't need to go—I know all that stuff. The manger, the shepherds, the wise men, the Cross. I don't need to hear it again.

TONY: OK, smart aleck. If you know it all, then you know when Jesus was first mentioned in the Bible, right?

KELLY: Sure. Let's see...Matthew. That's it. You thought I didn't know, didn't you?

TONY: Yeah, I thought you didn't know. Now I KNOW that you don't know.

KELLY: Oh, yeah? Well if you're so smart, when WAS Jesus first mentioned?

TONY: In Genesis.

KELLY: Yeah, right. This must be some kind of brilliant Sunday School class you go to. Jesus doesn't come around until the New Testament.

TONY: Have you ever heard of Adam and Eve?

KELLY: What is this, kindergarten? Everyone's heard of Adam and Eve.

TONY: Then you remember that God made a perfect world, and He created Adam and Eve to live in it.

KELLY: Yeah. And Eve ate the apple because the snake told her to...

TONY: This would probably go faster if you wouldn't interrupt. Who said Eve ate an apple?

KELLY: Everybody knows Eve ate an apple and then God zapped her for it.

TONY: Well, maybe everybody is wrong. The Bible doesn't say anything about an apple.

KELLY: OK, so maybe it wasn't an apple. Maybe it was a peach. Who cares? The point is, what does that have to do with Jesus?

TONY: It has everything to do with Jesus. Remember that Adam and Eve only had one rule to obey in their perfect world...

KELLY: That doesn't sound perfect to me. Perfect would be NO rules.

TONY: Have you ever tried to play a game where there were no rules?

KELLY: No. Let me think about it. *(Pause.)* If there are no rules, then everyone does what ever he wants to do. That might be pretty confusing.

TONY: All right! You're beginning to get it. So God gave them lots of privileges and one rule: Don't eat the fruit of the tree of knowledge that was in the middle of the garden.

KELLY: This is the part about the snake. You don't really believe that Eve was out talking to a snake, do you? That's just a fairy tale.

TONY: Yes, I do believe it. The Bible says that the snake was Satan in disguise. And Satan told Eve that God made the rule because He was afraid if people ate from that tree, God would have some competition. But that was a lie that Satan told her just to make her sin. Once she and Adam ate the fruit, the world wasn't perfect any more.

KELLY: You told me all this had something to do with Jesus. I haven't heard His name yet.

TONY: I'm almost there. God made plans for correcting the damage that Adam and Eve did. He promised that the seed of woman would bruise the head of the serpent and the serpent would bruise the heel of the woman's seed.

KELLY: So? What's that supposed to mean?

TONY: That's Genesis 3:15. That's God's promise that a Savior would come into the world and Satan would hurt Him a little, but the Savior would destroy Satan. That Savior is Jesus. The name Jesus isn't used, but that's who the passage is talking about.

KELLY: OK. So Jesus is mentioned in Genesis. So what?

TONY: It's not the only time Jesus is mentioned. The Old Testament is filled with references about Him. And it's important, because it shows how much God loves us.

KELLY: Because He's going to send a Savior? Why didn't He just stop Adam and Eve from sinning in the first place?

TONY: If He had stopped Adam and Eve, then we'd be robots, not people. God wants us to do right because we want to, not because He forced us to. So, God not only promised to send us a Savior, but He told us what the Savior would be like, and how we could recognize Him. God sent lots of prophets to tell different things about the promised Savior.

KELLY: You mean like those people on TV who tell what's going to happen next year.

TONY: No, not at all. If God's prophets said that something would happen, it had to happen exactly the way they said. That's how we know we can trust the things they have to say about the future. Do you want to know what the prophets had to say about the Savior?

KELLY: OK, I'm curious. What did they have to say about the Savior?

TONY: Well, God told the prophets whose earthly family the Savior would belong to. Jeremiah prophesied that the Savior would come from the family of King David.

KELLY: That's the guy who killed Goliath, right?

TONY: That's right. Another prophet, Isaiah, told us what some of His titles would be. Isaiah said the Savior would be called Wonderful, Counselor, the Mighty God, the Everlasting Father and the Prince of Peace.

KELLY: I've heard some of those before. What else did the prophets say?

TONY: Another prophet, Micah, told where the Savior would be born. Micah said that even though Bethlehem was one of the smallest places in Judah, God's chosen Savior would be born there.

KELLY: Anything else?

TONY: Yes. In Isaiah, chapter fifty-three, God tells why the Savior is coming.

KELLY: A savior comes to save. You need a whole chapter to say that?

TONY: But remember, God wanted us to know for certain who the Savior would be. God said, through Isaiah, that people are like sheep who go straying off, and God would put all of our wrong on the Savior. The Savior would take the punishment we deserve for the wrong things we've done.

KELLY: But that's not fair! Why would somebody want to be punished for something that somebody else did? I got in trouble at school because someone else was goofing off and the teacher thought it was me. That really made me mad. Why would God make somebody else suffer because I did something wrong? Why doesn't He punish the ones who do wrong and leave the others alone?

TONY: God didn't MAKE anyone suffer for other people's sins. Jesus willingly took the punishment that everyone else deserved. Romans chapter five, says that one man's disobedience made many sinners. Do you know who that's talking about?

KELLY: Adam, I guess. That's when everything stopped being perfect.

TONY: That's right. It also says that by the obedience of one, many shall be made righteous.

KELLY: I guess that's talking about Jesus. But why didn't everyone pay for their own sins? Then Jesus wouldn't have had to die on the cross.

TONY: Because the payment for sin is separation from God, and God wants us to be united with Him, not separated. Because Jesus was perfect, He could pay the price for our sins and only be separated from God the Father for a short time. If we had to pay for our own sins, we would be separated from God forever.

KELLY: But what about people who don't sin? Aren't they being treated unfairly?

TONY: But that's just it! Everybody sins! Sinning doesn't just mean doing horrible things like committing murder. Sinning just means not being perfect. Do you know anybody who is perfect?

KELLY: Well...no.

TONY: OK. So Jesus came to pay the price for the sins of everybody who ever lived and everybody who ever will live. That way, we ALL can have our sins forgiven and be able to live with God forever.

KELLY: I guess maybe I don't know as much as I thought I did. I mean, if Jesus did so much for me, maybe I should learn more about it. Is that invitation still open?

TONY: It sure is.

DEVILS' RETREAT

SCRIPTURE: Genesis 2; 3; 6—8; 37; 45; Exodus 11; 12:31—14; Numbers 14:36-38; Esther; Jeremiah 26; Daniel 3; Matthew 1:18—2:8; Luke 4:1-11

SUGGESTED TOPICS: Salvation; Christian unity; testing the spirits

BIBLE BACKGROUND

Since the beginning of time, Satan has been trying to foil God's plan of a perfect creation. In the Garden of Eden, he deceived Eve into doubting God's word (see Genesis 3:4). All through the ages, Satan and his minions worked behind the scenes. Satan attempted to entice Jesus into compromising His mission and His authority (see Matthew 4:1-11).

Finally, Satan was successful—or so he thought. The Savior was ignominiously hung from a cross, dead at the age of thirty-three. What had God's Chosen One been able to accomplish? At first glance, it would appear that Jesus had been a colossal failure. All but a small handful of His followers had scattered in fear after His arrest and trial. Surely it would not take long for Him to be completely forgotten.

Satan's "victory" was short lived. Throughout His life on earth, Jesus showed us truth about God, relationships with others and love in action. Through His death, He paid the price for our sin. Redemption had become reality. God's promise had been fulfilled. The resurrection of Jesus dramatically shattered Satan's plans.

PERFORMANCE TIPS

1. Suggested props: table and chairs, briefcase for Satan, papers to represent reports, pads and pencils for the demons to take notes, mirror.

2. Satan and his minions are formidable adversaries. Do not portray them as buffoons.

3. Part of the demons' problems result from their inability to support each other. All should nod in agreement when someone else is blamed for failure.

DISCUSSION QUESTIONS

1. How can you be sure Jesus is the promised Savior? What evidence do we have?

2. Satan is out to destroy what Jesus has done. How can we help God's plan of salvation?

3. What things do we do that might contribute more to Satan's plan than to God's plan?

4. Read James 4:7. How can you resist the devil?

DEVILS' RETREAT

CHARACTERS

SATAN
MALEFICENT (mal-EF-ih-sent)
NONSEQUITUR (non-SEK-wih-tur)
TAROT (TARE-oh)
DISGRUNTLE

SATAN: *(Stands.)* Bad evening, cruel ones. I trust your stay here at our retreat has been miserable.

MALEFICENT: It's been ROTTEN. All I could want.

NONSEQUITUR: Couldn't be worse.

TAROT: Disgusting. Bed's far too uncomfortable to sleep.

SATAN: It pleases me to hear it.

DISGRUNTLE: I've got a complaint.

SATAN: Speak.

DISGRUNTLE: The food's been too good—YECCH. I haven't had indigestion yet.

SATAN: Make a note. Fire the cook. And when I say fire, I mean FIRE. *(Mimics flames with his hands. Demons laugh.)* Anything else before we begin?

OTHERS: No.

SATAN: Then, let's begin. As you know, we're here to review our overall performance. Take time to get the big picture and glory in our past victories. And, of course, my favorite—we're here to assign blame for failures. So. From the beginning. Anyone?

TAROT: I think I speak for us all when I say the serpent in the Garden of Eden was a masterful touch on your part, Chief.

OTHERS *(applauding)***:** Hear, hear!

SATAN: Of course it was, you apple-polisher! *(To audience.)* No pun intended. *(To his GROUP.)* EVERYTHING I do is masterful. However, it wasn't completely successful. Adam and Eve COULD have eaten from the Tree of Life, too. Imagine—people living in sin forever! *(Smiles.)* Oooooh. The thought gives me goose bumps. But MY brilliant work was UNDERMINED. WHO failed to get them to eat it?

MALEFICENT: Nonsequitur, Chief. He fouled up the works.

NONSEQUITUR: *(Rises angrily.)* How can you suggest such a thing?

MALEFICENT: *(Rises.)* You tried to make them believe God couldn't see them if they hid. But you didn't confuse them into thinking that what they had done was alright. You spent so much time on having them hide, you gave them time to feel guilty. You should have KEPT them from feeling guilty.

SATAN: No, no. Guilt comes with the territory, sooner or later—one of HIS rules. *(Smiles.)* But I have twisted it to my advantage, millions of times! Nonsequitur, YOU are to blame for not USING their guilt wisely. We could have used it to control those humans—if it hadn't been for HIM.

NONSEQUITUR: Yeah! It's HIS fault! He should have KILLED them. *(Whines.)* Why is He LIKE that? All He did was make them leave the garden and work for a living! And to top it off, He made those—UGH!—PROMISES.

DISGRUNTLE: Yeah. How did it go, Chief? You'd bruise some guy's heel but He'd bash your brains in when you did...

SATAN *(outraged)***:** SHUT UP! IDIOT! Don't you know ANYTHING? We've been trying to eliminate the chance of that Promised One ever coming, EVERY DAY since He said that! No wonder you're incompetent! You don't even understand our game plan!

DISGRUNTLE: *(Looks down in shame and mumbles.)* It was all Nonsequitur's fault!

SATAN: He was as slow as YOU are. *(Writes.)* One mark against Nonsequitur.

MALEFICENT: But look at MY success rate after that! I had everybody hating his neighbor.

DISGRUNTLE *(snarling and sarcastically)***:** Yeah? What about the—UGH!—obedient boat builder? How did you happen to miss him?

MALEFICENT: Look. *(Nervous.)* One obedient guy in a whole world—I can't be everywhere!

DISGRUNTLE: Come on! He's building a boat the size of a FOOTBALL FIELD! And you don't notice. What were you doing? SLEEPING?

MALEFICENT: You can't pin this on me! *(Points upward.)* HE sent the flood! *(Snaps fingers.)* Just like that—hundreds of years of work for NOTHING! Nothing left but a bunch of animals and eight humans who—ulp!—loved HIM.

SATAN: Disgruntle's right this time, even if he is an idiot. *(Writes.)* Maleficent, this falls on your shoulders. *(Looks up and sighs.)* Do I have to do everything myself?

TAROT: *(Stands.)* But Chief, with my brilliant work, we got the humans back to idol worship in no time flat. Every last one of them...

DISGRUNTLE *(sarcastically)***:** Like Abraham? Look at all the PROMISES he got. Why didn't you stop him before he obeyed?

TAROT: Who would figure he'd listen to HIM? Abraham had lots of gods to choose from. But he just packed up his tents and left. Go figure.

MALEFICENT: If I hadn't stirred up strife in his family, we would have failed completely.

DISGRUNTLE: Big deal. *(Points upward.)* It just made HIM give the guy more PROMISES!

MALEFICENT *(irritated)***:** Hey! I worked VERY hard in that family for generations. And what do I get? Joseph! I never expected the *F* word from him. Not after all the things I'd gotten his brothers to put him through!

DISGRUNTLE *(sarcastically)***:** Ooooh! The dreaded *F* word.

MALEFICENT *(panicked)***:** No! Don't SAY it!

DISGRUNTLE: Forgiveness! FORGIVENESS! *(Points.)* You blew it, Maleficent!

SATAN: I have to agree with Disgruntle. *(Writes.)* Another mark against Maleficent. You had to let his brothers think it would be better to sell him into slavery than to kill him. If you had followed the original plan...

DISGRUNTLE: Then I wouldn't have had to be so busy in Egypt.

MALEFICENT: YOU? I was the one who kept the Egyptians angry. I was the one who had all the male babies killed.

DISGRUNTLE: And if you hadn't missed Moses, I wouldn't have had to keep the Israelites arguing among themselves.

TAROT: Don't take all the credit. I had them worshiping Molech all the way to the Promised Land!

SATAN: Not ALL of them. Caleb and Joshua still obeyed HIM. Even the giants didn't scare them off. *(Bangs table.)* How can He always find SOMEBODY who'll do RIGHT?!

NONSEQUITUR: But Chief, remember? I got them ALL for a while with my "do your own thing" deception! I even got rid of Samuel and everyone like him. *(Whines.)* How was I to know that making them want a KING would work into HIS plan?

SATAN: You DID manage quite a few despicable kings. BUT—and this is a BIG one—you never managed to do away with the House of David! That was CRUCIAL to our plans!

NONSEQUITUR: Uh, look, Chief, I got more royal family members killed off than either one of us can count! I threw myself into that one!

SATAN: *(To NONSEQUITUR.)* Even ONE obedient ruler is too many! They never forgot HIS ways completely! *(To himself.)* And those prophets! Some of them were absolutely INTOLERABLE! *(Begins to pace.)* Torture them, put them in holes, deceive people into ignoring them—and still HE manages to get somebody to listen. EVERY TIME!

TAROT: Even when we got the whole bunch shipped off to Babylon, He seemed to be, well...one step ahead of us. Again.

DISGRUNTLE: My crew worked day and night on that Jeremiah situation. We got people worked up against him, got him thrown into jail. Best of all, we brought in a big group of false prophets to tell the people they'd be free and back in the land in no time. We did our job.

NONSEQUITUR: Maybe your false prophets did their job TOO well. Too many of those Israelites stayed separate from the people who deported them. You should have convinced ALL of them to join in, be one of the boys! Look at Daniel. Look at Shadrach, Meshach and Abednego. Couldn't you have let them be content with their position? No. You had to keep pushing!

DISGRUNTLE: That wasn't my doing.

SATAN: Don't try to worm out of it. You FAILED. *(Writes.)* But we could have gotten rid of the whole nation in one bloody day while they were in Babylon! Who blew THAT one, when we had Haman right in our pocket?

MALEFICENT: Yeah, who messed up? That's what I want to know! Just show me his face.

TAROT: *(Hands MALEFICENT a mirror.)* Here you go.

MALEFICENT: What's this for?

TAROT: I'm showing you the bungler's face!

MALEFICENT: Rot. I NEVER bungle.

TAROT: You did on this one. You got Haman so worked up against Mordecai, he lost all common sense. He couldn't think straight and look what happened. He lost his head! *(To audience.)* No pun intended.

MALEFICENT: That's not MY doing! Nonsequitur should have brought his "it's not my problem" deception down on Queen Esther right away. But, NO! He was late again! She had the—YUK!—truth in front of the king before Haman could say, "Kill the Jews!"

NONSEQUITUR: I was busy. She wasn't the only person around to deceive!

SATAN: Maleficent, that's THREE for you. And to think...you're lusting after MY job! You'll have to do better than this!

MALEFICENT *(shocked that he's been caught)*: How...how did you know?

SATAN: I have informants. *(Leans over MALEFICENT.)* Never forget, you scheming slime, they don't call ME the "father of lies" for nothing! *(To group.)* Ahem. The last item on our agenda is the most crucial. Our Eternal Enemy is at it again.

MALEFICENT: Not again.

NONSEQUITUR: Doesn't He ever quit?

TAROT: Doesn't He ever get tired?

DISGRUNTLE: Uh-oh. You're not going to say that dreaded *R* word!

SATAN: *(Into DISGRUNTLE's ear.)* Redemption! REDEMPTION! There! It's a beautiful word but SOMEBODY had to say it.

ALL: Yecch!

SATAN: This time, the situation is critical. Our spy chain has just reported. The Promised One is about to come into the world.

MALEFICENT: How?

SATAN: Virgin birth.

TAROT: Crafty. Very crafty.

NONSEQUITUR: How does our Eternal Enemy come up with these ideas?

DISGRUNTLE: Just think of what we could accomplish if ONE of us was omniscient.

SATAN: Stop whining! We need a plan!

NONSEQUITUR: You say virgin birth. Single parent?

SATAN: *(Consults notes.)* Kid named Mary. Good family, engaged to Joseph.

NONSEQUITUR: Simple. I'll get to Joseph. Convince him to divorce her.

SATAN: Good luck. The man's in love!

NONSEQUITUR: Leave it to me. Deception and misleading thoughts are my specialty.

SATAN: OK, you've got Joseph. DON'T BLOW IT! But we need backup plans. Anyone?

TAROT: How does the Eternal Enemy plan to announce the birth? He must have some big sign or wonder.

SATAN: *(Consults notes.)* The reports say a new star. A bright one.

TAROT: Excellent. I have some astrologers working in the East.

SATAN: I thought they were His.

TAROT: So do they. Isn't it WONDERFUL? I tell them what to do and they give all the credit to HIM. It's one of my better plans.

SATAN: Let's hope it makes up for your Abraham blunder. So, what will you do?

TAROT: I'll have them misread the star. Send them to the wrong place. They'll announce a different savior. At the very least, it'll confuse the issue.

MALEFICENT: This goes against everything I believe in but, Tarot, how about you and I...cooperate?

OTHERS: Yecch! The *C* word.

MALEFICENT: Desperate times call for desperate measures. Listen, I've got a plan. The king of Judea is in my pocket. The Savior is going to come from around there, right?

SATAN: *(Consults notes.)* Bethlehem. Just outside of Jerusalem.

MALEFICENT: Perfect! This King Herod is ripe for the picking. Tarot, what if you lead your astrologers to Jerusalem?

TAROT: Easy enough. Why?

MALEFICENT: Those stargazers will be searching for a king, right?

TAROT: Naturally.

SATAN: I think I see where you're headed. I like it.

MALEFICENT: So they'll go to the palace and ask to see the new king.

TAROT: Of course.

MALEFICENT: If I know my Herod, he'll go wild!

SATAN: Magnificent, Maleficent!

TAROT: I don't get it.

MALEFICENT: Listen, we'll lead your astrologers to the RIGHT baby. They'll report back to my king.

TAROT: *(Rubs hands together.)* Ah, I see.

MALEFICENT: He sends his soldiers out. Kills the kid. Poof! No Savior.

SATAN: Brilliant! Can't miss! Disgruntle. We haven't heard from you.

DISGRUNTLE: These plans sound bad. But some of our most HORRIBLE plans have failed before.

SATAN: You're being a pessimist. I like that.

DISGRUNTLE: So I've got a contingency plan. Suppose Herod misses the Savior? Remember Moses! The worst case scenario is this: HE always seems to be one step ahead of us. HE always has ONE obedient person...

OTHERS: Bite your tongue! You're going to start sounding like one of THEM!

DISGRUNTLE: Look, I'm only saying, "What if."

SATAN *(outraged)***:** WHAT IF? You're talking "WHAT IF" to ME? That's enough! There's only one thing to do. If Herod doesn't get Him, I'M going in myself. I'll take my time. I'll watch and wait. And I'll get to Him when He's at His WEAKEST. I'll offer Him everything He wants—for a PRICE. I'll make a deal with Him that's so sweet He'll be in the palm of my hand before He knows what hit Him! I WILL BE WORSHIPED! I WILL BE KING!

(Murmurs of "Uh-oh!" and "Oh, wow!" from GROUP.)

SATAN: *(Regains composure.)* Now. Let's get going. Everyone know his job?

OTHERS: Got it.

(ALL rise and begin to leave.)

SATAN *(calling after them)***:** And this time, DO IT RIGHT!

SHOW ME

SCRIPTURE: Genesis 6; Exodus 2:1-10; Hebrews 11

SUGGESTED TOPICS: Showing faith; trusting God

BIBLE BACKGROUND

A well-known story tells of a famous acrobat who announced he would cross Niagara Falls on a tightrope, pushing a wheelbarrow. Naturally, a crowd assembled to watch his feat. "Who believes I can do this?" he asked the crowd. "We do!" was the enthusiastic response. "Who will ride in the wheelbarrow while I push it across?" he asked the assembly. He was greeted with dead silence.

Whether or not the above story is true, it clearly delineates the difference between belief and faith. One can passively believe; but if one has faith, it must be demonstrated. Hebrews 11 tells of the heroes of the faith and what they did to demonstrate their faith. Noah, in faith, built an ark. Abraham left his home in faith, and journeyed to a land he had never seen. Later, in faith, he prepared to offer up his only son as a sacrifice. Moses' parents, in faith, hid him for three months. Moses, in faith, forsook Egypt and his place there as Pharaoh's adopted grandson. Rahab, in faith, hid the Israelite spies. In each case, faith moved the person to action. Without demonstration, faith does not exist.

PERFORMANCE TIPS

1. Suggested props: Bible-times costumes, wood for Noah to move, sticks or reeds for Moses' mother to weave.

2. Noah should be working confidently; Noah's wife, exasperated with him.

DISCUSSION QUESTIONS

1. What is faith? Can you have faith without demonstrating it? Why or why not?

2. Read Hebrews 11. What are some ways different Old Testament people showed faith?

3. How do we know it is safe to place our faith in God?

4. What are some ways we can demonstrate our faith in God?

SHOW ME

CHARACTERS

NOAH
NOAH'S WIFE
MOSES' MOTHER
MOSES' FATHER

SCENE ONE

(NOAH walks onstage carrying wood. NOAH'S WIFE enters behind him, talking.)

NOAH'S WIFE: What are you doing?

NOAH: Gathering wood for lumber.

NOAH'S WIFE: I can see that. Why are you gathering lumber?

NOAH: To build.

NOAH'S WIFE: To build what?

NOAH: An ark.

NOAH'S WIFE: What's an ark?

NOAH: It's a boat.

NOAH'S WIFE: You've got enough lumber there to build twenty boats. Why do you want to build a boat, anyway? We live miles from the beach. Where are you planning to sail it?

NOAH: I don't have enough lumber. I need enough to build a boat four hundred and fifty feet long, seventy feet wide and forty-five feet high.

NOAH'S WIFE: Ridiculous! A boat THAT big could hold two of every kind of animal on earth!

NOAH: And seven of each of the clean.

NOAH'S WIFE: Clean, unclean—who cares? All I know is, you're making a mess in the front yard. What will the neighbors think?

NOAH: They will think what they wish. Probably evil.

NOAH'S WIFE: I'll tell you what they'll think. They'll think, "Noah's really lost it this time. He's gone over the deep end. One hundred percent bananas."

NOAH: Bananas! Good thinking! They will need food.

NOAH'S WIFE: WHO will need food?

NOAH: The animals.

NOAH'S WIFE: Which animals?

NOAH: The ones in the ark.

NOAH'S WIFE: Stop! *(NOAH stops.)* Why are you building this big boat?

NOAH: I TOLD you. To carry two of every kind of animal. Seven of the clean.

NOAH'S WIFE: But why build it at all?

NOAH: Because God told me to.

NOAH'S WIFE: God told you? Why would He tell you to build a huge boat?

NOAH: Because He wants the animals saved.

NOAH'S WIFE: From what?

NOAH: The flood.

NOAH'S WIFE: What flood? There's no water here to flood!

NOAH: It's coming.

NOAH'S WIFE: From where? *(Points.)* Look over there. Do you see any water? Over there? How about over there? Where is the water? Show me some water.

NOAH: I don't know where the water is. But God said He's going to flood the earth.

NOAH'S WIFE: How? There's not enough water to flood the earth!

NOAH: I don't know. God only told me what to do. That's what I'm doing.

NOAH'S WIFE: *(To sky.)* After five hundred-odd years, he's finally gone completely crazy.

NOAH: Back to work. Lots to do before the flood.

NOAH'S WIFE: Where will the water come from? We're on dry ground. Are you going to tell me there's water under the ground that will spring up?

NOAH: Perhaps. I don't know.

NOAH'S WIFE: Or maybe water will fall from the sky?

NOAH: Why not?

NOAH'S WIFE: Because it's never happened before. That's why.

NOAH: Doesn't mean it won't happen.

NOAH'S WIFE: I give up. *(Sarcastically.)* Will I have time to make supper before this flood happens?

NOAH: Oh, sure. Lots to do yet.

NOAH'S WIFE: When you come in, bring some water from the well with you. If the FLOOD isn't coming today, we'll need some water brought to the house. *(To herself.)* Now there's an idea—have water come into the house so you don't have to go out and fetch it! No. Water in a house? It'll never happen.

SCENE TWO

(FATHER paces frantically; MOTHER calmly weaves basket throughout scene.)

FATHER: This can't go on any longer. I don't think I can stand the strain.

MOTHER: The strain?

FATHER: Yes, the strain! Will the baby cry? Will Pharaoh's soldiers hear?

MOTHER: Oh, that strain.

FATHER: Yes! That strain! For three months. Something must be done!

MOTHER: I agree.

FATHER: I don't believe this. I'm going crazy and you're sitting there, calmly weaving reeds. Where's Miriam?

MOTHER: Gone to get more reeds. I don't have enough.

FATHER: What are you weaving?

MOTHER: A basket.

FATHER: For what? We're slaves. We don't have enough of ANYTHING to put in such a big basket.

MOTHER: On the contrary. We have something very important to put in this basket. Our son.

FATHER: You think putting him into a basket will keep him safe? The strain has made you even crazier than I am!

MOTHER: I'm not crazy. Look, we can't keep the baby quiet all the time.

FATHER: I know this. That's what's making me crazy!

MOTHER: Sooner or later, Pharaoh's men will hear him.

FATHER: And when they find we have hidden a male baby, they'll kill us AND him.

MOTHER: What if they don't find a baby here?

FATHER: You said yourself, they'll find him.

MOTHER: If we trust ourselves, yes. But maybe not, if we trust God.

FATHER: What do you think we've been doing?

MOTHER: But not fully. Here's my plan. I weave a basket.

FATHER: To keep your mind off our danger?

MOTHER: Listen. I cover it with tar to make it waterproof.

FATHER: So the baby won't drown when it rains?

MOTHER: No. So it will float on the river. We give the baby to God's care.

FATHER: I don't know. It frightens me. He could drown if any water gets in. He could be found by Pharaoh's men and be killed.

MOTHER: We have trusted God these three months. Should we stop trusting Him now?

FATHER: You're right. We must have faith. But I would go crazy, not knowing what has happened to our son.

MOTHER: So would I. But I have an idea.

FATHER: What is it?

MOTHER: Miriam can help me take the basket to the river. Then she can hide and see what happens. Then she can come home and tell us.

FATHER: Yes. At least we will know what has happened to him. But it's so...difficult.

MOTHER: Yes, it's difficult. But if we can't trust God, whom do you think we should trust?

PASSOVER ME BY

SCRIPTURE: Exodus 7—11

SUGGESTED TOPICS: Listening to God; accepting and learning from God's correction; obedience to God

BIBLE BACKGROUND

God promised to make Abraham a great and mighty nation. He also promised a land in which His people could live. However, God was amazingly patient with the people who were already living there. Their iniquity (marked by worship of false gods, child sacrifice, religious prostitution, witchcraft, etc., mentioned in Deuteronomy 18:9-12) was not yet complete (see Genesis 15:16-21). God told Abraham that the path to the Promised Land would be filled with curious twists and turns. Before Abraham's descendants could take possession of their own land, they first would be oppressed in a land (Egypt) which was not theirs (see Genesis 15:13).

Getting the Israelites into Egypt was no mean feat. It required a young man who stirred great jealousy in his brothers, an undeserved prison sentence, three strange dreams, a terrible famine and remarkable forgiveness. Getting the Israelites out again was even more difficult. God had to prove to His own people and to the Egyptians that He was the only God; that Egypt's gods could not begin to match Him in power. Finally, after four hundred and thirty years in Egypt (see Exodus 12:40), the Israelites were ready to begin moving toward the fulfillment of God's promise to Abraham.

PERFORMANCE TIPS

1. Suggested props: a very large book, bookshelf, two chairs.
2. Before the skit, briefly explain to the class how the Israelites got to Egypt in the first place and why they were now being oppressed.
3. The Advisor has been awakened from sleep but is afraid to admit it. He stifles yawns when Pharaoh isn't looking. He has a large boil on his face.
4. A number of people can cry out to cause commotion when the firstborn sons are slain. They should continue for the rest of the skit but keep the noise down enough for the actors to be heard.

DISCUSSION QUESTIONS

1. Why do you think Pharaoh would ignore nine plagues from God?
2. What kinds of promises does God make to us in the Bible? What are some things He warns us not to do?
3. The Bible says God hardened Pharaoh's heart (see Exodus 10:1). Does it sound fair for God to punish someone for something God did? Here's an experiment to try:
   a. Get a little bit of mud and put it on some foil.
   b. Get a piece of hard chocolate and put it on some foil.
   c. Put the mud and the chocolate under a light, close to the bulb. (A one hundred watt bulb works best.)
   d. Observe what happens to both the mud and the chocolate. Say, "God does not make us do things. His power only shows what we are like inside. We respond to Him according to the kind of people we are, just as the mud and the chocolate responded to the light."

PASSOVER ME BY

CHARACTERS

PHARAOH
ADVISOR

PRONUNCIATION GUIDE

draught (draft)

PHARAOH: Goodness, but it's dark. Not as dark as a few days ago, but dark. I wish I could get some sleep. Advisor!

ADVISOR: *(Enters, rubbing sleep from his eyes.)* Yes, my king.

PHARAOH: Were you asleep?

ADVISOR: *(Stops rubbing eyes suddenly.)* Me? Asleep while Pharaoh is awake? Oh, no. Never, never, never.

PHARAOH: Then why were you rubbing your eyes?

ADVISOR: Why? Umm, why was I rubbing my eyes. Something. I was rubbing. Why? Aha! I was rubbing my eyes because something was in my eye. Dust? A louse? That's it. I had a speck of louse in my eye.

PHARAOH: Just so you weren't asleep. I can't sleep.

ADVISOR: Perhaps you need a sleeping draught, O King.

PHARAOH: You mean a draft where I stand by my bed and open a window and the wind blows over a hammer which falls and hits me on the head?

ADVISOR: It works every time, Great Pharaoh.

PHARAOH: But I have such a headache in the morning! One of these days, someone will invent a better method of inducing sleep.

ADVISOR: But never a more effective one.

PHARAOH: Never mind. I have an alternate plan for getting some sleep.

ADVISOR *(horrified)***:** Not...

PHARAOH: Yes. The historical method. Read to me from the history book.

> *(ADVISOR stumbles to shelf and brings out very large book.)*

ADVISOR: Is there any special part Pharaoh would care to hear?

PHARAOH: Anywhere is fine.

ADVISOR: *(Opens book and begins reading.)* ...and it came to pass that Joseph...

PHARAOH: Joseph! Again with this Joseph! Who is Joseph?

ADVISOR: I don't know.

PHARAOH: Well, find out!

(ADVISOR flips backward through book, mumbling as though reading quickly.)

PHARAOH: Well, who IS he? Moses talks about him. The history books tell of him.

ADVISOR: Ah, I have it. (Reads.) "...and the Hebrew prisoner, Joseph, was elevated in rank and set in charge of collecting twenty percent of all the food produced in Egypt." He seems to have been a tax collector, Sire.

PHARAOH: All this fuss over a tax collector? Amazing.

ADVISOR (consulting book)**:** And he apparently saved Egypt from great famine.

PHARAOH: Oh. A hero. How long ago did this happen?

ADVISOR: About four hundred and thirty years ago, Sire.

PHARAOH: Oh. Ancient history. Nothing for me to worry about, then.

ADVISOR: No, Your Highness.

PHARAOH: (Stands.) Reading isn't helping. Maybe a midnight snack. What have we got?

ADVISOR: Frog legs, Sire.

PHARAOH: STILL?

ADVISOR: They were plentiful this year, Your Majesty.

PHARAOH: Well, I'm tired of them.

ADVISOR: As are we all.

PHARAOH: (Sits.) As long as I can't sleep, I might as well get some work done.

ADVISOR: (Starts to leave.) I'll leave you to it, then.

PHARAOH: No. Stay. I need advice. (Stares at ADVISOR.) Your face.

ADVISOR: I should advise my face to stay where it is, my lord?

PHARAOH: No! What's that hideous thing on your face?

ADVISOR: (Touches cheek.) A boil, Your Highness. Leftover from Plague Number Six.

PHARAOH: Oh. Well, do something about it tomorrow. It offends me.

ADVISOR: I have heard that sleep can remove boils, O Pharaoh. I shall attend to it immediately.

(Turns to go.)

PHARAOH: TOMORROW will be soon enough.

ADVISOR: (Aside.) I was afraid of that.

PHARAOH: What about this latest threat from Moses?

ADVISOR: Has he come to make another? I haven't seen him since the great darkness.

PHARAOH: Of course he hasn't come. I told him I'd kill him if I saw him again.

ADVISOR: Then what threat are we discussing?

PHARAOH: You haven't heard the rumors?

ADVISOR: Oh, rumors. Nothing to worry about.

PHARAOH: But the Hebrews are spreading BLOOD all over their houses.

ADVISOR: Just so they're not shedding blood in Egyptian houses, there's nothing to worry about.

PHARAOH: Then you think I'm doing the right thing, keeping the Hebrews in Egypt?

ADVISOR: But of course, Sire. Where else will you find a slave labor force of six hundred thousand men? You have building projects to complete! You need the manpower!

PHARAOH: True. But some Egyptians are taking the rumors seriously.

ADVISOR: Such utter nonsense. NO god can find the firstborn of every family in Egypt. And not only people, but animals. Pharaoh, not even the SUN can do this. There's nothing to worry about.

PHARAOH: Well, I don't like all that blood. Makes the country look messy.

ADVISOR: Then teach the Hebrews a lesson. Tomorrow, make them clean up all the blood AND make their full quota of bricks. Lean on them. Show them who's in charge.

PHARAOH: Hmm. That could work. Put a stop to all this trouble Moses has been causing.

(Loud screams and crying from offstage.)

PHARAOH: What's happening? Go find out!

(ADVISOR exits; crying continues. ADVISOR enters looking worried.)

PHARAOH: Well, what is it?

ADVISOR: Um...well, uh...nothing too serious. Just a little accident.

PHARAOH: There seems to be a lot of commotion for a little accident. Who's been hurt?

ADVISOR: Ahem. Well. *(Counts on fingers.)* The heir to the throne seems to have died. And the chambermaid's firstborn. And that of the queen's attendants. And the oldest of the palace cat's litter. The oldest of the footman, the butcher, the baker, the candlestick maker, the...

(PHARAOH runs offstage.)

MAKE A DEAL

SCRIPTURE: Joshua 2

SUGGESTED TOPICS: Godly vs. worldly values; trusting in God's guidance

BIBLE BACKGROUND

For forty years, the Israelites had wandered through the wilderness. Everyone (except for Caleb and Joshua) who was older than twenty years when Israel first saw the Promised Land had perished during the years of wandering. At last God said it was time for Israel to enter the land. In preparation for crossing the Jordan River, Joshua assigned two men to spy out the walled city of Jericho.

We know little of what they discovered about the city's military situation. Instead, the sacred writer focused on the prostitute, Rahab. We learn of her assistance to the spies and their promise of protection in the coming battle. Why so little attention to the major issues of strategy and policy? Why this emphasis on one woman? Perhaps it is to illustrate God's concern for each individual, no matter how seemingly insignificant or unworthy. Perhaps it is to honor Rahab's remarkable confession of faith in the God of Israel (see Joshua 2:8-11; Hebrews 11:31; James 2:25). And perhaps it is because Rahab became part of the lineage of King David and ultimately of Jesus Christ (see Matthew 1:5). Compared with matters such as those, military strategy seems insignificant.

PERFORMANCE TIPS

1. Suggested props: play money for Mammon to give to participants.
2. Most of your group will be familiar with the format of game shows. Both the announcer and Mammon should speak excitedly.
3. The entire group can participate as the audience. Determine a signal to prompt the audience to yell, "Make a deal!"

DISCUSSION QUESTIONS

1. How valuable did the scarlet cord turn out to be to Rahab?
2. How valuable was the bunch of flax to the Israelite spies?
3. Which is more important, God's directions or money? Why?
4. What are some situations in which people need God's guidance?
5. How does God guide you?

MAKE A DEAL

CHARACTERS
ANNOUNCER

AUDIENCE

MAMMON (MAA-mon)

RAHAB (RAY-hab)

SPY ONE

SPY TWO

KING

ANNOUNCER: It's time, once again, for Jericho's favorite game show—

AUDIENCE: MAKE A DEAL!

ANNOUNCER: And now, here's everybody's favorite host, the host with the most, Mammon, the Man Who Can—

AUDIENCE: MAKE A DEAL!

MAMMON: Thank you, thank you, thank you. You're beautiful. You, the lovely lady right here, I'll give you two shekels if you can show me a piece of scarlet cord.

RAHAB: I have one. Right here.

MAMMON: She has one! I like that cord. Tell you what. I'll give you five more shekels if you'll give me the cord.

RAHAB: No. I'd like to keep the cord.

MAMMON: You drive a hard bargain. Ten shekels.

RAHAB: No. I'll keep the cord.

MAMMON: Last chance. One full talent....

AUDIENCE: *(Gasps.)*

MAMMON: That's right. One full talent for that scarlet cord.

RAHAB: No. I prefer to keep the cord. I might need it for something.

MAMMON: OK. You've got your two shekels and the cord. Let's see if we can find someone else who wants to—

AUDIENCE: MAKE A DEAL!

MAMMON: You two. I love those costumes. You almost look like Israelites. But what would Israelites be doing in Jericho? You're going to have to tell me. What are you two supposed to be?

SPY ONE: Uh, spies?

SPY TWO: That's it. Spies. We're pretending to be Israelite spies who are trying to look like they belong in Jericho.

MAMMON: Well, you're doing great. You even have the accent. Here's the deal. Just because I like you, I'm going to give you each ten shekels. And because your accents are so well done, I'm going to throw in five more shekels.

The Big Book of Bible Skits ©1997 Gospel Light. Permission to photocopy granted.

BOTH SPIES: Wow!

MAMMON: You like the deal so far?

SPY ONE: Great!

SPY TWO: Terrific!

MAMMON: But—

BOTH SPIES: But what?

MAMMON: Because I like you, I'm going to give you a chance to—

AUDIENCE: MAKE A DEAL!

MAMMON: That's right. You can keep your fifteen shekels or you can take what's behind the curtain. But you have to agree. So what will it be, fifteen shekels or the curtain? *(SPIES mutter between each other.)*

MAMMON: OK. Time's up. What will it be?

SPIES: We're going to take what's behind the curtain, Mammon.

MAMMON: OK. Open up the curtain and let's see what's there.

ANNOUNCER: It's...flax. That's right. Stalks of flax. Great for processing and turning into linen tablecloths. All you need is the flax we're giving you, another five bushels, lots of skilled weavers, and you too can have a fine linen tablecloth. Retail value of this prize, one shekel.

MAMMON: Too bad. But what can Israelite spies expect in Jericho? Now, I need someone who has a crown. Does anyone in the audience have a crown? You, sir.

KING: That's sire.

MAMMON: What a great costume. You look just like the king.

KING: I am the king.

MAMMON: And you sound like him, too. Same pompous attitude. Are you ready to—

AUDIENCE: MAKE A DEAL!

KING: I am always ready to make a deal that will benefit Jericho. Except, of course, with the Israelites. I would never make a deal with them.

MAMMON: OK. If you can show me a royal seal, I'll give you two talents of gold. Can you show me a royal seal?

KING: Of course I can. I never go anywhere without my seal, in case I need to make an important proclamation. There. See? Right there on my finger.

MAMMON: And here are your two talents of gold. Now you can keep the money, or you can trade it for whatever's behind the curtain.

KING: What a decision. This is a lot of money.

MAMMON: Time's running. What will it be? The money or the curtain?

KING: I think, I'll keep...no, wait! I'll trade...no, uh, I'll...trade.

MAMMON: A tough decision. Is it the right one? What's behind the curtain?

ANNOUNCER: It's a network of stool pigeons, spies and informants. Yes, know what's happening in your country or household by keeping up-to-date on all the latest developments. Three hundred men, guaranteed to snoop around, stick their noses in where they don't belong, and then come tell you everything they've seen. A prize fit for a king. Retail value of this prize...four talents!

MAMMON: Well, we're almost out of time. It's time for the big final gamble. Let's see if any of our winners want to—

AUDIENCE: MAKE A DEAL!

MAMMON: Our king made the best deal so far. What about it, king? Do you want to keep your deal or gamble it on something better?

KING: I'm happy with my deal. I'll keep it.

MAMMON: Rahab. You made the next best deal. Do you want to keep your two shekels or gamble them on a final deal?

RAHAB: I'll trade, Mammon.

MAMMON: All right, Rahab! Come on over here. Give me the shekels and choose. Do you want Door Number One, Door Number Two or Door Number Three?

RAHAB: Oh, it's so hard. I want Door Number...

MAMMON: Which one? One, Two or Three?

RAHAB: Door Number...Three.

ANNOUNCER: It's...amnesty! Yes, Rahab. You have received the gift of amnesty. In the event the Israelites attack and destroy Jericho, you and all who are with you and your family will be saved!

MAMMON: Hard to tell if you made a good deal or not. But we'd better get approval from the Israelites. Where are those spies?

BOTH SPIES: Here, Mammon.

MAMMON: To seal the deal, you two should make a covenant with Rahab.

SPY ONE: But what is the covenant to be?

RAHAB: Let's see. If you are spying out the land and some of the king's informers should happen to see you, I promise that you can find sanctuary in my house. I will hide you and keep you safe from the king and all others who would seek to kill you. For I know that the Lord has given you this land.

SPY TWO: Our life for yours. If you do not speak of hiding us and seeing us...

SPY ONE: ...then when the Lord gives us this land, we will deal kindly with you.

SPY TWO: You may bring your father, your mother, your brothers and sisters and all your father's household into your house.

SPY ONE: Any who remain in your house will be spared.

SPY TWO: But any who leave your house to venture onto the street will not be protected.

SPY ONE: To be certain that all Israel will recognize your house and honor this covenant...

SPY TWO: ...take a scarlet cord and hang it from your window.

RAHAB: Let it be according to your words.

MAMMON: Just to seal this covenant, something should change hands. How about you boys give her the flax. She can keep it on her roof. Now then, I have a shekel for anyone who can show me an idol. Does anyone have an idol with him? Any kind of an idol, and you can—

AUDIENCE: MAKE A DEAL!

PROBLEMS, PROBLEMS, PROBLEMS

SCRIPTURE: Joshua 3; 4

SUGGESTED TOPICS: Trusting in God's guidance; obedience resulting from trust

BIBLE BACKGROUND

Forty years previously, the Israelites had been challenged to cross the Jordan River into the Promised Land. They had been dissuaded then by reports of giants in the land (see Numbers 13,14). After forty years, the giants were still in their fortified cities. However, this time, the Israelites elected to follow God and to cross the river.

Both groups of Israelites had witnessed God's power to do what seemed impossible. The earlier generation had seen Pharaoh agree to release two million slaves, ultimately begging Israel to leave Egypt. The latter generation had lived for forty years in the desert with God's provision of food and water for the wandering multitude. Whether the Israelites had really learned to trust God's promises or they had simply had all they could take of life in the desert, they finally were willing to step forward, following the priests who carried the Ark of the Covenant into the waters of the Jordan.

A considerable body of false information concerning the Ark of the Covenant has arisen over the years. The Bible is clear concerning the nature of this object. It was a wooden box, overlaid with gold, having rings through which poles were placed to carry the box (see Exodus 25:10-22). It was not a radio transmitter, it did not shoot bolts of lightning, it was never an artifact of magic. It was always a physical symbol of the reality of God's presence among His people.

PERFORMANCE TIPS

1. Suggested props: twelve rocks stacked in a mound.
2. Set the scene for your group. Indicate an area of the room to represent the swollen river which separated the land from the people.
3. Before the skit, ask, "If you were the Israelites' leader, Joshua, how would you bring two million people across a river where there is no bridge? Remember—babies, grandmothers and grandfathers are part of the crowd."

DISCUSSION QUESTIONS

1. Do you have a friend you trust? Why do you trust that friend?
2. What kinds of problems do you have in your life?
3. Think of one particular problem. How might God help you with that problem? Why can you trust God?
4. How can God guide you today? What methods might He use?

Problems, Problems, Problems

CHARACTERS

CHILD

FATHER

BENJAMIN

ADAM

JOSHUA

CHILD: Father, why are these stones here by the Jordan River?

FATHER: Interesting that you should ask. They were put here when I was about your age, as a sign and a remembrance.

CHILD: What kind of a sign? You mean like a stop sign or a warning?

FATHER: No. More like a joyful occasion. Like candles on a birthday cake.

CHILD: This was to celebrate someone's birthday?

FATHER: No, child. I see I am not explaining this very well. Let me start at the beginning. When I was a boy, we were preparing to enter into the Promised Land…

(FATHER and CHILD exit or freeze. BENJAMIN and ADAM enter.)

BENJAMIN: Father, what's everybody so excited for?

ADAM: We have been given the order to go into the Promised Land.

BENJAMIN: But, Father, the Promised Land is on the other side of the river!

ADAM: The Jordan. A magnificent river. Look how fast the current flows. At this time of year, the river is flooded. It is so deep, so wide, so treacherous.

BENJAMIN: How will we get across? Will Joshua build an ark, like Noah did?

ADAM: I don't know how we will cross. We have been told to follow the priests—those who bear the Ark of the Covenant.

BENJAMIN: But that ark is only a small box.

ADAM: No, Son. It is much more than that.

BENJAMIN: You mean, it's magic?

ADAM: No, my son. Not magic. True, it is a wooden box, overlaid with gold, but it is more than that. It is a symbol, God's promise to us that we are His people and that He will work His plan for His people.

BENJAMIN: But how will all the people get across the river? All the old people and the little babies. They can't swim across the river.

ADAM: And you can, my son?

BENJAMIN: Well…I could swim farther than Grandma.

ADAM: But you would still not be able to swim the full distance. You would be swept away and drowned, the same as the old people and the babies.

BENJAMIN: Then God brought us to the river to die?

ADAM: No, Son. God brought us to the Promised Land to show us that He is our God and we should trust and obey Him.

BENJAMIN: But if we all die in the river...

ADAM: We will not die, my son. God will protect us. You'll see. Are you frightened?

BENJAMIN: Of course not. I'm ten years old, and I'm not frightened of anything.

ADAM: Then I have not taught you well. There are many things to fear.

BENJAMIN: Are you afraid, Father?

ADAM: Yes. But in spite of my fear, I will obey. When Joshua calls us, I will follow.

BENJAMIN: But isn't being afraid the same as not having faith?

ADAM: No, my son. Faith is following God, even when you are afraid. Many years ago, our fathers were preparing to enter the Promised Land. But they allowed their fear to stop them from obeying God.

BENJAMIN: But if they were here, why are we only now entering the Promised Land? Why are we not already in our new home?

ADAM: Because our fathers did not obey God. This will not be an easy task, conquering this new land. God knows the difficulties that lie ahead. He knows that if we are not ready to obey Him, we will fail. That is why we have spent the last forty years in the wilderness. We have been learning to trust and to obey God.

BENJAMIN: How have we been doing that?

ADAM: By watching what God does. When we were in the wilderness, how did we eat?

BENJAMIN: We gathered manna. How else does anybody eat?

ADAM: No other people gather manna. God knew that when we were traveling in the wilderness, we would need food. He solved the problem by sending manna for us to eat. When we obeyed Him, we had enough for the day. But when we disobeyed and gathered more than we needed, the excess became moldy and not fit to eat.

BENJAMIN: So we learned that God would provide food for us?

ADAM: True. And where does one find water in the desert?

BENJAMIN: You just go to where it is.

ADAM: But where is it? Most places in the desert do not have water. Nobody knew where there was water. So we had another problem. But God led Moses to water. Once again, God solved our problem.

BENJAMIN: And now we have another problem.

ADAM: Right. We have to cross a river that nobody could possibly cross. So even though we are afraid, we will remember what God has done. We will trust and follow Him.

(JOSHUA enters.)

JOSHUA: Priests, raise up the Ark of the Covenant.

ADAM: Now, Benjamin, we will obey and see God work.

JOSHUA: Priests, walk into the waters of the Jordan.

BENJAMIN: Father! Look! The river is standing up!

ADAM: It looks that way, does it not? All the waters flowing down have made a huge wall!

JOSHUA: People of Israel, move across the river and into the land that God promised to Abraham. One man from each tribe will be chosen to pick up a rock from the bed of the Jordan and carry it to shore. Adam, will you represent your tribe?

ADAM: I would be honored, Joshua.

BENJAMIN: Father, shouldn't the river bed be all muddy?

ADAM: Yes, my son, it should be.

BENJAMIN: But it isn't. It's dry ground!

ADAM: Very true. Ah, here is a good rock. I will take this one.

JOSHUA: Is everybody across the river? Priests! Come across!

ADAM: You see, Son. I told you we would be safe.

BENJAMIN: Father! Look! When the priests left the river bed, the river rushed back along its course. That Ark of the Covenant MUST be magic.

ADAM: No, Son. What you saw was not magic. It was God's power. God simply used the Ark to remind the people that He was at work here.

JOSHUA: People of Israel, you see the stones taken from the waters of the Jordan where the priests held the Ark of the Covenant. These stones are a sign to you, so that in days to come, when children ask their fathers, "Why are these stones here?" you will be able to tell them all that happened here today. These stones will be a memorial to you...

(BENJAMIN, ADAM and JOSHUA freeze or exit. FATHER and CHILD enter or unfreeze.)

FATHER: ...a symbol of all that God has done for us.

CHILD: So when we have problems, we can remember that God loves us and cares about us?

FATHER: That's right. We can remember what He has done in the past and know that He will help us with our problems today. And that is the meaning of these stones along the river.

SUCH SOUND

SCRIPTURE: Joshua 6:1-21

SUGGESTED TOPICS: Trusting in God's guidance; following instructions; obedience resulting from trust

BIBLE BACKGROUND

The Israelites crossed the Jordan River, ready to begin their conquest of the Promised Land. Joshua began the campaign by circumcising the soldiers, effectively putting the entire army out of commission for a few days. He then faced the task of conquering Jericho. How to attack a city fortified with a double wall all around? There was no way; Jericho would never be defeated by human means. But with God, all things are possible.

Scholars disagree concerning the timing of the forty years of wandering in the wilderness. Some say the Israelites entered Canaan forty years after leaving Egypt; others, forty years after seeing the Promised Land but not entering for fear of giants. The skit chooses the latter view.

PERFORMANCE TIPS

1. Suggested props: microphone for VJ, kazoos or rolled-up pieces of paper as trumpets for the priests to play, large cardboard boxes or blocks to represent the walls of Jericho.
2. Select a few members of the group to be priests. If you have "trumpets," have the priests "play" a familiar tune, such as "When the Saints Go Marching In," as they lead the Israelites in marching around the room.
3. Designate one side of the room as Jericho. Have the Israelite camp on the other side of the room.

DISCUSSION QUESTIONS

1. What made the walls of Jericho fall? What do you think would have happened if Joshua had not followed God's plan?
2. God gives everyone instructions. How do you find out God's instructions?
3. Why should you follow God's instructions?
4. What can you do to pay better attention to God's instructions?

SUCH SOUND

CHARACTERS
GROUP OF ISRAELITES

VJ

JOSHUA

VJ: Hi and welcome to the nation's music video station, "Such Sound." Today we have a special treat: the Israelites' new music video. We all remember their last video—still a classic—the "Song of Moses." Now, some forty-two years later, we have the group's second video. Of course, in forty-two years, some changes have occurred. Lead singer, Moses, has been replaced by Joshua. Only two members of the original band are still playing with the Israelites: Joshua and Caleb. As an extra treat today, Joshua is with us in the studio. Welcome, Joshua.

JOSHUA: Thank you, Zophar. Always a pleasure to be here.

VJ: Tell us about this new song. First, the time span. Forty-two years between records. Why the long wait?

JOSHUA: Well, you might say that the last forty-two years have been a dry period for the group. We were reviewing our situation, deciding who to follow. Strengthening the band for our current status.

VJ: Tell us about the group's development. I understand that some major changes have taken place over the years.

JOSHUA: That's true. We were planning to release this record forty years ago, but there was some disagreement as to how we should go about making it.

VJ: So, there was dissension in the group?

JOSHUA: That's right. Caleb and I were ready to begin recording, but the others were afraid that the giants from the other labels might hear of our plans and retaliate. Destroy us.

VJ: But you and Caleb thought otherwise?

JOSHUA: Yes. We knew that God wanted us to proceed with the record, but fear won out. We wandered in the wilderness for forty years, learning again that God was the one we should follow. Finally, when only Caleb and myself were still alive out of the original group, God told us it was time.

VJ: And now, we have the new video. Tell us about the song itself. Is this video going to be as spectacular as your last? I'm thinking particularly of the special effects: the parting of the Red Sea, drowning the Egyptian army, the pillar of fire. Will we see more of this?

JOSHUA: Not exactly. But there will be some surprises.

VJ: Don't want to give it away, right? OK. Let's take a look at the Israelites' latest video, "Jericho, Bye Bye." It's a long one, seven parts, so we'll watch each part separately. Here goes "Jericho, Bye Bye," Part One.

(ISRAELITES quietly march around the room and return to their seats.)

VJ: Well, as Joshua said, there were some surprises. I don't recall seeing anything quite like this before. I like the trumpet music, but can you explain the lack of lyrics, Joshua?

JOSHUA: I can't say that I truly understand it myself. I only know that God instructed us to march quietly around Jericho and then to return to our camp.

VJ: OK. A mystery that will probably never be solved. Let's continue and see what surprises Part Two has in store.

(ISRAELITES quietly march around the room and return to their seats.)

VJ: Interesting concept. Two parts, identical in all respects. Would it be fair to say that you are symbolically showing that God is always the same? I notice that the trumpeters are all priests. The music is the same, the movement is the same, the only sound comes from the priests' trumpets. God is the same. That's the symbolism, right?

JOSHUA: I never thought about that. I only know that God instructed us to quietly march around Jericho and then return to our camp.

VJ: Another mystery. This will have music historians scratching their heads for years to come. Let's continue now with "Jericho, Bye Bye," Part Three.

(ISRAELITES quietly march around the room and return to their seats.)

VJ: I think I'm beginning to understand. Your first video was filled with all those spectacular special effects. That pillar of fire was especially impressive. Now you're showing that even though there has been flash in the lives of the Israelites, they're really ordinary people, no different from anybody else. They commute to work, return home. A remarkable insight into the everyday existence of everyday people.

JOSHUA: I never thought about that. I only know that God instructed us to quietly march around Jericho and then return to our camp.

VJ: For the lead singer, you know remarkably little about your own video. Oh, well. Let's continue with "Jericho, Bye Bye," Part Four.

(ISRAELITES quietly march around the room and return to their seats.)

VJ: It is amazing. Four parts, all the same. And every time I see it, I see something that I had previously missed. Take, for example, that big wooden box carried by the priests that come right behind the priests with the trumpets.

JOSHUA: The Ark of the Covenant.

VJ: Is that what it's called? Angels on top of it, one on each end with their wings touching. This must indicate that the Israelites are a united people. The two angels probably represent men and women. Or possibly, old and young. Or, being angels, perhaps they represent all things that are opposites in people and show that, in the case of the Israelites, they join together. Differences united into similarity. That's what this video is all about, right?

JOSHUA: I never thought about that. I only know that God instructed us to quietly march around Jericho and then return to our camp.

VJ: Give me some help here, Joshua. You want this video to be a hit, and I'm doing my best, but there's only so much that can be said about a long hike with priests playing the same trumpet tune over and over. There is something hidden in here that we have to dig out. Maybe Part Five will give us the missing clue. "Jericho, Bye Bye," Part Five.

(ISRAELITES quietly march around the room and return to their seats.)

VJ: It's beginning to make sense. I notice that all the men of war precede all the other people of Israel. War first, followed by peace, obviously indicating that people should be peace-loving, for war does not solve our problems. By having the long walk, with war in front, you are showing that problems can be eventually solved only by noncombatants. The women of the land and the children, not yet grown.

JOSHUA: I never thought about that. I only know that God instructed us to quietly march around Jericho and then return to our camp.

VJ: Well, in spite of your inability to assist us in uncovering the deep meanings contained within this work, I think that we're beginning to see the light. Part Six is bound to add to the total picture. "Jericho, Bye Bye," Part Six.

(ISRAELITES quietly march around the room and return to their seats.)

VJ: What a masterful stroke of symbolism. How did I miss it before?

JOSHUA: What's that?

VJ: The city itself. Look at the cold, grey, lifeless walls. Gates completely shut up. Nobody coming or going. Symbolically showing that if people shut themselves out, not allowing others to enter or get close, they become as cold and lifeless as the stone walls of Jericho. And then, in all this bleakness, we see the scarlet cord hanging down against the grey stone, showing that even though the exterior is grey and dead, there is life inside. The scarlet cord symbolizes the life blood that flows through living creatures. Life is not lost; there is hope. Masterful!

JOSHUA: I never thought about that. I only know that God instructed us to quietly march around Jericho and then return to our camp.

VJ: I'm excited about this video, now. In spite of no special effects, in spite of its length, this video will go down as one of the great videos of all time. Let's tie up all the loose ends now with "Jericho, Bye Bye," Part Seven.

(ISRAELITES quietly march around Jericho seven times, then JOSHUA cries, "Shout; for the Lord has given you the city!" and all the ISRAELITES shout.)

VJ: Wow! Look at those special effects! Look how the walls of the city fell away! I knew that Part Seven would bring everything into the light! Your song clearly says that God tears down the stone of our lives to let in the light. This has to be the most exciting video in the last hundred years. Congratulations, Joshua! That one burst of lyric has more meaning than all the songs ever written. We will have to watch this again and again.

JOSHUA: Actually, I believe that the video is saying that you should follow and obey the Lord.

VJ: Nonsense. Don't try to belittle the great work that you've done to unravel the human condition. We're out of time, but be sure to stay tuned for Elah's Comedy Hour, next on the nation's music video station, "Such Sound."

ACHAN BRINGS HOME THE BACON

SCRIPTURE: Joshua 7:1-23

SUGGESTED TOPICS: Telling the truth; obeying God; results of sin; greed; theft

BIBLE BACKGROUND

The Israelites had just finished forty years of wandering in the desert, the result of not believing God and being disobedient to His word. Surely, they had learned to trust and obey. God's instructions to the Israelites for the conquering of Jericho, the first Canaanite city to be faced, was to take no plunder for themselves. God was going to bring victory, not so the Israelites could enrich themselves, but as a validation of God's claim to possess the land. All the soldiers listened to the words of Joshua, except for Achan.

The Bible does not specifically say Achan's family knew he had taken any plunder from the city of Jericho. However, this was the first battle in the conquering of the Promised Land. Surely, the families of the soldiers would be anxiously waiting for the return of their husbands, brothers and sons. Also, they were living in tents; tents that could be easily transported on a long journey. How does somebody hide something in a one-room tent so that the other inhabitants are not aware of its existence?

However, even if they did not know Achan had taken the plunder, his family would still have suffered. This is a basic biblical principle. The actions of any individual have an impact on others; most especially do a leader's actions bring consequences to those under that authority.

PERFORMANCE TIPS

1. Suggested props: a multicolored cape or piece of cloth, wood or cardboard wedge spray painted gold or wrapped with gold foil, a bag of silver coins.

2. Very briefly discuss the instructions of God to Joshua concerning the battle of Jericho. Some students may not remember or may never have heard the story before.

3. Point out to the class that the Bible does not tell us Achan's family knew that the gold, silver and cloth were hidden in the tent. It is important for children to understand that their actions can hurt innocent people as well as themselves.

4. Focus attention on the fact that honesty in our personal relationships is essential for a good life.

DISCUSSION QUESTIONS

1. Have you ever done something you knew was wrong but pretended that what you did was all right? Could you ever make yourself believe that it was all right?

2. In the skit, Achan claims that he did not disobey any of the ten commandments. Look at each one (see Exodus 20:1-17). Which ones do you think he broke?

3. What were the consequences of Achan's disobedience? Have you ever told a lie? What happened when the lie was discovered?

4. Has anybody ever told you a lie? How did you feel when you discovered the lie?

5. Why is honesty important?

ACHAN BRINGS HOME THE BACON

CHARACTERS
ACHAN (AY-kan)
ACHAN'S WIFE
ACHAN'S SON
ACHAN'S DAUGHTER

ACHAN: Wife! Look! You'll never guess what I have.

WIFE: So, if I won't guess, how about you tell me.

CHILDREN: Me, too! Me, too! I want to know, too!

ACHAN: Look at this garment.

WIFE: Oh, Achan! It's gorgeous! Look at all those beautiful colors all interwoven. It's so beautiful! Where did you get it?

ACHAN: The same place that I got these.

CHILDREN: Wow! Look at all that silver! There must be forty years of allowance there. And that wedge of gold! Wow!

WIFE: But Achan, where did you get all these things? They must be worth a fortune.

ACHAN: Where else would one get all these riches in Canaan? I got them from the Canaanites. We'll be rich. Rich!

CHILDREN: Can we have an increase in our allowance now, Dad?

WIFE: Hush, children. Your father and I have to talk. Now, Achan, what do you mean, you got them from the Canaanites? I thought that you were fighting at Jericho all day.

ACHAN: I was. But who do you think lives in Jericho?

SON: Jerichoians?

DAUGHTER: Jerichoites?

CHILDREN: Jericho-ovians?

WIFE: Silence, children. Achan? Are you trying to tell me that you got these things from some Canaanite people in Jericho?

ACHAN: In a manner of speaking. Yes.

WIFE: You mean that you took a bribe so that some of the Jerichoites, Jerichoians… oh, children! Now you have me doing it. So that some of the people in Jericho could escape?

ACHAN: Of course not! What do you think I am—a traitor? Did our leader, Joshua, not say that we must drive out all of the Canaanites from the land? Were we not specifically commanded to destroy all the residents of Jericho, except for those in Rahab's house? I would not take a bribe to let some of the accursed of God live.

WIFE: Then how did you get these things from the Canaanites?

ACHAN: We were fighting through Jericho and I saw a rich man's house. And such a beautiful house it was, too. So, I thought to myself, *What if somebody is hiding in that house?* I went in, looked around and found nobody. But such wealth! Boy! Did I find wealth!

CHILDREN: So what happened, Dad?

ACHAN: I'll tell you. I looked all around. Nobody had come in with me. Nobody knew how much this wealthy Canaanite had. So I hid a little silver, a little gold, this garment and took it with me when we left the rubble that used to be Jericho.

WIFE: But isn't that wrong, Achan? Joshua said we were not to keep anything from Jericho. Joshua said to destroy everything.

CHILDREN: Yeah, Dad. Isn't that wrong?

ACHAN: What could be wrong with it? Look! It's only a little bit of what was there. And look at this beautiful garment. You will look so gorgeous in it. To destroy such a garment as this, that would be wrong. And a little silver and gold. What is wrong with a man trying to better himself so that his children can have some better things?

CHILDREN: Right! There's nothing wrong with bigger allowances.

WIFE: But it doesn't seem right. Isn't it against the Law?

ACHAN: How can it be against the Law? Look! Law number one. "You shall have no other gods before me." I'm not having other gods. Only a little silver and gold.

WIFE: That's true.

ACHAN: Number two. "You shall not make for yourself an idol." Am I making any idols? Number three. "You shall not misuse the name of the Lord your God." I have not misused His name.

CHILDREN: Right on, Dad! Nothing wrong there.

ACHAN: "Remember the Sabbath day by keeping it holy. Honor your father and your mother. You shall not murder. You shall not commit adultery." Does keeping a few little trinkets break any of those laws?

WIFE: Well...no. Number eight. "You shall not steal." How about that one?

ACHAN: What stealing? This is the spoils of war. The only person to have any claim on it was the rich Canaanite, and he doesn't need it now.

WIFE: Well...I suppose.

ACHAN: "You shall not give false testimony against your neighbor." Am I lying about anything that my neighbor did? "You shall not covet...anything that belongs to your neighbor." Does any of this belong to my neighbor? No! It belongs to me. *(Singing.)* "Oh, if I were a rich man..."

WIFE: Hush. You should not sing that song.

ACHAN: Why not?

CHILDREN: Because you don't sing very well.

WIFE: Children! That is no way to speak to your father. No. There are two reasons that you should not sing that song.

ACHAN: What is the first?

WIFE: If anyone should hear you, he might suspect that you have taken some booty from Jericho.

CHILDREN: And then you might have to give it back.

ACHAN: A very good reason. What is the second?

WIFE: The song has not yet been written. It will not be written for more than three thousand years. You should not sing songs that do not exist.

ACHAN: I suppose you're right. Somebody might think that it was fortune-telling or something if I were to sing a song that didn't exist. Oh, well. You must make this garment over into something nice for yourself.

WIFE: It would make a lovely evening gown. But, Achan. If I go out tomorrow with a new fancy dress, what will people say?

DAUGHTER: The women will all be envious and they will say, "Oh! What a lovely dress! Where did you get it?"

WIFE: Precisely.

ACHAN: I see your point, my dear. There could be some embarrassing questions about it. I have it! We will hide what I have taken from Jericho. Then, after a few more conquests, when we have taken some more booty, it will not be so noticeable that we have some new things. Everybody will have new things. But where can we hide this so that nobody will see it?

SON: How about under the floor of the tent, Dad? Nobody would come in with a shovel to look under anybody else's floor.

ACHAN: Ah! That's my son! A true thinking man. Come. We'll do it together. *(Singing.)* "Oh, if I were a rich man...."

Ai!

SCRIPTURE: Joshua 6:19; 7:1-4

SUGGESTED TOPICS: Sin hurts others; consequences of disobedience; following God's instructions

BIBLE BACKGROUND

Mighty Jericho had fallen. The power of God caused the city's walls to tumble down. Jericho was destroyed, never to return to her former glory. Next on the campaign trail was Ai, a much smaller city in the central hills of Palestine. The Israelites were confident, the Canaanites worried. If Jericho fell, how could Ai stand?

The Bible does not tell us whether Achan went or stayed behind when the Israelites went to battle Ai. Perhaps he went, wanting to be able to haul out his booty from Jericho under the guise of the spoils of the battle of Ai. Perhaps he would have gone because he was afraid he would be branded a coward if he did not volunteer to fight. The skit chooses to show Achan as avaricious in the extreme, wanting to stay back and admire what he took from Jericho.

PERFORMANCE TIPS

After the skit, tell the story of the battle at Ai (see Joshua 7:2-5). Read Joshua 7:20,21 to find out Achan's actions.

DISCUSSION QUESTIONS

1. What was Achan's sin? What happened because of his sin?

2. In what ways do you sometimes not follow God's instructions?

3. This story shows how sin hurts others. In what ways can your sins hurt other people?

Ai!

CHARACTERS

JOSHUA
FIRST SOLDIER
SECOND SOLDIER
THIRD SOLDIER
ACHAN (AY-ken)

PRONUNCIATION GUIDE

Ai (AY-eye)
Canaan (KAY-nun)

JOSHUA: Great battle, men. Jericho is soundly whipped.

SOLDIERS: Three cheers for us. Hip, hip, hooray! Hip, hip...

JOSHUA: Sorry to break up your celebration, boys, but we still have the rest of Canaan to conquer.

SOLDIERS: No problem. We're tough. We're rough. We'll beat 'em, thump em...

JOSHUA: Let's not forget that the Lord is with us. He really won the battle.

SOLDIERS: Oh, yeah. Right. Forgot about that.

JOSHUA: Now, let's review our previous strategy.

FIRST SOLDIER: We march...

SECOND SOLDIER: Silently...

THIRD SOLDIER: Around the city seven times...

SOLDIERS: Then blow the trumpets, shout and watch the walls fall down.

JOSHUA: And then...

SOLDIERS: Then?

ACHAN: I know, I know.

JOSHUA: Yes, Achan.

ACHAN: We burn everything and don't keep any plunder for ourselves.

JOSHUA: Right. Those were the Lord's instructions that we all obeyed. Right?

FIRST SOLDIER: Right!

SECOND SOLDIER: Right!

THIRD SOLDIER: Right!

ACHAN: Uh, *(pause)* right.

JOSHUA: That was the previous battle. From now on, we behave more like soldiers and fight our battles according to military strategy.

SOLDIERS: And we get to keep the spoils of our victories?

JOSHUA: Right.

SOLDIERS: Three cheers for Joshua. Hip, hip...

JOSHUA: Those are the Lord's commands, not mine. I don't need any cheers. Now, come closer. We need to make plans to conquer the next city.

FIRST SOLDIER: Ai!

JOSHUA: What's wrong?

FIRST SOLDIER: Nothing. Why do you ask?

JOSHUA: I thought you screamed. I must have been mistaken. Now, the next city...

SECOND SOLDIER: Ai!

JOSHUA: What's wrong?

SECOND SOLDIER: Nothing. Why do you ask?

JOSHUA: I thought you screamed. I must have been mistaken. Now, the next city...

THIRD SOLDIER: Ai!

JOSHUA: OK, what's the deal here? Every time I talk about going to the next battle, you scream. Are you cowards, or what?

SOLDIERS: No! We're just calling out the name of the next city. Ai.

JOSHUA: Oh. OK. Let's plan our strategy for conquering Ai.

FIRST SOLDIER: No problem.

SECOND SOLDIER: It's a tiny, little place up in the hills.

THIRD SOLDIER: We won't need the whole army.

JOSHUA: You're suggesting that some of the army stay here, in camp?

ACHAN: I'll volunteer to stay. I have, uh, things to do here in camp.

JOSHUA: Why not send the entire army? End the battle quickly?

FIRST SOLDIER: We've spied out the place.

SECOND SOLDIER: It doesn't have great defenses.

THIRD SOLDIER: Not many men defending it.

ACHAN: No sense in tiring the whole army on a march to such a little city. Why, it couldn't have much to offer in booty—I mean, be difficult to conquer.

JOSHUA: How many men should be sent to fight the battle?

FIRST SOLDIER: No more than a few thousand.

SECOND SOLDIER: How about three thousand? I've always liked the number three.

THIRD SOLDIER: Sure. That'll be plenty.

JOSHUA: What do you think, Achan?

ACHAN: Three thousand. I like it. Has a nice ring to it.

JOSHUA: Right. Then gather three thousand soldiers...

FIRST SOLDIER: I can get one thousand.

SECOND SOLDIER: I can get another thousand.

THIRD SOLDIER: I can get the third thousand.

ACHAN: And I'll be in my tent, counting gold—I mean, planning our next attack.

JOSHUA: It's good to know the Lord has men like you, ready to do His will when we go into battle. Go! And may the Lord be with you.

CANAAN TV NEWS

SCRIPTURE: Judges 4; 5

SUGGESTED TOPICS: Prejudice; disobedience vs. obedience

BIBLE BACKGROUND

The Israelites had conquered Canaan. However, contrary to God's command, not all the former inhabitants had been driven out (see Judges 1). The result of this incomplete victory was a vicious cycle that continually repeated itself for centuries: Israel would worship God and prosper; then Israel would be drawn away from the worship of God and would eventually be oppressed by its neighbors; finally, God would raise up a judge to call Israel back to the worship of the true God. Othniel, Ehud and Shamgar were the first of the judges to deliver Israel. However, for twenty years Israel was cruelly dominated by Jabin, the king of Canaan, seeking to restore Canaanite rule which had been ended by Joshua (see Joshua 11:1,10). Jabin may have been the name of a dynasty of Canaanite kings. During this bleak period Deborah, a prophetess, became Israel's next judge.

PERFORMANCE TIPS

1. Suggested props: one or more microphones for newscasters; large, potted palm tree to represent "Deborah's Palm"; sheet of paper for Barke.

2. This skit is best used with older groups. Younger groups may find the skit long and difficult to follow.

3. Distribute the skit in advance. Do not attempt to have the group perform it without practice.

4. Introduce the skit by saying, "We're about to see TV news from long ago. Watch closely and see if you can understand all that happened." After the skit, ask the group to tell you the story based on what they saw. Be prepared to supplement information they might have missed.

5. The commercials are just for fun. If you have creative participants who would enjoy the challenge, ask them to write their own commercials.

6. If your church is having a special event, you might use the commercial time to advertise it.

DISCUSSION QUESTIONS

1. What were the religious beliefs of the newscasters? How might the newscast have been different if they had been Jewish?

2. Were the Israelites in Canaan intolerant? Is intolerance always bad? When might intolerance be good and when might it be bad?

3. How should you treat people with beliefs different from yours?

4. Why do you believe Christianity is true?

CANAAN TV NEWS

CHARACTERS
ZAMAN (ZAY-mun)
ZORAH (ZOH-ruh)
HAMATH (HAY-muth)
TEREZ (teh-REZ)
TABOR (TAY-bur)
BARKE (BAR-keh)
ANNOUNCER

PRONUNCIATION GUIDE
Amalek (AM-uh-lek)
Barak (bah-RAHK)
Kishon (KEE-shon)
Manasseh (muh-NAA-suh)
Naphtali (NAF-tuh-lye)
Phoenicia (foe-NEE-sha)
Sisera (SIS-er-ah)
Zebulon (ZEH-byoo-lun)

ZAMAN: Good evening. I'm Zaman...

ZORAH: And I'm Zorah....

ZAMAN: And this is the twelfth-hour Canaan TV news.

ZORAH: Tonight's top story: Deborah is missing! But first, this message.

ANNOUNCER: After a long, hard day, do you find that your feet feel like they have wandered forty years in the wilderness? There's probably nothing wrong with your feet! It's your sandals! Yes! End aching feet forever with a pair of Dr. Samuel's sensational sandals! Your feet will love you for it!

ZAMAN: Welcome back to the news. Our feature story tonight: one of Canaan's true characters, Deborah, the judge and prophet of the Israelites. As everyone in Israel knows, Deborah spends most days sitting under a palm tree. However, for the past few days she has not been at her usual location. For an on-the-spot report, we go to Hamath at the palm tree. Hamath?

HAMATH: Thank you, Zaman. Today, Deborah did not appear at the palm at her appointed time. Hard-nosed investigation has revealed that she has not been here for several days. Unusual, to say the least. What has happened to her? Is she the victim of foul play?

ZAMAN: Have there been rumors about the cause of her absence?

HAMATH: There certainly have! Some of Deborah's critics suggests that she has run off with Barak, captain of Israel's army. When we went to her home and questioned her husband, Lappidoth, he became unreasonably upset, a reaction that leads some to suspect the rumor may be true.

ZAMAN: Thank you for your in-depth analysis, Hamath. Another fine job of reporting. Zorah?

ZORAH: Racial intolerance has once again reared its ugly head in our fair land. With us tonight is Professor Terez of Jezreel University. Welcome to the program, Professor.

TEREZ: Thank you, Zorah. It's a pleasure to be here.

ZORAH: Professor, can you shed any light on this latest round of racial prejudice?

TEREZ: Certainly, Zorah. For centuries there was never any racial strife in Canaan. Oh, we had our little squabbles and disputes, the same as anybody else, but basically, we got along pretty well. If your neighbor chose to worship a rock while you worshiped a tree, fine. Nobody worried about it. If you chose to sacrifice your children to Baal while I chose to sacrifice mine to Molech, what was the big deal? Everyone was happy. Content.

ZORAH: What happened to change this, Professor?

TEREZ: The Israelites arrived. Naturally, the people already here were concerned about the new arrivals. But it was expected that after a few years, the Israelites would come to accept our ways as reasonable. After all, everybody else who moved in had.

ZORAH: You're saying this has not been the case with Israel?

TEREZ: It certainly has not! Do you remember the name Joshua?

ZORAH: Only too well, Professor. The Scourge of Canaan, I believe he is called in the history scrolls.

TEREZ: Joshua, as you remember, led the first Israelites here, and as soon as he did, there was war. Every day, another city was being attacked by the Israelites. Jericho, Ai, the list is almost endless.

ZORAH: Why was Joshua so intent on destroying Canaan, Professor?

TEREZ: The man was obviously imbalanced. He claimed something about the land being promised to them by God. His rallying cry to his troops was, "Drive out those God has cursed!" That kind of thing.

ZORAH: What I don't understand, Professor, is why people were afraid of someone who claimed to be obeying a god. After all, aren't all gods just about the same?

TEREZ: The Israelites have always claimed to have a different god than everybody else. They say things like, "Remember the God of Abraham, Isaac and Jacob." I know this sounds peculiar to anybody with an ounce of sense, but they actually believe there is only one god.

ZORAH: In this enlightened age, doesn't everyone accept that everything around us is a god and that everyone has his own god to help him? Why don't the Israelites understand something that simple?

TEREZ: Well, over the years, the Israelites realized that trying to worship one god was ridiculous. Most of them accepted the gods of the people living around them. Life actually became peaceful.

ZORAH: Then why do the Israelites always seem responsible when racial—and I suppose, religious—prejudices crop up?

TEREZ: About every forty years or so, some Israelite claims to be a messenger from God and calls the Israelites to forsake the gods of Canaan. When that happens, look out. The Israelites forget the reasonableness of many gods and go back to only one god. When THAT happens, the only possible outcome is war.

ZORAH: Are you suggesting that we might have another conflict in Canaan?

TEREZ: I'm afraid it's a very real possibility. That's the problem with intolerance. It always leads to violence.

ZORAH: Thank you again for being our guest, Professor.

TEREZ: Any time, Zorah.

ZORAH: There you have it. It appears that we could be in for more unnecessary violence in our fair land. Zaman.

ZAMAN: Our last story tonight also involves the Israelites. Eyewitnesses report a mass migration of Israelites, something on the order of ten thousand men, moving from the north country into the south. It's a well-known fact that Israelites tend to be home-bodies. Sounds as though something strange is brewing up north. Stay tuned. Tabor will be right back with the weather.

ANNOUNCER: Is your camel getting old? Do you find yourself having to add water at every oasis along the way? Are you getting fewer miles per pound of grain? Then it's time to trade up, and now is the time to deal! Ahab can't afford to haggle! He's over-stocked! Get down to Ahab's today! Make your best deal and ride away on the camel of your choice! Single hump, double hump, compact, full-size—whatever you need, Ahab has it!

ZAMAN: And now, here's Tabor with the weather.

TABOR: Thank you, Zaman. Before tonight's weather, I want to apologize to all of you. I told you that the weather would be sunny and warm. As you know now, I was wrong. Somewhere out in the Great Sea, the wind god and the cloud god got into some kind of big argument. That caused hundreds of bushels of water to pour down, especially around Kishon Valley.

Things are looking up for tomorrow, however. I consulted the priests of the weather gods, and they say all have made peace with one another. So tomorrow, we should have the pleasant weather we expected today. Get outside and enjoy yourselves, because who knows when the gods will begin fighting again. Good night and good weather.

ZAMAN: Thanks for that report, Tabor. We'll be back with sports after this word from our sponsor.

ANNOUNCER: Has all this bad weather from the gods given you a nasty cough, aching throat, runny nose? Well, don't worry! Bothersome colds can now be a thing of the past with Zadok's new Elixir of Health. Approved by the god of health, this elixir will give you health, wealth, happiness—everything that makes life worth living! Order yours today. This special TV offer cannot be found in stores. Send seven drachmas for each bottle to Elixir, Box 7750, Station A, Beth-Shan. Don't wait! Do it now!

ZORAH: Welcome back. And now, here's Barke with the sports.

BARKE: Thank you, Zorah. Well, it's been a big day in sports. Let's review what happened around the leagues.

Egypt was a big loser against Amalek, and that's what we've come to expect. Egypt is no longer a great powerhouse since it has lost the leadership of Rameses II. A close game between Ammon and Midian saw Ammon squeaking out the narrowest of victories. Moab beat the Philistines in overtime.

Today's big game went on at Megiddo Stadium in the Kishon Valley. Weather conditions were not ideal. Rain, thunder, lightning—you name it, we had it. And we had some other surprises, as well. Coach Jabin had his team ready. You could see it in the eyes of his captain, Sisera. The home team was well prepared and well equipped. They had the best chariots, horses and weapons that money could buy. Nine hundred chariots! And Sisera was ready to use them.

The visiting Israelites fielded an amazingly large team for them: approximately ten thousand men. However, they were poorly equipped and poorly trained. Their captain, Barak, made a surprise change in personnel for this game. Everyone in the know was certain he would select his team from the tribe of Manasseh, men who live in the area and know the terrain. But in an unprecedented move, he chose his entire team from the tribes of Naphtali and Zebulon. What's more, he had a woman on the sidelines with him. Nobody seems to know just who she was, but she seemed to be in on the decision making during the game.

Anyway, back to the game itself. Sisera had his game planned out for a dry afternoon, but you know what happened. The gods fought in the heavens and dumped water all over the field. Sisera's chariots were stuck in mud and couldn't move. Instead of being an asset, they were a liability. And the gods, not content with simple rain, threw in blinding flashes of lightning and ear-splitting thunder. The war horses reared up in terror, throwing their riders and running in panic. Coach Jabin's team was totally confused, even the experienced Captain Sisera. To make a long story short, Sisera was thumped by Barak and the unknown woman. *(BARKE is handed a sheet of paper.)*

This late-breaking story just in. It seems that Sisera, having fled the field at Megiddo, sought shelter at the tent of Heber. Heber wasn't home but his wife, Jael, let Sisera in anyway. Bad move on Sisera's part. We don't know Jael's motive—maybe she dropped a bundle betting on the game—but when Sisera was asleep, Jael drove a tent spike through his head. This is a sad day for sports, indeed. One of Canaan's great players, Sisera, first defeated and now dead at the hands of women. One hardly knows what the far-reaching effects of this development will be, but I expect that Jabin will no longer be the force he once was. For now, that's all in sports.

ZORAH: Another development just in. It seems that Deborah has returned home. Her disappearance was nothing more than a little trip to watch a sporting contest. We're glad you're home safe and sound, Deborah. That's all for tonight. Until tomorrow, I'm Zorah—

ZAMAN: And I'm Zaman—

ZORAH: Good night.

THE CALL OF GIDEON

SCRIPTURE: Judges 6

SUGGESTED TOPICS: Handling fear; trusting God in spite of fear

BIBLE BACKGROUND

Forty years after Deborah's term as judge, the Israelites again fell away from God. As a result of their disobedience, they were conquered by the Midianites (see Judges 6:1), a nomadic people who formed alliances with the Amalekites and Moabites. Most of the crops Israel grew were taken by the Midianites, leaving Israel impoverished. In their anguish, the Israelites cried out to God. In His mercy, God responded by raising up another judge.

Gideon heard God's call, but did not believe at first (see Judges 6:17). Even Gideon's own family had built, and probably maintained, an altar to Baal. In spite of Gideon's disbelief and his family's acceptance of idol worship, the Lord used him to redeem Israel.

Purah, Gideon's servant, has been included as the second character in the skit because, other than Gideon's father, Purah is the only other name mentioned in the biblical account. Although the Bible does not specifically say he was among the ten servants who took part in tearing down the idol of Baal, the skit assumes he did because of his close position to Gideon.

PERFORMANCE TIPS

Introduce the skit by setting the scene: "Often in the history of the Israelite people, we see a pattern develop. The Israelites started out by obeying God, but then gradually began to worship false gods. As a result, God withdrew His protection, and the enemies of the Israelites caused trouble for them. Then the Israelites cried to the one, true God for help. Because God loved the Israelites, He answered their cries and sent them a strong leader. This skit tells the story of one of God's greatest leaders, Gideon."

DISCUSSION QUESTIONS

1. Why was Gideon afraid? How do you think he felt when the other Israelites tried to kill him for tearing down Baal's altar?

2. Are you ever afraid? What sort of things scare you?

3. Does trusting God mean you will never be afraid again? Why or why not?

4. What should you do when you feel afraid?

THE CALL OF GIDEON

CHARACTERS
PURAH (POO-rah)
GIDEON (GID-ee-un)

PRONUNCIATION GUIDE
Manasseh (muh-NAA-suh)
Naphtali (NAF-tuh-lye)
Zebulon (ZEH-byoo-lun)

PURAH: May I ask you a question, Gideon?

GIDEON: Yes, but that's already a question.

PURAH: Quit clowning around. You know what I mean.

GIDEON: What's the question?

PURAH: Could you please tell me how you know we're supposed to fight the Midianites?

GIDEON: Purah! You're my servant! I'm the boss. You're supposed to do what I say without asking a lot of questions.

PURAH: I know. But I'd feel better if you could tell me why we're going to do this.

GIDEON: (Sighs.) OK. If it will make you feel better. I was threshing wheat in the winepress...

PURAH: How come?

GIDEON: Because if you don't thresh it, you get a lot of dirt in with the grain.

PURAH: I mean, how come you were threshing wheat in a winepress? Wouldn't it be easier to thresh it outside?

GIDEON: Of course it would! But if I threshed it out in the open, then the Midianites would have come and taken it away. Remember the Midianites? They're the enemy.

PURAH: You don't have to be sarcastic. So, you were threshing wheat...

GIDEON: In the winepress. Then, suddenly, I heard a voice. Was I ever scared!

PURAH: Why? There's nothing illegal about threshing wheat in a winepress. It's a little strange, maybe, but not illegal.

GIDEON: I wasn't afraid of breaking any law. I thought the Midianites had found me and that they would take away all the wheat.

PURAH: Oh, Gideon! Don't let them take away your wheat! If you do, your family will starve to death and I won't ever see you again...

GIDEON: Purah.

PURAH: ...and we won't ever be together again...

GIDEON: Purah.

PURAH: ...and I'll be all alone and so unhappy...

GIDEON: Purah!

PURAH: Yes?

GIDEON: I'm telling a story. There are no Midianites here. And I couldn't change the story anyway. So be quiet and listen.

PURAH: I'm listening.

GIDEON: Good. As I said, I was scared. I heard the voice, but I hadn't really heard what it said. You know what I mean?

PURAH: Sure. Because it was talking in a foreign language.

GIDEON: No! Not like that. I understood the language. But I was so afraid that I didn't hear the words. My brain was so busy thinking the Midianites had found me, it wouldn't decipher the words I was hearing.

PURAH: Oh. Then how did you finally know what it was saying?

GIDEON: My brain finally figured out that the voice was not a Midianite. Then I stopped to think about what it had said.

PURAH: And what did the voice say?

GIDEON: It said, "The Lord is with you, oh mighty man of valor."

PURAH: That's funny, Gideon.

GIDEON: What's funny?

PURAH: You were quaking in your boots and somebody says, "Hey there, you're a tough soldier, a brave fighter..."

GIDEON: Do you want to hear the story, or not?

PURAH: Sorry. But I still think it's funny.

GIDEON: Anyway, I peeked out from the winepress, and I saw an angel.

PURAH: An angel?

GIDEON: Right.

PURAH: With wings and a shiny halo?

GIDEON: No! Angels don't look like that.

PURAH: Then what did it look like?

GIDEON: It looked kind of like a man...

PURAH: Then how did you know it was an angel? Did it walk around and say, "Behold, mighty quaking-in-your-boots man of valor! I am an angel. Listen to what I say..."

GIDEON: You're making fun again.

PURAH: Look, Gideon. I'm your main servant, right? But I have trouble believing that you saw an angel. Angels don't exist! They're like boogeymen. Only nicer.

GIDEON: I'm telling you what happened. If you don't believe it...

PURAH: Go ahead. I'll pretend to believe it for now.

GIDEON: OK. Well, I saw this angel. And I had trouble believing what it had said about the Lord being with me.

PURAH: And you're giving me a hard time about not believing?

GIDEON: OK, OK. But I said to the angel, "If the Lord is with us, then where are all the miracles that our fathers told us about? If the Lord is with us, why are we oppressed by the Midianites?"

PURAH: Hah! That's telling him. By the way, are angels hims?

GIDEON: I don't know. I guess so.

PURAH: Doesn't matter. You sure told him a thing or two. Hah, angel. *(Pause.)* But, Gideon, if that was an angel, should you have been speaking to it that way?

GIDEON: No. But I didn't know at the time that it was an angel.

PURAH: But you said you saw an angel.

GIDEON: Yes. I saw an angel, only I thought it was a man at the time. That's why I wasn't afraid to be a little bit rude.

PURAH: So how did you figure out that it was an angel?

GIDEON: When it touched the bread with its staff, and it all burned up.

PURAH: What bread?

GIDEON: The bread that was with the meat.

PURAH: What meat?

GIDEON: The meat that I served the angel.

PURAH: Do angels eat bread and meat?

GIDEON: No.

PURAH: Then why did you serve the angel bread and meat?

GIDEON: Because I didn't know that it was an angel! How about if I tell the story in its proper order? Then you might understand everything.

PURAH: Good idea. Go for it.

GIDEON: This angel that I thought was just a man said, "Go and save Israel from the Midianites. I am sending you."

PURAH: And you believed him?

GIDEON: Not right away. But I thought that maybe he was a prophet and he had got the wrong person. So I told him, "You've got the wrong guy. My family isn't important. We're poor. And I'm the youngest. Who is it that you're looking for? Maybe I can give you directions to his house."

PURAH: That makes sense. Israel needs a leader we can all look up to...

GIDEON: I'm telling this.

PURAH: Sorry. But you're not the kind of guy who looks like a leader, you know?

GIDEON: Well...you're right. Anyway, the angel that I thought was maybe a prophet said, "I will be with you. And you will strike down the Midianites as if they were only one man."

PURAH: That's weird.

GIDEON: What's weird?

PURAH: Some guy tells you that the two of you are going to fight the Midianites and you'll outnumber them two to one.

GIDEON: You don't understand the way prophets speak. What he meant was God would be fighting beside me and so the Midianites would be destroyed because they cannot stand up to God.

PURAH: So, prophets talk weird. What did you do?

GIDEON: I thought if he was a prophet he could do something to show me that he meant what he said. So I asked him to show me a sign that he really meant me. But I thought I should try to make up for being rude earlier, so I asked him to wait while I got him something to eat.

PURAH: But angels don't eat.

GIDEON: But I thought that he was a man.

PURAH: Right. I forgot.

GIDEON: So I brought him some bread and meat.

PURAH: I bet your mom was mad at you. Giving the family supper to a stranger.

GIDEON: You'd be surprised at my parents. They're pretty cool. Anyway, that was when he touched the meat and bread with his staff and it all just burned up.

PURAH: You should have known better than to put it on something flammable. These sudden fires have happened before, you know.

GIDEON: I didn't put it on something flammable. I put it on a rock. When fire came up out of the rock, I realized I had been talking to an angel. And that's when I got really scared. I was sure that I was going to die.

PURAH: So what happened? Did you die?

GIDEON: Look at me. Do I look dead?

PURAH: To tell you the truth, you have looked better. You're a little pale...

GIDEON: No! I didn't die. But God told me to do something.

PURAH: God told you to do something?

GIDEON: Right, He told...

PURAH: First an angel, now God. Are you sure you're feeling alright, Gideon?

GIDEON: I never felt better. Anyway, God told me to do something.

PURAH: And...

GIDEON: I did it.

PURAH: What?

GIDEON: What God told me.

PURAH: Which was?

GIDEON: I thought you knew. You were there. When we tore down the idol of Baal.

PURAH: Oh, that! I thought that was some kind of Halloween joke.

GIDEON: It was no joke. And Halloween hasn't been invented yet.

PURAH: I thought we were goners the next day. That was some lynch mob.

GIDEON: But Dad stood up for us.

PURAH: Yeah. Even after he found out you'd killed his bull. If it had been my dad, we'd be dead meat by now.

GIDEON: Back to the story. That was when the Midianites joined with the Amalekites and brought a huge army up to the Valley of Jezreel. God told me to gather an army from the tribes of Manasseh, Asher, Zebulon and Naphtali.

PURAH: God spoke to you again?

GIDEON: Right.

PURAH: And you jumped right to it?

GIDEON: Well...not right away. I wanted to be sure that I hadn't misunderstood.

PURAH: Good thinking. Might have just been a dream.

GIDEON: So I laid a fleece out all night.

PURAH: That's it? You put a sheepskin on the ground?

GIDEON: And what do you think happened?

PURAH: The Midianites came in the night and stole it?

GIDEON: No! The next morning, I wrung a bowlful of water out of the fleece.

PURAH: And...

GIDEON: And what?

PURAH: You were getting a sign. What happened to the water? Did it turn red, or did fish appear in it, or what?

GIDEON: Nothing else happened to the water.

PURAH: Then what was the sign?

GIDEON: The water was the sign.

PURAH: The water.

GIDEON: Right. The water.

PURAH: You know, Gideon. This may come as a bit of a surprise to you, but on a summer's eve in Israel when you leave something out overnight, it always gets wet. It's called dew, Gideon. The fleece got wet because of dew.

GIDEON: But the ground around it was dry. Bone dry. Still, I was not certain myself. So I asked for another sign.

PURAH: Good idea. Showers of gold or something like that?

GIDEON: No. I laid the fleece out again.

PURAH: And it got wet again. You've got no imagination, Gideon.

GIDEON: That's just it. This time, the ground all around the fleece was wet, but the fleece itself was as dry as dust.

PURAH: OK. I'll admit it. That was a good trick. So now what?

GIDEON: So now we're going to meet the army that I've gathered.

PURAH: To fight the Midianites?

GIDEON: Right.

PURAH: Have you told them your story yet?

GIDEON: Not yet.

PURAH: A word of advice, then.

GIDEON: Which is?

PURAH: When you do, go easy on the angel and the talking with God and the sheepskin. If you tell them those parts, you're not going to have much of an army left.

GIDEON'S ARMY

SCRIPTURE: Judges 7

SUGGESTED TOPICS: Trusting God when outmatched;
obedience resulting from trust

BIBLE BACKGROUND

For seven years, the Midianites had viciously oppressed the Israelites. The Midianites had the technology for processing iron and, consequently, had the latest in military hardware. They formed a powerful coalition with Amalek and other nearby nations. Judges 7:12 records that together they were like a swarm of locusts in number—unable to be counted. Against these odds, Gideon was to take an army which had access to only very primitive weapons. The Israelites were still working with wood and stone. Even so, when the Israelites assembled to fight the Midianites, most must have expected some form of military protocol to be followed. What must have been the reaction to Gideon's seemingly offhand method of breaking every rule of war found in the military handbook?

Every army has its sergeants; surely Gideon's army was no different—one man cannot possibly hope to give orders to thirty-two thousand men without some help. Since no other name is mentioned in the biblical account, Gideon's servant, Purah, has been chosen to be one of the sergeants in this skit. Although Purah is presented as a comic character, consider how much loyalty a man must have to follow a leader who, from a worldly viewpoint, is going about things all wrong.

PERFORMANCE TIPS

1. Suggested props: several rocks and thick, wooden sticks for troops to carry.
2. Before the skit, describe the military strength of the Midianites. (See Bible Background.) Make certain the group understands the hopelessness of the Israelites in their fight against Midian.
3. The skit ends before Gideon and Purah travel to the enemy camp. Tell the rest of the story to the group, emphasizing how God encouraged Gideon in the face of insurmountable odds.
4. In Gideon's time, fighting at night was not common. It was too easy to kill your own soldiers. Help the class understand that the strategy God gave to Gideon worked because of the confusion caused by a nighttime battle.

DISCUSSION QUESTIONS

1. Have you ever seen a swarm of grasshoppers? What are other phrases that would describe a group of people too large to be counted?
2. There is a very fine line between being foolish and being brave. Was Gideon brave or foolish? Why?
3. How would you feel if you were Purah? The Bible tells us that Purah went with Gideon to the Midianites' camp before the battle started. Would you be ready to fight the Midianites if you were Purah? Was Purah brave or foolish? Why?
4. How can the story of Gideon help us today? When have you faced a situation in which it was difficult to obey God? How can God help you when you are afraid to obey Him?

GIDEON'S ARMY

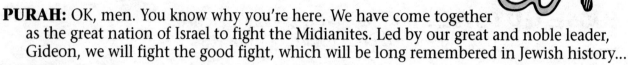

CHARACTERS
PURAH (POO-rah)

GIDEON (GID-ee-un)

ISRAELITE TROOPS

PURAH: OK, men. You know why you're here. We have come together as the great nation of Israel to fight the Midianites. Led by our great and noble leader, Gideon, we will fight the good fight, which will be long remembered in Jewish history...

GIDEON: Purah.

PURAH: Our children will sing songs of our gallant bravery! They will sing of our memory! Those who bravely die in battle...

GIDEON: Purah.

PURAH: Their exploits will be remembered long after their bodies are rotting in the grave. As their souls cry out in Sheol...

GIDEON: Purah!

PURAH: No! Their souls will not cry out, "Purah!" Who said that?

GIDEON: I did.

PURAH: Why are you making fun of me in front of the men, Gideon?

GIDEON: I didn't make fun of you, Purah.

PURAH: You certainly did. When I was giving my stirring speech to the troops, you said the souls in Sheol would cry out, "Purah!"

GIDEON: No I didn't. I was calling out your name to get your attention.

PURAH: Oh. Just a minute then. OK, men! Take five! Smoke if you have them!

GIDEON: What does that mean?

PURAH: I have no idea. But sergeants always yell that to the troops.

GIDEON: In the future, I think you should know what you're saying before you say it.

PURAH: OK. You're the boss. You wanted to see me about something?

GIDEON: Yes. I'm going off to pray, to ask God's guidance...

PURAH: Shh!

GIDEON: What? Did you hear something?

PURAH: No. But you should hold back on that talking to God stuff in front of the men. They might think you're a few bricks short of a load and go home. There'll be nobody left to fight the Midianites except you and me.

GIDEON: You're worrying for nothing. These are brave men, the finest in all of Israel. They won't desert us. And they SHOULD know that God is our leader, not me.

PURAH: Don't say that, Gideon! The men need somebody to follow that they can see.

GIDEON: No they don't. It's always better to follow God than to follow a person. Anyway, while I'm off praying, I want you to check out our weapons situation.

PURAH: Right! You've got it, boss. OK men! Fall in!

TROOPS: Fall in what?

PURAH: That's army talk. It means, "Get over here, now!" Now then. How many of you men brought weapons with you? How many brought a sword? Anybody? *(Pause.)* No. OK then. We have no swords. How about spears with iron tips? How many of you have spears with you? Anybody? *(Pause.)* Hmm. No spears. Shields! We do have shields, right? How many of you have shields? *(Pause.)* None? You must have brought something! Pointed sticks? How many have pointed sticks?

TROOPS: Yo!

PURAH: OK. Now we're cooking. How about rocks? Did anybody bring rocks with him?

TROOPS: Yo!

PURAH: Alright! Pointed sticks and rocks! How about wooden clubs?

TROOPS: Yo!

PURAH: Great! We have sticks and rocks and clubs. Everything an army could want.

GIDEON: How are things going, Purah?

PURAH: Terrific! Couldn't be better. Every man here has at least one weapon. Some have pointed sticks, some have rocks, some have wooden clubs...

GIDEON: Men, I would like to speak to you.

PURAH: OK you jokers! The general's about to speak! Listen up!

GIDEON: Thank you, Purah.

PURAH: Don't mention it.

GIDEON: Men, I have been talking with God.

PURAH *(whining)***:** Gideon. Ixnay on the odgay stuff.

GIDEON: It has been brought to my attention that although you are willing to fight, some of you are afraid. If you have any fears at all, please feel free to go home. Nobody will think less of you if you decide to leave now.

PURAH: Hold it! Don't nobody go nowhere! Gideon, could I talk to you, please?

GIDEON: Certainly, Purah. *(They step away from troops.)*

PURAH: Gideon, are you out of your ever-lovin' mind?

GIDEON: What do you mean, Purah?

PURAH: Do you know how many men we have here?

GIDEON: At a guess, maybe thirty-one or thirty-two thousand.

PURAH: Right! And how many men do the Midianites have?

GIDEON: Hard to say. They're like a swarm of locusts. There's so many of them that they're impossible to count.

PURAH: Right! And what kind of weapons do they have?

GIDEON: Swords, shields, spears, suits of armor. The usual stuff.

PURAH: Right! So we're hopelessly out-manned, hopelessly out-armed, and you want to send some of our soldiers home.

GIDEON: That's right.

PURAH: But why?

GIDEON: Because God told me to.

PURAH: Why would God do that? I thought He wanted us to win.

GIDEON: He does. But He wants us to realize that it's His victory, not ours. If we go into battle with thirty-two thousand men and win, Israel will boast that its soldiers are such great fighters that we can defeat anybody. God wants us to realize we won because He won the battle for us.

PURAH: It still doesn't make sense to me, but if you say so. At least we won't have as many casualties as we would if everyone stayed. Men! You heard our illustrious leader! If you're chicken-livered, yellow-bellied cowards...

GIDEON: Purah!

PURAH: If any of you have any doubts as to the wisdom of your being here, feel free to go home. But leave your sticks and rocks and clubs for the real soldiers.

GIDEON: Purah! I said they would not be criticized, and I meant it.

PURAH: Look at them all leaving! Most of them are splitting! Two thirds or more! Gideon, there's only going to be about ten thousand men left.

GIDEON: I'm going to pray again. While I'm gone, you can redistribute the weapons.

PURAH: OK! We've got lots of weapons now! Everybody should have at least one rock, one stick and one club. If you have an extra club, tie it to your waist as a spare, in case you break the first one.

GIDEON: Purah.

PURAH: Yes, Gideon.

GIDEON: Have the men go down to the spring.

PURAH: Good idea. We shouldn't go into battle thirsty. Are any of you men thirsty?

TROOPS: Yo!

PURAH: OK then! Everybody to the spring. Drink lots, because there won't be any time for drinking while the Midianites are slaughtering...I mean, while we're fighting the enemy.

(TROOPS move to spring. GIDEON and PURAH observe them.)

GIDEON: Do you notice how the men have different styles of drinking, Purah?

PURAH: They're not drinking Purah. They're drinking water. I think maybe you've been standing outside in the sun a little long, Gideon.

GIDEON: I didn't say they were drinking Purah. I was calling you by name, again.

PURAH: Oh. What was the question again?

GIDEON: Do you notice the different drinking styles that the men use?

PURAH: Yeah. Some of them are kneeling, scooping up a little bit of water in their hands. They can't get a decent mouthful that way. But most of them bend right over and get their faces down near the water. That's the way to get a good drink.

GIDEON: Men. I'd like to have a word with you.

PURAH: OK you mangy dogs! Listen up! The general's talking!

GIDEON: Thank you, Purah.

PURAH: Don't mention it.

GIDEON: I was speaking with God, again...

PURAH *(whining)*: Gideon.

GIDEON: I want to thank all of you for being willing to risk your lives in the service of your country, but God wants a somewhat smaller army than we currently have. So all you men who drank directly from the stream may go home.

PURAH: Hold it! Don't nobody go nowhere! May I talk to you again, Gideon?

GIDEON: Certainly, Purah. What is it?

PURAH: I don't want you to think that I'm trying to undermine you, Gideon...

GIDEON: I wouldn't think that, Purah.

PURAH: But are you sure you heard God right?

GIDEON: Yes, I'm sure. He said ten thousand men was too many, and Israel would boast of its greatness if an army of ten thousand defeated the Midianites. He told me we need to have a smaller army.

PURAH: But our army will be down to only about three hundred men if you send home the others.

GIDEON: That's right. God is going to win the victory. We just have to be there.

PURAH: OK. If you say so. Listen up, men! You guys who drank from out of your hands, stay! The rest of you can go home! But leave your weapons behind. We need all the help we can get now!

GIDEON: I'm going to pray one more time. Redistribute the weapons while I'm gone.

PURAH: OK! We've got lots of weapons now! Everybody carry as many clubs and pointed sticks as you can! If the rocks are too heavy, you can leave those behind! We can find more! Everybody got that?

TROOPS: Yo!

GIDEON: Purah.

PURAH: Yo! I mean, yes, Gideon?

GIDEON: Give every man a torch, a pitcher and a trumpet.

PURAH: But, Gideon. If they're carrying that stuff, how are they going to carry their weapons?

GIDEON: They won't.

PURAH: They won't what?

GIDEON: They won't be carrying weapons.

PURAH: Let me get this straight. We're going to fight a superior force...

GIDEON: Right.

PURAH: An army that has superior weapons...

GIDEON: Right.

PURAH: And we're going into battle without weapons...

GIDEON: Right.

PURAH: And you expect to win.

GIDEON: Right.

PURAH: And how will this miracle take place?

GIDEON: At last. You understand!

PURAH: Understand? Understand what?

GIDEON: That a miracle is going to happen. God will win the battle.

PURAH: All I understand is that we're about to go on a fool's mission. OK men! This is it! Drop your weapons and get your torches, pitchers and trumpets! Maybe if we play badly enough, we'll scare them to death! Oh, Gideon. One more thing.

GIDEON: What's that, Purah?

PURAH: Do you think we could get this fight started before you talk to God again?

SAMSON: THE EARLY YEARS

SCRIPTURE: Judges 13; 14

SUGGESTED TOPICS: Talents and abilities; consequences of disobedience; wisdom

BIBLE BACKGROUND

After Gideon came Abimelech, Tola, Jair, Jephthah, Ibzan, Elan and Abdon. After Abdon's death, the Israelites again did evil in God's sight. Consequently, they were delivered into the hands of the Philistines for forty years (see Judges 13:1). Once again, the Israelites cried out to God and God raised up the thirteenth judge, Samson.

Samson is one of the most difficult biblical characters to understand. He did not seem to have much consideration for the laws of God, respect for his parents or even common sense. In spite of these shortcomings, God used Samson as a hero of the faith (see Hebrews 11:32).

In the skit, Samson is portrayed as being totally self-centered. What he wants matters; nothing else does. He is shown as breaking every part of his Nazirite vow with the exception of cutting his hair (see Numbers 6:1-21). The Bible does not indicate that he drank wine or ate grapes but this is assumed as having happened from observing his other actions.

PERFORMANCE TIPS

1. Suggested props: chair and newspaper for Manoah, jar of honey for Samson.
2. If you have a large group, the Philistine man can be played by three or four men who follow Samson around and talk among themselves.
3. For comic effect, have the Philistine man (or group of men) follow right on Samson's heels just prior to his introduction.
4. Before the skit, read Numbers 6:2-6 to find out about the Nazirite vow.

DISCUSSION QUESTIONS

1. How did Samson use his great strength to obey God? How did he use it to disobey God?
2. What happened when Samson obeyed God? What happened when he didn't?
3. God gives everybody some kind of special ability or abilities. What special abilities do you have?
4. How can you use your abilities to obey God?

SAMSON: THE EARLY YEARS

CHARACTERS
MANOAH'S WIFE

MANOAH

SAMSON

SAMSON'S BRIDE

MAN

NARRATOR

PRONUNCIATION GUIDE
Nazirite (NAA-zer-ite)

Philistine (FIL-ih-steen)

WIFE: Manoah, will you please put your paper down? I have something very important to discuss with you.

MANOAH: What is it, my dear?

WIFE: I don't know if you've noticed or not, but we don't have any children.

MANOAH: It would be hard not to notice. Is there a point to your comment?

WIFE: Yes. We are going to have a son very soon.

MANOAH: You sound very sure of yourself. Are you absolutely certain about this? Not the child part. I know you can be certain about that. But what makes you think it will be a boy? People have girl babies, too, you know.

WIFE: An angel of the Lord appeared to me and said I would have a son. I am one hundred percent certain that the angel would not lie to me.

MANOAH: Do me a favor, please. Don't tell the neighbors you were speaking to an angel. I mean, why would an angel speak to you, or to me for that matter? We are not famous, like Moses or Joshua or even Gideon. Angels don't speak to nobodies.

WIFE: But those three you just mentioned were nobodies. They are famous because God or His angels spoke to them.

MANOAH: You have a point there. OK, I believe that an angel spoke to you. Did he tell you anything special about our son?

WIFE: He said that our son would deliver Israel from the Philistines and that he is to be a Nazirite.

MANOAH: Now I have a problem with what the angel told you. We're from the tribe of Dan and don't live anywhere near Nazareth. How can our son be a Nazirite?

WIFE: You're thinking of Nazarene. Our son is to take the Nazirite vow from birth. You know. The vow in the Law.

MANOAH: Oh, right! That vow! Maybe you could refresh my memory a little.

WIFE: Remember? A person devotes himself entirely to the Lord. He doesn't drink wine...

MANOAH: I could stand my son not being a drunkard.

WIFE: And he is not to approach any dead body...

MANOAH: If we want a decent funeral, we better have more children.

WIFE: And a razor is never to touch his hair.

MANOAH: Hold on, now! I don't know that I like that part. I mean, what's he going to look like in twenty years? Hair all over the place! How long is this Nazirite vow supposed to last?

WIFE: All of his life.

MANOAH: I don't know. I would like to meet this angel and make sure that you got all the instructions straight. Maybe I will ask God to have the angel come again so that I could ask some questions.

NARRATOR: A son was born to Manoah and his wife, just as the angel said. Years pass, and one day the young man, whose name is Samson, came to his parents...

SAMSON: Mom! Dad! Guess what? I met the girl of my dreams and I'm going to marry her!

WIFE: Isn't this lovely, Manoah? Our little boy is all grown up and is going to get married. Who's the girl? Is she pretty? Does she come from a good family?

MANOAH: Yes. That is important. Where does she live and when can we meet her and her family?

SAMSON: She lives in Timnah. And you can come with me tonight and meet her family.

MANOAH: That's a strange place for an Israelite family to live.

WIFE: Isn't Timnah a Philistine city? Why would an Israelite family live there.

SAMSON: Who said she's an Israelite?

WIFE: You mean you're planning to marry a Philistine? Oh, my son! How can you do this to your father and me? Can you not find a nice Israelite girl to marry? Surely there are many who would love to be your wife.

SAMSON: Maybe so. But there aren't any that I want to marry! I want to marry this Philistine girl. And nothing you can say will make me change my mind. I'm going to see her now. If you don't want to come along, that's fine with me! Good-bye! Don't wait up. I'll probably be quite late.

NARRATOR: Samson leaves his parents to go to Timnah. But on the way...

SAMSON: My parents. What a couple of relics from the dark ages. I guess they mean well, but what a drag they are sometimes. This Nazirite vow thing is a perfect example. Not cutting my hair and my beard is OK. That's kind of a status symbol. But not drinking any wine? How can you have a decent party without a little wine? And if that's not bad enough, I'm not even supposed to have any grapes. Well, really! Is it any wonder that I prefer to visit in another city where nobody knows I have a restricted diet? Boy, sometimes my parents really make me mad! Do this! Don't do that! I wish there was something I could tear to pieces! There's never a phone book around when you need one. Wait a minute. What's that lion doing? It thinks it's going to have me for supper. I'll show it a thing or two. Take that, lion! Ha! That was no tougher than beating up a baby goat. Well, that's one less lion for the shepherds to worry about.

NARRATOR: Meanwhile, in Timnah...

BRIDE: Oh, this is the happiest day of my life. Not only am I getting married soon, but to the strongest man in the entire country. The only problem is that his father has not come to see my father yet. Oh well, that's minor. Still, it will be a whole lot easier to make all the wedding plans if the two fathers would get together and finalize every thing. Really! How difficult can it be? I am so beautiful and he is so strong that it's easy to see we were made for each other. His hair is a bit of a problem, but maybe I can convince him to get it cut for the wedding. Here he comes now. Hello, Sammy!

SAMSON: Greetings, my beauty, my love. Did you miss me while I was gone?

BRIDE: I miss you every minute you're not near me. Did you talk to your parents?

SAMSON: Of course I did. I said I would.

BRIDE: How did they take the news?

SAMSON: Oh, like typical parents. You know how parents are. "She's not good enough for you." All that kind of stuff. But they'll come around. Don't worry. The wedding will come off as planned.

NARRATOR: Samson continued to visit his Philistine love, and one day, while returning home...

SAMSON: Look at this. Here's the carcass of that lion I killed a few days ago. There seems to be a lot of activity around it. Lots of buzzing. I think I'll go over and have a look. Well, I'll be! Look at that! A swarm of bees has taken over the body for a nest and has already started to make honey. I think I'll take some home for Mom and Dad.

WIFE: Manoah. Our boy is coming home. And it looks like he's carrying something.

MANOAH: How can you call him "our boy"? Planning on marrying a Philistine girl. I'm thinking of disowning him.

SAMSON: Mom! Dad! I'm home. Look, I brought you a present. Some nice, fresh honey, straight from the hive.

WIFE: That's so sweet of you, Son. Wasn't that thoughtful of him, Manoah? Where did you find it?

SAMSON: Oh...it was just...lying around.

MANOAH: So, have you given this marriage business any more thought? Like maybe deciding to call it off?

SAMSON: Yes, I have given it more thought. And no, I'm not going to call it off. At least come and meet her, OK? You'll see that she's a very nice girl. Much nicer than the Israelite girls.

MANOAH: Alright. I guess there's nothing I can do to stop the wedding anyway.

NARRATOR: So Samson's father met Samson's intended. And Samson made plans for a great feast....

BRIDE: Oh, Sammy! Isn't this nice? Look at all the people who stop us on the street to congratulate us. Just think, in seven days, I will be your wife. Isn't that wonderful?

SAMSON: I'm sure looking forward to it. Say! Who are these thirty men who keep following us around?

BRIDE: They're your groomsmen. You don't think I'm going to have the smallest wedding in Canaan, do you? I'm having one of the largest bridal parties you've ever seen, and how many of your Israelite friends are going to come? So Daddy arranged for some of the local boys to come out to be your groomsmen.

SAMSON: I'm glad to meet you fellows. Say! Do you like riddles?

MAN: Sure. Who doesn't?

SAMSON: Well, I've got a good one. You'll never guess it in a million years.

MAN: What will you give us if we guess it?

SAMSON: Well, let's see. There are thirty of you. If you guess it, I will give each of you a complete change of clothes and a linen sheet. But if you fail, each one of you will give me a change of clothes and a linen sheet. How about it?

MAN: I don't know. What do you think, guys? We're pretty good at solving riddles. Let's take the bet. OK, you're on. What's the riddle?

BRIDE: Oh, this is so exciting! Already Sammy is making friends in my town. We'll be able to live next door to Mommy and Daddy and we'll live happily ever after.

SAMSON: This is the riddle. Out of the eater came something to eat. Out of the strong came something sweet. Now! Solve it.

MAN: How long do we have to work on this? Because it's a tough riddle. We shouldn't have to solve it this minute.

SAMSON: Until the seventh day of the wedding feast. That'll give you fourteen days.

MAN: That sounds fair enough. Let's see...out of the eater.... What is an eater? A wolf! But we don't eat wolves. Tigers, lions, bears? Same problem. Sheep and cattle, we do eat. But we don't get sweet things from them.... This is tough! But we'll have it solved in fourteen days, don't you worry about that.

SAMSON: I'm not worried. I know the answer and you don't. And I'm sure that you'll never guess it.

BRIDE: Oh, my Sammy! Not only is he brave and strong but he's smart enough to think of clever riddles, too.

NARRATOR: For three days the Philistines tried to think of the answer....

MAN: We've been working on this riddle for days now, and we're no closer to solving it than we were on the day we first heard it. I think we better get some inside help on this.

BRIDE: Hi, guys. What are you doing here? I thought you would be working on Sammy's riddle.

MAN: We are working on it. That's why we're here. You're going to help us solve the riddle.

BRIDE: Oh, I'm not very good at riddles. I wouldn't be any help to you at all.

MAN: You don't understand. You're going to get the answer from that Israelite boyfriend of yours and then you're going to tell us the answer.

BRIDE: Oh, I would never do that! Why do you think I would do that to my Sammy?

MAN: Because if you don't, we're going to burn down your father's house, with you and your family inside.

BRIDE: Well, if you put it that way, I'll see what I can do. We wouldn't want an Israelite to appear smarter than a Philistine, would we?

NARRATOR: So, every day until the final day of the feast, Samson's sweetheart wept in front of him and begged him to tell her the answer to the riddle.

BRIDE: If you really loved me, you would tell me the answer to the riddle. Come on. Be a sport. Tell me the answer. Husbands and wives shouldn't have secrets from each other.

SAMSON: I haven't even told the answer to my parents. Why should I tell you the answer? You'll learn the answer later today.

BRIDE: But I don't want to know the answer later. I want to know it before anybody else. Please! Pretty please! Let me know the answer.

SAMSON: Woman, you've pestered me almost to death for nearly a week now. OK, I'll tell you the answer. I killed a lion and some bees made honey in the carcass of the lion. That's the answer to the riddle. Hey! Where are you going in such a hurry?

BRIDE: Oh...I just thought of some last minute things that need to be done. See you at supper tonight.

SAMSON: I don't think I'll ever understand women. Well, well, well. Here comes my wedding party. Coming to outfit me for my honeymoon with thirty new suits, no doubt. Hello, fellows! How goes the riddle solving?

MAN: We think we've got it solved. Now. What's the strongest eating animal around? Obviously, the lion. And as for the sweet part, what could possibly be sweeter than honey? We think you found a lion that was killed that had a hive of bees making honey in it. How about it? Is that the correct answer?

SAMSON: The only way you could have known that was if my woman had told you. Well, I didn't say you couldn't use her help in solving the riddle. You wait here, and I'll go and get your new clothes. But if you see that woman I was supposed to marry, tell her the wedding's off!

MAN: But you can't just leave her at the altar. She's all set to get married today. What's she going to do?

SAMSON: Tell her to marry the best man who'll have her.

MAN: What's that? Did he say let his best man marry her? Well, I don't see any problem with that, do you fellows? Let's go and finish off what's left of the food and celebrate this new wedding.

SAMSON'S DOWNFALL

SCRIPTURE: Judges 15; 16

SUGGESTED TOPICS: Talents and abilities; consequences of disobedience; wisdom

BIBLE BACKGROUND

Samson had left Timnah angrily after killing thirty Philistines to pay off his bet. Later he relented and returned to claim his bride.

Wedding customs were substantially different from what they are today. Samson was legally married to the Philistine girl on the first day of the feast. However, his walking away on the seventh day of the feast was sufficient to constitute a legal divorce under the Philistine law. From their viewpoint, she was free to remarry.

Israelite women in biblical times had a considerably exalted status in comparison to the women of neighboring countries. Mosaic law required a certificate of divorce to be given to a woman if a marriage broke up; a man could not just walk away from her and later walk back and claim nothing had happened. If she had not been given the certificate, the man was responsible to meet her needs as his wife. Samson, by walking away from the marriage and then trying to take his wife back, again shows his disregard for both God's law and the customs of human society.

The fact that the Philistines wanted to know the secret of Samson's strength suggests that Samson did not have a substantially different physique from that of most other men. If he had massive muscles, would the source of his strength not be obvious to the most casual observer? To learn the source of Samson's strength, the Philistine leaders approached Samson's latest flame, Delilah. Although Delilah proved herself faithless on three different occasions, Samson finally gave in and revealed the secret.

PERFORMANCE TIPS

1. Suggested props: several chairs placed together to represent the couch at Delilah's house, ropes to loosely tie around Samson's wrists.

2. Older Samson is the narrator. If your room has enough space, have Samson slowly walk in a circle (as though grinding the Philistines' grain) as he speaks.

3. During the final scene, have someone lead Samson around the room. Let Samson bump into walls and objects to indicate his blindness.

DISCUSSION QUESTIONS

1. Read Colossians 3:23,24. God calls us to do things with all our heart. What does the phrase "with all our heart" mean?

2. How does doing things with all your heart show that you love and obey God?

3. What was Samson's job? How would you evaluate his performance?

4. What jobs do you have in your daily life? How can you do them to show that you love and obey God?

SAMSON'S DOWNFALL

CHARACTERS

OLDER SAMSON

YOUNG SAMSON

FIRST PHILISTINE

SECOND PHILISTINE

ISRAELITE

DELILAH

SCENE ONE

OLDER SAMSON: Oh, what disgrace. Here am I, the mighty Samson, formerly the scourge of the Philistines, now blinded and their slave. How could this happen? How could such a strong man be brought so low? Because of my own foolishness, that's how! Why didn't I listen to my parents? Why didn't I listen to God? Why did I have to hang out with the Philistines? Why am I talking to myself, now? Why not? I'm the only one who will listen to me anymore. I guess my downfall began when I went back to Timnah to be reconciled with my bride....

YOUNG SAMSON: Hey there, father-in-law. It is I, Samson, the best son any father could ever hope for. I've decided to forgive my bride. I'll just go into her room and surprise her. What's that? You gave her to my best man to marry? Why did you do something stupid like that? You thought I hated her? Why would I hate her? I married her, didn't I? You'll just have to call off the second marriage. What do you mean, you can't do that? It's simple. Just tell her she's married to me and the other marriage doesn't count. No! I don't want to marry her younger sister! I want my wife! You won't let me have her? Then forget it! But don't blame me for what happens. Blame yourself!

OLDER SAMSON: I was angry. And when I was angry, I did rash things....

FIRST PHILISTINE: Isn't it great to be a Philistine? Just look at all these beautiful wheat fields. Plenty to last all winter. Maybe even into next harvest.

SECOND PHILISTINE: It sure is great! And you're right about the wheat, too. But don't forget, if we don't have enough, we can always take some from the Israelites. Now that's something I wouldn't want to be, an Israelite. Except maybe to be that Samson fellow.

FIRST PHILISTINE: I know what you mean. He's the one man in Canaan who does whatever he wants, goes wherever he wants and never has to worry about what other people think. Nobody wants to get into a fight with him. If he gets mad at you, look out!

SECOND PHILISTINE: I'll say. You've heard the talk around the Israelites that he was supposed to be their next savior, haven't you? I'm sure glad he hasn't tried to fill that role, yet.

FIRST PHILISTINE: You and me, both. If he ever decided to wipe out the Philistines, you wouldn't be able to find enough of us to form a crowd at a...hey! What's going on in that wheat field?

SECOND PHILISTINE: It looks like a bunch of foxes running through the field. And their tails are on fire! No, that's not exactly it...

FIRST PHILISTINE: There must be three hundred foxes. In pairs. With their tails tied together. And a firebrand tied to their tails. They're setting the fields on fire! We better go get some help to put out the fire or we'll lose the entire crop!

OLDER SAMSON: But they were too late. Not only all their wheat was destroyed but, also their corn, grapes and olives.

SECOND PHILISTINE: Who would do this to us? Foxes don't tie their own tails together with firebrands. I suspect we're the victims of foul play.

FIRST PHILISTINE: I was talking to that old man over there. The one that was going to be Samson's father-in-law. He says Samson was here earlier today, and get this—the old man threw Samson out on his ear. He told Samson that his daughter was married to somebody else and Samson couldn't have her. He says Samson went away mad!

SECOND PHILISTINE: So this old man caused all our trouble. Well, we'll fix him. Our crops were all burned. Put the old man and his daughter in their house, and we'll burn it down. Let's see what he thinks of fire.

(PHILISTINES exit. YOUNG SAMSON enters.)

YOUNG SAMSON: Boy! Was that fun! Catching those foxes and setting that fire. What a blaze! I bet it goes down in history as the most famous fire ever. Hey! There's a guy I know. What did you think of the great Philistine blaze? What do you mean, which one? No, I didn't hear about the one in Timnah. Tell me about it. *(Exits.)*

OLDER SAMSON: And once again, my anger was kindled. To avenge the death of my wife and father-in-law, I went into Philistine territory and slaughtered many Philistines.

(PHILISTINES enter.)

FIRST PHILISTINE: OK! That does it! I've had it up to here with Samson! He's only a man. Get as many men together as you can. We're going to teach that boy a lesson in manners!

SECOND PHILISTINE: We've got a whole army here. What are we going to do?

FIRST PHILISTINE: We're going to march into Israelite territory and demand that they turn him over to us! After tying him up, of course.

SECOND PHILISTINE: How will that help us? Nobody can tie up Samson if he doesn't want to be tied up.

FIRST PHILISTINE: Oh, it will work just fine. Samson may be a jerk, but he does have a soft spot when it comes to other Israelites. You'll notice he's never hurt any of them. He'll have to let them tie him up because if he doesn't, we'll destroy Israel.

SECOND PHILISTINE: Alright! I like this plan. I won't be afraid of a Samson who is securely tied.

FIRST PHILISTINE: Well, here we are. You there! Israelites! We want Samson and we want him now! Take some men, go tie him up securely, and bring him here to us! If you don't, we wipe out Israel! Well, what are you standing there for? Go get him!

SECOND PHILISTINE: That's telling them. *(PHILISTINES exit.)*

YOUNG SAMSON: Well, well, well. Look at this. There's a party of men, all Israelites, I'd say. There must be three thousand men there. It looks like they're coming to see me. Hi, guys. What's happening?

ISRAELITE: Hi, Samson. We have a little favor to ask of you.

YOUNG SAMSON: Well, go ahead and ask. Have I ever turned you down before?

ISRAELITE: No. But we've never asked for a favor before.

YOUNG SAMSON: That's true. But there's always a first time, right? Now, what's the little favor you want?

ISRAELITE: I'm not sure how to word this...

YOUNG SAMSON: Take your time. Get the words all straight. I'll play with these two new ropes you brought. Do you want to see a neat rope trick? You take two cords, like these, tie a special knot in them...

ISRAELITE: We didn't bring the ropes for you to do tricks with. OK, I'll put it to you straight. There's a bunch of angry Philistines down in the valley. If we don't tie you up and take you down to them, they say they will destroy all of Israel. We have to ask you to let us tie you up and take you to them.

YOUNG SAMSON: What do they want with me?

ISRAELITE: They didn't say, exactly. But the word barbecue did come up in their conversation once or twice.

YOUNG SAMSON: So I'm supposed to let you tie me up. Then you'll take me as a prisoner and hand me over to the Philistines. Have I got this straight?

ISRAELITE: That's pretty much it.

YOUNG SAMSON: There's nothing fancy in this idea, is there? Nothing like you planning to kill me yourselves?

ISRAELITE: No. We just tie you up and take you to the Philistines. Just between you and me, I think if we delivered your dead body to them, they would be madder than they are now. I think they want the pleasure—sorry, wrong word...uh, honor of killing you themselves.

YOUNG SAMSON: If all you want to do is to tie me up, go ahead. No problem. Make sure that you've got some good, solid knots there. If there's one thing I can't stand, it's shoddy workmanship. *(ISRAELITES begin tying.)* That's good! You fellows really tie some fine knots....

OLDER SAMSON: Samson's finest hour! That's what it should have been called. There I was. All tied up, waiting for the wrath of the Philistines to be cast upon me. But that's not the way the scene played. When I got to the Philistine camp, I saw the bones of a donkey lying on the ground. Just the bones, you understand. The donkey was long gone. Well, the Philistines shouted at me, called me all sorts of mean, nasty, ugly names. They told me what they were going to do to me, things that shouldn't be repeated in mixed company. But the Spirit of the Lord came upon me, and I broke those strong, new ropes as if they were fire-weakened flax. Then, I picked up that donkey's jawbone and used it as a mighty war club. I killed more than a thousand Philistines that day. I must say, it was a fitting weapon. A jackass using a jackass's jawbone to destroy his enemies. You would think I would have learned by then that God wanted to use me to destroy the Philistines. But no! Samson is too smart! He doesn't need anybody to tell him what to do. I continued to associate with the Philistines. They kept making plans to kill me, and I kept outwitting them. Then, I met Delilah....

SCENE TWO

FIRST PHILISTINE: Delilah, we've got a job for you.

DELILAH: Oh, yeah? What?

SECOND PHILISTINE: Nothing tough. You've heard of Samson, right?

DELILAH: He comes around from time to time. So what?

FIRST PHILISTINE: You know that he's a pretty strong boy.

DELILAH: One of history's great understatements. So what?

SECOND PHILISTINE: You've probably heard about the time we had him trapped in Gaza one night. And how we surrounded the city, knowing he couldn't leave until morning, but then he ripped the gates off the city wall and walked away with them...

DELILAH: I've heard the stories. Do you have a point to make or not?

FIRST PHILISTINE: We're getting there. The point is, the reason Samson is such a nuisance to us is because of his great strength...

DELILAH: All that buildup for such a simple statement. Samson is stronger than all of the Philistines put together. Again I say, so what?

SECOND PHILISTINE: So, we remember a time, some years ago, when Samson had a secret. He wouldn't reveal the answer to anybody, except for the woman he was planning to marry...

FIRST PHILISTINE: And Samson is pretty close to you...

SECOND PHILISTINE: And will tell you things he wouldn't tell anybody else...

FIRST PHILISTINE: So you could learn the secret of his great strength...

SECOND PHILISTINE: Then we fix it so that he isn't strong any more...

FIRST PHILISTINE: And capture him.

DELILAH *(bored)*: Terrific. What's in it for me?

SECOND PHILISTINE: The knowledge of a job well done.

DELILAH *(sarcastically)*: How wonderful.

FIRST PHILISTINE: The gratitude of Philistines everywhere.

DELILAH *(more sarcastically)*: Marvelous.

SECOND PHILISTINE: And eleven hundred pieces of silver from every Philistine lord.

DELILAH *(enthusiastically)*: Now you're talking my language! Look! Here he comes now. Go out the back way. I'll learn his secret and tell it to you tomorrow.

YOUNG SAMSON: Hi there, Delilah. You got anything to eat here?

DELILAH: All kinds of things. You know, Samson, I was thinking. If we're going to be good friends, we should know things about each other. You go first.

YOUNG SAMSON: Did I ever tell you about the time I killed a lion?

DELILAH: Often.

YOUNG SAMSON: How about the great fire?

DELILAH: I've heard it.

YOUNG SAMSON: How about the time I killed a thousand men...

DELILAH: With the jawbone of a donkey. Heard it. I was thinking of something a little more personal. Take your great strength, as an example. What makes you so strong? You don't look different from any other man. Why can't anything be used to bind you? C'mon. Be a sport. Tell me. Is there anything that could be used to tie you up?

YOUNG SAMSON: You promise not to tell anybody?

DELILAH: Cross my heart and hope to...well, cross my heart.

YOUNG SAMSON: You know those really thin branches on vines? The ones that can be tied. If I were tied up with seven of them, then I'd be as helpless as a newborn lamb.

DELILAH: I'd love for you to stay and talk, but I've got a lot of things to do. You go now, and I'll see you tomorrow night.

YOUNG SAMSON: But we didn't talk about you.

DELILAH: That's alright. You're more interesting than me, anyway.

YOUNG SAMSON: That's true. OK, I'll see you tomorrow. Good-bye.

OLDER SAMSON: The next day...

FIRST PHILISTINE: Seven green branches from the vine. You're sure of this?

SECOND PHILISTINE: It sounds too easy to me.

DELILAH: Has anybody tried it before?

SECOND PHILISTINE: No, but it still sounds too easy.

DELILAH: Trust me. You have some men hiding in the back room at my place and when Samson is powerless, grab him!

FIRST PHILISTINE: They'll be there. You just be sure he's tied up.

OLDER SAMSON: Later, that evening...

YOUNG SAMSON: Hi there, Delilah. What's happening?

DELILAH: Nothing much. How about coming in and lying down? You look a little tired.

YOUNG SAMSON: Food and sleep. Everything a man could want. *(He lies down and sleeps, while Delilah ties him up.)*

DELILAH: He's finally drifted off and he's tied up. All that money is as good as mine. Here goes nothing. Samson! Wake up! The Philistines are coming to capture you!

YOUNG SAMSON: *(Breaks the vines.)* Huh? Who? What? Where?

DELILAH: Samson! You lied to me! You told me that seven green branches would secure you and look what happened. You broke them as if they were a piece of string stretched across a fire. If we're going to have any kind of relationship, we have to be honest with each other. So tell me the truth. Isn't there anything that could make you weak?

YOUNG SAMSON: OK. So you caught on to my little joke. There's nothing special about my strength that new ropes that have never been used before wouldn't cure.

DELILAH: That's it? Just use new ropes?

YOUNG SAMSON: Sure. Nothing to it. Now, where's something to eat?

DELILAH: You'll have to find something at home. I just remembered some things I need.

OLDER SAMSON: The next day...

FIRST PHILISTINE: You're sure about it, this time? We have to use brand new ropes. There's nothing tricky about the knots or anything?

The Big Book of Bible Skits ©1997 Gospel Light. Permission to photocopy granted.

SECOND PHILISTINE: Didn't those Israelites use new ropes when we tried to capture him before?

FIRST PHILISTINE: They said they did. But you can't trust Israelites for anything. They were probably making it up just to impress us.

SECOND PHILISTINE: Are you sure he's not kidding you again, Delilah?

DELILAH: Why would he? He knows I tested him last time. Even Samson isn't stupid enough to lie to me again.

FIRST PHILISTINE: OK. The men will bring the ropes when they come to your place. You get Samson tied up and we'll have him.

OLDER SAMSON: Later, that evening...

DELILAH: Well, I've got him trussed up like a Thanksgiving turkey. What will I buy with all that money that will soon be mine? I'd better test this before I call those men in here. Samson! Wake up! The Philistines!

YOUNG SAMSON: *(Breaks the ropes.)* Huh? Who? What? Where?

DELILAH: I can't believe it! You lied to me again! Those were some of the best ropes money could buy, and you've ruined them. This joke of yours is getting tiresome, Samson. Are you going to tell me what makes you stronger than other men or not?

YOUNG SAMSON: Women! They've got no sense of humor. A guy tries to make a little joke and they get all huffy. Maybe I'll tell you and maybe I won't.

DELILAH *(sweetly)***:** I'm sorry that I yelled at you. I just don't want there to be any secrets between us. C'mon. Tell me the secret of your strength.

YOUNG SAMSON: OK. It has to do with my hair. If you were to weave the seven locks of my hair together, I would be as helpless as the proverbial kitten up a tree.

DELILAH: There. That wasn't so hard, was it? You go back to sleep now. I have some weaving to do. *(She begins braiding his hair.)* Weaving. That's it! Clothes! That's what I'll do with all that beautiful Philistine money. New clothes. There. I'm finished. Now. Let's try it. Samson! The Philistines!

YOUNG SAMSON: Huh? Who? What? Where?

DELILAH: OK! That does it, buddy! We're through! You want to come here again, you tell me the real secret! If you tell me another lie, I'll never speak to you again! You got that?

OLDER SAMSON: So I told her the real secret. And while I was asleep with my head in her lap, she called in a barber. He shaved me as bald as an egg. No more hair. No more beard. I really was helpless then. The Lord was no longer with me. I had completely violated my Nazarite vow. The Philistines blinded me, put me in brass fetters and have been using me as a slave to grind their grain. But nobody seems to notice that my hair has been growing again. And with it, I can feel my strength returning. Wait! Somebody's calling me. Oh, it's only the jailer. What's that? *(Pause.)* The Philistine lords and their ladies are in Dagon's temple. Who cares? Let them worship their god, Dagon, if they want to. What do they want me there for? Probably to laugh at. That's about all I'm good for, now. Yeah, keep your shirt on. I'm coming. But somebody will have to lead me there. Oh. There's a boy here to be my guide. Right. Lead on, MacDuff. There's a lot of noise in this place. How many people are here? No kidding. Three thousand? Where's the pillars that support this place? Lead me over to them, would you? I'm tired and I need to lean on something to rest. Hey, kid! Do you like riddles? Here's one for you. What do you call a Nazarite whose hair has grown back? You don't know? Well, listen close. Because the answer to this one is going to bring the house down.

I've Been Working...

SCRIPTURE: Ruth 1—3

SUGGESTED TOPICS: Value of work; responsibility; loyalty

BIBLE BACKGROUND

A woman's position during ancient times was perilous, to say the least. In most countries, she was little more than property; something which could be bought and sold. Her value might be deemed less than that of an ox or horse. A widow was particularly vulnerable. The laws of most countries afforded her neither protection nor ability to earn a living. Ruth's decision to be a daughter to Naomi and leave Moab was not one to be made lightly. By leaving her homeland to go with Naomi, she renounced all protection that might be afforded her by her father or other relatives.

Compared to women in the surrounding nations, the women of Israel had a relatively generous lot. For example, numerous references call for the protection and provision of widows. Among the laws set down by Moses which provided for the needs of women was that of gleaning (see Leviticus 19:9,10; Deuteronomy 24:19-21). Israel was clearly required to be generous in what was left behind for the widows and strangers in the land.

PERFORMANCE TIPS

1. Suggested props: Bible-times costumes.
2. Ruth should be shy. Rarely will she lift her eyes to look at Boaz. She is overwhelmed that a man would talk to her. This was not common in those times.
3. Boaz is portrayed as something of a rough-and-tumble sort. He speaks sometimes without thinking, but he has a good and generous heart.
4. After the skit, finish the story of Boaz and Ruth.
5. Also read or tell the story of the talents (see Matthew 25:14-30). Jesus also spoke of the importance of using our abilities wisely.

DISCUSSION QUESTIONS

1. Why might Ruth have reason to be afraid of Boaz?
2. What are the things Boaz commends in Ruth?
3. Read Proverbs 10:4. What does the Bible say about our attitude toward work?
4. What are some of the benefits of work?
5. What sort of jobs are you responsible to do?
6. Why is it important to do the best job we can, no matter what the job is?

The Big Book of Bible Skits ©1997 Gospel Light. Permission to photocopy granted.

I'VE BEEN WORKING...

CHARACTERS
RUTH
BOAZ (BOH-az)

BOAZ: Hello.

RUTH *(keeping her eyes down)*: My lord.

BOAZ: I hear you've been gleaning in my fields.

RUTH: Is this wrong, my lord? I'm sorry. I'll stop.

BOAZ: Did I say it was wrong?

RUTH: No, sir.

BOAZ: My servant tells me you come from Moab.

RUTH: Yes, my lord. Forgive me. I'll leave your fields.

BOAZ: Why would you do that? Did I say to leave?

RUTH: No, sir. But I'm from Moab. I'm a foreigner.

BOAZ: So you are. What are you doing in Israel?

RUTH: Gleaning in your fields, my lord.

BOAZ *(laughing)*: So you are. So you are. Let's try again. Why are you in Israel when you come from Moab?

RUTH: I came with my mother-in-law. She is from your country.

BOAZ: And who is your mother-in-law?

RUTH: She is called Naomi, who was married to Elimelech.

BOAZ: Well, there you go! We're relatives, you and I. I'm a kinsman of Elimelech.

RUTH: *(Glances up, with interest.)* Yes, my lord. I know.

BOAZ: Where is your husband? A married woman should not be gleaning. Her husband should be supporting her.

RUTH: I have no husband, my lord.

BOAZ: Well of course you do! You can't have a mother-in-law if you're not married!

RUTH: I'm a widow, sir.

BOAZ: *(Slaps forehead.)* Oh. I'm sorry! Clumsy of me. I seem to suffer from foot-in-mouth disease.

RUTH: You have done no harm, sir.

BOAZ: Well, I should be more careful. How is the esteemed Naomi?

RUTH: She is well, now that she is in her own country.

BOAZ: But how about you? You're not in your country.

RUTH: This is now my country, even if it does not accept me.

BOAZ: How can this be your country? You're from Moab.

RUTH: I left Moab with Naomi. To her, I swore an oath: "Where you live, I will live. Your people will be my people. Your God, my God. And where you are buried, there will I be buried."

BOAZ: So now, you're almost a woman without a country?

RUTH: I don't understand, my lord.

BOAZ: You've left Moab. But not all the Israelites accept you, do they?

RUTH: Not all. But many are kind to me.

BOAZ: Just as you have shown kindness to your mother-in-law. Well, there's one more who accepts you as an Israelite. Welcome home, kinswoman.

RUTH: You are too kind, my lord.

BOAZ: Nonsense. What are your plans for the rest of the day?

RUTH: I shall continue gleaning the fields. There are many more.

BOAZ: Nonsense. Look over there. That's my field. And over there? That's mine, too. And that one. And I have lots of others. You don't need to glean in anyone else's fields. Stay in my fields.

RUTH: But how will I know for certain it is your field, my lord?

BOAZ: You see those women over there? They work for me.

RUTH: Yes?

BOAZ: You stay with them. They only work in my fields. You can glean where they reap. And if you get thirsty, help yourself to the water my men draw.

RUTH: But the gleaners are not allowed to drink the water of the workers.

BOAZ: They're MY workers and it's MY water. What I say goes. I'll tell them not to harm you. Now you do as I say.

RUTH: Why are you so kind to me, a stranger in your land?

BOAZ: Stranger? What stranger? You left your home to take care of Naomi, an older woman who had no family to look after her. You work hard gleaning the fields to support the two of you. May the Lord God bless you in the same measure you have blessed Naomi.

RUTH: Thank you for your kind blessing.

BOAZ: It's no more than you deserve. Back to work. We've all got work to do. Bye for now. But I've got a funny feeling we'll be seeing more of each other.

YOU WERE SAYING?

SCRIPTURE: 1 Samuel 3

SUGGESTED TOPICS: Listening to God; respect for elders; obeying God

BIBLE BACKGROUND

An Israelite man, Elkanah, had two wives: Peninnah and Hannah. The first bore Elkanah children, but Hannah was barren. In ancient societies, the inability to bear children was a deplorable situation for a woman. At best, she was scorned as being an unworthy wife; at worst, she was seen as being punished by God. In spite of Hannah's situation, Elkanah apparently loved her deeply (see 1 Samuel 1:5-8). However, Elkanah's affection for her was not sufficient to overcome Hannah's unhappiness. Hannah deeply wanted a child, specifically a son. In her anguish, she cried out to the Lord and promised that if He would grant her a son, the boy would be dedicated to the Lord to serve Him all of his days.

Hannah was living when the leadership of the judges in Israel was nearing an end. Eli was high priest and his two sons, Hophni and Phinehas, were judges over Israel. However, in spite of Eli's goodness, his sons were corrupt. But God, in His infinite wisdom and mercy, did not desert Eli. Instead, while answering the prayer of Hannah, God gave Eli a third child to raise up and instruct in His ways, a child who would listen.

PERFORMANCE TIPS

1. Suggested props: a scroll, a table, a cot for Eli (if a cot is not available, improvise by placing three or four chairs together).

2. Samuel is young and energetic; Eli is old. Their movements should reflect their ages.

3. Prior to the skit, explain Samuel's presence in the Tabernacle by summarizing the story of Hannah's prayer and Eli's response. Or start with the skit, then backtrack. Say, "Let's see why Samuel was living in the Tabernacle."

4. After the skit, continue Samuel's story to show how he listened to God. Have someone read 1 Samuel 7:3,4.

DISCUSSION QUESTIONS

1. What things can interfere with listening?

2. Do you need to be an adult to serve God? Why or why not?

3. Samuel heard God's voice call him. What other ways does God speak to His people?

4. Many people who do terrible things claim that God talks to them and that they are following God. How can you be sure God is speaking to you? How can you judge if someone else is listening to God?

5. What can you do to obey God this week? Think of one specific way you can obey God.

YOU WERE SAYING?

CHARACTERS
SAMUEL
ELI

ELI: Samuel!

SAMUEL: Here I am, sir. What do you want?

ELI: The scroll I had with me—where is it? I laid it down right here, and now I can't find it.

SAMUEL: It's right over there, sir. On the table.

ELI: On the table? That's right. I remember. That's where I put it.

SAMUEL: Shall I get it for you, sir?

ELI: No. I won't need it until morning. My eyes are no longer strong enough to read by candlelight. Finish your chores and then go to bed.

SAMUEL: Very good, sir. I'm almost finished.

ELI: Good boy. *(Pats SAMUEL affectionately.)*

    (SAMUEL exits.)

ELI: *(Yawns.)* There's nothing for me to do until the sun comes up. I guess I'll go to sleep. *(Snores for several seconds.)*

SAMUEL: *(Enters.)* Here I am, sir!

ELI: Huh? What? Who?

SAMUEL: It's me, sir. I was just drifting off to sleep when I heard you call.

ELI: I didn't call. I was sleeping.

SAMUEL: But you must have called, sir. There's no one else in the Tabernacle.

ELI: I tell you, I was sleeping! It was probably just the wind making noise. Go back to your room and get some sleep.

SAMUEL: Yes, sir. *(Exits.)*

ELI: Young people! Can't tell the voice of the wind from the voice of a man. Now, then. Back to sleep. Ba-ack to slee-eep. *(Snores.)*

SAMUEL: *(Enters.)* Here I am, sir!

ELI: Huh? What? Who?

SAMUEL: It's me, sir. I was sleeping, but I heard you call.

ELI: Why do you disturb my slumbers? I am an old man. I need my rest.

SAMUEL: Yes, sir. You do, sir. But you DID call. I heard you.

ELI: I did nothing of the sort. You must have been dreaming. What did you have for supper tonight?

SAMUEL: Nothing unusual. Vegetables, meat, a little goat's milk.

ELI: Hmm. You used pepper, didn't you?

SAMUEL: Yes, sir. I like pepper.

ELI: That'll do it. Spicy food before bed. You were having a dream.

         The Big Book of Bible Skits ©1997 Gospel Light. Permission to photocopy granted.

SAMUEL: But I didn't use very MUCH pepper, sir.

ELI: It doesn't take much. Now go to bed and let me get some sleep!

SAMUEL: Yes, sir. *(Exits.)*

ELI: These foolish young people. Always putting things on their food. Mixing things together. If this keeps up, soon they'll be putting tomato sauce and cheese on bread and baking it. Terrible thought. Ah, sleep. *(Snores.)*

SAMUEL: *(Enters.)* Here I am, sir!

ELI: Huh? What? Who?

SAMUEL: It's me, sir. I know you called me. I heard you very distinctly.

ELI: How many times must I tell you...

SAMUEL: But you called. I heard my name called. "Samuel!" Just like that. It wasn't a dream and it wasn't the wind.

ELI: Have pity on a tired old man. How could I call you when I was asleep?

SAMUEL: Perhaps you called me in your sleep, sir?

ELI: I don't talk in my sleep. You are hearing things. Hallucinations.

SAMUEL: What?

ELI: You're hearing things that aren't real. Hallucinations.

SAMUEL: Hallucinations?

ELI: Yes. Something like visions. Now go to bed.

SAMUEL: Yes, sir. *(Starts to leave.)*

ELI: Hallucinations. Visions. Wait! Come back!

SAMUEL: Yes, sir?

ELI: What did this vision say to you?

SAMUEL: Nothing, sir. I only heard my name being called.

ELI: What you are hearing is not a hallucination. It is a vision.

SAMUEL: A vision?

ELI: Yes. The Lord is speaking to you.

SAMUEL: But, how can that be? I've never had visions. Besides, surely the Lord would speak to you, His high priest!

ELI: The Lord speaks to whom He chooses. Now, listen closely.

SAMUEL: Yes, sir?

ELI: If the voice should call again, you must answer, "Speak, Lord; for your servant hears." Repeat it.

SAMUEL: Speak, Lord; for your servant hears.

ELI: That's right. *(Pats SAMUEL.)* And when He speaks, LISTEN. For He must have chosen you for some important purpose. Go back to bed now. And remember, when the Lord speaks, listen.

SAMUEL: *(Exiting.)* Speak, Lord; for your servant hears. Speak, Lord; for your servant hears.

ELI: Aah! *(Smiles and rubs chin.)* The Lord is speaking to Samuel! He is still with His people. Now I know I can really rest. *(Snores.)*

JUDGE, NOT!

SCRIPTURE: 1 Samuel 8

SUGGESTED TOPICS: Obedience to God; importance of Bible reading; ignoring God's instructions; effects of sin

BIBLE BACKGROUND

Upon the death of Eli and his sons (see 1 Samuel 4:14-18), Samuel was quickly recognized as the undisputed leader of Israel. He ruled wisely and, under his leadership, Israel prospered. After many years of faithful service, old age overtook Samuel. The job of judging Israel was too much for him and he passed the mantle of responsibility on to his sons, Joel and Abijah. Having seen the problems that could happen from having judges that did not listen to God (Phinehas and Hophni), one would expect that Samuel would have ensured that his two sons were well versed in the law and were honorable men who would take their responsibility seriously. However, this was not to be. For whatever reason, Samuel allowed two bribe-takers to assume the role of judge, and the people of Israel rebelled against their injustice. Then, against all warnings from Samuel (see 1 Samuel 8:11-18), the people demanded a king to rule over them.

PERFORMANCE TIPS

1. Suggested props: chairs for Joel and Abijah, a table to sit behind, a gavel.

2. If there has been a scandal reported in the news recently involving abuse of power, use it as an example of how greed and injustice continue as they did in Samuel's time.

3. Joel and Abijah are portrayed as being lazy. Have the students playing those parts act as if they are unwilling to give any effort to their jobs.

4. Mammon should be self-assured. He is rich and knows that money can buy anything.

5. Hadad should be very humble. He has come to plead his case.

6. The entire class can participate as the people. Have a few scripts available to distribute throughout the class.

7. After the skit, finish telling the story of the choosing of a king in Israel.

DISCUSSION QUESTIONS

1. Have you ever been treated unfairly? How did it make you feel?

2. What can a kid your age do to keep from being unfair?

3. What do people mean when they say, "Treat others as you want to be treated"? Do you agree? Why or why not?

4. What are some ways we can show God's love to people around us?

The Big Book of Bible Skits ©1997 Gospel Light. Permission to photocopy granted.

JUDGE, NOT!

CHARACTERS

SAMUEL
JOEL
ABIJAH (ah-BUY-jah)
CLERK
MAMMON (MAM-on)
HADAD (HAY-dad)
BENJAMIN
PEOPLE

SCENE ONE

SAMUEL: *(Beckons with a stiff hand.)* Come here, my sons.

JOEL: Yeah, Dad?

ABIJAH: What is it, Dad?

SAMUEL: My sons, I am growing very old. Too old to be Israel's judge any longer. I want you to be the judges of Israel now.

JOEL: You mean both of us?

ABIJAH: Why not just one of us?

SAMUEL: It's a big job. There will be plenty for both of you to do.

JOEL: OK. We'll be the best judges...

ABIJAH: ...that money can buy.

SCENE TWO

JOEL: OK, what's the first case?

CLERK: Hadad versus Mammon.

JOEL: So what's the problem that needs to be settled?

MAMMON: This whining pimple borrowed money from me. Three shekels.

JOEL: And you claim that you did not borrow money from him?

HADAD: Oh, no! I did indeed borrow three shekels from him.

JOEL: Then what could possibly be the problem?

MAMMON: When I asked for my money back, he only gave me three shekels. He refused to pay me any interest.

HADAD: That's because the Law of Moses says you're not supposed to charge interest to a brother.

MAMMON: Well, there's no problem because you're not my brother. Now give me my money. All of it. Three shekels plus interest.

HADAD: Please, Joel. Give us a ruling that is fair. Mammon has much money and land

and does not need more. But if I am forced to pay interest, then I will be poor again and forced to borrow once more.

JOEL: This is a tough problem. Let me consult my brother for a minute.

ABIJAH: This is tough, Joel. I think what father would do is to read the Law and do what it says, but that sounds like a lot of work. Maybe we can think of something easier.

JOEL: I'm all for something that takes less work. But if we have to think, that sounds even harder than reading.

ABIJAH: Well, we have to do something.

MAMMON: If it will help you to decide, settle in my favor and half the interest is yours.

JOEL and ABIJAH: Are you trying to bribe us?

MAMMON: Well...uh...yes.

HADAD: You have made a big mistake. No son of Samuel would take a bribe. Now you have lost for certain.

JOEL and ABIJAH: We find in favor of Mammon.

HADAD: What?

JOEL: He made an excellent point. You are not his brother.

ABIJAH: And even if you were, I'm not certain that the old Law would apply anyway. It's probably outdated. Next case.

JOEL: This job is going to be easier than I thought.

ABIJAH: And better paying.

SCENE THREE

BENJAMIN: Samuel, we have a couple of problems.

SAMUEL: So take them to Joel and Abijah. They are your judges.

BENJAMIN: They are also our problems.

SAMUEL: What do you mean?

BENJAMIN: There is no longer justice in Israel. Only people who have enough money to bribe your sons can get judgments in their favor.

SAMUEL: This is terrible! I will dismiss them and appoint a new judge—one who will be fair.

PEOPLE: No! No more judges! We want a king!

SAMUEL: But if you have a king, he will rule over you with an iron fist. He will take your sons and daughters to be his servants. He will take the best of your crops for his use. You will be forced to plow his fields. You DON'T want a KING.

PEOPLE: We want a king! We want a king! We want a king!

SAMUEL: But if you have a king, he will make you miserable.

PEOPLE: We want a king! We want a king! We want a king!

SAMUEL: I will ask God. If He will permit it, I will appoint a king to reign over you. But when things go wrong because you have a king, don't go crying to God about it. I am old and I will soon be gone. But you will have to live with your choice.

PEOPLE: We want a king!

(SAMUEL shakes head slowly.)

GRUDGE MATCH

SCRIPTURE: 1 Samuel 15:1-24

SUGGESTED TOPICS: Obeying God's Word completely; ignoring God's instructions; making excuses

BIBLE BACKGROUND

Saul had been chosen king of Israel by God Himself (see 1 Samuel 9:15,16). Surely, if any man would obey God, a king chosen by God would be the man. Unfortunately, Saul quickly forgot who had given him power in Israel, and began to rely on his own understanding (see Proverbs 3:5). First, he offered sacrifices in direct contradiction to Samuel's instructions to him. Then, in his battle against the Amalekites, he again refused to listen to God's instructions and saved King Agag and the best of the spoils of the battle. When Samuel called him to task for his disobedience, Saul went so far as to blame the other Israelites (see 1 Samuel 15:21) instead of accepting responsibility for his own actions.

PERFORMANCE TIPS

1. Suggested props: microphones for the announcers.

2. Joram should start his commentary quietly, but become more and more excited as the "game" continues.

3. After the skit, finish the story of Saul's disobedience. Emphasize verse 22.

DISCUSSION QUESTIONS

1. How was Saul obedient to God? How did he disobey God?

2. What were the consequences of Saul's disobedience? (Also read 1 Samuel 16:1.)

3. When have you ever been disobedient? What are some excuses you have tried to give to explain your disobedience? Did anyone really believe your excuses?

4. What are some different ways you can learn what God wants you to do?

5. If you disobey God, what should you do? Why?

GRUDGE MATCH

CHARACTERS
JORAM (JO-ram)
PEKAH (PEE-kah)
SAMUEL

PRONUNCIATION GUIDE
Agag (AY-gag)
Amalekites (uh-MAL-uh-kites)
Kenites (KEY-nites)

JORAM: Hello, sports fans. It's a beautiful day for today's game. The temperature's in the low seventies, there's just a sight breeze and the sun's shining brightly. Joining me on today's telecast is our color commentator, Pekah. Pekah, tell us about today's matchup and who we should expect to be the leaders on each side for today's game.

PEKAH: Well, Joram, I don't think there's any doubt about who the leaders will be today. The Israelites have been unstoppable this season, and it has to be because of their new captain, Saul. Sure, they had some minor victories over the past few seasons, but this year, they've been THE dominant power on the field. Nobody except the Philistines have come close in any game this season. So for the Israelites to do well today, they will need a strong performance from their captain.

JORAM: What about Jonathan, the son of Saul? Some have suggested that his play has made Saul look better than he really is.

PEKAH: Well, there's no doubt that Jonathan is the player of the future. But right now, Saul is it. Saul is the hope of Israel.

JORAM: OK. So much for Israel. Now, how about your thoughts on the Amalekites? What should we look for from them?

PEKAH: The Amalekites are, and always have been, an also-ran team. Oh sure, they've had some success in the past, but they've never won the cup. And don't look for them to go very far in the playoffs this year. But any team can come up with a win on any given day and this could be their day.

JORAM: Who should we be watching for the Amalekites?

PEKAH: First and foremost, their captain, Agag. Like Saul, he is the heart and soul of his team. He's a guy who always gives a hundred percent on the field. Also, the Amalekites have bolstered their team with some new faces from the Kenites. These fellows are unknowns and may make their presence felt in a big way today.

JORAM: Thank you for your analysis of today's game. We're almost ready for the start. But first, let's get a few words with the Israelite's coach, Samuel. Samuel, welcome to today's telecast.

SAMUEL: Thank you, Joram.

JORAM: Coach, could you tell us a little bit about your game plan for today? How are you going to beat these fellows?

SAMUEL: Well, to tell you the truth, I haven't developed a game plan.

JORAM: Are you trying to tell us that you just send the team in without telling them how to defeat their opponents? How can you justify your salary if you aren't going to instruct your team?

SAMUEL: I have given them instructions on what to do when the game is won. But I do not have to give any special instructions on how to win, because it will be won in the ordinary manner—by the superior team.

JORAM: That sounds a little overconfident, but I guess Pekah said much the same thing in his commentary. Could you tell us about the special instructions you have given your team?

SAMUEL: They have been instructed to completely destroy the Amalekites and all that the Amalekites have.

JORAM: Wow, that's putting it right on the line. Thank you for taking some time to be with us today, Samuel. Pekah, could I get your reaction to Samuel's comments?

PEKAH: Well, Samuel is not really a very organized coach. He seems to prefer doing things on the spur of the moment. He calls it "being led by the Lord." If we look at his record in all fairness, the Israelites have never lost a game when they followed his game plan.

JORAM: But what about his special instructions? Don't you find them a bit surprising?

PEKAH: Yes and no. You must remember, this is a grudge match. Everyone remembers, of course, how bitterly the Amalekites tried to prevent the Israelites from moving into Canaan. You might almost say that Israel is now trying to return the favor.

JORAM: That would, of course, explain why Samuel wants the team wiped out. But to destroy all of the Amalekites' possessions as well? Why would he want to do that?

PEKAH: That part of his plan makes no sense to anyone. If I were Saul, I would ignore that part of Samuel's instructions.

JORAM: We're almost ready for the start of the game. And look at the size of Israel's team! I've never seen such a large team! How many men would you say they have, Pekah?

PEKAH: Saul has easily got two hundred thousand, maybe even two hundred and ten thousand men with him today. No wonder Samuel seemed so confident.

JORAM: The game has started. But Saul isn't swooping onto the Amalekites as quickly as we would have expected. What is he doing? Why is he waiting?

PEKAH: Saul has approached one of the problems we discussed in the pregame show. Didn't we say the Kenites would be an unknown factor in the game, that the Kenites could make the difference? As you can see, Saul has convinced them to leave the Amalekites. Right at the beginning of the game, Saul has made a brilliant play to weaken the Amalekite team.

JORAM: It doesn't take a genius to see that this game will be very short lived. All that remains to be seen is, will Saul obey Samuel's instructions?

PEKAH: I don't see Samuel on the sidelines. This has always been another knock against him as a coach. He seems to think that he has more important things to do than to stay and watch the game.

JORAM: Well, that should actually make Saul's job easier. I wouldn't want to be the captain of a team of two hundred thousand and tell them that after the game, they won't be receiving any more than their regular paycheck.

PEKAH: This is very true. Everybody knows that most of a player's salary comes from his share of the booty that is taken at the end of a game. However, Saul seems to be following Samuel's plan to a tee. Everyone and everything is being utterly destroyed.

JORAM: Wait! Look! Saul is doing what we thought would be best. Look behind that chariot. One of the best sheep has been saved by Saul. Yes! A superb play. He is saving the best of the animals. No doubt his teammates will appreciate this and will play even better for him next game, knowing that he is a player's captain.

PEKAH: Not only that—he has executed another major coup. Although he SEEMED to be following Samuel's instructions, he has spared the life of Agag!

JORAM: I don't understand. How was that a smart play?

PEKAH: Saul knows that the Amalekites do have friends. If he had killed all of the Amalekites, then their friends might form an alliance and try to destroy Israel. But by saving the captain, Saul is telling Amalek's allies, "Look. We can get along." If anything unusual does happen this season and the Israelites should be defeated, Saul may be counting on the victors remembering what Saul has done and sparing his life, also.

JORAM: Well, it's all over now except for the shouting. Israel has won another stunning victory. We have to go now. But remember: Follow Saul's example and always watch out for yourself!

LAST BUT NOT LEAST

SCRIPTURE: 1 Samuel 16:1-13

SUGGESTED TOPICS: Trustworthiness; using abilities given by God; inner character versus outer qualities

BIBLE BACKGROUND

Saul's reign as king was coming to an end. He had repeatedly ignored the law and instructions of God and so had proven unworthy to be king over God's people. God had searched the hearts of the Israelites and found a replacement, a young man after God's own heart: David.

Outwardly, David did not appear to be the man for the job. At the time of his anointing, he was little more than a boy. But God does not look at outward appearances. David had all the inner qualities God required for the king of His people: most importantly, a love and reverence for God.

PERFORMANCE TIPS

1. Suggested props: Bible-times costumes and an animal horn. If an animal horn is not available, roll a piece of construction paper in the shape of a cone.
2. If a cow costume is available, consider having someone play the cow.
3. If cast members are few, Jesse's other sons and the town elders could be played by two or three people alternating parts. Change headgear to indicate a different person.
4. Town elders can speak in unison or alternate lines individually.
5. David should be considerably shorter than other cast members. If no one is that short, consider strapping sandals to David's knees and have him "walk" in on his knees.

DISCUSSION QUESTIONS

1. What do you think are the two most important qualities a person can have?
2. Many people think that money, looks and intelligence are what make people important. Do you agree? Why or why not? Does God agree?
3. Jesus told His disciples they were not servants, but friends (see John 15:15). What can you do to show that you are Jesus' friend?

LAST BUT NOT LEAST

CHARACTERS
SAMUEL
JESSE
TOWN ELDERS
ELIAB (ee-LYE-ab)
ABINADAB (a-BIN-a-dab)
DAVID
JESSE'S OTHER SONS

SCENE ONE

SAMUEL *(straining on rope)*: Come on, Bossy.
Move those legs. I thought you were a cow, not a mule.

TOWN ELDERS: Samuel?

SAMUEL: Excellent! Help! Would some of you get behind this beast and push?

TOWN ELDERS: You are Samuel?

SAMUEL: Of course I am. Now, are you planning to stand around or help me?

TOWN ELDERS: That depends.

SAMUEL: On what?

TOWN ELDERS: On whether you come in peace.

SAMUEL: Of course I come in peace. I am the Lord's servant.

TOWN ELDERS: True. But Saul sometimes gets upset with you. You didn't come to do something that will anger Saul, did you?

SAMUEL: I came to Bethlehem to make a sacrifice to the Lord. How could that make Saul angry? Sanctify yourselves and come to the sacrifice. Oh—and bring Jesse and his sons with you. But first, help me move this beast.

SCENE TWO

JESSE: It was good of you to invite my family to the sacrifice. It is a great honor to be here with God's servant.

SAMUEL: But you are alone. Where are your sons?

JESSE: They're coming. Here they are. *(SONS other than DAVID enter.)*

SAMUEL: What fine-looking young men! You must be very proud of them.

JESSE: I am indeed! *(SONS strike different bodybuilder poses.)*

SAMUEL: Introduce me to them.

JESSE: This is the eldest, Eliab.

SAMUEL: Look at him. So tall and handsome. Truly I must be looking at Israel's next king. Good thing I brought my horn of anointing oil. *(Takes horn from belt, stops and* *cups his hand to his ear. Looks upward.)* Not him, Lord? But look at him. No? *(Pats ELIAB on back.)* I'm sure you're a fine young man.

JESSE: Then, of course, my next eldest, Abinadab.

SAMUEL: The very model of manhood. *(Takes horn from belt, stops and cups his hand to his ear. Looks upward.)* Not him, either? *(Pats ABINADAB on back.)*

JESSE: Then, Shammah.

SAMUEL: Oh, yes! *(Takes horn from belt, stops and cups his hand to his ear. Looks upward.)* No? *(Pats SHAMMAH on back.) (In pantomime, JESSE continues to introduce his other four SONS. Same actions as before.)*

SAMUEL: None of them. Could I have been mistaken? Maybe the Lord said go to Bethel, not Bethlehem. No, I'm sure He said Bethlehem. Jesse?

JESSE: Yes, Samuel?

SAMUEL: Have you any other sons?

JESSE: Only the youngest, the baby of the family. He's out tending the sheep.

SAMUEL: We cannot continue with the sacrifice until he comes. Please send for him.

JESSE: *(To SONS.)* Go and bring your brother.

ALL SONS: Yes, Father. *(Exit.)*

SAMUEL: Tell me about this boy, David.

JESSE: Well, there's not much to tell. He's the youngest.

SAMUEL: What does he look like?

JESSE: He's not very big. A little sunburned, from being out with the sheep all day. But, on the whole, he's reasonably handsome.

SAMUEL: Does he have any hobbies?

JESSE: Now that you mention it, he's a fine musician. He plays his harp so beautifully, you would think he was an angel.

SAMUEL: How about his work habits?

JESSE: Funny you should ask. Most conscientious. A more trustworthy lad you'd never find if you searched through all Israel. Keeps his eyes open and makes sure the sheep find good grazing land and quiet waters.

SAMUEL: But you must be worried; him alone with the sheep. So many dangers.

JESSE: I never thought about it before, but never has he lost so much as a single lamb. Even when the bear and the lion tried to snatch one away, did he run for help? Not David. Took the lion by the beard and slew it. Killed the bear, too, come to think of it.

SAMUEL: I think I truly want to meet this boy.

JESSE: Your wish is granted. Here they come now. *(SONS enter, with DAVID bringing up the rear.)*

SAMUEL: I must have been mistaken. The Lord must have said Bethel. *(Cups hand to ear and looks upward.)* Are you sure, Lord? But he's so young and so small. How could one such as this be a king? Very well. *(Takes horn from belt.)* David, come forth. The Lord has told me to anoint you king of Israel. May His Spirit be upon you all your days and His wisdom and power be with you.

DRAGNET FOR DAVID

SCRIPTURE: 1 Samuel 18

SUGGESTED TOPICS: Friendship and loyalty; sin of jealousy

BIBLE BACKGROUND

Saul was still king, but David had been anointed by Samuel to be king instead of Saul. David remained loyal to Saul, who should have felt honored to have a friend and subject such as David. However, David's popularity aroused such jealousy in Saul, it was as though a green mist passed over the king's eyes every time he saw the young warrior. Instead of seeing a soldier who won great victories on his king's behalf, Saul saw a usurper of whom the women sang, "Saul has slain his thousands, and David his tens of thousands" (1 Samuel 18:7).

Later events show that Saul had nothing to fear from David. Even when given the opportunity, David chose not to destroy Saul out of his reverence for God (see 1 Samuel 24:6).

The man who had cause to be jealous of David was Saul's son Jonathan. Jonathan would have been next in line to be king, but David had been anointed in his place. Even though Jonathan knew that David would become king (see 1 Samuel 23:17), friendship with David was more important to Jonathan than worldly acclaim and power.

PERFORMANCE TIPS

1. Suggested props: a palace wall with two holes in it, a notebook for Pete, a crown and purple robe for King Saul.
2. Joe should speak matter-of-factly, almost monotone. (Joe is a takeoff on the "Joe Friday" character from the "Dragnet" TV series.)
3. King Saul should be inconsistent, sometimes speaking rationally, sometimes ranting and raving.
4. If your class is not familiar with the story of David and Jonathan, explain what Jonathan was doing when he went out for archery practice.

DISCUSSION QUESTIONS

1. Do you agree with Joe concerning David's whereabouts? Why or why not?
2. Why do you think Saul was so intent on finding David?
3. What caused the two holes in the wall? What made Saul behave this way?
4. What does "jealousy" mean? Have you ever been jealous of someone?
5. If you are jealous of someone, what can you do about it?

DRAGNET FOR DAVID

CHARACTERS

JOE

PETE

SAUL

PRONUNCIATION GUIDE

Michal (MY-kul)

JOE: This is the city. It's the place where I work. I love it. In the city are a thousand stories. This is one of them.

PETE: Is it my turn yet?

JOE: Not yet. I'm still in the middle of my dramatic introduction. Now, where was I? Oh, yes. My name is Sabbath. Joe Sabbath. I'm a cop. Sgt. Jacobs and I had been called to the palace on a missing persons case.

PETE: Boy, this is sure exciting. Being on an important case for the king.

JOE: They're all exciting, Pete.

PETE: Yeah. But the king! How many people ever get a chance to talk to the king?

JOE: Probably more than you think. Let's go inside.

PETE: Shouldn't we ring the doorbell first?

JOE: No.

PETE: Why not?

JOE: Because we're here on authority. And doorbells haven't been invented yet.

PETE: Look! That's Jonathan, the king's son. What do you think he's doing?

JOE: I suspect that he's going hunting.

PETE: Why do you think that?

JOE: He has a BOW. And a quiver full of ARROWS. And a small boy to FETCH the arrows.

PETE: Maybe he's going to fight a mighty battle against the Philistines.

JOE: I doubt it.

PETE: Why not?

JOE: Because if he was going to battle, he would take soldiers with him. Not just a little boy.

PETE: Oh, yeah. Good thinking. So who do you think is missing?

JOE: I don't waste time in idle speculation when somebody can give me the facts. That's all I want. Just the facts.

PETE: But who is going to give us the facts?

JOE: The king.

PETE: But how are you going to find the king?

SAUL (from behind): You could try turning around.

PETE: Oh!

JOE: Your Majesty! We came as soon as we got your message. Now, please give us the facts. Who is missing?

SAUL (yelling): Servant!

PETE: We need a better description than that. Which servant?

SAUL: Which servant what?

JOE: Which servant is missing?

SAUL: None of my servants are missing.

PETE: Then why did you say that one was?

SAUL: Oh, no. I was calling for a servant to bring us some wine.

JOE: No, thank you. We're on duty. So who exactly is missing?

SAUL: David!

PETE: Can we get a description of this David?

JOE: We won't need one. Everybody in the city knows David.

SAUL (bitterly): They certainly do.

PETE: Are we talking about the David that killed Goliath?

SAUL: That's the one.

JOE: And now he's missing?

PETE: I've got a theory. Maybe he's afraid of being brought to trial for the murder of Goliath, and he ran away to hide.

SAUL: I hardly think that's likely.

PETE: Begging your pardon, Your Royalness. But you don't know how the criminal mind operates. Being trained policemen, we do.

SAUL: Why should he be afraid of being brought to trial for killing Goliath when he has already been promoted for that deed?

JOE: You're forgetting, Pete. Goliath was a Philistine.

PETE: Oh, yeah. Now I remember. I keep getting the two sides mixed up.

SAUL: Can we get on with this? I really need to find David.

JOE: Certainly, Your Majesty. I imagine that the loss of a hero is distressing to you.

PETE: A HERO? Do you mean that we're looking for the hero, David? The one that the women are always singing about? You've heard that song *(Sings.)*, "Saul has slain his thousands and David his tens of thousands," that the women are always singing in the streets. Is something wrong, Your Highnessest?

SAUL: What? Ah, no. No. Nothing. Why do you ask?

JOE: You had turned a little green there for a minute. Pete doesn't realize the effect that his singing has on most people. Now, Your Majesty, what can you tell us about David and his habits?

SAUL: Very little. His closest friend is my son, Jonathan. He could tell you things about David, but he's out taking a little target practice.

JOE: Maybe you could tell us all that you do know. Just the facts, sir.

SAUL: Well, he's my son-in-law. He's married to my daughter, Michal.

PETE: Joe.

SAUL: What?

PETE: Joe.

SAUL: What about Joe?

PETE: You just called him Michael.

SAUL: No, I didn't.

PETE: Yes, you did. I have it written down. When Mr. Sabbath asked you to tell us all you knew, you said that David was married to your daughter, and you called him Michael.

SAUL: No, I didn't. I called HER Michal.

PETE: Begging your pardon, Your Kingliness, but when you're talking about a man, you don't use the word "her."

JOE: Allow me, Your Majesty. Pete, the king's daughter's name is Michal.

PETE: Oh. There should be a law against giving a girl a boy's name. It gets very confusing.

JOE: You were saying that David is married to Michal. Has it been a happy marriage? Perhaps David just wanted to get away from the little woman for a while.

SAUL: I hardly think so. They've only been married a short time. And to get her, well, you should have seen the dowry that he gave.

JOE: I understand David was a shepherd before he became a soldier. Where would a shepherd get a large dowry?

SAUL: Oh, he didn't give me money. He killed two hundred Philistines to have her hand in marriage.

PETE: *(Sings softly.)* Saul has slain his thousands and David his tens of thousands.

SAUL: *(Yells and pulls hair.)* Arrghhh! *(Throws imaginary spear.)*

PETE: Wowee! Where did that spear come from? Whoowee! That nearly pinned me to the wall, just like a butterfly in a display case.

SAUL: Sorry. It's that wretched song—when I get upset, I throw things. Don't you do that sometimes?

JOE: Sometimes. But I always make sure that they don't have sharp-pointed ends and that nobody is in the way. However, Pete doesn't realize what his singing does to people. Any judge would have ruled it justifiable homicide.

PETE: Look at that! That spear went all the way through the wall!

SAUL: Can we please get back to the investigation?

JOE: Certainly, Your Majesty. What else can you tell us about David?

SAUL: Well, he's an excellent musician. Sometimes when I feel a little down, he sits over there and plays the harp for me. *(Points to wall.)*

JOE: Beside the wall with the two holes in it?

SAUL: That's right.

JOE: Hmmm. Thank you, Your Majesty. I think we have enough to begin our preliminary investigation. Come on, Pete. It's time to go.

PETE: Right through the wall! Boy! Is he strong. Wow!

JOE: It's time to go, Pete. Let's move it.

PETE: Do you think we've got enough to solve the case, Joe?

JOE: Sure. It's easy to figure out. A former shepherd, a musician, just married. Obviously, he's gone off into the hills to write a love song for his new bride. He'll be back in a few days. Nothing LIFE threatening. Well, Pete, another case wrapped up.

THE FUGITIVE

SCRIPTURE: 1 Samuel 21:1-9; 22:6-19; 24

SUGGESTED TOPICS: Compassion; respect for God's leaders; God's timing

BIBLE BACKGROUND

Saul's jealousy of David flared into a raging fire. No longer was David safe when he was anywhere near Saul. In spite of David's valor in battle against Saul's enemies, his marriage to Saul's daughter, his friendship with Saul's son, and his unswerving loyalty to Saul as king, David became a hunted criminal. His "crime" was two-fold: he was more popular than Saul (see 1 Samuel 18:8) and he had been annointed to be the next king of Israel.

David's actions during this conflict show why David was called a man after God's own heart (see 1 Samuel 13:14). With his popularity, he could have raised up an army to lead a rebellion against Saul. Instead, he fled and offered no opposition to Saul, trusting God to bring about His purpose in His own way. Even when given the opportunity to destroy Saul, David refused, not because Saul was king and David was afraid of the consequences of killing the secular head of the kingdom, but because Saul was "the Lord's anointed" (1 Samuel 24:6). David never lost sight of Saul's position in God's order, even when Saul proved himself unworthy of that position.

PERFORMANCE TIPS

1. Suggested props: a butter knife, a large sword for David, weapons for soldiers, a crown for Saul.

2. Soldiers and servants can double as David's men if actors are in short supply.

3. Saul's moods change rapidly. He should be played with large movements, sweeping gestures, etc.

DISCUSSION QUESTIONS

1. Why did Saul hate David? What had David done to Saul?

2. How do you think David felt when he was treated so unfairly? (Read Psalm 57. It is believed that David wrote this Psalm when Saul was chasing him.)

3. Often we let our feelings guide our actions. Did David do this? How did David control his feelings and act in a different manner?

4. Do you think Saul deserved David's friendship? Why or why not?

5. Why should you show friendship like David's?

6. As Christians, we are called to be like Christ. How did Jesus show His friendship to us? How can we show this kind of friendship to others?

THE FUGITIVE

CHARACTERS
NARRATOR
DAVID
AHIMELECH (ah-HIM-eh-lek)
SAUL
DOEG (DOH-egg)
SERVANTS and SOLDIERS
FIRST MAN
SECOND MAN

SCENE ONE

NARRATOR: Unjustly accused of treason, David has had to flee for his life. Aided by Saul's son, Jonathan, David escaped from the palace. For now, the sentence of death has been delayed. David is free. Free to jump at every shadow, free to hide from the king's men, free to roam from place to place hoping to find a haven to rest his weary head. Free to be...THE FUGITIVE.

(Sound of knocking on door.)

AHIMELECH: Who's knocking on my door so late at night? Go away! I'm trying to prepare my sermon.

DAVID *(whispering)***:** Ahimelech. It's David. Please, open your door.

AHIMELECH: David? Captain of the king's army? Trusted servant of Saul?

DAVID *(whispering)***:** Yeah. Open up, will you?

AHIMELECH: The king's favorite is always welcome here. But should you be out on a cool night when you have a touch of laryngitis?

DAVID *(whispering)***:** I don't have laryngitis. I'm just being careful.

AHIMELECH: Well, come in. Come in. It's safe to speak here. Why all the secrecy?

DAVID: *(Looks right and left and motions AHIMELECH closer.)* I'm on a secret mission for the king.

AHIMELECH: Say no more.

DAVID: I can say no more. But I need some provisions.

AHIMELECH: But would the king not have provided you with food?

DAVID: There was no time. This secret mission is of the greatest importance and I had to leave immediately. I had no time to stop for food.

AHIMELECH: Say no more.

DAVID: I can say no more. Can you spare five loaves of bread? Or anything you might have.

AHIMELECH: I have some communion bread. Yes, you may have it.

DAVID: What was that noise?

AHIMELECH: Doeg.

DAVID: I didn't know you had a dog.

AHIMELECH: Not dog. Doeg. Saul's chief herdsman.

DAVID: Did he see me?

AHIMELECH: Perhaps. But you're both the king's servants. What difference can it make whether he saw you or not?

DAVID: Maybe none. But my mission is top secret...

AHIMELECH: Say no more.

DAVID: I can say no more. Do you have any weapons I could take with me?

AHIMELECH: I am a man of God. Why would I have weapons? You're the soldier.

DAVID: Yes, but the king's business required haste. I had no time to stop for my own armament. You must have some weapon.

AHIMELECH: A butter knife? No, hardly satisfactory. Wait! I do have this museum piece. A GOLIATH sword. *(Produces a large sword.)*

DAVID: Excellent! There is none other like it in the land. Farewell, my friend. May you be rewarded for your friendship. Farewell! *(Exits.)*

AHIMELECH *(thoughtfully)*: A strange young man. But a good and faithful servant.

SCENE TWO

(SAUL enters court filled with SERVANTS and SOLDIERS.)

SAUL *(screaming with rage)*: You call yourselves servants?

SERVANTS and SOLDIERS *(mumbling)*: Yes, m'lord.

SAUL: Are you all conspiring with David against me?

SERVANTS and SOLDIERS: No, m'lord.

SAUL: *(To SERVANTS.)* Can David give you vineyards and fields?

SERVANTS: No, m'lord.

SAUL: *(To SOLDIERS.)* Can David give you promotions?

SOLDIERS: No, m'lord.

SAUL: Then why do you all conspire with him? *(Voice changes to whining.)* Doesn't anybody care? You all knew Jonathan, my own son, was helping him. And now he has four hundred men helping him. Everybody hates me. You're all no good. Isn't anybody sorry for me? Won't anybody help me? *(Buries face in hands and sobs.)*

DOEG: Yes, m'lord!

SAUL: (*Looks up.*) Who are you?

DOEG: Doeg.

SAUL: How dare you insult me! Call me a dog, will you?

DOEG: No, m'lord. My NAME is Do-eg.

SAUL: Oh, yes. Your name. Quite. Well, what do you want?

DOEG: I have important information for you.

SAUL: Nothing's important anymore. Nobody loves me. Everybody conceals things from me. Nobody will tell me where to find David so I can kill him.

DOEG: I will.

SAUL: You know where David is?

DOEG: No. But I know where he was. He was visiting Ahimelech. And Ahimelech helped David. He gave him food and a sword.

SAUL: Bring Ahimelech here!

    (*SERVANTS hurry out and return with AHIMELECH.*)

SAUL: So, you're the traitor. And you call yourself a priest.

AHIMELECH: I'm not a traitor, O King. How can you say such a thing?

SAUL: You aren't a traitor? Didn't you give David food and weapons?

AHIMELECH: Of course.

SAUL: Ha! You admit you're a traitor!

AHIMELECH: I'm not a traitor. Why shouldn't I give things to David? He is your son-in-law. He is the most faithful of all your men. He sits in an honored place in your home. How was I supposed to know you hated him?

SAUL: I won't have traitors in my country! Soldiers! Kill him!

SOLDIERS (*muttering among themselves*)**:** But he's a priest! We can't kill him.

DOEG: (*Jumps up and down.*) Me! Me! Let me! I'll kill him for you. And all the other priests who were with him and all his family and his cat and his dog and his sheep and...

SAUL: Why can't ALL my servants be as faithful as Doeg?

SCENE THREE

    (*Stage area is inside of cave. DAVID and MEN are in cave.*)

SAUL: (*From offstage.*) We've been searching all over these rocks for David. It's time to sleep. Hmm. Kind of looks like rain. Guards, you wait here and I'll sleep in this cave. (*Enters.*) It's kind of dark in here. But it's dry. Oh, chasing fugitives is so tiring. (*Lays down and covers himself.*)

     The Big Book of Bible Skits ©1997 Gospel Light. Permission to photocopy granted.

FIRST MAN: *(Punches DAVID's shoulder.)* Look! The day spoken of by the Lord has come to pass.

SECOND MAN: Yes. The Lord has delivered Saul into your hands!

FIRST MAN: You can do whatever you want to him.

SECOND MAN: You could kill him!

DAVID: Wait here. *(Creeps down to where SAUL sleeps and cuts off piece of cloak.)*

FIRST MAN: That's IT?

SECOND MAN: Why not cut off his whole coat, right about throat level?

DAVID: God forbid that I should hurt or kill His anointed. Let him rest and go in peace.

> *(DAVID and MEN crouch, watching SAUL. SAUL wakes and stretches.)*

SAUL: Oh, that's better. Nothing like a good night's sleep to restore the body. Now I can resume chasing that no-good, cowardly, lily-livered, traitorous David. *(Exits.)*

> *(DAVID rushes to mouth of cave.)*

DAVID: My lord, the king!

SAUL: Who's there?

DAVID: *(Bows down.)* Why do you listen to men who say, "David wants to hurt you"? I could have cut your throat as you lay sleeping in this cave. I have never sought to hurt you, and I never will. Look! This piece of your cloak I cut off could easily have been your THROAT!

SAUL: Is this the voice of my son, David?

DAVID: It is.

SAUL: Oh, how could I be so cruel and stupid? You have shown me how good you are. Now I KNOW the kingdom will be yours. Show your mercy to me, my son, and promise me one thing.

DAVID: You have but to ask.

SAUL: When the Lord gives you the kingdom, do not destroy all my family. Do not blot out my name from the earth.

DAVID: As surely as the Lord reigns, this I promise you.

NARRATOR: And so Saul went home. But David remained on the run, for he knew that Saul would soon forget his remorse and seek David's life again. This is the life of one on the run. Never to rest in complete peace, always vigilant against the threat of renewed efforts to kill him. Such is the life of...THE FUGITIVE.

GREETING CARDS

SCRIPTURE: 1 Samuel 25:1-19

SUGGESTED TOPICS: Ingratitude; thankfulness; wise and foolish actions; sharing

BIBLE BACKGROUND

David was on the run from Saul. Although Saul had temporarily sworn a peace treaty with David, David had seen Saul change his mind before. Wisely, David and his men chose to remain in the hills, away from Saul's power.

While living in the hills, David and his men assisted the hired shepherds of a wealthy Israelite from the house of Caleb, a man named Nabal (meaning "fool"). Nabal, in spite of his great wealth, compares poorly with both his famous ancestor and his "intelligent and beautiful" wife. At a festive time of year when most farmers were celebrating God's goodness, Nabal could not see beyond his profits. Shortsightedly, he saw no profit in sharing with one whom the king of Israel had been chasing through the hills. Rarely has lack of gratitude so vividly been the cause of a man's downfall.

PERFORMANCE TIPS

1. Suggested props: greeting cards, swords for David and his men.

2. Letter verses on the cards for the actors to read.

3. If some in the class have an artistic bent, have them decorate the front of the cards in an appropriate manner.

4. Complete the story. Show the class what happened to Nabal and Abigail as a result of their thankfulness or lack thereof.

DISCUSSION QUESTIONS

1. Why did David assume Nabal would be willing to share?

2. What might be some reasons Nabal was so selfish?

3. What was David's reaction to Nabal's selfishness? (See 1 Samuel 25:34.)

4. What good things has God given you? How have you repaid God?

5. How can you show God that you are thankful for what He has done?

GREETING CARDS

CHARACTERS
DAVID
NABAL (NAY-bal)
ABIGAIL
FIRST MAN
SECOND MAN
SERVANT

SCENE ONE

DAVID: What's all the noise?

FIRST MAN: Sheep.

DAVID: I know it's sheep. But why so MUCH noise?

SECOND MAN: Because it's sheep shearing time.

DAVID: Sheep shearing time! I remember it well. A time of festivity, rejoicing. Let's have a party!

FIRST MAN: I wish we could.

DAVID: Why not? I hereby decree this to be a feast day!

SECOND MAN: But we have nothing to feast with.

DAVID: True. We've been on the run from Saul. What DO we have?

FIRST MAN: A few loaves of bread...

SECOND MAN: A bit of dried fruit...

FIRST MAN: A little beef jerky...

DAVID: Not exactly a feast.

SECOND MAN: No.

DAVID: Aha! An idea. All the time we've been camped here, we've protected the flocks and the shepherds of Nabal. If someone had done this for my dad, he would have already sent a gift over to them.

FIRST MAN: Then, why didn't Nabal send us anything?

DAVID: He probably doesn't know what we've done. His shepherds just haven't reported it to him. Here! *(Hands card to MEN.)* Take this card to Nabal with our warmest greetings.

SCENE TWO

FIRST MAN *(walking)***:** Do you think Nabal will share some of his flock with us?

SECOND MAN *(walking)***:** Well, of course he will. He's rich! He has three thousand sheep and a thousand goats.

FIRST MAN: But you KNOW how rich people can be.

SECOND MAN: Nonsense! Rich people are just like other people.

FIRST MAN: But why would he share with us?

SECOND MAN: Because, if we hadn't been out there, protecting his flocks and shepherds, he would probably have lost lots of sheep and goats—if not to the wild animals, then to the Philistines.

FIRST MAN: That's true.

SECOND MAN: And we're coming from David. You know how well respected David is.

FIRST MAN: True again. You're right. Nabal will be more than happy to share with us.

SECOND MAN: Look! There he is. Remember, David said to be respectful.

FIRST MAN: *(Holds out hand.)* Hello, neighbor.

NABAL *(snarling)*: What do you want?

SECOND MAN: *(Hands card to Nabal.)* We come bringing the warmest regards of our master, David.

NABAL *(snarling)*: What's this? Some cheap card? Let's see. *(Reads card.)*

> "Peace be to you and to your house,
>
> Your children and your loving spouse.
>
> May all you touch turn into gold
>
> And all you give return tenfold."

So, what does David want in return for this cheap sentiment?

FIRST MAN: We have lived on the hills, among your shepherds...

SECOND MAN: During that time, we helped protect your flocks from all dangers...

FIRST MAN: In fact, during this past year, you haven't lost so much as a single lamb.

SECOND MAN: Don't take our word for it. Ask your men. They'll tell you.

NABAL *(snarling)*: Cut the fancy talk and get down to it. What do you want?

FIRST MAN: David only asks that if we have found favor in your sight...

SECOND MAN: Perhaps, during this glad time of harvest, you would be willing to share a small amount of your good fortune.

NABAL *(snarling)*: I thought so. Looking for a handout. Here! *(Hands men a card.)* Take THIS to your precious David. And tell him that's all he gets!

SCENE THREE

(MAN gives card to DAVID.)

DAVID: Let's see. What does Nabal have to say? *(Reads card.)*

> "Who is this man you say you serve?
>
> I've never met him or his kin.
>
> Because he's David, he thinks he deserves

The Big Book of Bible Skits ©1997 Gospel Light. Permission to photocopy granted.

Meat from my table or grain from my bin?

He's nothing more than a common thief

Who's run away from his master, Saul.

I'll give him nothing else but grief

And kick him out, should he come to call."

(Looks up.) Is this some kind of a joke?

FIRST MAN: I don't think so.

SECOND MAN: He seemed serious.

DAVID: Then he wants WAR. Everyone! Put on your swords! We've got work to do.

FIRST MAN: Swords?

SECOND MAN: Are we going into battle?

DAVID: We kept everything Nabal owns safe for the whole season. Is this our reward? I swear to you, by morning, he will be left with nothing!

SCENE FOUR

SERVANT: And that's what happened. Our master was most rude to David's men.

ABIGAIL: Did these men truly protect you and the flocks?

SERVANT: Truly, they did. They were like a strong, protective wall about us, night and day. We knew we were safe with them on guard.

ABIGAIL: I can't believe Nabal would treat David that way! But then again, knowing Nabal, I CAN believe it.

SERVANT: Madam, please think of something to do. Quickly! For David is a man of war. I don't think he will take this insult lightly.

ABIGAIL: You're right. Get me two hundred loaves of bread, two bottles of wine, the meat from five sheep, five measures of corn, one hundred clusters of raisins and, oh—two hundred cakes of figs. Load them onto donkeys and start toward David's camp. I'll follow, just as soon as I find the right card to give David.

SERVANT: Even as you speak, it is done, Madam. *(Exits.)*

ABIGAIL: Let's see. *(Pulls several cards from pocket and thumbs through them.)* Ah! Here's the perfect one. *(Reads card.)*

"David, my lord, long may you live;

Accept this humble gift I give.

Nabal's name translates as 'fool'

He lacks the sense God gave a mule!

Put Nabal's sin upon my soul

Then let our friendship be made whole."

I just hope this does the trick. *(Sighs.)* Men! Always ready to quarrel!

ISRAELI HOME SHOPPING CLUB

SCRIPTURE: 2 Samuel 2—3:1

SUGGESTED TOPICS: Loyalty to God, not men; making wise choices

BIBLE BACKGROUND

"The king is dead; long live the king!" This is a familiar phrase to any who live in a monarchy. When the old king dies, the country expresses its allegiance to the new king. Saul had committed suicide and three of his sons had been killed in battle against the Philistines (see 1 Samuel 31:2-4). Who then would be Israel's king?

Abner, the commander of Saul's army, threw his allegiance behind Ishbosheth. This was a logical choice, as Ishbosheth was a son of Saul. Tradition dictates that the new king be a son of the previous king, but God does not follow the traditions of men. He had already chosen David to be the new king of Israel. Because of Saul's sin, the kingdom was taken from his family by God (see 1 Samuel 15:28). Abner, a brave and skilled warrior, ignored God's clear intention, and the result of this unwise choice was destruction.

PERFORMANCE TIPS

1. Suggested props: purple robe (or piece of cloth), cardboard or wooden scepter.
2. Announcer is trying to sell cheap merchandise, passing it off as top quality. He should speak fairly quickly and excitedly.
3. After the skit, continue the story to show the wise choices David made.

DISCUSSION QUESTIONS

1. Did Abner make wise choices? What might have influenced him to make the choices he did?
2. What were some choices David made? Were they wise choices? Why or why not?
3. What kinds of decisions do you have to make? How can you help ensure wise choices?

ISRAELI HOME SHOPPING CLUB

CHARACTERS
ANNOUNCER
ABNER

PRONUNCIATION GUIDE
Ishbosheth (ISH-bow-sheth)

ANNOUNCER: It's great to be back on the air with you again at the Israeli Home Shopping Club! And do we have some bargains for you today! Let's not waste any more time. Look at the first item. *(Pause, allowing viewers to see the item.)* Look at that robe! All in royal purple with a hem sewn in genuine gold stitching! You would expect to pay up to a talent of gold for this item anywhere else but not if you're a member! Certainly not! Look at this low members' price. Seven shekels. That's right! No, we haven't gone totally crazy here at the Club, but we wanted to start off today's show with a real bargain. The phones have been ringing off the hooks on this one already. Let's talk to one of the shoppers. Hi, who am I talking to?

ABNER: This is Abner.

ANNOUNCER: Abner. Terrific name. Are you related to the Abner who was the captain of Saul's guard?

ABNER: That's me. I'm the same Abner.

ANNOUNCER: Well, that's great. Because having been around King Saul for so long, you would certainly know the value of a wonderful garment like the one we're offering!

ABNER: Well, yes. I have seen many beautiful robes in my time at the king's palace. And this one does look beautiful.

ANNOUNCER: It more than LOOKS beautiful. It IS beautiful! I mentioned the color before and the gold stitching, but this has almost too many features to mention!

ABNER: Go ahead. Mention some.

ANNOUNCER: Did I talk about the beautiful, royal, purple color?

ABNER: Yes.

ANNOUNCER: What about the gold stitching?

ABNER: Yes.

ANNOUNCER: What about this? ONE SIZE FITS ALL! That's right! It doesn't matter if you're as tall as Goliath or as short as David, this robe will fit you!

ABNER: Why did you mention David? Has HE ordered a robe, too?

ANNOUNCER: I was merely using a well-known metaphor here in Israel. Everybody knows that Goliath was huge and that David is short. But back to the robe. What sort of money would Saul have paid for a robe like this?

ABNER: Well, he was sometimes a bit extravagant when it came to clothes. Not unusually so, you understand. After all, he WAS the king. But I would never reveal any of the king's secrets.

ANNOUNCER: Abner. What are you afraid of? Saul is dead. He can't do anything to you for revealing an innocent secret. Come on. Tell us a little palace gossip. What sort of money would Saul have paid for a robe like this one?

ABNER: No. I can't betray the secrets of a king, even if he is no longer with us. But I CAN tell you that he would certainly have paid more than seven shekels for one.

ANNOUNCER: OK! Great! There you have it folks, a testimonial direct from the palace! This is one GREAT bargain! There's only a few seconds left to order your very own "kingly" robe. That's it! Time's up on this item. But we still have more terrific buys coming up on the Israeli Home Shopping Club. Here comes the next item now. There it is! *(Pause to allow time for audience to see.)* An ABSOLUTELY GORGEOUS, SOLID GOLD-PLATED scepter! You can see the beauty and craftsmanship built into this item. Fully three feet long and encrusted with ten genuine cubic zirconias. No king would dream of purchasing a scepter for less than two full talents of gold. But this one can be picked up for a psalm. Look at that members' price—TEN SHEKELS! I can't believe that one myself. I wish that you could be here in the studio with me to see this in person. Just think! For a mere ten shekels you will not only be king of your house, but you will have the scepter to prove it. If you want one of these beauties, you'd better call in quickly, or you'll miss out. Let's talk to one of our buyers. Hi! You're on the Israeli Home Shopping Club! So what do you think of this item that we're offering now?

ABNER: I think that it looks like a very good buy. That's why I'm buying it.

ANNOUNCER: You know, you sound a lot like a previous caller. Who is this?

ABNER: It's Abner.

ANNOUNCER: Well, you are doing a lot of shopping tonight, Abner. What's the big occasion? Are you planning to dress up and show the little woman that you're king of the home?

ABNER: Actually, I'm buying them for a friend. Ishbosheth.

ANNOUNCER: Bless you. That's a nasty sneeze you have there.

ABNER: I didn't sneeze. That's my friend's name. Ishbosheth.

ANNOUNCER: Well, I'm certainly glad that he didn't call in himself. I'd never have been able to pronounce his name. I'd probably have ended up calling him Sneezy.

ABNER: I wouldn't joke about his name too much. And I would learn how to pronounce it if I were you. Because he's going to be the next king of Israel.

ANNOUNCER: Politics really isn't my thing, but I thought that David was going to be the next king of Israel. That's what all MY neighbors are saying, anyway.

ABNER: Well, they're all wrong. Ishbosheth will be the next king.

ANNOUNCER: It's been nice chatting with you, Abner. But we're just about out of time on our portion of the show today. Stay tuned for Deborah. Deb's going to have some terrific buys for all you ladies out there. I'll be back tomorrow with some more "kingly" purchases for you men. Until then, so long and see you again.

O WORSHIP THE KING

SCRIPTURE: 2 Samuel 8:9—9:12; Psalm 96

SUGGESTED TOPICS: Keeping promises; friendship

BIBLE BACKGROUND

David's regard for the Lord caused his behavior to differ vastly from that of other kings of his time. Allowing the relatives, particularly sons and grandsons, of the former king to live was considered grave foolishness. As long as they lived, so did the possibility of a rebellion to restore the throne to the former dynasty. This fear sometimes grew to extreme paranoia, as evidenced by the actions of Athaliah (see 2 Kings 11:1-3). David, however, recognized that to worship God with words while being vindictive and unjust would be the worst form of hypocrisy. So David, being a man of his word, fulfilled his oath sworn to Jonathan years before (see 1 Samuel 20:42).

Joab was a man who swore his allegiance to David. However, he was not always sympathetic to what he saw as David's weaknesses (see 2 Samuel 3:23-27; 19:5-7). Although he is not mentioned as being present when David interviewed Ziba, the skit uses him as the one man in David's army who would not be afraid to question David's wisdom, and thereby prod David to explain the meaning of true worship.

PERFORMANCE TIPS

1. Suggested props: crown for David, chairs for David and Ziba, weapons for Joab (sword, spear, shield, etc.), Bible-times costumes.
2. Consider having readers read Psalm 96 when Joab refers to it.
3. Ziba should be suspicious of David and indicate this by his manner. He knows that new kings always killed off all the former king's sons and grandsons.
4. Joab is a man of war. He should act rough, with a loud voice and large gestures.

DISCUSSION QUESTIONS

1. Why do you think Ziba would be so afraid of David?
2. Why would Joab think David would want to kill Mephibosheth?
3. In the skit, what three ways did David use to worship God?
4. What other ways can you worship God?

O WORSHIP THE KING

CHARACTERS
DAVID
JOAB
ZIBA (ZEE-buh)

PRONUNCIATION GUIDE
Mephibosheth (muh-FIB-uh-sheth)
Tou (too)

JOAB: *(Hauls ZIBA into the court.)* Here! I found him, my lord!

DAVID: Joab! I asked you to BRING Ziba to me.

JOAB: Well? That's what I did.

DAVID: There are different ways of escorting a person. Now, Ziba...

ZIBA: *(Falls to his knees and pleads.)* Forgive me, my Lord. I didn't mean to do it. It wasn't my fault...

DAVID: Stop! Stop! Stop! What wasn't your fault?

ZIBA: Whatever it was that made you bring me here.

JOAB: Give me three minutes with him and he'll confess!

DAVID: Confess to WHAT?

JOAB: Whatever you want him to confess to.

DAVID: I don't want him to confess to anything!

JOAB: You don't?

ZIBA: You don't?

DAVID: No. Come. Get off your knees and sit here. *(ZIBA sits.)* Now. You were one of Saul's servants...

ZIBA: *(Falls to his knees.)* Forgive me, my lord. I was young and foolish. I didn't know what I was doing. Never would I do such a thing again...

DAVID: Stop! Stop! Stop! What's the matter with you?

ZIBA: I have a slight cold, but other than that...

DAVID: I mean, why are you acting so strangely? Get up and sit down.

The Big Book of Bible Skits ©1997 Gospel Light. Permission to photocopy granted.

JOAB: You heard the king! *(Pulls ZIBA up.)* Get to your feet and sit down. *(Forces ZIBA into chair.)*

DAVID: Thank you, Joab. But I think he could have managed himself. Now, Ziba. You were one of Saul's servants.

ZIBA *(cautiously)*: Yes.

DAVID: So you should know if any of Saul's grandchildren are still alive.

ZIBA *(cautiously)*: Yes.

DAVID: Well?

ZIBA: Well...

JOAB: Answer the king! Before I...

DAVID: Joab! Please. Tell me, Ziba. Are any still alive?

ZIBA: There is one, my lord. But he's no threat to you.

DAVID: Ah! So THAT'S it. Ziba, I mean no harm to him. I only ask because I wish to show kindness to him.

ZIBA: There is one named Mephibosheth. But he's lame, so you don't have to worry about him.

DAVID: I'm NOT worried about him. I told you. Because of my friendship with Jonathan, I want to show kindness to any of his sons who may still be living. Please, Ziba, go and bring him to me.

ZIBA: As you wish, my lord. *(Exits.)*

JOAB: I don't get it. *(Pauses.)* Oh! Now I get it. You are clever!

DAVID: What do you mean?

JOAB: He thought you wanted to harm this Muffy—whatever the kid's name is. So he's got him hidden and you couldn't find him. Now, you've got him convinced that you don't want to hurt the kid, so he'll come right to the palace. Then, you'll kill him.

DAVID: Why would I do that?

JOAB: Because that's what kings DO.

DAVID: Kings who don't worship God may do that. I do not.

JOAB: Sure you do.

DAVID: What?

JOAB: Sure you worship God. I've seen you pray and write poems to Him.

DAVID: I meant, other kings may kill the former king's grandchildren. I don't.

JOAB: Oh! See, I thought you said you didn't worship God. But what's worshiping God got to do with making a sound political decision?

DAVID: Everything! Worship is a part of life.

JOAB: Naw, it's only when you write poems to God. Like that "sing a new song to the Lord" one. I like that one. Has a real catchy tune.

DAVID: Oh, no. Worship is much more than that. Remember when King Tou sent me that gift of gold, silver and bronze!

JOAB: Yeah. *(Looks around.)* Whatever happened to it?

DAVID: As an act of worship, I gave it to the Lord.

JOAB: You mean it's in HEAVEN?

DAVID: No. It has been dedicated to the Lord, so it can only be used by the priests in the Tabernacle to help all of Israel worship God.

JOAB: That's a pretty expensive way to worship. I should think poetry would be enough.

DAVID: Nothing I could give would be enough. This was simply a token, a symbol to show God that I recognize where my strength comes from.

JOAB: OK, but what about this Messy-fish—whatever his name is? You're actually planning to let him live?

DAVID: Of course! He's Jonathan's son!

JOAB: Precisely my point.

DAVID: God gave me the best friend I ever had. Should I repay God for this kindness by destroying the son of that friend? Heaven forbid!

JOAB: But he's a threat.

DAVID: If God should choose to replace me on Israel's throne, so be it. But I will worship God by showing kindness to the son of Jonathan. He will be honored in this court as if he were my own son. Do I make myself clear?

JOAB: As clear as an open window on a cloudless summer day. I still don't understand it; but mine is not to reason why. I will obey your orders, as always, my king.

DAVID: Thank you, Joab. You are a good and trusted friend.

THE ORPAH SHOW (DAVID'S DESIRE)

SCRIPTURE: 2 Samuel 11:1—12:23

SUGGESTED TOPICS: Obeying God; consequences of sin; making wise choices

BIBLE BACKGROUND

King David was a man after God's own heart. But in spite of his efforts to please God in all ways, being human, David still sinned. The difference between David and Saul was their attitude towards their sin. Whereas Saul sought an alibi for his sin, David admitted and repented (although sometimes only after a prompting from God), begging God's forgiveness. David's desire to please God led to God's greatest promise: the Messiah would come from the seed of David (see 2 Samuel 7:5-16).

Naturally, in Bible times, there were no afternoon television talk shows. But if there had been, and David were a guest on the show, what topic would hold the most interest for the hostess and her viewers? Would it be the good life David had led, his wise leadership, his conquering the land and establishing a peaceful kingdom? Or would the focus of the program be on the darker side of his life, exploring the times he failed?

PERFORMANCE TIPS

1. Suggested props: a microphone for Orpah, a crown for David.
2. When the audience asks questions, Orpah should go over to the person, holding the microphone for him or her to speak into.
3. David should not be portrayed as angry with Orpah. Rather, he is disappointed with himself and ashamed of his former conduct.
4. Orpah should encourage the audience members who want to discuss Bathsheba by smiling, nodding her head, etc., while appearing bored by questions about David's good conduct and leadership.

DISCUSSION QUESTIONS

1. Have you ever watched a TV talk show? What topics were discussed on the show?
2. Which do you think would be more important to a talk show host and producer, a sensational topic or a nonsensational topic? Why?
3. How did Orpah lead the conversation to topics of her choosing?
4. If David was a God-centered king, why would he commit sins like adultery and murder?
5. How might David have prevented himself from sinning?
6. Do you always make the right decisions in your life? What things can cause you to make wrong choices?
7. What can you do to help yourself make wise choices?
8. When you do make a wrong choice (sin), what should you do?

The Big Book of Bible Skits ©1997 Gospel Light. Permission to photocopy granted. 113

THE ORPAH SHOW (DAVID'S DESIRE)

CHARACTERS
ORPAH
DAVID
ANNOUNCER
MEMBER ONE
MEMBER TWO
MEMBER THREE
AUDIENCE

ORPAH: *(Looks at watch.)* OK, King David. It's almost air time. Do you have any last-minute questions?

DAVID: I just want to be sure that I understand what we'll be talking about. We will be talking about my reign and how I've helped Israel to become a strong and mighty nation under God, right?

ORPAH: *(Big smile.)* Sure. That's it exactly. Look out! It's show time!

ANNOUNCER: And now, live from our studios in Shiloh, it's "The Orpah Show!" Orpah's guest today is the king of Israel, David!

AUDIENCE: *(Loud cheers.)*

ORPAH: Yes, we are pleased to have David as our guest today. David, it's no surprise to anybody who knows you that you have led Israel into being the great and mighty nation that it has become. But has it ever surprised you?

DAVID: No, it hasn't really, Orpah...

ORPAH: That sounds a little conceited. What do you think, audience?

AUDIENCE: *(General murmurs of agreement.)*

DAVID: Please, let me explain. When I was younger, God anointed me to be king of Israel. I knew if I obeyed Him, He would prosper Israel under my leadership.

ORPAH: And you always try to obey God.

DAVID: Yes, that's true.

ORPAH: *(Leans toward DAVID.)* Maybe you could explain how this little incident with Bathsheba was obeying God.

DAVID: *(Leans away.)* Well, that was an incident I would rather not talk about. I did an evil thing and people suffered because of it. However, that subject is now closed.

ORPAH: It sounds to me as though you're trying to cover something up. What do you think, audience? Don't we want to hear the details of this?

AUDIENCE: *(Cheers and applause.)*

DAVID: *(Wipes brow.)* I assure you, I am not trying to cover anything up. All Israel knows about it. It's just that it's a rather sordid affair that I would rather forget.

ORPAH: Well, not everybody here is from Israel, so why don't you just tell us the basic story and be done with it?

DAVID: There's really not much to tell. I saw a beautiful woman having her evening bath, I coveted her, we conceived a child together, and I had her husband killed so he wouldn't learn about it. Then, I married her myself. As I said, it's an ugly story. I'm not proud of it, and I would rather forget it.

ORPAH: We have to take a short break, but we'll be right back with King David.

DAVID: Are we off the air?

ORPAH: Yes. This show is going to be a great one!

DAVID: I thought you said that we would be talking about how Israel was becoming a strong and mighty nation. I do not intend to sit here and have you try to embarrass me and my family for the entertainment of your audience. I'm leaving. *(Gets up to leave.)*

ORPAH: *(Holds up hand.)* But you swore an oath that you would come on the show. Is your word nothing but empty sounds?

DAVID: But this is not the kind of show that I agreed to come on.

ORPAH: You didn't swear an oath to come on a special kind of show. You swore an oath to come on the Orpah Show. But, if you would rather leave and have all Israel say that their king's word is worthless....Besides, we're going to have audience questions now. I'm sure that many of them will want to know about the restoration of Israel's greatness.

DAVID: All right. I'll stay. But only because I swore an oath.

ANNOUNCER: And now, once again, here's Orpah!

ORPAH: Hi. We're back, talking with King David about how Israel has become a mighty nation once again, in spite of David's indiscretion with Bathsheba. Does our audience have any questions for King David?

MEMBER ONE: I'm not from Israel. But I understand that Israelites are not known for traveling around much. How did you manage to see Bathsheba without her husband learning about it?

DAVID: Please, I beseech you. This is something I'd rather not discuss.

ORPAH: *(Shoves mike in DAVID's face.)* Come on, King David, what are you trying to hide?

DAVID: I am NOT trying to hide anything! Very well. Her husband was one of my soldiers and they were out fighting Ammon at the time.

MEMBER ONE: But I thought that YOU always led your army into battle.

DAVID: Usually I did. But this once, I tarried in Jerusalem. *(Looks at ceiling.)* If only I had gone instead!

ORPAH: Let's take another question.

MEMBER TWO: How do you feel that God is leading Israel at this time?

DAVID: I believe that God is using me to subdue the surrounding countries so that Israel will have many years of rest and prosperity under her next king...

ORPAH: There's another question here?

MEMBER ONE: I don't understand this country and its customs. I thought that the women were modest. How did you see this Bathsheba woman bathing? Do you have public baths in Jerusalem?

DAVID: Must you continue this prying?

ORPAH: What are you trying to cover up, David?

DAVID: There is nothing to cover up! This is all public knowledge! I just hate talking about it. Very well. It is customary to bathe on the roof of one's house in the evening. It's usually quite private, but her house was next to mine and mine had a higher roof.

ORPAH: Another question?

MEMBER TWO: I was wondering...

ORPAH: Sorry. You've had a question before. Does somebody else have a question?

MEMBER THREE: Could you please tell us why you had Bathsheba's husband killed? You're the king! Why didn't you just take her for your wife and tell her husband that he would have to get another? That's the way civilized countries would do it.

DAVID: *(Sighs.)* Obviously I must resign myself to talking about this painful subject. Israel has different laws from all the other countries, because we worship the one true God. His ways are different from all others. I could not take Bathsheba away from Uriah, because God considers the marriage covenant to be sacred. Under Mosaic law, she was Uriah's wife until death.

MEMBER THREE: But you're the king! Why not just tell Uriah that you had blessed his family and that the child was yours? He should have been thrilled.

DAVID: By this time I had grown to love Bathsheba. Under Mosaic law, if a woman is found to be unfaithful in her marriage covenant, the punishment is death. I did not want Bathsheba to die.

MEMBER THREE: But why kill her husband, what's-his-name?

DAVID: Uriah.

MEMBER THREE: Yeah, him. Why kill him? Surely an intelligent man like you could trick him into thinking that the baby was his.

DAVID: I tried. But everything failed.

ORPAH: As long as we're discussing this anyway, how were you found out? Who would tattle on the king?

DAVID: Nobody tattled. I forgot during that time that nothing is hidden from God. He sent a prophet to rebuke me for my sin. Oh, the agony that I went through for the next seven days. And the trouble that still follows me.

ORPAH: Yes, you have another question?

MEMBER ONE: I'm going to be in Israel for a few more days. I wonder if, when I'm in Jerusalem, it would be possible to stop and see the child. If the mother is as beautiful as you say, and you are indeed a handsome man, why the child must be gorgeous!

DAVID: No! It's impossible! The child is dead! *(Buries face in hands.)* Oh, how long must I suffer for this sin? How long, O Lord?

ORPAH: I wish we could continue this show forever, but our time's up. Be with us tomorrow when all of David's sons will be here. We'll hear from each one why HE should already be crowned king. Until tomorrow, this is Orpah!

THE ORPAH SHOW II (DREAMS OF GLORY)

SCRIPTURE: 2 Samuel 15—18

SUGGESTED TOPICS: Respect for parents; family problems;
consequences of disobedience

BIBLE BACKGROUND

Although King David was a God-centered king, he did not always make wise choices. God makes it clear to us that, although He is merciful and ready to forgive, He is also righteous. God's righteousness cannot permit the presence of sin, since sin is a direct attack on God. God demonstrated this perfectly balanced nature with David. The child born through adultery with Bathsheba died; Solomon, born of Bathsheba in wedlock, became king of Israel and is honored as the wisest man who ever lived.

Not all consequences of sin are a direct punishment of God. God reminds us that making the wrong choices will naturally result in problems. For instance, gluttony leads to weight problems, which in turn lead to health problems. In David's case, his lack of guidance as a parent led to conflicts within his family as each son vied for the position of David's successor. Absalom even went so far as to lead a revolt while David was still alive.

If the mythical "Orpah Show" were on the air and David's sons were guests, how might each one act in public?

PERFORMANCE TIPS

1. Suggested props: a microphone for Orpah, Bible-times costumes.
2. Orpah should hold the microphone for audience members when they ask questions.
3. To achieve the right sound in the fight scene, Absalom could hit his palm with his fist to mimic the sound of hitting Amnon.
4. After the skit, finish the story of Absalom's revolt.

DISCUSSION QUESTIONS

1. From their appearance on the talk show, which of David's sons do you think would be the best candidate for king? Why?
2. How does Absalom try to win people to his side?
3. What can we learn about David as we watch and listen to his sons?
4. Read Exodus 20:12. What does it mean to honor your father and your mother?
5. Does the Bible say to honor your parents only if they are good parents? How can you honor them even if they do wrong things?

THE ORPAH SHOW II (DREAMS OF GLORY)

CHARACTERS
ORPAH
ADONIJAH (AD-ah-NYE-jah)
SOLOMON
AMNON
ABSALOM (AB-suh-lum)
MEMBER ONE
MEMBER TWO

PRONUNCIATION GUIDE
Tamar (TAY-mar)

ORPAH: We're here today with some of the sons of King David. Each one is going to explain to us why he should be the next king of Israel. Welcome to the show, Absalom, Amnon, Adonijah and Solomon.

SONS: Happy to be here.

ORPAH: Instead of my asking each of you different questions, I'm going to ask you all the same one. What is wrong with the monarchy today and how would you fix it if you were king? Adonijah?

ADONIJAH: The current king is too old and relies too strongly on the advice of old men, like Nathan. If I were king, I would change the administration so that younger, more forward-thinking men were in charge. Of course I would not throw out all of the older men—not those who recognize the importance of new thinking, like Joab and Abiathar.

SOLOMON: When you criticize the king, you are criticizing our father. That's not right.

ADONIJAH: Listen, mama's boy! The future belongs to the bold. And that's ME! *(Hits chest with fist.)*

AMNON: I think you're on the right track, Adonijah, but you're looking at it from the wrong perspective. We need younger men, that's true, but we need a complete overhaul of the legal system. I mean, look at all the laws we have now. They all date from MOSES' time! We particularly need to look at the laws concerning relations between stepbrothers and stepsisters.

ABSALOM: You come anywhere near my sister, Tamar, and you're a dead man.

AMNON: See? Even Absalom is a living relic of the past.

ABSALOM: *(Begins to rise.)* You come anywhere near Tamar and you'll soon be a DEAD relic.

SOLOMON: Brothers, let's not fight in public this way. Can't we settle any differences we may have in a peaceful manner?

ADONIJAH: Keep out, mama's boy. Let them tear each other apart!

ORPAH: We still haven't heard from you, Absalom. What would you do to improve the government in Israel?

ABSALOM: Unlike my brothers, I think that the basic laws are OK. What we need is better enforcement of existing laws. Dad did a great job in the past, but he's too old to effectively control his judges. What we need is someone who is young and vital enough to handle the problems that are being ignored by our public officials!

SOLOMON: Maybe we could be good sons and HELP our father.

AMNON: How can you help someone who won't change? He still thinks that those laws thought up by Moses are worth keeping!

ADONIJAH: *(Stands.)* If we want things to improve, we have to be ready to seize each opportunity that presents itself! Dad spends too much time seeking the advice of men like Nathan to get anywhere.

ABSALOM: I think that Solomon has a good point. I'm all for doing whatever I can to help Israel and her leaders.

ORPAH: We have to take a short break, but we'll be back with more from the sons of David after this message.

SOLOMON: But I didn't get a chance to say what I think needs to be done.

ORPAH: Sonny, all you've said so far is that things aren't too bad. That doesn't get ratings. People want to watch conflict, not wisdom and goodness. So get off your high horse and give us some fights worth watching!

SOLOMON: *(Stands.)* But it's not RIGHT.

ORPAH: *(Pushes him into seat.)* But it SELLS! And that's all that interests me. OK, boys. Sit down. We're ready to roll again....Hi. We're back. I wish you could all have been here during the break because we had a beautiful knock-down-drag-'em-out fight. Fortunately, we have it on videotape. Let's get a replay of that.

ABSALOM: I thought I told you to leave Tamar alone!

AMNON: All I SAID was that she's a good-looking woman!

ADONIJAH: What's the big deal, Absalom? She's my sister, too, and you don't see ME getting all worked up.

ABSALOM: *(Stands.)* Maybe you're just too stupid to know better! I'm warning you, Amnon. Leave her alone. *(Shakes fist.)* Don't even mention her NAME again!

AMNON: It's a relatively free country, stepbrother. And I'm a son of the king. I'll talk about and see whoever I want....Ow! *(ABSALOM exaggerates a right hook; AMNON staggers back, holding jaw.)*

ORPAH: Nice right hook, Absalom. OK, audience. Do you have any questions for our guests before they beat each other up?

MEMBER ONE: My brother is a bond servant to another Israelite and has been for over six years now. But his current master has not released him. What can you do about it?

AMNON: Well, that's too bad. But he shouldn't have got in debt in the first place.

ADONIJAH: Go and see your brother. Tell him that when the time is ripe, he should run away and free himself. After all, the future belongs to the quick and the brave.

ABSALOM: Where are you from, friend?

MEMBER ONE: Gibeon.

ABSALOM: This is a travesty. It's almost unbelievable that things like this could be happening in Gibeon. The law clearly states in Deuteronomy 15:12 that your brother should be freed. *(Looks up to heaven.)* Unfortunately, I can't help you because I'm not the king and do not have any real power. But if *I* were king, I would have heard your complaint and have already had your brother freed from bondage.

SOLOMON: I think...

ORPAH *(quickly)*: Is there another question?

MEMBER TWO: I had some financial trouble a short time ago and had to borrow some money from a rich neighbor. But when I went to pay him back what I had borrowed, he said it was not enough. He wants fifty percent interest! Can you help me?

ADONIJAH: *(Shakes fist.)* Stand up to him. Tell him that's all he gets. Punch him in the nose if you have to. Remember, the future belongs to the guys with guts!

AMNON: If he has a good-looking sister, get close to her. She could probably get him to drop the interest rate considerably.

ABSALOM: Where are you from, my friend?

MEMBER TWO: I'm from Bethel.

ABSALOM: Oh, the horror of it! Even BETHEL has forgotten the laws of our fathers. I would not have thought that such injustice could happen in Bethel. We all know that unfair loans are a crime. It's right there in Leviticus 25:36. You are perfectly right. He cannot charge you interest. If only I were the KING—then I could DO something for you. Oh, how my soul cries out for you. How long, O Lord, must your people suffer oppression?

SOLOMON: Perhaps if we went to see Father, he would...

ORPAH: *(Interrupts.)* We're out of time. Be sure to tune in tomorrow when we look at the problems of intergalactic marriage.

The Big Book of Bible Skits ©1997 Gospel Light. Permission to photocopy granted.

SHEPHERD'S PSALM

SCRIPTURE: 2 Samuel 23:8-17; Psalm 23

SUGGESTED TOPICS: Friendship; trusting in God; thankfulness

BIBLE BACKGROUND

David's life was not idyllic. Being the youngest of eight sons, he had often been regarded as the least important. When Samuel was sent to anoint the next king of Israel from among Jesse's sons, David was tending the flock and nobody thought to call him for the sacrifice. When Goliath scorned the Israelite army and David asked why no one would fight him, older brother Eliab suggested David only came down to get a thrill by watching a battle (see 1 Samuel 17:28). Faithfully serving Saul won David favor until he became more popular than the king. Then, Saul sought to kill him, forcing David into a life on the run as a fugitive.

Even when he became king, David's life had its valleys. The Lord was with him and helped him to overcome his enemies, but temptations beset him. In a moment of weakness, He coveted Bathsheba. The child born from their illicit union died at the hand of the Lord. David's sons continually fought among themselves and, eventually, Absalom attempted to overthrow his father.

Through his trials, David learned to depend upon the goodness of the Lord. When David sinned, he repented and asked for the Lord's forgiveness. And when David unintentionally sent three of his men on a fool's errand (to draw water from a well in enemy territory), he demonstrated his love and concern for his men by giving the water as an offering to the Lord, claiming the water represented the blood of the three soldiers who had risked their lives to obtain the water.

The Bible does not tell us when David wrote Psalm 23. He might have written it as a young man tending the flocks. More likely, he wrote it later in life, remembering peaceful times on the hill with his father's flock, likening the Lord's care for him to the ways he had cared for his family's sheep.

PERFORMANCE TIPS

1. Suggested props: pen and pad for David, Bible-times costumes.
2. The entire psalm may be written out on the pad for David to read.

DISCUSSION QUESTIONS

1. Why would David write a psalm using a shepherd as a metaphor (word picture)? If you wanted to express similar feelings, what kind of metaphor might you choose?

2. How do you think David's three mighty men would have felt when they first brought back the water from Bethlehem and gave it to David? Why?

3. David had many hardships in his life. How did they affect his attitude toward God?

4. If you have a friend who would risk his or her life for you, how could you show your gratitude to that person for his or her friendship?

5. Jesus gave His life on the cross for you. How can you give thanks to Jesus for His gift?

SHEPHERD'S PSALM

CHARACTERS
DAVID
BENAIAH (beh-NYE-ah)

PRONUNCIATION GUIDE
Josheb-Basshebeth (JAH-sheb-bah-SHEB-eth)
Eleazar (el-ee-AY-zur)
Shammah (SHAM-ah)

DAVID (*speaking as he writes*)**:** "...dwell in the house of the Lord forever."

BENAIAH: Hey, chief! Whatcha doin'?

DAVID: Writing a psalm.

BENAIAH: You got a catchy tune for this one?

DAVID: Not yet. I've just finished the lyrics. I haven't started on the tune yet.

BENAIAH: Can I hear it?

DAVID: Well, I'd like to wait until I have the music...

BENAIAH: Please? Pretty please? With sugar on it?

DAVID: OK. For a man of war you make some strange pleadings.

BENAIAH: Yeah. But they work. Lay the psalm on me.

DAVID: (*Clears throat.*)

BENAIAH (*looking at paper*)**:** How do you spell that?

DAVID: That's not part of the psalm. I was just clearing my throat.

BENAIAH: Oh.

DAVID: (*Reads.*) "The Lord is my shepherd, I shall not want."

BENAIAH (*gasping*)**:** Ah!

DAVID: (*Looks up.*) What? Did you hear something? Is the enemy approaching?

BENAIAH: No. I was just surprised by your poem.

DAVID: Why?

BENAIAH: You just said you didn't want the Lord to be your shepherd.

DAVID: No, I didn't.

BENAIAH: Sure you did. You said, "The Lord's a shepherd I don't want."

DAVID: No. I said "The Lord is my shepherd, I shall not want." Didn't you hear the pause after the word shepherd?

BENAIAH: Sure, but the words are still the same.

DAVID: You don't understand. These are two thoughts. First, I affirm that the Lord IS my shepherd. Then, I continue to say that he gives me all I need: "I shall not want."

BENAIAH: I still don't get it. "Want" means you wish something was different.

The Big Book of Bible Skits ©1997 Gospel Light. Permission to photocopy granted.

DAVID: Here's another way to say it. See if you can understand it. "The Lord leads me and gives me everything I need, so I do not want for anything."

BENAIAH: That I understand. You should change your psalm.

DAVID: But the other way is better poetry. Besides, if you hear the whole poem, you'll understand the meaning.

BENAIAH: OK. I'll listen, but I still think you ought to change that.

DAVID: OK, try this on for size: "The Lord is my shepherd, I shall not BE IN want."

BENAIAH: Yeah, much better. Go on.

DAVID: "He makes me lie down in green pastures, He leads me beside quiet waters."

BENAIAH: I don't know. Shouldn't He give you a bed to sleep in? And maybe some wine instead of just water?

DAVID: No. You don't understand. The psalm is a metaphor.

BENAIAH: You met a what?

DAVID: A metaphor. The psalm talks about the Lord as being my shepherd. That means, I am a...*(Waits for BENAIAH to fill in.)*

BENAIAH: Sheep. I get it. You're a little, woolly, dumb, fuzzy...

DAVID: OK. So. The psalm tells us this shepherd finds good places for His sheep to eat and drink. Green pastures and still waters.

BENAIAH: I get it. Metaphor. I'll have to remember that word.

DAVID: *(Reads.)* "The Lord is my shepherd, I shall not be in want.

He makes me lie down in green pastures,

He leads me beside quiet waters, He restores my soul.

He guides me in paths of righteousness for His name's sake.

Even though I walk through the valley of the shadow of death, I will fear no evil,

For You are with me; Your rod and Your staff, they comfort me."

BENAIAH: Where's that valley? I've never heard of it.

DAVID: It's part of the metaphor. See if you can figure it out.

BENAIAH: *(Scratches head, thinks hard.)* Oh!

DAVID: You understand?

BENAIAH: I think so. If you're in a valley then there's lots of shadows. And these shadows are all death. So, it's like, even if you're in danger, you're not really afraid because you know God's there.

DAVID: That's the idea.

BENAIAH: So that's why you haven't been afraid, even while Saul's been chasing you.

DAVID: That's it.

BENAIAH: Then, your men aren't important to you? You don't need us?

DAVID: Of course I need you. All of you. You men are part of the Lord's "rod and staff" to me. You are one of the wonderful gifts God has given me.

BENAIAH: But when Josheb-Basshebeth, Eleazar and Shammah gave you a gift, you threw it away.

DAVID: No, I didn't. I made an offering to the Lord.

BENAIAH: It looked to me like you poured the water they gave you on the ground.

DAVID: Yes, I did. Don't you understand why I did it?

BENAIAH: No. I was surprised that the guys weren't angry.

DAVID: They weren't angry because they understood. Remember what happened?

BENAIAH: Sure. You were sitting around having a pity party...I mean...

DAVID: No, you're right. I was only foolishly feeling sorry for myself.

BENAIAH: Well, we were near Bethlehem, near where you were born. But you couldn't go to Bethlehem because the Philistines set up their camp there.

DAVID: That's right. And because I was feeling sorry for myself, I began to complain. I said, "If only I could drink from Bethlehem's well. Boy! That's the best water in the whole world."

BENAIAH: So Josheb-Basshebeth, Eleazar and Shammah, risking their lives, crept through the enemy lines and got some water for you. And then you threw it away.

DAVID: No. I offered it to the Lord! You see, when I saw how much my soldiers would risk for me, I realized how I shouldn't complain. They risked being killed just to bring me a drink of water.

BENAIAH: Which you threw away.

DAVID: I couldn't drink that water! By risking their lives, my soldiers had made that water as precious as their blood. If I drank it, I would be saying "Go ahead, risk your lives for a glass of water. Your lives aren't important."

BENAIAH: Oh.

DAVID: So, I made an offering to the Lord. By pouring the water on the ground, I was thanking Him for giving me such good and faithful friends. Friends I didn't deserve.

BENAIAH: So that's why they weren't angry. Oh—the poem.

DAVID: It's right here.

BENAIAH: Yeah. Read me some more.

DAVID: It's almost finished.

"You prepare a table before me in the presence of my enemies.

You anoint my head with oil; my cup overflows."

BENAIAH: That doesn't sound like sheep. Oh, I get it. The metaphor about sheep is finished.

DAVID: Right.

BENAIAH: So you're saying the Lord shows you honor when your enemies are watching. And He gives you so much, it runs out of your cup.

DAVID: Right. To continue,

"Surely goodness and love will follow me all the days of my life,

And I will dwell in the house of the Lord forever."

BENAIAH: That's a good poem. I'm glad you told me all this. Now I know for sure that you care about us just like we care about you. Good night, David.

DAVID: Good night, Benaiah.

COUNT THE COST

SCRIPTURE: 2 Samuel 24; 1 Chronicles 21:1; 22; 28; 29:1-22

SUGGESTED TOPICS: Listening to God; ignoring God's instructions; repentance

BIBLE BACKGROUND

How often are we faced with decisions that seem simple, but are really complex? Often, a choice that seems so natural has deeper implications. What could possibly be wrong with a king conducting a census of his army? By and of itself, nothing; but underlying the action itself is the reason for the action. David was not just academically curious as to how many soldiers he had, nor was he trying to estimate how much he would need to pay his army and make a budget. He was estimating his chances of victory in upcoming conflicts based solely on the strength of his army.

God reminded David that his actions as the leader of Israel would affect all of Israel. Consequences of allowing himself to slip away from God's guidance would influence the well-being of every citizen. David's census was a clear act of turning away from trust in God. In spite of such repeated failings, David never turned against God, nor did he complain of the treatment he received. Instead, he gave God the honor and glory for his victories and, when he sinned, he always returned to the forgiveness God was ready to offer to the humbled heart.

PERFORMANCE TIPS

1. Suggested props: Bible-times costumes, blueprints and plans for the Temple.
2. Possibly end the skit by having David read 1 Chronicles 29:10-19 to show the class his prayer for Israel and Solomon.

DISCUSSION QUESTIONS

1. Why was David wrong to count the soldiers in his army? Why do you think the people of Israel had to suffer a plague for three days because of David's sin?
2. Everybody sins (see Romans 3:23). What kind of sin happens in the life of a kid your age? How does this sin affect you? How does it affect the people around you?
3. What good choices have you made? How did these choices affect you? How did they affect the people around you?

COUNT THE COST

CHARACTERS
DAVID
SOLOMON
GAD
GUARD

PRONUNCIATION GUIDE
Araunah (uh-RAW-nuh)
plague (playg)

SCENE ONE

GUARD: Someone to see you, Sire.

DAVID: Is Joab finished counting the troops? Good. Send him in.

GUARD: No, Sire.

DAVID: What do you mean, "No, Sire"? *(Points.)* I ORDER you to send Joab in.

GUARD: I can't do that, Sire. Joab isn't here.

DAVID: Then who is?

GUARD: Gad, Sire.

DAVID: Gad? Good! God's prophet. Send him in.

GUARD: Immediately, Sire. If not sooner. *(Exits and GAD enters.)*

DAVID: Gad, it's good to see you.

GAD: Perhaps so. Perhaps not.

DAVID: Hey! Why so downcast? You can't be worried about the Philistines attacking, can you? Don't worry. I'm having the troops counted now. I think we'll find we've got all the manpower we need to stop anyone.

GAD: You think so?

(GUARD enters.)

GUARD: Excuse the interruption, Sire. But Joab has finished the count. We've got eight hundred thousand soldiers in Israel and five hundred thousand in Judah.

DAVID: Wonderful! You see, Gad. We can defeat ANYONE with this army.

GAD: Can you defeat the Lord God Almighty?

DAVID: Of course not. I'm not at war with HIM.

The Big Book of Bible Skits ©1997 Gospel Light. Permission to photocopy granted.

GAD: You are NOW. Have you forgotten that the Lord is your sword and buckler? He goes out before you and defeats your enemies.

DAVID: Well, perhaps I overlooked it...

GAD: Why do you need to count your soldiers, to rely on their strength?

DAVID: Well, it's only human to want to know...

GAD: Exactly! Because you have sinned, the Lord is giving you three choices: you may choose three years, three months or three days.

DAVID: Well, that's very generous of Him...

GAD: You are to choose which Israel will have. Will it have three years of famine, three months of defeat at the hands of your enemies or three days of plague?

DAVID: What a choice. Oh, Lord, how could I have sinned? I beg you, Lord, put away the wrongdoing of your servant. I have done a foolish and wicked thing.

GAD: The Lord awaits your answer. Famine, defeat or plagues?

DAVID: Must I choose? MUST this punishment happen?

GAD: It must.

DAVID: Then I choose three days of plague. For the Lord is merciful. Let me fall into the hands of God, but let me not fall into the hands of my human enemies.

GAD: So be it. The Lord has heard your answer.

SCENE TWO

GUARD: Sire, the latest figures are in. Seventy thousand have died in the last three days.

DAVID: Why, oh why was I such a fool? *(Falls to his knees.)* Lord, *I* am the man responsible for the census of Israel. The people did nothing wrong. Take away the plague from them. Let me and my house be the ones to suffer.

(GAD enters.)

GAD: The Lord has heard your plea. He commands you to go to the threshing floor of Araunah and make an offering there.

DAVID: I shall do so. At once. Guard, do you think six hundred shekels of gold will be enough to buy a threshing floor? I will need to take enough with me to pay Araunah.

GUARD: Sire, live forever! But you will not need to buy the threshing floor. When you explain to Araunah why you want it, I'm sure he'll GIVE it to you. He might even throw in the wood and the oxen for the sacrifice.

DAVID: No. I will not take something from someone else to offer a sacrifice for my own sin. I failed to count the cost previously. No more. From now on, I THINK first. No longer will others pay for my folly. *(Beckons.)* Come! We must go and make the sacrifice immediately.

SCENE THREE

DAVID: *(Puts arm around SOLOMON.)* Solomon, I'm glad you're here. I have much to discuss with you.

SOLOMON: Fire away, Dad.

DAVID: As you know, for years I have wanted to build a house of worship in Jerusalem.

SOLOMON: Yes. Are you ready to start?

DAVID: No. The Lord will not allow me to build His house. For I am a man of war and the house of the Lord must be built by a man of peace. You are that man.

SOLOMON: Dad! I'm just a kid. I don't know how to build temples.

DAVID: I've thought of that. You don't have to worry. The Lord has promised to be with you. As He has been with me, so He will be with you. Remember what He has done for me; remember what He did for Moses. Be strong and of good courage.

SOLOMON: Well, I guess I could give it a shot. But how will I start?

DAVID: I have counted the cost. Look, here are blueprints for everything. Here's a complete list of the materials you'll need. And here's a detailed breakdown of the number of man hours necessary for completion.

SOLOMON: You seem to have thought of everything. Except for the money.

DAVID: I have counted the cost. I may never see the Temple completed, but I wish to contribute to it. Here's a little something to get you started. *(Indicates imaginary coins.)*

SOLOMON: *(Surprised.)* That's a hundred thousand talents of gold! And a million talents of silver!

DAVID: Not only that. There's so much bronze and iron available that I didn't even bother to weigh it. And there's timber and stones and the workmen necessary to fit and cut the materials.

SOLOMON: Then I have all I'll need!

DAVID: Nonsense. This is only the beginning. You'll need much more to complete a house of worship for the Almighty God. But all Israel will be at your command. Do you think, when they see what I have contributed, they will not also be moved to give what they can?

SOLOMON: This is such a huge task. I don't know if I can do it.

DAVID: *(Hand on SOLOMON's shoulder.)* You can, my son. Listen to God before you make decisions and you will be the wisest king the world will ever know. Count the cost. Listen to God and He will help you.

DECISIONS

SCRIPTURE: 1 Kings 3:1; 4:29-34; 9—11:12; 2 Chronicles 7:11—9:31

SUGGESTED TOPICS: Trusting in God; obeying God

BIBLE BACKGROUND

The early years of Solomon's reign were guided by the wisdom God gave him in answer to his request. While following God's wisdom, material riches abounded in Israel (see 1 Kings 10:14-29). However, as time went on, Solomon slowly replaced his reliance on God's wisdom with dependance on his own abilities. Instead of the great wisdom he had shown in the past, he began to make damaging mistakes, errors of faith which undermined his leadership. Eventually, God took the kingdom from his heirs. But one tribe was left to Solomon's son, out of respect for David, and because God had promised that the Messiah would come from the lineage of David.

PERFORMANCE TIPS

1. Suggested props: crown for Solomon, Bible-times costumes.
2. Begin the lesson with a discussion of the wealth of Solomon and the wisdom he had shown. Then introduce the skit by saying, "But Solomon had some tough decisions to make along the way."
3. After the skit, explain the choices Solomon made and the eventual consequences of his decisions.
4. Benaiah is constantly bowing. It's a habit he can't break.

DISCUSSION QUESTIONS

1. Does a wise person always make wise decisions? Why or why not?
2. What were some wise decisions Solomon made? What were some foolish decisions?
3. God's wisdom is available to all who will listen. How can you learn to listen to God?
4. Is it always easy to make right choices? Why or why not?

DECISIONS

CHARACTERS

SOLOMON

BENAIAH (beh-NYE-ah)

PRONUNCIATION GUIDE

rhetoric (RET-ur-ic)

SOLOMON: Benaiah!

BENAIAH *(walking and bowing)*: Here I am, My King. May your name be glorified forever. May peace follow you all of your days. May your enemies be crushed underfoot. May all your works show your power and might to the world. May songs be sung of you in Israel forever. What is it that you wish? Your word is my command.

SOLOMON: I need your advice on something.

BENAIAH: *(Bows.)* Ask, O King, and I will give you what little I have to offer.

SOLOMON: Cut the humility bit.

BENAIAH: *(Straightens up.)* As you wish.

SOLOMON: Would you say that my kingdom is secure?

BENAIAH: But of course it is! Have you not already subdued all that would harm you within Israel? Your kingdom is the most secure kingdom in the history of Israel.

SOLOMON: THAT'S not saying much. There have only been two kings before me.

BENAIAH: But you are well loved by the people. They would be ready to go into battle with you at the drop of a turban, may all your enemies be trodden underfoot. *(Bows.)*

SOLOMON: But that's just it. I don't WANT them to go into battle.

BENAIAH: O King, may you live forever, do not say that! If you go into battle alone, you will not survive. Just because Gideon defeated the Midianites with only three hundred men, you should not even consider fighting an entire army by yourself.

SOLOMON: I did not say that I would fight by myself.

BENAIAH: Forgive me for being an ignorant dog, but I thought you did.

SOLOMON: I want to present two ideas to you. Tell me which you think best.

BENAIAH: I am here at your service, My King. *(Bows.)* May your name be glorif—

SOLOMON: Cut the rhetoric and listen!

BENAIAH: Yes, My King.

SOLOMON: Now, our most dangerous potential enemy is Egypt. What would happen if I were to declare war on Egypt and go into battle?

BENAIAH: Do not ask me this, My King, for the answer is too distressing. If you insist on going into battle alone, choose a weaker enemy than Egypt.

SOLOMON: Not me alone! If I led an army against Egypt, what would happen?

BENAIAH: This also distresses me, My King. Please do not make me answer!

SOLOMON: As your king, I ORDER you to answer.

BENAIAH: Promise you won't be angry.

SOLOMON: I will not be angry.

BENAIAH: Promise you won't fly into a rage and try to pin me to the wall with a spear.

SOLOMON: *I* don't do that kind of thing. SAUL did that kind of thing.

BENAIAH: Promise?

SOLOMON: I promise.

BENAIAH: Well, Egypt is a mighty warrior nation. Pharaoh is a shrewd military leader. Israel's army would be cut to shreds in the first day.

SOLOMON: That's pretty much my assessment, also. Let me ask you this.

BENAIAH: Anything, my lord.

SOLOMON: If I should need assistance in a battle and asked Pharaoh for help, what would be his response?

BENAIAH: Do not ask me to be a mind reader, My King. Who can know the mind of another man unless he is a magician, which is illegal in Israel.

SOLOMON: What do you THINK his response would be?

BENAIAH *(bowing)*: May all those who would curse you be cursed. May all your enemies be trodden underfoot. May he who belittles the king of Israel be cast...

SOLOMON: Enough! What would be his response?

BENAIAH: He would laugh in your face.

SOLOMON: That also agrees with my assessment of the situation.

BENAIAH: Begging the king's pardon, but why are you asking these questions?

SOLOMON: All in good time, Benaiah. Another question. What would be the best way to secure the borders of Israel from attack?

BENAIAH: That is easy, My King. Secure a treaty with Egypt. That way, if anyone should attack you, he would be attacking Egypt at the same time. Nobody in his right mind would attack Egypt! Unless, of course, you are planning to attack Egypt. Then it would be a noble and just war.

SOLOMON: I am NOT planning to attack Egypt.

BENAIAH: *(Wipes brow.)* That's a relief.

SOLOMON: However, how can I make a treaty with Pharaoh? If I ask for his help, he would laugh in my face, as you said.

BENAIAH: Is this a riddle? I was never very good at those.

SOLOMON: Pharaoh has a daughter.

BENAIAH: Yes, he does.

SOLOMON: If I were to marry her, then I would be Pharaoh's son-in-law. THAT would secure a treaty with Egypt, would it not?

BENAIAH: Yes! Of course! The PERFECT solution.

SOLOMON: Except that Israelites are not supposed to have foreign wives.

BENAIAH: I was right. It is a riddle.

SOLOMON: Now come the two ideas. One is to hope that my borders are secure and do nothing. The other is to marry Pharaoh's daughter to secure a treaty. Which is the best idea? Which would give the country more security? Would the people feel that I had betrayed them by marrying a foreign woman or would they see the advantages of having Egypt as an ally?

BENAIAH: You're the king. I am glad this is not MY decision.

SOLOMON: I was hoping you would give me some guidance.

BENAIAH: I couldn't even hazard a guess. But if it is any help, I'm sure that you will make the right decision. May the God of Israel give you wisdom. *(Bows and exits.)*

SOLOMON: Oh. Right. Thanks anyway. *(Rubs head.)* Oy! Decisions, decisions, decisions.

MAKE A WISH

SCRIPTURE: 1 Kings 3

SUGGESTED TOPICS: Wisdom; seeking God's guidance

BIBLE BACKGROUND

During the long reign of David, the nation of Israel was united and able to triumph over her surrounding enemies. After years of war, the country was ready to enjoy peace, and needed a strong successor on David's throne. In spite of the machinations of David's other sons, Solomon was crowned king. David's last words to Solomon charged him to do what God wants and to walk in His ways (see 1 Kings 2:1-3).

Solomon did not feel adequately equipped for the task of king. He was still a young man, but he remembered his father's words and sought to follow the Lord. He traveled to Gibeon and burned incense before the Lord. During the night, God appeared to him in a dream. Whatever Solomon asked, the Lord would give. He could have chosen a long life, the lives of his enemies, great riches; but, instead, he asked the Lord to grant him the wisdom he would need to rule God's people. Shortly thereafter, God's answer was put to the test.

PERFORMANCE TIPS

1. Suggested props: throne and crown for Solomon, doll to represent the living baby, sword for the soldier.

2. The soldier can be one actor or there can be many soldiers.

3. The two women argue vehemently. However, they always address the king respectfully. Rachel should be struggling to keep herself from crying when speaking with Solomon.

4. In spite of the chaos around him, Solomon should always remain calm.

5. Begin the skit by relating the story of Solomon's dream (see 1 Kings 3:5-14).

DISCUSSION QUESTIONS

1. Read Proverbs 9:10. What do you think it means?

2. Name some decisions in your life that need to be wise ones.

3. How can you have God's wisdom to guide you? What different ways could God speak to you to help you make decisions?

4. Can you expect God to help you be wise if you are not part of His family? Why or why not?

MAKE A WISH

CHARACTERS

SOLOMON

RACHEL

NAOMI (nay-OH-mee)

SOLDIERS

SOLOMON: Next case.

>   (*RACHEL and NAOMI come into court, noisily arguing. NAOMI carries baby.*)

SOLDIER: Quiet! Cut the noise!

>   (*WOMEN stop arguing.*)

SOLOMON: Thank you. Now, what seems to be the matter?

>   (*WOMEN speak loudly, at the same time.*)

SOLDIER: Quiet! Cut the noise!

>   (*WOMEN stop arguing.*)

SOLOMON: Thank you. One at a time, if you please. You.

RACHEL: Yes, Sire?

SOLOMON: What's the story?

NAOMI: Don't listen to her! She tells lies!

SOLOMON: She hasn't said anything yet.

NAOMI: But she will! She'll tell lies! She always does!

SOLOMON: Quiet. You'll have your chance to speak. Now then...

RACHEL: Rachel, Sire.

SOLOMON: Rachel. There seems to be a disagreement between the two of you.

RACHEL: Yes, Sire.

SOLOMON: Describe it. Briefly.

RACHEL: Well, we live in the same house, Naomi and I.

SOLOMON: Yes.

RACHEL: And we each have babies. Both about the same age. Just three days apart.

SOLOMON: Two babies. Three days' difference in age. Go on.

RACHEL: Last night, when we were asleep, Naomi rolled over...

NAOMI: She lies! I didn't roll over! I never roll over! I sleep like a log!

RACHEL: You did, too! You always do! You toss and turn all night, sometimes!

NAOMI: Do not! Do not! Liar...

SOLDIER: Quiet! Cut the noise! *(WOMEN stop arguing.)*

SOLOMON: Thank you. *(To NAOMI.)* Please keep quiet. You will have your say. Rachel, continue. You were saying?

RACHEL: Yes, Sire. Well, she rolled over in her sleep and smothered her baby.

NAOMI: She lies! I wouldn't...

SOLOMON: *(Holds up palm to interrupt NAOMI.)* Rachel?

RACHEL: She must have. Her baby died. She must have rolled over and accidentally smothered it. Then, during the night, she took my Timmy from my arms as I lay sleeping and replaced him with her dead son.

NAOMI: What a liar! She tells lies! She always lies about me!

SOLOMON: You will have your chance, madam. Rachel?

RACHEL: That's all, Sire. But you have to make her give me back my Timmy.

SOLOMON: I see. *(To NAOMI.)* Now then...

NAOMI: Naomi.

SOLOMON: Naomi. What have you to say?

NAOMI: Well, she told some truth. But mostly she told lies.

SOLOMON: Then YOU tell me the truth.

NAOMI: Well, we do live together. And we both have babies. But she's the one who always tosses and turns. She's the one who smothered her baby. Now she's trying to rob me of my Nathan.

RACHEL: No! That's not true! He's my Timmy!

SOLOMON: Please! You've had your say. Go on, Naomi.

NAOMI: There's nothing more to tell. Except for you to tell her to peddle her papers elsewhere.

SOLOMON: I see. Two babies. One alive, one dead. Both about the same age. I have it. Where are the fathers? They should be able to identify the babies.

SOLDIER: There ain't no men with these women, Sire.

SOLOMON: Well, have them brought in! Where do your husbands work?

RACHEL: Well...

NAOMI: Uhh...

SOLOMON: I'm waiting. Where are your husbands?

RACHEL: I have no husband, Sire.

NAOMI: Nor do I.

SOLOMON: Oh. Wait here a moment. *(Leaves throne, walks a short distance from WOMEN and looks upward.)* Lord, I have asked you for wisdom. Please give me the wisdom to decide this case fairly. *(Returns to throne.)* Guard!

SOLDIER: Yes, Sire.

SOLOMON: Bring me a sword.

SOLDIER: Got one right here, Sire. *(Draws sword.)*

SOLOMON: It is my decision that we shall never know who is the rightful mother of the living child. Therefore, split it in two and give each woman half.

RACHEL: *(Screams.)* NO!

NAOMI: Sounds fair to me.

RACHEL: *(Shields baby in NAOMI's arms from SOLDIER.)* No, Sire! Don't kill Timmy! If she wants him, let her keep him! But don't kill him!

NAOMI: You see what she's like, Sire. She can't appreciate a fair decision.

SOLOMON: Guard. Put away your sword. Bring me the baby.

(SOLDIER takes baby from NAOMI and gives to SOLOMON.)

SOLOMON: Rachel, come here and take your child. You are truly his mother.

RACHEL: *(Takes baby.)* Oh, thank you, Sire! Thank you!

NAOMI: Well, gotta run. Bye. *(Exits running.)*

THE IMPOSSIBLE DREAM

SCRIPTURE: 1 Kings 5—7; 2 Chronicles 2:1—5:1

SUGGESTED TOPICS: Acting wisely; planning

BIBLE BACKGROUND

King David had wanted, with all his heart, to build a splendid place for people to come and worship the one, true God. But God had refused to grant David's desire. God's house was to be a house of peace, and David had spent his life as a man of war. However, God had promised to give David a son who would be a man of peace, a man who would be allowed to build the Temple (see 1 Chronicles 22:8-10).

Nonetheless, the prohibition against building the Temple did not restrict David from planning the Temple. David had laid out elaborate plans and set aside a goodly sum from his own property to commence construction. By the fourth year of Solomon's reign, David's dream was ready to be turned into reality. Construction of the Temple was about to begin.

PERFORMANCE TIPS

1. Suggested props: crown for Solomon, two sets of blueprints, two papers to represent the letter from Solomon to Hiram and vice versa.

2. While discussing the difficulties, Solomon and Benaiah should be tracing their fingers along different areas of the blueprints to show they are carefully studying the plans.

3. Consider reading aloud 1 Chronicles 22:8-10 prior to the skit.

DISCUSSION QUESTIONS

1. What difficulties did Solomon have to think about when planning to build the Temple? What might have happened if he didn't plan, but just plunged into the project?

2. What were some of the wise decisions Solomon made when planning the project?

3. What are some of the instructions God gives us to live our lives in His will?

4. Some of God's instructions are tough to obey. How can we show wisdom when called to make tough choices? What ways does God help us to make those choices?

THE IMPOSSIBLE DREAM

CHARACTERS

SOLOMON

BENAIAH (beh-NYE-ah)

SOLOMON: Benaiah!

BENAIAH: *(Bows.)* Always present. Ever awaiting your instruction, m'lord.

SOLOMON: I have a plan...

BENAIAH: A plan! How wonderful. I'm sure it's marvelous.

SOLOMON: ...that my father gave me. *(Unrolls blueprints.)* A plan to build a Temple in Jerusalem.

BENAIAH: Oh! *(Looks over SOLOMON's shoulder.)* That looks wonderful! It looks marvelous! It looks—impossible.

SOLOMON: Impossible? Surely not.

BENAIAH: Oh! *(Bows.)* Forgive me. Not impossible. Improbable?

SOLOMON: Explain yourself.

BENAIAH: Well, look at the size of it. Ninety feet long, thirty feet wide, forty-five feet high!

SOLOMON: Yes.

BENAIAH: Well, think of the COST. Where will we find the money?

SOLOMON: Gold and silver are as plentiful as stones in Jerusalem. Besides, Dad left a legacy to be used for construction. That'll give us a good start.

BENAIAH: True. But materials. Where will we get the materials? This is no mud-and-straw hut you have planned.

SOLOMON: True. But plans are already underway. Here's a copy of a letter I sent to King Hiram of Tyre. And here's his reply. *(Reads.)* "Pleased to hear that you have succeeded to your father's throne. Am sending timber as requested. Furthermore, am sending skilled woodworkers to assist you."

BENAIAH: Good! There's no finer lumber than the cedars of Lebanon. And no better woodworkers than those in Tyre. But we'll need general laborers. Got it! We'll go to war, take a bunch of prisoners—and THEY can do the laboring.

SOLOMON: Afraid not.

BENAIAH: No? But it's such a good plan. And with Egypt to help us, we can't lose.

SOLOMON: The Temple is to be built by a man of peace. The laborers will have to come from Israel.

138

The Big Book of Bible Skits ©1997 Gospel Light. Permission to photocopy granted.

BENAIAH: But it's impossible! You'll need THOUSANDS of workers!

SOLOMON: Thirty thousand should do it.

BENAIAH: Oh, I think we could probably get by with ten thousand. But where will we find ten thousand men who can be away for all that time?

SOLOMON: We can't. But ten thousand can be away for a month at a time. We'll work three shifts of ten thousand each. One month on the job, two months at home.

BENAIAH: *(Points to plan.)* But look at all that stone work. It can't be done! After those stones have been hewn and brought to Jerusalem, there'll have to be chipping and fitting. The rubble will take YEARS to haul away!

SOLOMON: The Lord has provided skilled stone masons. They assure me they will be able to make all necessary fittings at the quarry. No tool will be needed to fit the stones in Jerusalem.

BENAIAH: They ALL say that.

SOLOMON: I've seen their work. I think they can do it.

BENAIAH: But what about all the implements for use in the Temple? Where will you ever find them? We don't have a Temple supply house to run out to and buy what we need.

SOLOMON: We have many in use now in the Tabernacle. And what we don't have, we'll make. There are goldsmiths, silversmiths and iron workers. We have the necessary resources.

BENAIAH: It looks like you've figured everything out. But this will take YEARS.

SOLOMON: Seven years should do it. We should be finished just about the time of the Feast of Tabernacles. That will be an appropriate time for a Temple dedication.

BENAIAH: Well, m'lord, I guess so. If everything works exactly right. If nothing goes wrong. If everyone pulls his weight. And if we cancel all other building projects, we might do it.

SOLOMON: Speaking of other projects, did I show you the plans for my new house? *(Pulls out second set of plans.)* We'll be building it at the same time as the Temple. It's going to be one hundred and fifty feet long, seventy-five feet wide, forty-five feet high. Windows, windows, windows! See the porch? Pillars everywhere! And, of course, we'll need a special area for my Egyptian wife. The daughter of Pharaoh can't just sleep anywhere. And the harem room over here...

BENAIAH *(holding his head)***:** Aagggh! PLEASE, your majesty!

YOU CAN BE KING

SCRIPTURE: 1 Kings 12—14; 2 Chronicles 10—12

SUGGESTED TOPICS: Making wise choices; listening to wise advice; obeying God

BIBLE BACKGROUND

David was a man after God's own heart. He attempted to instill the same values in his son, Solomon, and succeeded to a great extent. Unfortunately, the son was not as close to God as was the father. Later in his life, Solomon built altars and high places for the gods of his idolatrous wives. The result of this ungodly behavior was a stern prophecy from God that the kingdom would be torn from Solomon's grasp. However, even in His anger, God showed His mercy. Because of David's heart and the promise God had sworn to David, the kingdom would not be entirely removed from Solomon's successors. The kingdom would be split. Ten tribes and the northern half of the kingdom would be taken away from Solomon's heir, but David's seed would retain the southern tribe of Judah and the portion of the kingdom containing the city of Jerusalem.

PERFORMANCE TIPS

1. Suggested props: microphone for Rezon, crowns to be awarded to Jeroboam and Rehoboam, chair for Ahijah.

2. Rezon speaks quickly, Jeroboam and Rehoboam speak more slowly, as if considering their answers.

3. Announcer can be an offstage personality, a voice only.

4. Other members of the class can be audience. Make an applause sign to signal for the cheering.

DISCUSSION QUESTIONS

1. What wise decisions did Jeroboam make? What unwise ones?

2. What wise decisions did Rehoboam make? What unwise ones?

3. What are some things a kid your age might choose to do to be popular? Which choices are wise, and which ones are unwise?

4. What should you do when you feel like making an unwise choice just to be popular?

YOU CAN BE KING

CHARACTERS

ANNOUNCER

REZON (REE-zahn)

REHOBOAM (REE-uh-BOH-am)

JEROBOAM (JER-uh-BOH-am)

AHIJAH (ah-HYE-jah)

AUDIENCE

ANNOUNCER: And now it's time for everyone's favorite show, the show that can make you ruler in your own house, the show that can give you a feeling of absolute authority, YOU CAN BE KING! And here's the man who gives you the reason to want to be king, REZON!

AUDIENCE: *(Cheers.)*

REZON: Thank you, thank you, thank you! You're too kind. Well, not really. I deserve it! After all, how many other people can help you become king? Well, audience, it's time to play "You Can Be King." Who are our contestants today?

ANNOUNCER: First, a man who knows what it's like to hold the reins of power. One of the sons of former king Solomon, REHOBOAM! *(AUDIENCE cheers as REHOBOAM enters.)* Next, a mighty man of valor, one who has had some experience at being in charge of the House of Joseph, JEROBOAM! *(AUDIENCE cheers as JEROBOAM enters.)*

REZON: Well, it sounds like we have two good contestants today. Two men used to making decisions. Let's find out a little bit about them. Rehoboam, it says here that you're a son of Solomon.

REHOBOAM: That's right. I've been raised all my life to be a king.

REZON: That's wonderful. A natural for our game if ever there was one. Jeroboam, it says you were in charge of the House of Joseph. One house doesn't sound like a big responsibility.

JEROBOAM: Well, that really means that I was governor over a tribe descended from Joseph. So it really was a big responsibility.

REZON: All right. Two worthy opponents. And let's meet our judge, the prophet Ahijah. *(AHIJAH waves and AUDIENCE cheers.)* OK. It's time to play "You Can Be King." You know the rules. You're given a skill-testing question. If you give the right answer, you score one hundred points! Ahijah judges whether or not answers are correct. His decision is final. Now, lets find out what kingdom we'll be playing for today.

ANNOUNCER: It's the Kingdom of ISRAEL! Yes, answer correctly and YOU could be the proud owner of this fabulous kingdom. Begun by Saul, consolidated and prospered under David and BOOMING under Solomon, this kingdom features beautiful beaches along the Great Sea, the fast-flowing River of Jordan, all the salt you could want from the Dead Sea and, of course, the fabulous city of Jerusalem and the breathtakingly beautiful Temple built by Solomon!

AUDIENCE: *(Cheers.)*

REZON: A prize, dare I say it, fit for a king! And it could be all yours. OK. First question to you, Rehoboam. Suppose your people come to you complaining of their heavy tax burden. What would you do?

REHOBOAM: That's a tough question. First, I'd take time to consider. Say, three days. I'd consult with my advisors. Then, I'd make my decision.

REZON: And your decision would be?

REHOBOAM: My three days aren't up yet.

REZON: Sorry, you don't have three days. Only one minute. What would you do?

REHOBOAM: Well, the old men would probably advise that I lower taxes. But my young advisors would probably say, "Why lower taxes? That will only lower your income and make the people think you're weak. Stick it to them! Don't lower taxes; raise them!" That's what I'd do. I'd raise the taxes higher.

REZON: It sounds like a good decision to me, but I'm not the judge. Ahijah?

AHIJAH: You should have listened to the older men. Such action as this will only infuriate your people. It could lead to a revolution. No points.

REZON: Too bad, but you can't be right all the time. Jeroboam, suppose a prophet called you to lead a nation. How would you get the people to follow you?

JEROBOAM: Well, first I'd find something the people didn't like. Then, I'd call on the king with a large group of men. We'd demand changes. If the king made the changes, I'd be a hero and be in position to take over when he died. If he didn't, I could promise to make the changes and the people would follow me.

REZON: That almost sounds like treason. What about it, judge?

AHIJAH: You have spoken wisely. It is much easier to lead if your people follow willingly. One hundred points.

REZON: Rehoboam, you've got some catching up to do! Second question: Suppose you were king of Israel and your people rebelled. What would you do?

REHOBOAM: Man, that's tough. My first reaction would be to gather up an army and quell the revolt. Kill the revolutionaries. But all the people are related and God might not want us to fight. I'd...

REZON: Yes?

REHOBOAM: I'd let those who wanted to separate leave and concentrate on improving relations with those who remained loyal.

REZON: Not very decisive. I would have thought the king would be tougher. Ahijah?

AHIJAH: The Lord God of Israel loves His people. He would not want them fighting among themselves. You have chosen wisely. One hundred points.

REZON: Back to you, Jeroboam. You have a country, but the people are used to going out of your country to worship their God. What do you do?

JEROBOAM: Well, that's easy! You don't want all that money leaving the country. So you make a new place to worship. Just to make sure that the people will come to the new place, you make new gods. Calves of gold are always good.

REZON: Keep the money where it belongs. Good answer. Right, Ahijah?

AHIJAH: Only one nation has a single place of worship. That nation is Israel. The God of Abraham, Isaac and Jacob does not approve of idol worship. Since He gave you the power, you should obey Him. No points.

REZON: We're down to our last questions. Rehoboam, suppose the king of Egypt attacked you and took away all the gold and silver from the Temple. What would you do?

REHOBOAM: What COULD I do? Nobody can stand up to Egypt. I'd let them go and replace them with brass or bronze. Much less valuable. And I'd encourage the people to worship other gods so there wouldn't be so much treasure all in one place.

REZON: Sensible. Ahijah?

AHIJAH: You were not listening to the previous answer. The God of Israel would not approve and He is the One who gives power to princes. No points.

REZON: Last question, Jeroboam. Say you have had an altar built, and a prophet of God appears. He says God disapproves and will destroy the altar. You lay your hand on the altar and your hand shrivels up and the altar falls apart. What do you do?

JEROBOAM: First, I'd get the prophet to heal my hand by promising to repent. Then, when my hand was healed, I'd do whatever I wanted. After all, this is a one-in-a-million thing.

REZON: *(Nods head.)* Play the odds. Rule with might. Ahijah?

AHIJAH: *(Shakes head.)* You have learned little. The Lord God's warnings should not be scorned. No points.

REZON: Well! We're just about out of time. Ahijah's adding up the points. And the winner is?

AHIJAH: It's a tie. One hundred points to one hundred points.

REZON: A tie? How will we award the prize?

AHIJAH: The prize will be split. Each will be awarded a crown. *(REZON takes crown to JEROBOAM.)* Jeroboam, you will be given ten of the tribes of Israel. Most of the people will follow you. *(REZON takes crown to REHOBOAM.)* Rehoboam, although you will not rule over most of the people, you will retain the tribe of Judah. With it, you will rule over the city of Jerusalem and thereby have most of the wealth.

REZON: A fair compromise. We're out of time. Join us again tomorrow when we play "YOU CAN BE KING!"

AUDIENCE: *(Cheers.)*

AHAB'S MOUNT CARMEL PRESS CONFERENCE

SCRIPTURE: 1 Kings 18; 19:1

SUGGESTED TOPICS: Trusting God; listening to God; obeying God; courage

BIBLE BACKGROUND

Under the evil influence of Queen Jezebel, King Ahab had instituted idol worship in Israel. As a sign that He alone was the only true God, Jehovah withheld rain from Israel for three years. Since Elijah was God's prophet who foretold this disaster, Ahab and Jezebel blamed Elijah for all of Israel's problems. They hunted everywhere for him, wishing to execute him. They were shocked when Elijah came out of hiding and proposed an extraordinary showdown between Baal and Jehovah.

PERFORMANCE TIPS

1. Suggested props: podium for Ahab to stand behind, notebooks for the reporters.

2. Ahab's opening address is long. Give your actor time to look over the part. If performing the skit from memory, Ahab could be allowed to read the opening address.

3. Prior to performing the skit, discuss press conferences and their purposes with the class. Be sure they understand that some press conferences are not intended to give out information but to give someone a chance to alibi a situation which might make him look bad.

4. After the press conference, have the class explain what they understand happened. Be prepared to fill in parts the class might have missed.

DISCUSSION QUESTIONS

1. What do you think the word "influence" means?

2. How did Ahab and Jezebel influence their country?

3. How did Elijah influence the country?

4. What things influence a kid your age to do good things? evil things?

5. Name ways you can pay attention to the good influences and ignore the bad ones.

AHAB'S MOUNT CARMEL PRESS CONFERENCE

CHARACTERS
AHAB
REPORTER ONE
REPORTER TWO

PRONUNCIATION GUIDE
Baal (bale)
Elijah (ee-LIE-juh)
Hamath (HAY-math)
Jezebel (JEZ-uh-bel)
Obadiah (OH-buh-DIE-uh)

AHAB: I want to thank all of you for coming out—well, both of you—on such a rainy and stormy night as we're having tonight. I haven't seen rain like this for over three years, ha, ha. Before I entertain questions from you, I would like to read a prepared statement that should do away with many unnecessary questions that would only waste our time. *(Clears throat.)*

"For three years now, Israel has been without rain and has been experiencing one of the darkest hours in its history. This administration recognizes the importance of the family farm to our illustrious nation's economy and has been spending significant resources to end the drought that has imperiled the livelihood of this significant factor of our great nation. Although some of the experiments attempted to alleviate the drought were resoundingly unsuccessful, this is not to say that they were a waste of taxpayers' money. If nothing else, they have been entered into the *Chronicles of King Ahab* and it will not be necessary for other kings to try these procedures should a similar situation occur.

"Of particular note was the cloud-seeding experiment suggested by Hamath, minister of science. The press was quick to ridicule the minister for this timely experiment, implying that firing arrows at the clouds was a waste of the kingdom's money and manpower. Although this experiment did not bring forth the desired rain, it did lead to major improvements in the bow and the strength of the bowmen, which should keep Israel in the fore of military might for decades to come.

"We are pleased to announce that the terrible drought which has been afflicting the country has come to an end. Contrary to the mutterings of certain doomsayers, this is NOT signaling a forthcoming flood of proportions not seen since the days of Noah.

On the contrary, this rain is the very thing this country has needed for the past three years. In the event of any flooding in the lowlands which might imperil life of person or animal, the military is on the alert and will respond with the speed and diligence that has made Israel's proud fighting man the envy of the surrounding nations.

"Although we are naturally pleased with the end of the drought, we are also saddened by the senseless death of eight hundred and fifty kindly and gentle men of Israel. I am, of course, referring to the prophets of Baal and the groves who had been blamed by certain rabble-rousers and publicity-seekers for Israel's problems. This only shows what can happen when justice falls into the hands of a mob instead of resting in the duly constituted authority of the king. In light of the large number of men responsible for the death of these prophets and the resulting disaster which would befall the country if all should be arrested and imprisoned, they are being given a full pardon by this administration. The only one who will be punished, as an example to the many, is the ringleader of the mob, Elijah—if we ever catch him. Although his whereabouts are unknown at this time, Israel's finest soldiers are out scouring the countryside for him at this very moment."

That is the end of the prepared statement. I will now entertain any questions that you gentlemen might have.

REPORTER ONE: Is it your contention, O King, that the drought we have experienced was not caused by Israel's sin but by some as yet unknown natural cause?

AHAB: Could you elaborate on that phrase you used, "Israel's sin"?

REPORTER ONE: Certainly. I am referring to the fact that most of Israel has stopped following the God of Abraham, Isaac and Jacob and is, instead, bowing down to idols, most of which are championed by the queen, Jezebel.

AHAB: In the first place, I must caution you about your lack of honor for the name of the queen. That is treason. I am sure you meant no harm so I will overlook it this time. But don't let it happen again. Concerning the worship of gods in Israel: Every nation in the world worships many gods. The backwardness of Israel in worshiping only one god has held it back from occupying its true place as one of the great nations of the world. The queen and myself have simply been trying to correct this problem and to enlighten the people under our control—er, authority.

REPORTER TWO: I understand that Elijah has been an outlaw in Israel for many years, but according to reports received by our editor, Elijah was in full view of the king and his soldiers today at Mount Carmel and was not arrested at that time. Would the king please explain why a known outlaw was not taken into custody?

AHAB: I would be delighted to answer your question. You know Obadiah....

REPORTER TWO: Certainly. He is one of your servants.

AHAB: He is one of my most TRUSTED servants. As you know, he is one of the keenest-eyed men in all of Israel. He and I were out searching for water, a little brook or a minor fountain, or perhaps some green grass to feed the livestock to keep them alive for a short time.

REPORTER TWO: I wouldn't think you'd need a keen-eyed man for that. Surely any green would stand out like a sore thumb in this land where everything has turned brown?

AHAB: At any rate, Obadiah ran into this Elijah. As you know, Obadiah is not a soldier or one of my guards. Being the brave man that he is, Obadiah was ready to attempt a citizen's arrest of this notorious criminal....

REPORTER TWO: I had never heard that Elijah had ever hurt anyone.

AHAB: But before he could make the arrest, Elijah told him to go and tell me that he, Elijah, wanted to meet with me. Naturally, Obadiah was reluctant to leave a known criminal, thinking that he might hide again, but my faithful servant did bring me the message that Elijah wanted to meet with me. I considered coming for my soldiers but decided that I would be able to handle this arrest myself.

REPORTER ONE: Concerning Obadiah's reluctance to leave Elijah and take his message to you: There is a rumor that if you had gone to meet with Elijah and he was not there, your ferocious anger would have been kindled and you would have taken it out on Obadiah, possibly killing him on the spot for bringing you a false report. Would you comment on that, please?

AHAB: I have not finished answering the previous question, but I cannot leave so vicious a rumor unanswered. All who know me, those close to me, know that I have been maligned by my political opponents. In truth, I am a gentle man, and had Elijah not been there, I would have reprimanded Obadiah for leaving a known criminal to run free, but I would have understood his motives and acted accordingly.

REPORTER TWO: Are we to understand, then, that you saw this outlaw not only at Mount Carmel, but also earlier in the week?

AHAB: Yes. I met with him.

REPORTER TWO: And yet you did not arrest him at that time. Could you please explain your motives in allowing him to go free?

AHAB: That would be simplicity itself. At our meeting, he gave me to understand that all of Israel's troubles could be solved if I would meet him at Mount Carmel with the four hundred and fifty prophets of Baal and the four hundred prophets of the groves. Naturally, Israel's troubles were all related to the drought that had been in existence for the past three years. Because we had been dealing with this problem unsuccessfully for so long, I thought it in the best interests of Israel to meet with him and the other prophets at Mount Carmel.

REPORTER ONE: Are you saying that Elijah is a prophet? I thought he was an outlaw. Which is it?

AHAB: I was merely patronizing him. Of course he is not a REAL prophet, but he likes to think of himself as one. I was merely stating his point of view.

REPORTER TWO: But all of Israel knows Elijah does not believe that the prophets who eat at the queen's table are true prophets. Didn't you question his motives in wanting to meet with them? Didn't you think it strange that he also wanted you to summon all of Israel to witness what would happen at Mount Carmel?

AHAB: Certainly I was curious about his wanting all the other prophets there. But I restrained my curiosity for two reasons. First, any chance of ending the drought had to be taken, even if it was being spearheaded by a criminal. Second, I was hoping that he'd come to his senses and was gathering a giant prayer meeting to implore the gods to send rain. And I did not have to order the people of Israel to come. Their curiosity was so aroused, I doubt I would have been able to keep them away.

REPORTER ONE: Once he started to speak, did you not realize that he was hoping to incite a riot? His very manner suggested that he wanted mob rule to be the order of the day, did it not? Weren't you worried by his attitude?

AHAB: Not at all. I knew he was playing for a showdown, but there were many soldiers there. Also, I knew that when his God failed to provide relief for the people, they would realize that Elijah was just another religious fanatic whose day had finally ended. I had hoped that this would put an end to the dangerous brand of religious fervor that he advocated. Unfortunately, I miscalculated. But it was an honest error that any king seeking the best for his subjects would have made.

REPORTER TWO: Would the king please comment on his feelings about the show put on by the prophets of Baal at Mount Carmel today?

AHAB: It was one of the most impressive spectacles I have ever witnessed in my life. No adjective in our language could adequately describe my feelings at the time. I suppose "glorious" is the closest—the dancing, the singing, the cutting themselves with knives. Of course, any king loves to see the sight of blood—unless it's his own or that of his soldiers.

REPORTER TWO: Would the king then explain why, if he was so impressed with the performance of the prophets of Baal, he allowed this Elijah to make fools of them? To laugh at them? To imply that they were wasting their time trying to arouse a god that could not hear?

AHAB: I was, of course, letting him dig his own grave. Everybody there knew the test set out was impossible. The longer I let him ridicule the prophets of Baal, the greater would be his downfall when he also failed. It was simple psychology that any king worth his salt would have used.

REPORTER ONE: Would the king please express his thoughts about the amount of water Elijah wasted when Israel was in the middle of the worst drought in its history? How could the king stand idly by while Elijah had twelve barrels of water poured on his altar? Did not the king feel that the water could be better used elsewhere?

The Big Book of Bible Skits ©1997 Gospel Light. Permission to photocopy granted.

AHAB: No. What amazed me was that the people of Israel did not see that the prophets of Baal must have succeeded. Not in getting fire but having water appear instead. I have no idea where so much water was found. That is just another example of what can happen when a large number of good men gather to pray.

REPORTER ONE: Then you're saying the prophets of Baal made the water appear?

AHAB: I certainly can't think of where else it might have come from. Can you?

REPORTER ONE: Discretion being the better part of valor, I would not even suggest to the king that maybe Elijah's God produced it for him.

AHAB: You are wise not to suggest such a possibility to me.

REPORTER TWO: When the fire appeared from heaven and consumed not only the sacrifice that Elijah had placed on his altar but also the altar itself, the water running around the altar and the dust, what were your feelings?

AHAB: Naturally, I was awestruck. If it would not have been undignified, I would have fallen to the ground with the rest of the people of Israel.

REPORTER ONE: Would the king explain why he did not stop the senseless slaughter of the unsuccessful prophets on the mountain? Why did you not exert your authority and make the people go home?

AHAB: You were there. You saw how the mob suddenly followed everything that Elijah suggested. There were too many people and not enough soldiers to stop the ensuing slaughter. You were lucky that Elijah had a grudge against Baal's prophets and not reporters.

REPORTER ONE: (Aside.) Or kings.

REPORTER TWO: Would the king please explain why it took so long to arrive back in Jezreel after the catastrophic violence that took place?

AHAB: I had to stop and think. There was much to ponder concerning what was to be done in the aftermath. With all those people there, it was impossible to arrest Elijah. I could not punish all of the participants in the massacre. I had to decide what to do.

REPORTER ONE: There is a rumor that the reason the king took so long to arrive back in Jezreel is that he was afraid to face Jezebel and tell her that her favorite prophets had all been slain at the command of Elijah. Would the king care to comment?

AHAB: That is simply another of the vicious rumors started by my political opponents in an attempt to embarrass me and to make me a laughingstock in Israel. It is a ploy which shall never succeed because it is unfounded. Imagine any man, much less the king, being afraid of his wife. This press conference is now over. Thank you for coming.

REPORTERS (together): Thank you, Your Majesty. (REPORTERS exit.)

AHAB: Now then, how AM I going to explain this to Jezebel?

FOOD FOR THOUGHT

SCRIPTURE: 2 Kings 2:1-22; 4:38-44

SUGGESTED TOPICS: Positive influences; complaining; trusting God

BIBLE BACKGROUND

Elijah took a young student, Elisha, under his wing. By observing Elijah in the crucible of the world, Elisha learned that God's promises were true and could be trusted. When the time came for Elijah to be taken from this world, Elisha refused to abandon his mentor and friend. The faithful Elisha received Elijah's mantle and became God's voice in Israel.

Part of Elisha's role was teacher to a group of students. Likely, they were all attentive, realizing the importance of their teacher's words. However, human nature seems to try to find fault. The complaining student in the skit is typical of the common human tendency to criticize.

PERFORMANCE TIPS

1. Suggested props: Bible-times costumes, two chairs.
2. Student One is a complainer. His whining voice and frequent sighs should indicate this.
3. Student Two is enthusiastic. His voice and energetic body language should indicate this.
4. Students could pantomime gathering firewood, cleaning house or some other manual task as they talk.

DISCUSSION QUESTIONS

1. Why do people complain?
2. What things do kids your age complain about? Are those things really that bad?
3. Think of all the good things you have. Do you give thanks for them as often as you complain about the things you don't like?
4. Who or what are some of the teachers God has given to you? What sorts of things do you learn from them?
5. What can you do to thank the people who are good influences on you?

FOOD FOR THOUGHT

CHARACTERS
STUDENT ONE
STUDENT TWO

PRONUNCIATION GUIDE

Elisha (ee-LIE-shuh)

STUDENT ONE: *(Sighs heavily.)* I sure get tired of the same old food, day after day.

STUDENT TWO: Why complain? Many people have no food at all.

STUDENT ONE: Yeah. But all we get these days seems to be bread.

STUDENT TWO: We have other things.

STUDENT ONE: Yeah, like yesterday. Poisoned stew.

STUDENT TWO: Well, it started out poisoned, but Elisha fixed it. Then it was delicious!

STUDENT ONE: We were lucky we weren't all killed.

STUDENT TWO: We weren't LUCKY—we're with Elisha. And GOD is with Elisha.

STUDENT ONE: If we aren't lucky, what are we?

STUDENT TWO: We're BLESSED.

STUDENT ONE: Hah! Blessed. Sure.

STUDENT TWO: Sure we are. Even if we didn't have enough to eat, think of the other things we have.

STUDENT ONE: Name one.

STUDENT TWO: Most importantly, Elisha's teaching.

STUDENT ONE: It's just like the food—same thing day after day! *(Rolls eyes.)* Follow God. Follow God. Follow God. Why can't we have something different?

STUDENT TWO: We have the best, and you want something different?

STUDENT ONE: Well, yeah. How about a MIRACLE? I keep hearing about them, but I don't see any.

STUDENT TWO: You wouldn't know a miracle if it leapt out and bit you! You've seen lots of miracles.

STUDENT ONE: Oh yeah? Like what?

STUDENT TWO: Like what? You were almost poisoned yesterday. Everyone knew the stew had been poisoned and we would all die. But DID we?

STUDENT ONE: You're telling the story. *(Sarcastically.)* DID we die?

STUDENT TWO: Of course not. We're alive, aren't we?

STUDENT ONE: If you can call this living.

STUDENT TWO: This is the best life ANYONE could have! Learning from a man of God!

STUDENT ONE: Yeah? Just wait until the food runs out. Then we'll see who's so happy to be learning from Elisha. If your belly wasn't full, your mind wouldn't care.

STUDENT TWO: That's where you're wrong. But I'll never get a chance to prove it— because Elisha always makes sure our needs are met.

STUDENT ONE: He's not meeting MY needs.

STUDENT TWO: Sure he is! He may not be meeting all your WANTS, but he's meeting your NEEDS.

STUDENT ONE: Needs, wants—same thing to me. *(Sarcastically.)* But I can hardly wait for supper.

STUDENT TWO: Why? I thought you said you were tired of the same thing.

STUDENT ONE: Oh, tonight will be different. I saw supper arrive.

STUDENT TWO: What is it?

STUDENT ONE: Bread and grain.

STUDENT TWO: That sounds like what we usually have.

STUDENT ONE: The quantity is different. Tonight, there won't be enough for HALF the people here. But, since you don't care about food as long as Elisha is teaching, I'll have YOUR share.

STUDENT TWO: Fair enough. You eat until you're full. If there's any left over, I'll eat.

STUDENT ONE: *(Laughs.)* Tonight, you starve. And tomorrow during classes, your little tummy will be growling. We'll see if you pay attention to teaching tomorrow.

STUDENT TWO: *(Rises.)* There's the dinner bell. Let's go. We'll feed the body tonight and the mind tomorrow.

STUDENT ONE: You mean, I'LL feed the body tonight. Who KNOWS what we'll get tomorrow!

MAD ABOUT ELISHA

SCRIPTURE: 2 Kings 6:24,25,31-33; 7:1-20; 13:14-19

SUGGESTED TOPICS: Setting a good example; obedience to God

BIBLE BACKGROUND

The mantle of Elijah had fallen upon Elisha. He was now the most influential prophet in Israel. He could have used this position for great personal power and wealth. Many prophets were welcomed at the king's court, provided they would tell the king what he wanted to hear. Elisha, however, remained true to his calling. In spite of personal danger, he remained faithful to the God he was called to serve. Elisha's faithfulness resulted in God's supernatural protection for him (see 2 Kings 6:17). The king of Syria wanted Elisha dead because he believed Elisha was responsible for Israel's repeated success in battles against Syria. Ironically, the king of Israel later blamed all of Israel's problems on Elisha and also sought to kill him.

PERFORMANCE TIPS

1. Suggested props: trench coat and notebook for Dan, crown for the king.

2. The king is under a lot of pressure. He should appear short-tempered and impatient.

3. Dan is methodically doing his job. His speech should be matter-of-fact, almost monotone.

4. Finish the story by telling about God's miraculous intervention on Israel's behalf.

DISCUSSION QUESTIONS

1. The king blamed Elisha for Israel's problems. Was Elisha to blame? Why or why not?

2. How was Elisha a good influence on those he met?

3. Read 1 Timothy 4:12. How can you be a good influence on the people you meet?

MAD ABOUT ELISHA

CHARACTERS
DAN
KING

PRONUNCIATION GUIDE
bunco (BUN-coe)
Dothan (DOE-thun)
Samaria (suh-MARE-ee-uh)
Syrian (SEER-ee-un)

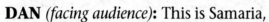

DAN *(facing audience)*: This is Samaria, known to us as "The City." In The City are a million stories— well, a few thousand, anyway. This is one of them. My name is Dan. I'm a policeman. The following story is true. Really. I'm a policeman. Would I lie to you? It all started when I was summoned to the king's palace...*(Turns to KING and pulls out notebook.)*

KING: Dan, I've been told you're the best man on the Samaritan police force.

DAN: I'm happy that you've heard such good reports, Your Majesty, but I'm sure you didn't summon me here to tell me that.

KING: You're right. I didn't. I need your help.

DAN: What seems to be the problem, Your Majesty?

KING: Elisha!

DAN: Bless you. That's quite a cold you have there. But I'm not a physician. You need a doctor, not a policeman.

KING: I don't have a cold. My PROBLEM is a man named Elisha.

DAN: Has he been threatening you? Threats are not colds. Threats would be a police problem. *(Flips open notebook and begins to take notes.)* How long has this—could you spell the name of the man who's been threatening you?

KING: E-L-I-S-H-A!

DAN: Thank you. How long has he been threatening you?

KING: He hasn't ACTUALLY been THREATENING me.

DAN: Maybe you'd better give me the facts, sir. Just the facts. Who is this Elisha?

KING: He's a prophet.

DAN: You mean like a fortune-teller? You've called the wrong department, Your Majesty. You should have called bunco. I usually deal with more violent crimes.

KING: No! Elisha is not like a fortune-teller. Sometimes he DOES predict the future; and when he predicts something, it comes TRUE.

DAN: That would make a bunco rap tough to fasten on him. If you don't want him arrested as some sort of con man, what do you want? Just the facts, Your Majesty.

KING: I'm not sure what I want. That's why I need your help. Maybe if I tell you what happened, you'd be better able to advise me.

DAN: That's a good idea. Facts are always useful. What has this prophet done to hurt you?

KING: It started some time ago when the Syrian army was encamped against the town of Dothan.

DAN: If he was fighting for the Syrians, then a charge of treason would be appropriate. By the way, you wouldn't happen to have a spare cup of coffee, would you?

KING: No. I wouldn't.

DAN: OK. Back to Elisha. Fighting for the Syrians would be treason. That should be no problem to pin on him.

KING: He wasn't fighting for the Syrians.

DAN: Oh. Then treason's no good. What was this guy doing?

KING: He was the reason the Syrians were attacking Dothan. They wanted to KILL him.

DAN: This Elisha sounds like one terrific troublemaker. Both the king of Syria and the king of Israel want to kill him. That's the first thing you two have ever agreed on, isn't it? How about some fruit?

KING: No. I don't think fruit comes into the story anywhere.

DAN: I meant to eat. *(Looks around.)* Do you have any spare fruit around? It doesn't have to be a lot of fruit. A handful of grapes would do. Even raisins.

KING: No, I don't have any spare fruit! Can we get on with this?

DAN: Certainly. What happened at Dothan?

KING: The Syrian army was BLINDED. Couldn't see their spears in front of their faces!

DAN: And this Elisha had something to do with it?

KING: He is rumored to be responsible for it. Yes.

DAN: Then I think we've got him. Assault causing bodily harm. Should be good for five to ten in the dungeon. Sort of ironic.

KING: What is?

DAN: He blinds an army but he's the one who ends up in the dark! *(Chuckles.)*

KING: I don't think we can charge him with anything for blinding the Syrian army. Hurting Syrians is not a crime in Israel.

DAN: You're right. I guess that's why you're king and I'm not. Let's continue. What did he do with this army of blind men?

KING: He led them into Samaria.

DAN: Ah! Illegal immigration! Probably charged each one a pretty price for the privilege. I'm not sure whose jurisdiction this falls under.

KING: They weren't immigrating. He led them here to be my prisoners!

DAN: Got him—slave trading! *(Pauses.)* No. That's not a crime yet. What happened to these prisoners?

KING: I was ready to kill them. I figured THAT would teach the king of Syria to send an army against Israel. But Elisha wouldn't let me!

DAN: He physically restrained you? Common assault should stick for that.

KING: No. He didn't touch me. He just told me that I shouldn't kill them.

DAN: What did you do then, sir? Just the facts, please. Did you torture them?

KING: No. Elisha told me to give them bread and water and to send them back to Syria.

DAN: Bread?

KING: Yes, bread.

DAN: Where?

KING: Well, it's gone now. They ate it!

DAN: No, I mean now. Have you any bread to spare?

KING *(glaring)*: No, I don't!

DAN: It doesn't have to be good bread. If it's a little moldy, that would be fine with me. I missed breakfast this morning.

KING: I don't have any bread to spare! Stop worrying about your stomach and start worrying about my problem!

DAN: So far, I don't see that he's caused you any problems.

KING: You don't see any PROBLEMS? Look around you! We're having the worst famine in our history in this city. People are eating their own children to stay alive, and you don't see that he's causing any PROBLEMS?

DAN: Black marketing. While the city is starving, he's making a big profit by selling storeholds of food at steep prices. Rather ironic.

KING: How so?

DAN: While the people starve, the prophet profits. *(Laughs at own joke.)*

KING *(irritated)*: He's NOT profiting. He's NOT selling food on the black market! He DOESN'T have food stashed away.

DAN: Then how do you figure that he's responsible for the famine?

KING: The famine is caused by the Syrian army camped around Samaria. If Elisha hadn't made me release them before, they wouldn't be here NOW.

DAN: Strange. I don't remember a large group of Syrians being around here recently. When did you release this army?

KING: Oh, years and years ago.

DAN: Then we can't charge him on that one. The statute of limitations would have already expired.

KING: Well, you have to do SOMETHING about him! You're the police!

DAN: That's the problem. I have to uphold the law. He hasn't broken it. If he were in the palace and you had him executed, that would solve your problem.

KING: But then you'd come and arrest me for murder.

DAN: No, I couldn't do that. The king's palace is outside of my jurisdiction. Anything that happens inside with the king's consent is legal. Well, if there are no more facts, I think I'll go and try to find a little something to eat.

KING: You do that. *(Calls in other direction.)* Servant! Come here! I want you to take a message to Elisha!

The Big Book of Bible Skits ©1997 Gospel Light. Permission to photocopy granted.

TRUST AND OBEY

SCRIPTURE: 2 Kings 15:1-7; 2 Chronicles 26; Isaiah 6

SUGGESTED TOPICS: Obedience to God; pride; consequences of sin

BIBLE BACKGROUND

After the split of the kingdom of Israel into Israel and Judah, a series of kings held power for varying amounts of time. All the kings of Israel and many of the kings of Judah had evil reigns, leading their people into idolatry. As a result, the job of prophet in Israel or Judah was hazardous. The king would inquire of the prophet, "Should I go to battle?" If the prophet told him "No, the Lord is not with you," the king might easily order the prophet killed as a traitor to the crown. If he said yes, and the king lost but was able to return, the prophet might be killed for lying to the king. Occasionally, a good king arose in Judah; one who would listen to the prophets of God and act accordingly.

However, even a good king can forget his position in life and allow his successes to go to his head. Uzziah was such a king. Second Chronicles 26:4 states that Uzziah did what was right in the sight of the Lord. The verses that follow list his considerable accomplishments. The list continues until verse 16 which begins with the dreaded word "but." We find that Uzziah, when he was strong, lifted up his heart to destruction. Against all advice, Uzziah tried to usurp the rightful role of God's priest, and he paid dearly for his folly.

PERFORMANCE TIPS

1. Suggested props: a crown and throne for Uzziah, a large book for Jeiel, a bottle to represent the incense, a curtain or sheet to mark the Holy of Holies.

2. The stage could be divided into two parts: the throne room and the Temple. If your stage is too small, have Uzziah and Jeiel walk while the scene changes from the throne room to the Temple.

3. Uzziah should be played as smug and self-satisfied.

4. Jeiel is always deferential toward Uzziah and bows often, out of habit. But he is sarcastic behind Uzziah's back.

5. The high priest takes his job seriously. He is not impressed with human kings.

6. After the skit, read or tell the story in Isaiah 6 to contrast the two men's attitudes toward God.

DISCUSSION QUESTIONS

1. What were some of the sins Uzziah committed? (Remember, sin means "missing the mark.")

2. What was Uzziah's attitude when his sin was pointed out to him?

3. The high priest's responses to King Uzziah were taken from Job 38 and 39. (Assign short passages to students to read and paraphrase.) What should Uzziah's attitude have been?

4. Read Isaiah 6:5. What was Isaiah's attitude when reminded of his sin?

5. We all sin and need to be corrected. How do you react when somebody points out something you have done wrong?

6. How can you learn to be more like Isaiah? Think of practical things you can do each day.

TRUST AND OBEY

CHARACTERS

UZZIAH (yoo-ZYE-ah)

HIGH PRIEST

JEIEL (JAY-el)

UZZIAH: Where is Jeiel? I want my scribe! Where is he?

JEIEL: *(Runs in, bowing.)* Coming hastily, O Mighty Monarch.

UZZIAH: Have you got the *Book of the Chronicles of Uzziah*?

JEIEL: In my hand. Held most preciously, O Righteous Ruler.

UZZIAH: Good. I feel in need of some good literature. Read about the things I have done.

JEIEL: Where would you have me begin, O Powerful Potentate?

UZZIAH: Anywhere at all. The beginning is always a good place.

JEIEL: And at what point should I cease reading, O Kindly King?

UZZIAH: Just keep reading. I'll tell you when I get tired.

JEIEL *(softly, to audience)***:** Oh dear. The whole book, again.

UZZIAH: What was that?

JEIEL: I said, "Good cheer. Uzziah reigns."

UZZIAH: Very good. Begin.

JEIEL: Ahem. *(Reads.)* "Uzziah's celebrated reign began in his sixteenth year of life. Son of good King Amaziah and Queen Jecoliah..."

UZZIAH: You can skip the family history. That stuff always bores me.

JEIEL: But of course, Munificent Majesty.

UZZIAH: Continue with the good stuff.

JEIEL: "Having sought the Lord God, the God of Abraham, Isaac and Jacob, He who brought us up from the land of Egypt in the days of Moses..."

UZZIAH: Let me see that book. *(JEIEL hands book to UZZIAH.)* That part could be edited a bit. Let's cross out all that bit about Abraham, Isaac, Jacob and Moses.

JEIEL: As you wish, Illustrious Imperator. *(Aside.)* I don't know what that means, but it sounds good. *(Crosses out part of writing.)*

UZZIAH: Continue.

JEIEL: "Mighty Uzziah, Conqueror of Nations, Worker of Wisdom, went to battle..."

UZZIAH: *(Interrupts.)* Is that ALL?

JEIEL: No, Supreme Ruler of All He Surveys. There is much more about your deeds.

UZZIAH: I mean, descriptions of me. There's only two.

JEIEL: Yes.

UZZIAH: Well, we crossed out all of that Abraham, Isaac, Jacob, Moses stuff. So we can put in more about me. See to it when you leave.

JEIEL: Your every wish is my command, O Living Legend.

UZZIAH: Continue.

JEIEL: "...went to battle. Under his Fabulous Feet, Uzziah trampled the grapes of Philistine manhood into the sweet wine of success to be savored upon the lips of His Illustrious Highness..."

UZZIAH: What's all that mean?

JEIEL: It is a poetic way to say you conquered the Philistines, O Conquering Commander in Chief. I could change it to say "Uzziah conquered Philistia."

UZZIAH: No, the other way sounds better. Continue.

JEIEL: "The deeds of His Royal Highness, Emperor of the Minions, Protector of the Defenseless, Wielder of the Weapons of War, have spread across the breadth of the world. The Ammonites..."

UZZIAH: You can skip that part. Go on to my building projects.

JEIEL: *(Aside.)* Good. The abridged version.

UZZIAH: What was that?

JEIEL: I said, "Good bridges"—referring to your most capable construction.

UZZIAH *(surprised)*: Have I built bridges? I must have. I've done everything else. *(Waves hand.)* Continue.

JEIEL: "Uzziah, Builder of Billions, Mason of Might, Woodworker of Wonder, set his hand to the ageless aggrandizement of His Noble Nation..."

UZZIAH: I like that, "Woodworker of Wonder." By the way, send in the royal physician when you leave. I got a splinter in my finger from the throne.

JEIEL: As my feet leave the throne room, my lips shall impart your most majestic message.

UZZIAH: Continue.

JEIEL: "...tirelessly toiling, the Undaunted Uzziah effortlessly erected towers at the Corner Gate, at the Valley Gate and at the turning of the wall. Fearlessly fortifying the formidable fortresses, His Most Unrelenting Uzziah has prospered the portals of the House of Judah with peace everlasting."

UZZIAH: Stop! Something has occurred to me.

JEIEL: Yes, Omnipotent One.

UZZIAH: All this has happened because I sought the advice of the Lord?

JEIEL: I believe that is in the preface. I can erase that part, should you wish.

UZZIAH: No! It's not that. But what have I done to give thanks? Have I offered thanks at the Temple?

JEIEL: Most assuredly, Majestic Majesty. Every year, you and all the people gather to give the sacrifices to God...

UZZIAH: I'm not talking about that! How utterly boring, sacrificing with the RABBLE. I should do something special. After all, God will surely be pleased with a thank offering from ME. I'm so important! Not like the common people.

JEIEL: *(Aside.)* May the Lord be praised.

UZZIAH: What was that?

JEIEL: I said, "Magnificently raised." Above the level of the common people.

UZZIAH: Quite. Come with me. We'll go to the Temple now.

(UZZIAH and JEIEL go to the Temple.)

UZZIAH: High Priest! Thank your lucky stars. I have come to sacrifice.

HIGH PRIEST: Have I missed something? Is it time for the sacrifice, already?

UZZIAH: No! This is a special sacrifice, because I'M special.

HIGH PRIEST: This is not the attitude one should have before God.

JEIEL: Careful, High Priest. You're speaking to His Imperial Majesty.

HIGH PRIEST: Then he should stop sounding like His Doddering Donkey. Come to the Lord with thanksgiving and with a humble spirit.

UZZIAH: Nonsense. Humility is fine for those who should be humble, but I'm special. I'm important. I am the KING. I am the Great Builder!

HIGH PRIEST: Where were you when Jehovah laid the foundations of the earth? Have you the ability to measure the earth? Have you stretched a measuring line across its width?

JEIEL *(quietly, to HIGH PRIEST)*: Careful. Don't get him angry!

UZZIAH: I am Uzziah, King of Judah! I have laid waste to vast nations.

HIGH PRIEST: Have you taken hold of the ends of the earth, that the wicked could be shaken out? Have the gates of death been opened to you?

JEIEL: *(To HIGH PRIEST.)* Don't make him angry. You won't LIKE him when he's angry!

UZZIAH: Not since the days of Solomon has such wealth been seen in Judah! I have great herds of sheep and oxen! Vast numbers of horses!

HIGH PRIEST: Who set the wild donkey free? His pasture includes all the mountains. Will the wild ox allow itself to be tamed by you? Have you given the horse its strength? Do hawks and eagles fly because you command them?

JEIEL: *(Rolls eyes.)* Too late. He's mad.

UZZIAH: I WILL sacrifice and the Lord WILL be pleased. He will be pleased because *I* am making the sacrifice.

HIGH PRIEST: *(Crosses arms.)* When you have this attitude, you cannot sacrifice.

UZZIAH: Who says I can't! Give me that incense! *(Grabs incense and exits.)* I will burn incense to God!

HIGH PRIEST *(shocked)*: No! You must not! You must not go into the Holy Place! Only the sons of Aaron have been appointed to enter and burn incense. You are trespassing! *(Runs after UZZIAH.)* What you are doing will neither bring honor to God nor to yourself.

(UZZIAH stomps into the Holy Place.)

UZZIAH *(screaming)*: AAH! *(Stumbles out of the Holy Place.)*

JEIEL: What is it, my king? What's wrong?

HIGH PRIEST: *(Jumps back.)* It's leprosy! Quick! Cast him out of the Temple! The Temple must not be defiled!

JEIEL *(leading a defeated UZZIAH)*: Don't worry, Leprous Leader. I'll find some way to write this out so that it will sound good.

HECKLING HEZEKIAH

SCRIPTURE: 2 Kings 18; 2 Chronicles 32:1-19; Isaiah 36

SUGGESTED TOPICS: Trusting in God; revering God; discouragement; courage

BIBLE BACKGROUND

Hezekiah inherited a mess. His father, Ahaz, had made Judah a nation of idolatry during his sixteen-year reign. Because Syria and Israel had joined forces against him, Ahaz made a pact with the strongest nation of the time, Assyria. As a present to Tiglath-pilesar, King of Assyria, Ahaz sent a tribute which included all the silver and gold in the Temple as well as what he himself owned. In spite of the alliance, Judah was beset on all sides (see 2 Chronicles 28:16-22). At the time of Ahaz's death, the Temple of God had been closed up and altars to every heathen god imaginable were set up throughout the land. Children were being sacrificed to appease the strange gods.

In spite of the actions of his father (or perhaps because of them), Hezekiah began his twenty-nine-year reign in a very different manner. In the first month, he reopened the Temple and had it cleansed. He tore down all the altars and high places for idol worship. He commanded Judah to come together for a great sacrifice to God, to ask Him to remove their sin. He reinstituted the Passover. Also, he stopped paying tribute to Assyria. After fourteen years, Assyria's new king, Sennacherib, decided enough was enough and launched a major campaign against Hezekiah.

PERFORMANCE TIPS

1. Suggested props: a crown and a chair for Sennacherib, a writing pad for the counselors, a very large book for Rabshakeh, weapons (swords, spears, shields, etc.).

2. Set Sennacherib's camp to one side of the stage. Soldiers and counselors will enter from the near wings. Jerusalem will be offstage in the far wings.

3. When Rabshakeh addresses the people of Jerusalem, he should walk to the opposite side of the stage from Sennacherib. He can simulate shouting by cupping his hands widely around his mouth.

4. Prior to the skit, tell about the cleansing of the Temple, the revival in Judah and the fact that Hezekiah stopped paying tribute. After the skit, ask "What would you do if you had to go to war against the strongest country in the world when your army was one of the weakest?" Then read or tell about Hezekiah's prayer, Isaiah's counsel and God's answer.

DISCUSSION QUESTIONS

1. Why would Hezekiah insist on offering a sacrifice for the sins of the whole country of Judah?

2. Why does God hate idol worship so much? (Read 2 Chronicles 28:3 to see part of the answer.)

3. We don't worship statues of idols, but sometimes we have other gods. What other gods do we allow to creep into our lives?

4. One of Satan's strongest weapons is discouragement. What is discouragement? Why does Satan use it as a weapon?

5. How can God help you overcome discouragement? How can other people help? How can you help others?

Heckling Hezekiah

CHARACTERS

SENNACHERIB (seh-NACK-er-ib)
SOLDIER ONE
SOLDIER TWO
SOLDIER THREE
COUNSELOR ONE
COUNSELOR TWO
COUNSELOR THREE
RABSHAKEH (rab-SHAY-keh)

PRONUNCIATION GUIDE

Assyria (uh-SEER-ee-uh)
Hezekiah (hez-uh-KY-uh)

SOLDIER ONE: O Mighty King Sennacherib, may you live forever.

SENNACHERIB: Speak.

SOLDIER ONE: We have returned from our scouting expedition.

SOLDIER TWO: The city of Jerusalem is just beyond that next hill.

SOLDIER THREE: But our advance scouting reports were wrong.

SENNACHERIB: WRONG?

SOLDIER THREE: "Wrong" is maybe a bit harsh. Let's say "Mistaken."

SENNACHERIB: WRONG?

SOLDIER THREE: OK. Wrong.

SENNACHERIB: In what WAY were they wrong?

SOLDIER ONE: We were told there would be plenty of water flowing down from springs near Jerusalem.

SOLDIER TWO: We were told we would have all we needed to drink.

SOLDIER THREE: But the water is dried up. I think the people might have built a dam in Jerusalem to stop the water.

SENNACHERIB: The scurvy dogs! How dare they? Water is sacred! Counselor!

COUNSELOR ONE: *(Enters.)* Yes, Sire.

SENNACHERIB: Make a note. "Amend the rules of war: Changing the course of waterways will henceforth be prohibited." Got that?

COUNSELOR ONE: In its entirety, my lord. *(Exits.)*

SENNACHERIB: So. Hezekiah thinks he can stop me by shutting down one little waterway, does he? We're close enough to water and have enough men to shuttle the water back and forth. We'll have enough. Well? Are you still here?

SOLDIER ONE: There's more, Sire.

SENNACHERIB: More?

SOLDIER TWO: Yes, Sire. You remember the reports about the city walls?

SENNACHERIB: Certainly. They're in need of repair.

SOLDIER THREE: No longer, Sire. The inner wall has been built up to the towers.

SENNACHERIB: What do you mean, INNER wall?

SOLDIER ONE: They've built another wall outside of the first, Sire.

SENNACHERIB: A second wall? Counselor!

COUNSELOR TWO: *(Enters.)* Sire?

SENNACHERIB: Make a note. "In conjunction with the *Rules of War*, Article 5, Paragraph 7, Subparagraph 25. No additional fortifications shall be made to capital cities once war has been declared." Got that?

COUNSELOR TWO: From your lips to the page, my lord. *(Exits.)*

SENNACHERIB: Good. Well, Hezekiah's plans will do him no good. I'm the world champion of wall destruction. Any other problems?

SOLDIER ONE: No, O Mighty King.

SOLDIER TWO: None, O Valiant Warrior.

SOLDIER THREE: All is now well, O Terror of the Nations. *(SOLDIERS exit.)*

SENNACHERIB: Counselors!

COUNSELOR ONE: *(Enters.)* We come.

COUNSELOR TWO: *(Enters.)* Most hastily.

COUNSELOR THREE: *(Enters.)* Ever eager to serve.

SENNACHERIB: Yeah, yeah, yeah. What's the latest on our data about Judah?

COUNSELOR ONE: They have fallen away from the true faith. No longer do they worship many gods. They only worship one God.

SENNACHERIB: One God? Why, that's blasphemy! If I only worshiped one God, I'd be the laughingstock of the world.

COUNSELOR TWO: We know they have completely cleaned and repaired the Temple in Jerusalem. Hezekiah has ordered all of the high places to be destroyed. All worship will only happen in the Temple.

SENNACHERIB: And people call ME cruel. How are all the old people supposed to get to Jerusalem for worship?

COUNSELOR THREE: We have also learned that Hezekiah ordered sacrifices to this one God to ask forgiveness for the sin of Judah.

SENNACHERIB: He's not much of a psychologist. You're not supposed to tell people they've done bad things. You're just supposed to call it "alternative lifestyles." Any word on the payment of tribute?

COUNSELOR ONE: Yes, my lord. He has sent a tribute of silver and gold.

SENNACHERIB: The full amount? Three hundred talents of silver and thirty talents of gold?

COUNSELOR TWO: If not the full amount, very close to it.

SENNACHERIB: Ridiculous. Hezekiah hasn't got that much. Where did he get it?

COUNSELOR THREE: Our reports say he took all the gold and silver from the Temple treasury. All the gold and silver vessels from the Temple. He even cut the gold from the doors and the pillars.

SENNACHERIB: Hmm. Get me my lawyer!

RABSHAKEH: *(Enters.)* Here I am.

SENNACHERIB: I sent an ultimatum to Hezekiah. I told him, "Send me three hundred talents of silver and thirty talents of gold or I'll destroy you." And he sent me a bunch of gold and silver.

RABSHAKEH: Then, what's the problem?

SENNACHERIB: The problem is, I WANT to destroy him.

RABSHAKEH: Ah, I see. Let me consult a little volume I have with me. *(Two men carry out huge book. RABSHAKEH thumbs through it.)* Here it is. Torts.

SENNACHERIB: None for me, thanks. I'm watching the old waistline.

RABSHAKEH: Not dessert—damages for wrongful actions. His refusing to pay before you got here caused you to suffer grievous personal loss.

SENNACHERIB: It did?

RABSHAKEH: Work with me on this.

SENNACHERIB: Oh, it did. IT DID!

RABSHAKEH: Therefore, you're going to damage him for his wrongful actions.

SENNACHERIB: Excellent! I'll destroy him now.

RABSHAKEH: Let's do this by the book, shall we? We'll have to inform him of your intent. We also want to destroy his confidence at the same time. How about you leave this to me?

SENNACHERIB: You're the expert.

(RABSHAKEH walks to far side to show he has walked some distance.)

RABSHAKEH: Hey, Judeans! You in Jerusalem! I've got a message for Hezekiah from Sennacherib. Here's the message: Hey! Stupid! What's the matter with you?

SENNACHERIB: *(Stands where RABSHAKEH left him and delivers rest of lines to audience.)* Couldn't have put it better, myself.

RABSHAKEH: Who do you think is going to help you if the mighty king of Assyria is against you?

SENNACHERIB: He could have been a little more forceful. Mighty king of Assyria, Ruler of the Universe, Conqueror of All that Lives, Destroyer of Dogs Who Don't Pay Up. Things like that.

RABSHAKEH: Maybe you're planning to trust Egypt?

SENNACHERIB: He might be. Egypt is pretty strong.

RABSHAKEH: I say, hah! Egypt's strength is the same as a broken stick! If you lean on Egypt, you'll impale yourself!

SENNACHERIB: Nice touch.

RABSHAKEH: Maybe you're planning to trust in God? What? You got a penny that says "In God We Trust"? How can you trust God when Hezekiah destroyed all His places of worship?

SENNACHERIB: That'll teach Hezekiah to be a blasphemer.

RABSHAKEH: OK, here's the deal! You give us a damage deposit, say a few hostages, and Sennacherib will give you two thousand horses!

SENNACHERIB: Why would I do that?

RABSHAKEH: But only if you have enough soldiers to ride them!

SENNACHERIB: Oh! Excellent!

RABSHAKEH: Even if you have two thousand horsemen, do you think you could stop one Assyrian chariot? Hah! We're men of war! You are farmers!

SENNACHERIB: What do farmers have to do with anything? Some farmers are pretty tough.

RABSHAKEH: God told me to go up against Jerusalem and destroy it! Don't let Hezekiah fool you, Judeans! He can't save you!

SENNACHERIB: Good. Talk right to the people. Make them lose heart.

RABSHAKEH: OK! Here's the deal! Surrender to me, the king of Assyria! Bring me presents to show you really mean it! Then I will not harm you! Everyone will have his own farm and will live!

SENNACHERIB: THAT'S where the farms come in.

RABSHAKEH: Don't let Hezekiah fool you by telling you God will save you! What about the gods of all the other countries I have conquered? They couldn't stop me! And Hezekiah's God is no different! Surrender and live! Rebel and die!

SENNACHERIB: That was a good job. Now, I just have to wait a bit for the people to start fleeing the city. Then, I destroy it and all within. *(Laughs wickedly.)*

THIS IS THE LAW

SCRIPTURE: Deuteronomy 30:11—31:13; 2 Kings 22:1—23:3;
2 Chronicles 34:1-15

SUGGESTED TOPICS: Obedience to God's Word; following God's
instructions; importance of Bible reading

BIBLE BACKGROUND

The people of Israel had demanded a king. Saul, David and then Solomon ruled over the kingdom. Solomon's son, Rehoboam, saw the kingdom divided into the nations of Israel and Judah, each having its own king. Almost from the beginning, the worship of the true God was forgotten in both kingdoms. From time to time a king would remember God, but most of the kings worshiped idols. Some three hundred years after the kingdom split, Josiah ascended to the throne of Judah. Jerusalem was immersed in idolatry, and the Temple of God had deteriorated badly.

PERFORMANCE TIPS

1. Suggested props: a crown for Josiah, an old book to represent the Book of the Law.

2. Have Shaphan read Deuteronomy 28:58-68 when Josiah tells Shaphan to read the book.

3. After the skit, summarize Deuteronomy 30:15-20 to explain why Josiah was so worried.

DISCUSSION QUESTIONS

1. Why was Josiah so worried?

2. Why is it important to read the Bible?

3. Why should you obey God? What good things come from obeying God's law?

4. How can you learn God's law and promises?

THIS IS THE LAW

CHARACTERS
JOSIAH (jo-ZI-ah)
HILKIAH (hil-KI-ah)
NARRATOR
GUARD
SHAPHAN (SHAY-fan)
HULDAH

SCENE ONE

JOSIAH: Hilkiah, good of you to come.

HILKIAH: When the king requests an audience, even the high priest must obey.

JOSIAH: True enough. Hilkiah, how long have I been king?

HILKIAH: Eight years, my King. Half of your young life.

JOSIAH: And in those eight years, I have been given advice by many people.

HILKIAH: True, my King.

JOSIAH: However, some advice was better than others. Some was downright terrible.

HILKIAH: Unfortunately true, my King. Although you may fill a man with all the spices of the world, his advice still may not be sage.

JOSIAH: What? Oh. Another proverb. And true. But I have always found your advice trust worthy. *(Pause.)* Now, I have a problem. Many gods are worshiped in Jerusalem.

HILKIAH: Unfortunately, also true.

JOSIAH: But your advice has always been good and true. So I ask you—if I am to give allegiance to one of the gods worshiped in Jerusalem, which one should it be?

HILKIAH: That is simple, my King. Worship the true God, for there is only one.

JOSIAH: And you know this god?

HILKIAH: Of course, my King. I am His chief priest.

JOSIAH: Then teach me about Him, that I may know Him, too.

NARRATOR: For the next four years, Josiah learned about the God of Abraham, Isaac and Jacob from Hilkiah. Then, when he was twenty years old, in his twelfth year as king...

JOSIAH: Hilkiah, I have learned much about Jehovah from you in the past four years.

HILKIAH: All of which is the truth, my King.

JOSIAH: I believe you. Your conduct, your advice—all these things point toward your worshiping the one true God. But one thing you said puzzles me. You said Jehovah wants His people to worship only Him.

HILKIAH: Why should this puzzle you, my King? When people worship false gods, they obey false gods. They follow bad advice and live evil lives. Jehovah wants His people to have the best. To follow what is good and to truly live.

JOSIAH: Guard! *(GUARD enters.)*

GUARD: You screamed, oh King?

JOSIAH: I want you to take this hastily written decree...

GUARD: Most hastily, oh King.

JOSIAH: ...to the scribes. Have it copied many times and posted throughout Jerusalem...

GUARD: On every corner, oh King.

JOSIAH: I don't need THAT many. But post it so that all the citizens of Jerusalem can read it and obey it.

GUARD: It is already done, oh King.

JOSIAH: And then, I want a messenger to ride into every town in Judah to read the decree to all the citizens of my kingdom.

GUARD: This will take one man many years, oh King.

JOSIAH: Use as many messengers as are required. All of the kingdom of Judah must hear this decree immediately.

GUARD: Even as you speak, it is done, oh King.

JOSIAH: Then go! Do it! *(GUARD exits.)*

NARRATOR: What a decree this was. It contained instructions to rid Judah of all false gods. It ordered the destruction of the high places, the groves and wood and metal images. All were broken down into powder and scattered on the graves of those who had sacrificed to the false gods. He even burned the bones of the false priests on their own altars and then tore down the altars. Satisfied that all had been accomplished according to his will, Josiah returned to Jerusalem.

JOSIAH: There. It took six years, but I am certain that all has been put right. All the false gods have been pulverized. I can rest, knowing only Jehovah will be worshiped in Judah. All will come to His beautiful Temple—the TEMPLE! For years it has been in ruins. It must be restored.

NARRATOR: And what a job THAT was. The Levites gathered offerings from the people to begin the task of restoration. The rubble that had accumulated for decades had to be removed. Old stones that had chipped and broken had to be carefully removed from the walls and new ones put in their place. Old rotting timbers had to be replaced with new ones. And in the midst of the work...

(HILKIAH sifts through rubble while SHAPHAN watches.)

HILKIAH: Look what I have found. *(He holds out an old book.)* The king must know of this immediately. Where is Shaphan? The scribe must take this to the king at once. Shaphan! Shaphan!

SHAPHAN: Not so loud. I'm right behind you.

HILKIAH: I have found a treasure that must be taken to the king.

SHAPHAN: Then give it to one of the laborers to carry. I'm a scribe, not a porter.

HILKIAH: But this is a special treasure. One that a scribe would appreciate.

SHAPHAN: *(Gazes at Hilkiah's treasure.)* I see what you mean! I will take it to the king immediately. *(Exits the Temple.)*

SCENE TWO

GUARD: Oh King, may you live forever. There is one here who wishes an audience with Your Most Blessed Majesty.

JOSIAH: I told you I was busy. No visitors today.

SHAPHAN: *(Enters.)* Forgive me, my King, but Hilkiah instructed me to deliver this most important treasure to you immediately.

JOSIAH: Shaphan! Of course I have time to see the one who is overseeing the restoration of the Temple. How does the work progress?

SHAPHAN: Well, my King. The money collected by the Levites has been paid to the workmen. But Hilkiah found this treasure in the midst of the rubble. *(He offers the book to JOSIAH.)*

JOSIAH: Treasure? It looks like nothing more than an old book.

SHAPHAN: It is an ancient manuscript, my King. But it is far more than that. When Hilkiah was instructing you in the ways of Jehovah, he spoke from memory. That which had been passed down from his father and his grandfather, he passed along to you. But now—*(pause)* the Book written by Moses, lost for many years, has been found.

JOSIAH: I may be young, but I wasn't born yesterday. Moses died centuries ago. Such a book would have rotted away by now.

SHAPHAN: Of course, my King. This is the last copy. The one that was faithfully copied from the one before, as has always been the custom in Judah. This is the Book of the Law, the very instructions that Jehovah gave to Moses.

JOSIAH: Then sit down, Shaphan, and read me the book.

NARRATOR: Shaphan did as the king ordered. He read to the king all the words of the Law, from Genesis to Deuteronomy.

JOSIAH: Is this true? Are these words that will come to pass for all in Judah and also in Israel? It cannot be! It MUST not be! *(He tears his clothes.)*

SHAPHAN: Why does the King cry out so? And why does the King rend his garment?

JOSIAH: You read the words! You heard the promises! Did you not also hear the curses? Were you deaf to what you read?

GUARD: I wouldn't worry about it. It's an old book, written in old language. It probably doesn't apply to life today. The words probably don't have the same meaning now.

JOSIAH: Which is why you are a guard and not an advisor. Shaphan, take some men and find someone who can inquire of the Lord—for me and for those left in Israel and in Judah—about the words of this Book. For great is the wrath of the Lord, poured out upon us, because our fathers have not kept the Lord's word.

NARRATOR: So the four men sought out Huldah, a prophetess of the Lord.

HULDAH: Thus says the Lord: "I will bring evil upon this place and upon its inhabitants, all of the curses written in the book that was read to the king of Judah, because they have forgotten me and have worshiped other gods. But say this to the king of Judah. Because your heart was tender and you humbled yourself before God, and wept and rent your clothes when you heard my words, you will not see my wrath in your lifetime."

NARRATOR: When Huldah's prophecy was reported to Josiah, he made a covenant before God to walk in His ways all the days of his life, and he commanded the people of Judah to also agree to the covenant. Josiah honored his promise and served God for the rest of his life, until his death when he was thirty-nine.

PROPHETS' ROUND TABLE

SCRIPTURE: Jeremiah 29,31; Selections from Ezra; Nehemiah; Malachi

SUGGESTED TOPICS: Listening to God; trusting God; reading God's Word

BIBLE BACKGROUND

Throughout history, God has chosen prophets—devout men and women called to proclaim His word to His people. But along with the prophets of God came false prophets. God's standards for His prophets were very high. God warned Israel not to follow a prophet just because something he predicted actually happened. If a prophet claimed, "You can see I am a prophet. I know what I'm talking about. Forget about Jehovah. I have a better way," he was to be put to death as a false prophet (see Deuteronomy 13:1-5). A true prophet always honors God.

Or if a prophet claimed to speak in the Lord's name, but the things predicted did not happen, he was a false prophet and was to be put to death (see Deuteronomy 18:20-22). If God says a thing will happen, it happens.

Unfortunately, being God's prophet was not the safest occupation, from a human standpoint. Elijah was chased throughout Israel by Ahab because he spoke God's condemnation to the king. Elisha had a death sentence placed on him by the king of Israel because the king blamed Israel's troubles on Elisha. Jeremiah was locked in stocks and imprisoned because he spoke God's truth. God's prophets were not always popular, since God does not always speak kindly to His people. When God's people needed correction, they often resisted the messenger and any warning message which God sent. However, behind such prophecies was always the promise that God would not forsake them. He would raise up a Savior.

PERFORMANCE TIPS

1. Suggested props: table and chairs, large name tags for all characters.

2. Set the table center stage for the current time. Have the prior time satellite to one side of the stage and the future time satellite to the other.

3. The false prophets should whine and complain.

DISCUSSION QUESTIONS

1. How would you describe a prophet?

2. Read Deuteronomy 13:2,3. How can you tell if someone is trying to lead you after other gods? What are some ways you can use to decide?

3. God has a great plan for humankind. Describe the plan in your own words.

PROPHETS' ROUND TABLE

CHARACTERS
MODERATOR
JEREMIAH
ZERUBBABEL (zuh-RUB-uh-bull)
EZRA
NEHEMIAH (NEE-uh-MY-uh)
MALACHI (MAL-a-kye)
PASHUR (PASH-er)
SHEMAIAH (shem-EYE-ah)

PRONUNCIATION GUIDE
Cyrus (SY-rus)
Artaxerxes (ar-tuh-ZERK-sees)

MODERATOR: Good evening and welcome to "Prophets' Round Table." Our guests tonight are not prophets, but they are men of character who have been influenced by prophets. Here at our table are Zerubbabel, Ezra and Nehemiah, three men instrumental in the rebuilding of Jerusalem. Welcome, gentlemen.

ZERUBBABEL, EZRA and NEHEMIAH: Thank you. Hello. Good to be here.

MODERATOR: We will have other guests with us via satellite later in the show. From our prior times satellite, we will be joined by Jeremiah, Pashur and Shemaiah. And from our future times satellite, Malachi. But first, our guests in the studio. Zerubbabel, you're something of a grassroots politician.

ZERUBBABEL: Yes, that's a pretty fair description of me. I'm a man of the people.

MODERATOR: It seems to me that you wouldn't require the services of a prophet.

ZERUBBABEL: That's where you're wrong. Fourteen years ago—is that all it is? It seems like such a long time ago, now. Anyway, fourteen years ago, I had an awesome responsibility. I was in charge of bringing nearly fifty thousand people back to Jerusalem.

MODERATOR: That's a lot of people. You say you brought them back. Where had you been?

ZERUBBABEL: We had been in captivity in Babylon. Then Babylon was defeated and so forth, but that's old history. Finally, Cyrus, king of Persia, allowed us to return to our home, Jerusalem.

MODERATOR: So you were chosen to lead these people?

ZERUBBABEL: Yes, and given the responsibility of the money to be brought back.

MODERATOR: How much could that be? You had been captives, slaves.

ZERUBBABEL: You'd be surprised. Cyrus was very generous. Gold, silver, all the implements from the Temple. There was a lot of wealth traveling with us.

MODERATOR: And how do prophets fit into this?

ZERUBBABEL: With all the problems, I had to continually ask myself, "Is this the right thing? Is this what God has planned?" Fortunately, I had the writings of Isaiah.

MODERATOR: He's a prophet from long ago.

ZERUBBABEL: Yes. Long before Judah was taken into captivity, before King Cyrus was even born, Isaiah prophesied, "Thus says the Lord of Cyrus. He is my shepherd. He will build Jerusalem and lay the foundation of the Temple."

MODERATOR: What's so special about that prophecy?

ZERUBBABEL: When he said it, Jerusalem was a city and the Temple was completely built. Later, the city and the Temple were torn down. So I could see his writings and know that God wanted Jerusalem and the Temple to be rebuilt. I was doing God's will.

MODERATOR: I see. Thank you. Nehemiah. You're a bit different. You're also in politics, but you're in the higher ranks of power. You were the cupbearer to King Artaxerxes. That's a powerful position.

NEHEMIAH: Yes, it is. It gave me direct access to the king every day.

MODERATOR: And you took it upon yourself to come out and help rebuild Jerusalem.

NEHEMIAH: Yes. Zerubbabel had made a good start but there was much left to do, even after fourteen years.

MODERATOR: Being that close to the king, you wouldn't need prophets to help you.

NEHEMIAH: On the contrary. The prophets were most important to me.

MODERATOR: But why?

NEHEMIAH: I also came out with a great deal of money for the project. And there were many people living around Jerusalem who wanted the project stopped. They sent false reports about me to the king.

MODERATOR: But you're his trusted advisor. Why would he believe false rumors?

NEHEMIAH: Trust doesn't go very far these days. I needed the words of the prophets to sustain my spirit. I needed to read the warnings for disobeying God's laws and the promises for obedience. That gave me the courage to correct my people when they were following false ideas.

MODERATOR: That leaves Ezra, priest of God. Surely YOU wouldn't need the prophets? You would instruct them.

EZRA: On the contrary. I, too, need to heed the prophets. I am but one man. I am capable of being wrong. God gives prophets so that the priest can look at himself to determine if he is following God.

MODERATOR: Can you give us an example?

EZRA: Of course. I had not asked the king to give us a guard for our journey. Was I wrong to not ask? I thought, "No. I can't ask for a guard. I told the king that God is our protector." But I needed confirmation. Fortunately, men of understanding...

MODERATOR: Prophets?

EZRA: Exactly. Men of understanding were with me. We fasted and prayed and God confirmed we were on the right course.

MODERATOR: There you have it. People in all walks of life need the prophets. Now, via satellite, let's talk to some prophets. Prophets of the past, are you there?

JEREMIAH: Yes, I'm here.

PASHUR: There you go again. Always setting yourself up as better than everyone else.

SHEMAIAH: That's right. You're not the only prophet here. There's three of us.

JEREMIAH: One who speaks falsely is not a prophet.

MODERATOR: Gentlemen, gentlemen. Do I sense some strife?

PASHUR: It's Jeremiah's fault. It's always his fault. He just wants to be a gloomy gus all the time.

SHEMAIAH: That's right. Is it our fault that we're optimists and he's a pessimist? Show us a donut, we see a donut. Show him a donut, he sees the hole.

JEREMIAH: Finally, you speak the truth.

PASHUR: Ah! He admits it.

JEREMIAH: Of course. When you look at a donut, you only see the cake. When I look at a donut, I see the whole donut. All of it. The cake and the hole in the center. You see the donut, I see the whole donut.

SHEMAIAH: There he goes, twisting our words around again.

PASHUR: You shouldn't have him on the show. He's nothing but trouble.

EZRA: Excuse me, but are you Jeremiah who prophesied in Jerusalem in the time of Jehoiakim until the captivity?

JEREMIAH: Yes, I am.

EZRA: I wish I could shake your hand. Your words have brought such comfort to me!

PASHUR: Comfort? HIS words? The man doesn't know the meaning of the word "uplifting."

SHEMAIAH: It's a sorry state of affairs when the priest is illiterate.

JEREMIAH (*ignoring others*)**:** I am glad my words were of benefit. Praise God!

MODERATOR: How did Jeremiah help you, Ezra?

EZRA: Jeremiah always spoke the truth, even if it hurt. He didn't try to make people believe the situation was better than it was. Therefore, when Jeremiah says, "Israel and Judah have not been forsaken by God," I can believe him. When we were in captivity, we knew God was still there.

PASHUR: But what about us?

SHEMAIAH: Yeah. We said God was with us.

ZERUBBABEL: But you told lies.

NEHEMIAH: And did evil things.

EZRA: You, Pashur. You, a son of a priest and a governor, should have listened to Jeremiah and called the people to repentance. But what did you do?

NEHEMIAH: You had him beaten instead.

ZERUBBABEL: And had him put in stocks.

SHEMAIAH *(whining)*: A LOT of people want to be in stocks—and bonds!

PASHUR *(whining)*: And he called me names. He called me "Fear Around Him" and said my friends would die. He should have been punished.

JEREMIAH: I only gave you that name at the Lord's command—after you had injured me. If you would have listened and called the people to repentance, would the Lord not have listened?

EZRA: And you, Shemaiah—if we had listened to you, our hearts would have failed us.

NEHEMIAH: Yes. Jeremiah told us the captivity would be long. That we should build houses and plan to be in exile for some time.

ZERUBBABEL: You wanted us to believe we would be freed at any time, Shemaiah.

EZRA: If we had listened to YOU, we would have given up long ago.

MODERATOR: Thank you for being with us, gentlemen. We have one more prophet to speak to—Malachi. Malachi, you will be prophesying in the future. In fact, if our research is accurate, in the very near future. What sort of things do you foresee?

MALACHI: My job is a little different from that of Jeremiah. God has sent me to lift up the hearts of the exiles returning to Jerusalem.

MODERATOR: So not all true prophets predict gloom and doom?

MALACHI: Of course not. We tell the people what God tells us. Because people sin, we often have to remind them what happens when they sin. But God loves His people and has a plan.

EZRA: God has revealed His plan to you, Malachi?

MALACHI: Sort of. I don't understand all of it, myself. But what God says, I report.

NEHEMIAH: What sort of things, Malachi? Tell us, please.

MALACHI: The Lord says, "I send My messenger before Me and he shall prepare the way. Then the Lord whom you seek will come to His Temple."

ZERUBBABEL: Of what does he speak?

NEHEMIAH: I don't know. Ezra, what does this mean?

EZRA: The Lord is renewing His promise. He is reminding us that He will come.

MALACHI: Yes, I think that's what it means. He has also said some things about Elijah returning. I will write it down. What we don't understand, future generations may.

MODERATOR: Thank you, gentlemen, for being here. (Looks at audience.) Tune in next week when eight hundred and fifty prophets of the groves and Baal will be here to tell us of all the advantages of eating at the queen's table.

DUMB, DUMB, DUMB

SCRIPTURE: Ezra 7—10

SUGGESTED TOPICS: Obeying God; respect for God; repentance

BIBLE BACKGROUND

The people of Israel and Judah had been carried into captivity because of their sin. The worst sin was the idolatry that had infested the people of God as they intermarried with the people of the surrounding nations. Now, approximately sixty years after the first contingent of Jews had made their way back to their homeland, Ezra followed with a king's ransom to help rebuild the land.

Ezra expected to find a nation committed to the God of its forefathers. Instead, he found a nation that had slipped back into its idolatrous past. The cancer which had nearly destroyed the nation had returned. But with the skill of a surgeon, Ezra prepared to operate on that cancer and make the nation whole.

PERFORMANCE TIPS

1. Suggested props: table and chairs, papers (reports) for Ezra to look through.

2. Eliezer thinks the hard part's finished. He's relaxed, casual.

3. Ezra knows much is left to be done. He's intense.

DISCUSSION QUESTIONS

1. Why was Ezra so worried?

2. What kinds of sin were the people of Israel committing?

3. What did the people of Israel do to show they respected God? (See Ezra 10:9-19.)

4. Why is confession of sin a way to show respect to God?

5. What are some practical ways to show repentance for unconfessed sin in your life?

DUMB, DUMB, DUMB

CHARACTERS

EZRA

ELIEZER (EL-ee-AY-zer)

PRONUNCIATION GUIDE

Artaxerxes (ar-tuh-ZERK-sees)

ELIEZER: Well, everything's just about done.

EZRA (*studying paper*)**:** Hmm?

ELIEZER: Well, the hard part's done. We got here with all the gold and silver. I still think it was dumb not to ask Artaxerxes for a regiment of soldiers to go with us.

EZRA: I couldn't.

ELIEZER: Why not? We could have used protection. We were carrying almost twenty-nine tons of silver. And thirty pounds of gold. That's enough to tempt any thief.

EZRA: What? I'm supposed to go to Artaxerxes and say, "Please, kind King. Since we have so much to carry, could you please send all the soldiers you can spare to protect us?"

ELIEZER: It sounds reasonable to me.

EZRA: That would have been dumb. Hadn't I told Artaxerxes of the great power of God?

ELIEZER: But...

EZRA: But, but, but. Would Artaxerxes have had any respect for a God who needs the protection of a man? Shouldn't it be the other way around?

ELIEZER: Well, of course. But a little extra couldn't hurt.

EZRA: It couldn't? Don't you read history?

ELIEZER: Not all the time.

EZRA: Read it. Then we'll talk. See how God wants His people to recognize His protection.

ELIEZER: Well, anyway. Now we can relax.

EZRA: Relax? Are you crazy?

ELIEZER: It's done! The priests have all the money. Everything's been delivered. Time to put up the old feet, sit back and...

EZRA: Get to work. We have been entrusted by Artaxerxes to see that everything is done according to his decree. More importantly, we must see that things are done by God's decree.

ELIEZER: Oh, well. That should be no problem.

EZRA: No problem? Look at this! *(Hands paper to ELIEZER.)*

ELIEZER: Marriage certificate. Everything seems to be in order.

EZRA: In order? How can you say, "In order"? The man is a Levite.

ELIEZER: Sure. But priests can marry.

EZRA: The woman is a Canaanite!

ELIEZER: *(Studies paper more closely.)* Are you sure?

EZRA: I only wish there was room for doubt. How dumb can these people be?

ELIEZER: *(Hands paper back.)* Don't make a big deal out of it. It's only one couple.

EZRA: Haven't you heard that one bad apple can ruin the whole barrel?

ELIEZER: Well, yes.

EZRA: A little yeast makes all the dough rise?

ELIEZER: Well...yes.

EZRA: And this is not an isolated case. There must be hundreds, maybe thousands of marriages between God's people and other races.

ELIEZER: Hey, maybe it's not so bad. Maybe all the heathen women are learning to respect God.

EZRA: Read your history. The road to righteousness is narrow and difficult. The road to evil is wide and easy. I have reports of the activities of the men of Israel. Already, they are forgetting the decrees of God.

ELIEZER: So remind them.

EZRA: Don't you see? We were taken into captivity for the very sin now being committed! We must end this matter, now! I have prayed and confessed our sin to God.

ELIEZER: OUR sin? YOU didn't do anything wrong!

EZRA: If the people of Israel sin, the leaders have also sinned. We must make this right. Call all the people together.

ELIEZER: Now?

EZRA: This very second!

ELIEZER: But it's raining. Cats and dogs. Even stronger than that. Horses and cows. We'll get pneumonia!

EZRA: Which is worse, a few sniffles or the destruction of Israel? Call the people!

ELIEZER: OK. But they aren't going to like it.

ELIEZER: They would worry about WEATHER when they face the wrath of GOD? *(To himself.)* Dumb, dumb, dumb.

KEEP ON KEEPING ON

SCRIPTURE: Nehemiah 1—2:10; 4—6

SUGGESTED TOPICS: Perseverance; reliance on God

BIBLE BACKGROUND

Nehemiah was cupbearer to the king. This was a much more important job than simply serving beverages to the king. It was even more involved than being a food taster to ensure the king was not poisoned. Being in close proximity to the king, the cupbearer often became a confidant of and advisor to the king. Rule number one for the cupbearer was: always look happy. The king wanted pleasant countenances surrounding him. If you could not control your visage, you might lose your head completely. Therefore, when Nehemiah appeared downhearted before Artaxerxes (see Nehemiah 2:1,2), Nehemiah had a great deal to fear. Not only was he already in danger of death, but he then compounded the danger by asking for a leave of absence.

Nehemiah's story is one of bravery, wisdom and perseverance. Against all odds, he set out to restore Israel to her former glory. Along the way, he had to contend with ridicule, threats, lies and the sin of his own people.

PERFORMANCE TIPS

1. Suggested props: a table and chairs, papers for Nehemiah to look through.

2. Ezer should appear tired. He has been working long, hard hours.

DISCUSSION QUESTIONS

1. How did Nehemiah show wisdom in his preparations to rebuild Jerusalem?

2. What were some of the obstacles Nehemiah had to overcome in his task?

3. What evidence do we have that Nehemiah had studied the Jewish Scriptures?

4. What are some reasons we should read the Bible?

5. What obstacles do you face in your life? How can you overcome them?

KEEP ON KEEPING ON

CHARACTERS
NEHEMIAH (NEE-eh-MYE-uh)
EZER (EE-zer)

PRONUNCIATION GUIDE
Sanballat (san-BAL-lut)
Sousa (SOO-suh)

EZER: *(Enters, brushing off clothes.)* What a dirty job!

NEHEMIAH: But somebody has to do it.

EZER: I like that. "It's a dirty job, but somebody has to do it." That could be a famous quote someday. I think I'll write it down. *(Looks around for pen and paper.)*

NEHEMIAH: There are more pressing matters at hand.

EZER: True. I'll write it down later.

NEHEMIAH: Now then. What are the reports?

EZER: The work on the wall is progressing nicely. Should be completely finished today. If it hadn't been for Sanballat, we might already be done.

NEHEMIAH: You know, sometimes I thank God for Sanballat.

EZER: If that's a joke, I missed the punch line. Sanballat's given you nothing but headaches! First, he laughed at you. Told you that you were crazy to think you could actually rebuild the wall.

NEHEMIAH: Every now and then, I thought he might have been right.

EZER: Then, we got reports that he might attack us. So, we've had to work with one hand while we remained armed and ready to fight with the other.

NEHEMIAH: Fortunately, that seems to have been an idle threat.

EZER: Then, when he knows he can't stop the building, he invites you out to have a conference with him. But all the time, he plans to kill you. And you thank God?

NEHEMIAH: Yes. I wonder if we would have had the strength to continue were he not here to remind us that we have enemies all around us.

EZER: *(Shakes head.)* I guess that's one way to look at it. So, now that the wall's done, I guess you'll be heading back to Sousa and that cushy job you had before.

NEHEMIAH: Head back? When there's so much left to do?

EZER: Like what?

NEHEMIAH: Bringing the Law back to the people.

EZER: Well, out here in the old west, we pretty much live by the law of the sword.

NEHEMIAH: If by that curious phrase you mean that whoever HAS power USES it, that's unfortunately true.

EZER: Yeah. Well, that's just the way it is.

NEHEMIAH: But not the way it WILL be. If we are to be a nation, we must remember who we are. We are the chosen people of the Most High God! It's time for us to act like we believe this.

EZER: You can't change people, Nehemiah.

NEHEMIAH: I know *I* can't. But GOD can—and He will! First on my list is this money-lending business. The rich get richer and the poor stay poor. This will change.

EZER: Lots of luck. The one time people NEVER change is if it's going to cost them money. Oh, well. Back to work. It's a dirty job, but that's life. No. That's not the quote I was going to write down. What was it again? "When the going gets tough, the tough get going"? Nope. "It never rains but it pours"? That's not it, either.

NEHEMIAH: God's speed on your dirty job.

EZER: Thanks. Someone's got to do it, you know. *(To himself.)* What WAS that quote? *(Exits.)*

RISKY BUSINESS

SCRIPTURE: Esther 1—6:11

SUGGESTED TOPICS: Courage; thankfulness; humility

BIBLE BACKGROUND

The book of Esther was written to give the history of the Jewish holiday, Purim. It almost did not receive canonical status for the simple reason that God is never directly mentioned in it. In spite of this omission, the book clearly shows how God protects His people. If Vashti had not been banished, Esther would not have been chosen queen. If Esther had not been queen, Mordecai would have had no pipeline to the palace to warn Xerxes of the plot against his life nor to request the second decree (see Esther 8:8-14). And if Esther and Mordecai had not been devoted to their people, nor possessed the courage to risk their lives on their behalf, the evil plot of Haman would have wreaked a terrible fate on God's people living in Persia. God had long ago promised that a faithful remnant would endure, and to fulfill the promise, God protected His people.

PERFORMANCE TIPS

1. Suggested props: a throne, a crown and a scepter for Xerxes.
2. Each scene takes place in the throne room of Xerxes. Have one side of the stage reserved for the vestibule leading to the room. The beginning of Scenes Two and Three take place in the vestibule and then Esther and Haman enter the throne room proper.
3. When Haman is considering headgear in Scene Three, perhaps have three different types of hats for him to try on as he thinks of how he might look. If so, adjust the script to suit the hats you have available.
4. Haman is arrogant. Esther is quietly confident. Keep them in character.
5. During her scene in the vestibule, Esther is frightened. Be sure she gives the appearance of worry (wringing her hands, pacing back and forth, etc.).
6. During the asides, the characters might lean or turn toward the audience to indicate that the other characters do not hear what is said.

DISCUSSION QUESTIONS

1. How did Esther show respect to the king? To Mordecai? To her people?
2. What risks did Esther take by appearing before the king?
3. At the second banquet, Esther had to demonstrate to the king that he had behaved foolishly by allowing Haman to write a decree to have the Jews killed. What risks might she have been taking by doing this?
4. What sorts of things that you are required to do feel risky to you? What might be some of the consequences of taking these risks?
5. Often, an action is worth the risk. That does not diminish the fear we might face in taking the action. What can you do to help keep the fear under control?

Risky Business

CHARACTERS

ESTHER
HAMAN (HAY-man)
XERXES (ZERK-sees)

PRONUNCIATION GUIDE

Mordecai (MOR-duh-kye)

SCENE ONE

HAMAN: (*Strides in.*) O Mighty King, may you live forever.

XERXES: Haman, my most honored advisor. Do you have some advice for me?

HAMAN: O Mighty One, ruler of the Medes and Persians, Conqueror of the World...

XERXES: All that, and more. Come close and bring me your advice.

HAMAN: I am afraid I have most distressing news, O King.

XERXES: Distressing?

HAMAN: Enough to cause one's hair to fall from one's head.

XERXES: Sounds serious. What is it?

HAMAN: There is a certain people in your kingdom, scattered through all the provinces...

XERXES: I should have thought many people were scattered through the provinces.

HAMAN: Yes, many. But only one people are the problem.

XERXES: Speak to me of the problem.

HAMAN: Their laws are different from those of all other people.

XERXES: That is wrong. Everyone should follow MY laws.

HAMAN: Precisely my point, O King. They are of no benefit to you.

XERXES: I shall make a new law, immediately. All people shall obey my laws.

HAMAN: That law is already in place, O King.

XERXES: It is? Then why do these people not obey it?

HAMAN: Because, O King, their laws are different from those of other people.

XERXES: I see. What do you propose I do about it?

HAMAN: Nothing too radical, O King.

XERXES: Good. I don't like radicals.

HAMAN: Here is my plot—I mean, plan. They must be eradicated!

XERXES: Turned into radicals?

HAMAN: No. Eradicated. Wiped out!

XERXES: Ah, yes. Wiped out. How much will this cost?

HAMAN: A mere ten thousand talents of silver should do it. But don't worry. As a special favor to you, I'll pay the cost from my own pocket.

XERXES: Very good of you, but the treasury can afford it. Write out a decree. Word it however you think best. Here, take my ring to seal the decree. That will give it full force of law.

HAMAN: Very good, O King. *(Bows and backs toward exit. Stops to speak aside to audience.)* He fell for it. I don't care about all of the Jews. Just one. Mordecai. He refuses to bow down to me. Well, now I can have him killed LEGALLY! Ha, ha! All the Jews will be destroyed because of him.

SCENE TWO

ESTHER *(pacing):* This is terrible. Terrible! All my people are to be destroyed. Uncle Mordecai was right when he reminded me that I, too, will be killed. Why would Xerxes MAKE such a decree? OK. I'm going in. But Xerxes hasn't invited me. If I go in and he's in a bad mood, he could have me killed! But if I don't, ALL the Jews will be killed! *(Takes deep breath.)* Here goes nothing. *(Steps into throne room.)*

XERXES: *(Sees ESTHER and holds out sceptre.)* Enter and draw near.

ESTHER: *(Enters and touches sceptre.)* My Lord.

XERXES: *(Aside to audience.)* I wonder what's on her mind? It must be important, for her to risk her life this way. *(To ESTHER.)* What do you wish, Queen Esther? You have but to ask and it shall be granted you. Anything up to half of the kingdom.

ESTHER: *(Aside.)* How do I word this? If I sound harsh, he will be displeased, and an angry king is a terrible thing indeed. *(To XERXES.)* If it pleases the king, will he and his advisor, Haman, come to a banquet I am preparing this evening?

XERXES: *(Aside.)* She is putting off her request. I'll humor her. Tonight, I'll ask her again. *(To ESTHER.)* Of course! I shall send for Haman at once. We shall certainly be there.

SCENE THREE

HAMAN: *(To audience.)* I am the second most important man in the kingdom. You want proof? Last night, the queen had a private banquet; today, she's having another. Do you know who was invited? The king and I. That's all. No princes, no foreign royalty. I would be the happiest man in the world were it not for Mordecai. Well, THAT'S about to end. The gallows have already been built. I go in and ask the king for permission to hang Mordecai. What reason do I give? Any one I choose. He is one of those accursed whom the king has already condemned to death. He'll simply meet his just reward a little sooner than the others. Is my hair in place? Good. In to see the king. *(Enters throne room.)*

XERXES: Goodness! Is it time for the banquet, already?

HAMAN: No, O King. I came a bit early.

XERXES: Good! I have something to discuss with you.

HAMAN: My King?

XERXES: There is a man in the kingdom whom I wish to honor.

HAMAN: *(Aside.)* He must mean me. Who else?

XERXES: Everyone in the kingdom must know how much esteem I have for this man.

HAMAN: *(Aside.)* Me! Without doubt, me!

XERXES: You're good with this pageantry stuff. What should I do for this man?

HAMAN: *(Aside.)* Oh! I'm about to be honored. Rapture! And I get to choose the method. Ecstasy! What shall I ask for? *(To XERXES.)* O King, may you live forever.

XERXES: Of course.

HAMAN: This man, of course I have no idea who he may BE, must be displayed royally through the entire city.

XERXES: Yes. Of course.

HAMAN: This man, WHOEVER he may be, won't have good enough clothing for such a procession. So, YOU should give him some of your royal clothing to wear. Something that everyone will recognize as yours.

XERXES: Such as my purple robe?

HAMAN: Perfect! I would look—I mean, HE would look so good in the purple robe. Now then, such a man could not be expected to WALK through the streets.

XERXES: No. That wouldn't look right.

HAMAN: I, that is, HE must ride. But not any old nag. The king's horse.

XERXES: MY horse?

HAMAN: Naturally. You do want to honor me, uh, him?

XERXES: Very well. He shall ride my horse.

HAMAN: What am I thinking? If I—HE is wearing royal robes, he cannot wear any old rag on his head. He'll need something special in the way of headgear.

XERXES: A new top hat?

HAMAN: Hmmmmmm, no. That wouldn't look right.

XERXES: A new stetson?

HAMAN: Hmmmmmm, no. I can't quite see it.

XERXES: I have it! A sombrero with gold threads woven into it!

HAMAN: Hmmmmmm, no. Not quite the right atmosphere. But what am I thinking?

XERXES: *I* don't know. Shall I call for the mind readers?

HAMAN: Only one kind of hat would be suitable for a man wearing royal robes and seated on the royal steed. The king's crown.

XERXES: MY CROWN?

HAMAN: It will only be for a short time, O King.

XERXES: Very well. So shall it be.

HAMAN: Oh dear! An awful thought!

XERXES: What? What is it?

HAMAN: If I'm, that is, the man the king honors is wearing the king's clothing and crown and riding the king's horse, people might think he stole them.

XERXES: That would be unfortunate. He could wear a sign around his neck saying, "The king said I could wear these."

HAMAN: That is one solution. But it might wrinkle the king's robe. Ah!

XERXES: You have another solution?

HAMAN: What do you think of this? You deliver the robe, crown and horse to one of your most noble princes. He takes everything to my, er, the man's house. Then, this most noble prince leads the man whom the king wishes to honor around the streets of the city.

XERXES: That should bring some attention.

HAMAN: Now, we need some kind of proclamation. The noble prince should speak these words: "Here is a man whom the king honors! This is what the king does for the man he esteems!" The noble prince would, of course, repeat this over and over.

XERXES: Excellent! Perfect! Haman, take this crown. Go and get the purple robe and my horse and take them to Mordecai.

HAMAN: To MORDECAI? But HE isn't a noble prince.

XERXES: No, but YOU are. Put the royal crown and robe on Mordecai. Lead him through the city, just as you have said. Do everything just like we've planned.

HAMAN: MORDECAI?

XERXES: Yes. You won't believe this, but many months ago, he overheard a plot against my life and had me warned. Well, in the confusion of the trial and all that, I totally forgot to reward him. If I hadn't been unable to sleep last night, I wouldn't have had my *Book of Chronicles* read to me and I might never have remembered to reward him.

HAMAN: *(Aside.)* Make a note. Invent some kind of sleeping powder to give the king before bedtime.

THIS IS COMFORT?

SCRIPTURE: Selections from Job

SUGGESTED TOPICS: Trust in God; man's inability to understand God perfectly; God's greatness and wisdom

BIBLE BACKGROUND

Job is believed to be one of the oldest books (if not the oldest) of the Old Testament. Its theme is the evil which can fall upon the just as well as the unjust here on earth. Job's comforters contend that his great suffering is obviously the result of some great sin Job has committed. However, Job never wavers from proclaiming his innocence, and ultimately God agrees with him. In the end, all is restored to Job in greater abundance than he'd previously had.

We often hear of "the patience of Job," but his reaction to severe hardship is not an uncommon one. His misery is so great that he practically begs God to kill him and end his suffering. However, in spite of not understanding the cause of his pain, Job places his trust in God and refuses to curse God for his troubles. He does, however, plead his case with God. "If only You would listen, I'd tell you all I've done," he says. God's answer is not gentle. In essence, God says, "Who are you to question Me?" Finally Job recognizes how much greater God is than he had ever imagined. Job willingly submits to God's far greater wisdom, and God heals Job and causes him to prosper again.

PERFORMANCE TIPS

1. Suggested props: Bible-time costumes.

2. Tell the story to the point of Satan's second attack on Job. Then begin the skit.

3. Job sits throughout the skit.

4. After the skit, finish the story by telling God's answer to Job's questions.

DISCUSSION QUESTIONS

1. Why do you think bad things happen to good people? What explanation does the story of Job provide?

2. Even in his worst times, Job trusted God. How can you learn to trust God in tough situations?

3. Sometimes friends do more harm than good in tough situations. If this happens to you, what should you do? Why?

THIS IS COMFORT?

CHARACTERS

JOB
ELIPHAZ (eh-LYE-faz)
BILDAD (BILL-dad)
ZOPHAR (ZOH-far)

(JOB sits with profile to audience; his back is turned toward OTHERS. The THREE FRIENDS stand at a distance.)

JOB: Oh, why? Oh, why was I born? Oh, why do I live?

ELIPHAZ: Poor Job.

BILDAD: I feel so sorry for him.

ZOPHAR: He's lost everything.

JOB: Oh, why? Oh, why was I born? Oh, why do I live?

ELIPHAZ: First, he lost his livestock. If they weren't killed, they were stolen.

BILDAD: Then, that terrible storm. Blew down the house of his oldest boy. And all Job's sons and daughters were in the house at the time. Killed, every last one. Terrible, terrible, I tell you!

ZOPHAR: And now look at him. Stricken with some hideous disease. Boils and sores all over his body. Ugh!

JOB: Oh, why? Oh, why was I born? Oh, why do I live?

ELIPHAZ: Poor Job.

BILDAD: Poor, poor Job.

ZOPHAR: I've got an idea. Let's go and cheer him up. *(OTHERS indicate that ELIPHAZ should go first. ELIPHAZ walks over to JOB.)*

JOB *(head in hands)***:** Oh, why? Oh, why was I born? Oh, why do I live?

ELIPHAZ: Job. Oh, poor Job. Never fear. We're here.

JOB: My good friend, Eliphaz. Is it you?

ELIPHAZ: It is. Oh, Job, look at you. You who have helped so many. When someone's heart was failing, you were always there to encourage him.

JOB: *(Looks up.)* Thank you, Eliphaz.

ELIPHAZ: And now look at you. A little inconvenience and you forget everything you ever said. You hypocrite!

JOB (*stunned*): What?

ELIPHAZ: You sit here moping and feeling sorry for yourself. You know that only the WICKED suffer. Repent, man! You can do it!

JOB: What are you talking about? What sin? What wickedness?

ELIPHAZ: How should I know? But take heart. Be happy. God is doing this for your own good, to correct you. Listen to Him! Repent! *(Walks away.)*

JOB: What do YOU know about ANYTHING? Have you suffered like this? If I had sinned so greatly, wouldn't I KNOW about it? Oh, why was I born? Why can't I just die?

BILDAD: Nice going, Eliphaz. You were no help at all. Watch THIS. *(Walks to JOB.)* Job?

JOB: Bildad? Is that your voice, Bildad, come to comfort me in my time of grief?

BILDAD: It is I, good friend Job. How are you?

JOB: I suffer greatly, Bildad. You can't KNOW how I suffer.

BILDAD: Well, of COURSE you're suffering, dummy. How long will you tell these lies to God?

JOB: *(Looks up, stunned.)* What?

BILDAD: What are you trying to cover up, Job? God doesn't punish the innocent.

JOB: What are you saying?

BILDAD: Isn't it obvious, Job? If you were as good as you pretend to be, don't you think God would notice what's happening and make it better?

JOB: Are you accusing me?

BILDAD: I don't accuse, good friend. I merely point out to you that God doesn't help evil people and He doesn't harm the righteous.

JOB: You're telling me that I have sinned greatly?

BILDAD: You and your children! I don't accuse, Job. I merely say, "If the shoe fits..."

JOB: There might be some truth in what you say.

BILDAD: Well, of course there is.

JOB: But how can a man compare himself with God? No matter how good I've been, is it good enough to compare to Him who can shake the earth from its foundations?

BILDAD: I think you're missing the point. *(Shakes finger.)* Confess your sin.

JOB: How can I confess what I don't know? If God had pointed out sin to me, don't you think I would have begged forgiveness rather than go through this? *(Drops head into hands.)* Oh, why was I born? Why can't I die?

    (BILDAD walks away.)

ZOPHAR (*loudly*): What kind of people ARE you? Have you helped this poor man one iota? *(Walks over to JOB.)*

JOB: Zophar? I hear Zophar's voice. Oh, what a comfort your voice is to me!

ZOPHAR: Job, I've heard everything that was said. All the nonsense...

JOB: Thank you, Zophar.

ZOPHAR: ...that YOU'VE been spouting! Can I just stand here and listen to your lies? When you mock God, shall I just stand here and not put you to shame?

JOB: *(Rubs head wearily.)* I beg your pardon?

ZOPHAR: Don't beg MY pardon. You didn't offend ME. You offended GOD. Beg HIS pardon.

JOB: I don't understand.

ZOPHAR: What's not to understand? You sit there saying, "Poor me. My heart is pure." Oh, if only God would speak. He'd tell you what a despicable liar you are.

JOB: Liar?

ZOPHAR: I know it's difficult to understand. God's wisdom is higher than the heavens and deeper than the depths of hell. You can't even begin to know.

JOB: And YOU can?

ZOPHAR: Apparently better than you. MY animals have not all disappeared. MY children were not all killed. MY body isn't covered with sores. Repent, you foul sinner! Count your blessings that God has given you this reminder of your sin and repent! *(Walks away.)*

JOB: *(Turns and calls after the OTHERS.)* No doubt you three are the only wise people on earth. I'm sure, when you die, all wisdom will pass away with you.

ELIPHAZ: *(Crosses arms.)* Well, I never.

JOB: No doubt my intellect is inferior to yours. I must be so stupid compared to the three of you.

BILDAD *(chin up)***:** There's no need to be sarcastic!

JOB: In fact, the only things on earth smarter than you three are the birds and animals. They know how the world works better than YOU do.

ZOPHAR: *(Shakes head.)* How rude!

JOB: I would love to speak with God! I want to reason with Him. But you three would show much more wisdom if you'd only shut up.

ELIPHAZ: I've never been so insulted in my life.

BILDAD: That's gratitude for you. After all we did for him.

ZOPHAR: You just can't reason with some people.

JOB: *(Turns back on OTHERS, drops head into hands.)* Oh, why? Oh, why was I born? Oh, why do I live?

THE BIG BOOK OF BIBLE SKITS

THE WRITING ON THE WALL

SCRIPTURE: Daniel 5

SUGGESTED TOPICS: Obeying God; honesty; courage

BIBLE BACKGROUND

Because of the sin of Israel and Judah, God allowed both to be taken into captivity by Assyria and Babylon respectively. When Babylon conquered a country, the royalty, nobility and well-educated were either killed or carried off in captivity. These captives were then trained in the ways of the Chaldeans so they could serve the king of Babylon. The commoners were left to tend the land under the supervision of governors placed there by Babylon.

Among the young men who were carried off for training was Daniel. In spite of the attempts of Babylon to indoctrinate him into its culture, he remained faithful to the God of Israel. His responsible actions were honored by God who granted him such great wisdom and insight that he soon rose to a position of influence and respect in Babylon. For many years, Daniel served as a trusted advisor to King Nebuchadnezzar, but when Belshazzar succeeded to the throne, Daniel's value was overlooked until the night of a fateful banquet.

PERFORMANCE TIPS

1. Suggested props: table, dishes (preferably unbreakable, some wrapped in foil to simulate gold and silver), chairs, crown for Belshazzar.

2. When repeating the name of Nebuchadnezzar, the tone should be solemn, honoring his memory.

3. For comedic purposes, Belshazzar and the wise men can let their knees knock in an exaggerated manner when they see the writing on the wall.

4. If you wish, continue the skit by having Daniel enter and interpret the writing. If not, finish the story either by reading it from the Bible or simply telling it.

5. Consider introducing the skit by telling the story of Daniel's instruction in Babylonian ways and the telling of Nebuchadnezzar's dream. Explain that the new king either didn't know about Daniel or had forgotten how much he had helped Nebuchadnezzar.

DISCUSSION QUESTIONS

1. In Daniel 1, Daniel and his three friends refused to eat certain things from the king's table. Why?

2. If the king had been angry about this, what might have happened to the four young men?

3. Belshazzar did not know about Daniel, even though he had helped Belshazzar's father. Why might Belshazzar have forgotten about Daniel?

4. What was Daniel's reward for telling the meaning of the writing? What was the danger in telling Belshazzar what the writing meant?

5. What are some situations in which a kid your age might need courage? How can someone find the necessary courage?

THE WRITING ON THE WALL

CHARACTERS

BELSHAZZAR (bell-SHAZ-ur)
WISE MAN ONE
WISE MAN TWO
WISE MAN THREE
SERVANT
QUEEN

PRONUNCIATION GUIDE

Mene (MEE-nee)
Nebuchadnezzar (NEB-uh-kad-NEZ-er)
Parsin (PAR-sun)
Tekel (TEE-kul)

BELSHAZZAR: Gentlemen, gentlemen, gentlemen! Unaccustomed as I am to public speaking, nonetheless I say this: Eat, drink, be merry! For tomorrow we diet! But seriously, eat and drink all you want. This feast has seven days. Or more, if we're having FUN. Thank you. *(Sits down beside WISE MAN.)*

WISE MAN ONE: A fine feast, my liege.

BELSHAZZAR: Thank you. But I can't help but feel it's missing something.

WISE MAN TWO: Good food. Good wine. What else?

BELSHAZZAR: I don't know. Better entertainment, perhaps.

WISE MAN THREE: If I may speak, my lord?

BELSHAZZAR: Please do.

WISE MAN THREE: The food and drink are excellent. Likewise, the entertainment. The problem lies in the place settings.

BELSHAZZAR: The DISHES?

WISE MAN ONE: He may be on to something.

WISE MAN TWO: True.

BELSHAZZAR: But these are the palace's best dishes!

WISE MAN THREE: That may be. But we've all SEEN them before. They were used at all the feasts given by your esteemed father, Nebuchadnezzar.

BELSHAZZAR and WISE MEN: *(Rise and place hands over hearts.)* Nebuchadnezzar. *(ALL sit.)*

WISE MAN THREE: You need something different.

BELSHAZZAR: Would you have me go to the peasants and beg for dishes?

WISE MAN THREE: Of course not. To use peasants' dishes would insult your guests. I do not propose a solution. I merely point out the problem.

BELSHAZZAR: I see. If I get the potters working on new dishes immediately...

WISE MAN ONE: They will not be ready until the next feast, my liege.

BELSHAZZAR: It takes that long?

WISE MAN ONE: I'm afraid so.

BELSHAZZAR: Then what can I do to liven up THIS feast?

WISE MAN TWO: If I may be so impertinent, my king?

BELSHAZZAR: Go ahead. Impert.

WISE MAN TWO: I would suggest that his majesty change the dishes.

BELSHAZZAR: But with WHAT? These are the best in the palace!

WISE MAN TWO: But not in the LAND, my king.

WISE MAN ONE: Ah.

WISE MAN THREE: Of course.

BELSHAZZAR: Look! I know you guys are paid to be mysterious, but could you give me a hint? Is it bigger than a bread box?

WISE MAN ONE: In the museum, my liege...

WISE MAN TWO: Treasures from other lands, my king...

WISE MAN THREE: Removed, my lord, by your esteemed father, Nebuchadnezzar.

BELSHAZZAR and WISE MEN: *(Rise and place hands over hearts.)* Nebuchadnezzar. *(ALL sit.)*

BELSHAZZAR: What about the museum?

WISE MAN TWO: Included in the treasures are dishes of gold, silver, brass, iron, wood and stone...

WISE MAN ONE: Taken from the Temple in Jerusalem...

WISE MAN THREE: By your illustrious father, Nebuchadnezzar.

BELSHAZZAR and WISE MEN: *(Rise and place hands over hearts.)* Nebuchadnezzar. *(ALL sit.)*

BELSHAZZAR: So?

WISE MAN ONE: Have the vessels brought to the feast.

WISE MAN TWO: Place them before your wives and concubines and princes.

WISE MAN THREE: And, of course, your most illustrious majesty himself.

BELSHAZZAR: Eat and drink from the dishes of a god? What a splendid idea! I, of course, will have the gold dishes.

WISE MAN ONE: Naturally.

BELSHAZZAR: Wood and stone will be good enough for the women.

WISE MEN: Naturally.

BELSHAZZAR: Even as you have suggested, let it be done.

> *(SERVANT brings in dishes. Party continues.)*

BELSHAZZAR: *(Stares at wall, grabs throat and screams.)* Aaaagh!

WISE MAN ONE: What is it, my liege?

WISE MAN TWO: He must have something stuck in his throat.

WISE MAN THREE: Quick. The hemlock maneuver.

WISE MAN TWO: You mean, the Heimlich maneuver.

WISE MAN THREE: No. The hemlock maneuver. Pour hemlock down his throat. Hemlock is poison; he throws up; his throat is clear.

WISE MAN ONE: But what if he dies from the poison?

WISE MAN THREE: At least it's faster than choking to death.

WISE MAN TWO: True. Bring hemlock!

BELSHAZZAR: No! *(Points.)* Look!

WISE MEN: *(Look in direction he points, grab throats and scream.)* Aaagh!

BELSHAZZAR: That hand! Those words! What can it mean?

WISE MAN ONE: Eenie, meenie...Looks like some kind of children's rhyme.

WISE MAN TWO: That's not what it says! It says MENE, MENE, TEKEL, PARSIN. It's calling someone cruel for tickling a parson. Not the king, surely. But it IS his wall.

WISE MAN THREE: That's not what it means. It would be spelled differently if it was talking about being nasty. Aha. It's a warning about an uprising. Many, many tekels will be uprising.

WISE MAN ONE: What's a tekel?

WISE MAN THREE: I don't explain everything. I just read it.

WISE MAN TWO: Well, I don't like your reading any better than mine.

WISE MAN THREE: Nonetheless, we must warn the king. My lord, the tekels are about to revolt.

BELSHAZZAR: The only revolting thing here is you three. You're supposed to be smart. What does this mean?

QUEEN (*entering*)**:** What is all the commotion in here? We women in the next room can't here ourselves think.

BELSHAZZAR: *(Points to wall.)* Look!

QUEEN: What? Graffiti? Honestly! You men get a little wine in you and you're worse than children! You've chiselled that right into the wall. It'll take weeks to sand that out!

BELSHAZZAR: But we didn't do it!

QUEEN (*sarcastically*)**:** Oh? I suppose a giant hand came down and wrote it?

BELSHAZZAR: Yes.

QUEEN: Oh, really. You've been drinking and then want me to believe a crazy story like....Wait a minute. You're serious, aren't you?

BELSHAZZAR (*nodding head*)**:** Uh-huh.

QUEEN (*turning to WISE MEN*)**:** Well? You're the wise guys. What does it mean?

WISE MAN ONE: As near as we can tell, it's either a children's rhyme...

WISE MAN TWO: Or some nasty person is tickling a parson...

WISE MAN THREE: Or the tekels are planning a rebellion.

QUEEN: You three are like garlic in a leg of mutton...

WISE MEN: Huh?

QUEEN: You stink up the joint. Listen, Belshazzar, you want to know what that writing means?

BELSHAZZAR: Of course I do.

QUEEN: Then deep-six these losers and do what I tell you. There's a man who used to advise your father, Nebuchadnezzar.

BELSHAZZAR and WISE MEN: *(Rise and place hands over hearts.)* Nebuchadnezzar. *(ALL sit.)*

QUEEN: This guy understands dreams before people even tell him what the dream was. Go find him. He'll tell you what it means. But I'm warning you ahead of time, you may not like what he says. He's not always popular, but he's always honest.

THE BIRTH OF JOHN

SCRIPTURE: Matthew 1:18-25; Luke 1:5-45,57-66

SUGGESTED TOPICS: The Savior; responding to God's Word

BIBLE BACKGROUND

The time for the Savior's birth was almost at hand. But first, God had a few necessary announcements.

God does nothing on the sly. If something is important for us to know, God ensures we will have access to the knowledge. The birth of the Savior was the beginning of the most important series of events in the history of mankind. God did not want this to be misunderstood. Among the things God wanted understood at the Savior's birth were the prophecies which were being fulfilled.

For example, prophets had foretold that Elijah must return (see Malachi 4:5,6). John the Baptist was a partial fulfillment of this prophecy—not that John was Elijah, but his ministry and spirit was so like Elijah's it was correct to say, "Elijah has come and will come" (Matthew 17:10-12).

To further fulfill prophecy, the Savior must be born of a virgin (see Isaiah 7:14). God wanted the people involved to understand God's plan and their roles in it. Since people do not have God's understanding, He sent His messengers to tell Zechariah, Mary and Joseph what they must do.

PERFORMANCE TIPS

1. .Suggested props: a slate and chalk or paper and felt pen for Zechariah. (Have Zechariah write in large letters "His name is John" as directed in the skit.)

2. During the skit Zechariah is struck mute. The person playing the part of Zechariah should be prepared to pantomime a need for writing materials.

3. The skit is written with Mary as an off-stage character. If desired, Mary could be visible but without spoken lines. Or, write lines for Mary to use in response to the angel and to Elizabeth. Refer to Luke 1:26-45.

DISCUSSION QUESTIONS

1. Girls, suppose you were Mary. How would you feel if you learned you would have a baby before you were married?

2. Boys, suppose you were Joseph. Would you have believed Mary's story about the angel? Why or why not?

3. Why did God send angels to speak to Zechariah, Mary and Joseph?

4. What are some ways God speaks to you today? When might it be hard to believe God's messages?

THE BIRTH OF JOHN

CHARACTERS

ZECHARIAH (zek-uh-RYE-uh)

ANGEL

ELIZABETH

NARRATOR

ZECHARIAH: Here I am in the Temple. What an honor to serve God in this way. I just wish Elizabeth and I had some children who could continue as priests before the Lord. But, I guess you can't have everything. Now then, where is that incense? Ah! There it is. Wait a minute! Who are you?

ANGEL: I am an angel of the Lord, Zechariah. I have come to deliver a message to you from God.

ZECHARIAH: You know, just the other day, I was telling Elizabeth that we lived in a boring village where nothing ever happened. Now, I come into the Temple, and I meet a crazy person.

ANGEL: I am not a crazy person, Zechariah. I am an angel of the Lord. I repeat, I have a message for you from God. Do you want to hear it or not?

ZECHARIAH: I might as well. I have nothing to lose. Go ahead crazy person—I mean, angel. What's the message?

ANGEL: The Lord has heard the prayer that you and your wife, Elizabeth, have been praying for many years. God is going to give you a son.

ZECHARIAH: Hold it! You don't need to go any farther. I know you're not an angel. That bit's been done before.

ANGEL: I beg your pardon?

ZECHARIAH: Does the name Abraham mean anything to you? He was very old and so was Sarah, but God promised to give them a son.

ANGEL: So? What's your problem?

ZECHARIAH: Well now. That's called a miracle. Do you know what a miracle is? It's something that only happens once. God already did that one. So now I'm SURE you're a crazy person.

ANGEL: What makes you think a miracle can only happen once?

ZECHARIAH: Well, if something happens again and again, it's hardly unusual. It's natural. And miracles are supernatural.

ANGEL: How long ago did this miracle happen to Abraham?

ZECHARIAH: Well, I'm not sure. About two thousand years ago?

ANGEL: Do you call something that happens once every two thousand years commonplace?

ZECHARIAH: Well, no...

The Big Book of Bible Skits ©1997 Gospel Light. Permission to photocopy granted.

ANGEL: Then please stop interrupting me and let me get on with the message. *(Formally.)* You will have a son and you will name him John. He will never drink wine nor strong drink. From the time he is conceived, he will be filled with the Holy Spirit of God. Because of him, many of the children of Israel will turn back to God. He will speak with the spirit and the power of Elijah to prepare the people to meet the Lord.

ZECHARIAH: *(Pause.)* I must admit, that is some message. My son—a great prophet and preacher. But there is still the problem of my age, and Elizabeth's. How can I be sure you are an angel? What happens if I run out and tell everybody an angel told me I'll have a son, and three years later, nothing? People will tap their heads when they see me and say, "There goes crazy, old Zechariah who talks to angels." So, if you don't mind, I'll hold off on the birth announcements for a while.

ANGEL: Zechariah! I am Gabriel, who stands in the presence of God. I was sent to speak to you. But don't worry—you will not be making any birth announcements. As a sign to you that what I say is, indeed, a message from God, from this moment until all these things have happened, you will not be able to speak.

NARRATOR: And at that very moment, Zechariah became mute. He could not utter a word, not even when he left Jerusalem and returned home....

ELIZABETH: Hello, my husband. Welcome home. Did you have a nice time in Jerusalem? What's the matter? *(ZECHARIAH pretends to write something.)* Wait! A game! We're going to play a guessing game. OK, give me a clue. You're writing something. A book. This is the name of a book. No? A writer. That's it. You're a writer. No? You're not very good at this game. You just do the same thing over and over. Wait! *(Pause.)* This ISN'T a guessing game. You want to write something and you need a pen and paper. Well, why didn't you say so? Speak up, man. What is it? *(Pause.)* You want some paper and pen.

NARRATOR: The angel Gabriel visited others besides Zechariah.

ANGEL: Fear not, Mary, for you have found great favor with God. I am the angel, Gabriel, and have been sent to bring you this good news. You will bear a child and shall call His name Jesus. *(Pause.)* Yes, I am well aware you have never been with a man. But the Spirit of God will come upon you, and the Holy Child born of you shall be called the Son of God.

NARRATOR: Bubbling with excitement, Mary went to visit her elderly relative, Elizabeth.

ELIZABETH: Hello, Mary. Why, you look positively radiant. What brings you all this way to visit? Not that I'm complaining, mind you. That husband of mine hasn't said a word since he came back from Jerusalem six months ago. But you don't have to tell me why you're here. I know you're going to have a baby, too. A baby specially blessed by God. And, Mary, the baby inside me jumped for joy when I heard your voice. But I'm hurt. Why didn't you invite us to the wedding? *(Pause.)* What do you mean, there hasn't been a wedding yet? But you and Joseph—NOT you and Joseph? Does Joseph know about this? Come into the house. We have a lot of catching up to do. When are you planning to tell Joseph about it? Do you think he'll believe you?

NARRATOR: Mary stayed with Elizabeth for about three months. In the meantime, God was making SURE that Joseph would believe what Mary told him.

ANGEL: Joseph! I am an angel of the Lord. Do not be afraid to take Mary to be your wife. The child inside her is from the Holy Spirit. This baby will be a boy, and you shall name Him Jesus, for He will save His people from their sins.

NARRATOR: Soon, Elizabeth's child was born.

ELIZABETH: *(Talks to someone offstage.)* Yes, we're excited and so pleased. Just think. Already he is eight days old. *(Pause.)* We're going to name him John. *(Pause.)* I know that no one in our family has ever had that name. But John will be his name. You'll have to ask his father. *(Sighs.)* Zechariah, our friends think it's strange that you haven't spoken since you got back from Jerusalem, nine months ago. They think it's even stranger that we're naming the baby John. Please tell them, Zechariah. *(Sighs again.)* I mean, write for them. Everyone look. *(She points over Zechariah's shoulder as he writes.)* He's writing, "His...name...is...John."

ZECHARIAH: At last! I can speak again! Praise God! It's just as the angel said it would be! God is sending us a Savior, and this child will prepare His way! Oh, praise be to God in the highest...

ELIZABETH: *(Shrugs.)* Well, there goes the peace and quiet.

CHRISTMAS QUIZ

SCRIPTURE: Isaiah 9:6; 53:3-6; Jeremiah 23:5,6; Micah 5:2; Matthew 2:1,2,11; Luke 1:30-32; 2:8,25-30,36-38

SUGGESTED TOPICS: Fulfillment of prophecy; coming of the Savior; God's love for His people

BIBLE BACKGROUND

From the moment of the Fall, God had a plan for our salvation. The Old Testament sets the scene for God's dealing with His people and people's inability to live up to God's standards. Throughout history, one fact stands out above all others. If people were ever to be rescued from sin and the vast damages it has caused, God would have to do it Himself. This is the good news, the gospel of our Lord Jesus Christ. God loved the world so much that He gave His one and only Son (see John 3:16). Without the willing sacrifice of the perfect Son of God (i.e., God Himself), all people would be condemned to eternal punishment. But in the fullness of time, the Savior came to all who would receive Him.

PERFORMANCE TIPS

1. Suggested props: loud sports jacket and tie for the Quiz Master; Bible, chair and table for the judge; question cards for the Quiz Master; bells or buzzers for the contestants.

2. Have the teacher play the part of the Quiz Master. If possible, have the judge played by the pastor, an elder, a deacon or some other prominent person in the church. Contestants may respond as a group, or you may designate teams or individuals to compete against each other. Be creative!

3. Much of the skit will have to be ad-libbed, as the knowledge levels of each class will be different. Don't be afraid to give clues if necessary.

4. Answers may be oral or written. You might want to make up answer cards to give students multiple-choice answers and have the students hold up what they believe is the correct answer.

5. The skit could be used in conjunction with a Christmas party.

6. To extend the quiz, supplement with extra questions found on page 200 or write your own.

DISCUSSION QUESTIONS

1. What special event do we celebrate at Christmas? Why?

2. Why did God need to send a Savior?

3. Why was it important for God to give Old Testament promises and prophecies about the Savior?

4. What is sin? Is there sin in your life? Do you know anyone who never sinned?

5. How can you show God you are glad for His great gift given to us on that first Christmas?

EXTRA QUESTIONS FOR CHRISTMAS QUIZ

1. Why was Jesus born in a stable? (No room in the inn. See Luke 2:7.)

2. To whom did the angel tell the meaning of the name "Jesus"? (Joseph. See Matthew 1:21.) And why did the angel tell Joseph to give Him this name? (He would save His people from their sins. See Matthew 1:21.)

3. Who was the king in Jerusalem around the time of Jesus' birth? (Herod. See Matthew 2:1,2.) And how did Herod say he felt about the new King? (He said he wanted to worship Him. See Matthew 2:8.)

4. What was the name of the angel who came to Zechariah to tell him about the birth of John? (Gabriel. See Luke 1:19.)

5. How long did Mary stay with her cousin Elizabeth when she went to visit? (Three months. See Luke 1:56.)

CHRISTMAS QUIZ

CHARACTERS

QUIZ MASTER

JUDGE

CONTESTANTS (All audience members)

QUIZ MASTER: Welcome to everyone's favorite game show, Holiday Quiz! I'm your favorite game show host, *(give name).* Our contestants today are *(name contestants).* This week's special holiday is...

(Give CONTESTANTS time to answer.)

QUIZ MASTER: Correct! Everybody scores one point! Now the contest really begins. First question, who is the Messiah?

(Give CONTESTANTS time to answer.)

QUIZ MASTER: Excellent! We have some truly great contestants today. Now, a multiple answer. For one point each, what are the names given to the Messiah in Isaiah, chapter 9?

(Give CONTESTANTS time to answer.)

QUIZ MASTER: This one's too tough for me. Judge, may we have the official answer?

JUDGE: *(Reads Isaiah 9:6.)*

QUIZ MASTER: Wow! There are four names there. How many got all four? OK. Next question. God promised to send the Messiah as Savior. According to Isaiah, why was God going to send the Savior?

(Give CONTESTANTS time to answer.)

QUIZ MASTER: What about it, Judge?

JUDGE: *(Reads Isaiah 53:3-6.)*

QUIZ MASTER: Wow! That's God's love for you! Ready for the next question? Alright! Who would be the Savior's most famous earthly ancestor?

(Give CONTESTANTS time to answer.)

QUIZ MASTER: Well, judge, right or wrong?

JUDGE: *(Reads Jeremiah 23:5,6.)*

QUIZ MASTER: So it was David. Now, the topic is geography. According to the book of Micah, in what town would the Savior be born?

(Give CONTESTANTS time to answer.)

QUIZ MASTER: Everybody sounds sure. Judge?

JUDGE: *(Reads Micah 5:2.)*

QUIZ MASTER: Lots of points to be awarded on that one. Now, shortly before the Savior was born, people wondered WHEN He would be born. God revealed this secret to someone. Who was the first person God told?

(CONTESTANTS answer. If nobody has an answer, give clues.)

QUIZ MASTER: Would God give such important news to a young girl? Judge?

JUDGE: *(Reads Luke 1:30-32.)*

QUIZ MASTER: So God does tell things to ordinary people. Now for an easy question. True or false? Jesus was born in a manger.

(Give CONTESTANTS time to answer.)

QUIZ MASTER: Judge?

JUDGE: Jesus was BORN in a stable and LAID in a manger. False.

QUIZ MASTER: Oh, ho! A trick question. You have to listen closely in this game. On the night Jesus was born, some people were outside in the dark. Who were they and what were they doing?

(Give CONTESTANTS time to answer.)

QUIZ MASTER: They sound pretty sure of themselves. How about it, Judge?

JUDGE: *(Reads Luke 2:8.)*

QUIZ MASTER: These contestants are too smart. We need a hard question. Aha! Here's one. When Jesus was forty days old, Mary and Joseph took him to the Temple to dedicate him. They also took an offering. What was their offering?

(Give CONTESTANTS time to answer.)

QUIZ MASTER: I thought that might stump you. Judge, what's the answer?

JUDGE: *(Reads Luke 2:24.)*

QUIZ MASTER: There, now we all know. Another tough question. Two people saw Jesus in the Temple: an elderly man and an elderly woman. What were their names?

(Give CONTESTANTS time to answer.)

QUIZ MASTER: Was anybody right?

JUDGE: *(Reads Luke 2:25-30 and 2:36-38.)*

QUIZ MASTER: Now, for another easy question. How many wise men came to see Jesus in the stable?

(Give CONTESTANTS time to answer.)

QUIZ MASTER: Let's hear the correct answer, Judge.

JUDGE: *(Reads Matthew 2:1,2 and 11. Emphasizes the word "house.")* That means NONE of the wise men saw Jesus in the stable.

QUIZ MASTER: There you have it. The three wise men saw Jesus in a house.

JUDGE: You weren't listening. The Bible doesn't say THREE wise men. It just says "wise men." It never tells us how many.

QUIZ MASTER: Oh. So I guess I have things to learn about Christmas, too. Let's tally up the scores and hand out the prizes.

HEROD

SCRIPTURE: Matthew 2

SUGGESTED TOPICS: The Savior; God's protection

BIBLE BACKGROUND

The fullness of time had come. The Savior was born in a small stable in an insignificant town in a conquered country. Rejoicing was heard throughout the heavens and in a few selected places in the world.

God sent His Son to save the world. All the world should have rejoiced; however, not everyone was excited about the good news. Herod was so concerned about the possibility he would lose prestige or power, that he feared the coming of Jesus, the Messiah. He was not prepared to change his ways, to surrender control of his life. To Herod, the good news was the worst news.

PERFORMANCE TIPS

1. Suggested props: crown for Herod, overcoats and sunglasses for spies.

2. Herod is an angry character and should speak loudly and forcefully.

3. If time permits, ask your group to work together to write a preamble to the skit. The wise men could discuss what they will need to bring for the long journey. Or, write dialog for Herod's meeting with the wise men.

4. After the skit, finish the story. Describe how God protected His Son or read Matthew 2:13-23.

DISCUSSION QUESTIONS

1. Read Micah 5:2. What does this verse tell about Bethlehem?

2. How many wise men came to see Jesus? Read Matthew 2:1,2 to check your answer.

3. What was Herod's response to the birth of Jesus? What was the response of the wise men? What is your response?

4. How can you show love and praise to God for His gift of Jesus?

HEROD

CHARACTERS
HEROD
SPY ONE
SPY TWO
SPY THREE

SCENE ONE

HEROD: Spies! Get in here! On the double!

SPY ONE: With the greatest of haste.

SPY TWO: Never wasting a second.

SPY THREE: At the instant of your command,

SPIES *(together)*: Your Highness.

HEROD: What's going on here?

SPY ONE: Concerning...

SPY TWO: ...what...

SPY THREE: ...matter...

SPIES *(together)*: Your Highness?

HEROD: What do you mean, concerning what matter? All of Jerusalem is in an uproar. I can hear it from here, through the palace windows. What's going on out there? Has Caesar declared a holiday that nobody told me about? Because if that's happened, heads will roll!

SPY ONE: We can assure you...

SPY TWO: ...no holiday has been declared...

SPY THREE: ...behind your most majestic back,

SPIES *(together)*: Your Highness.

HEROD: Then what's all the ruckus about?

SPY ONE: Wise men from the East...

SPY TWO: ...here, in Jerusalem...

SPY THREE: ...camels and donkeys carrying great wealth...

SPIES *(together)*: Your Highness.

HEROD: Wise men from the East. Hmm. Carrying great wealth. Hmm. They probably want to consult me about an important matter and brought me a few little gifts, as befits my great station in life. Find out what it is they want.

SPY ONE: With the greatest of haste.

SPY TWO: Never wasting a second.

SPY THREE: At the instant of your command,

SPIES *(together)*: Your Highness. *(Spies exit.)*

SCENE TWO

HEROD: This is most disconcerting, most distressing, most annoying! Spies, get in here!

SPY ONE: With the greatest of haste.

SPY TWO: Never wasting a second.

SPY THREE: At the instant of your command,

SPIES *(together)*: Your Highness.

HEROD: Why are those wise men asking, "Where is He, born King of the Jews?"

SPY ONE: Interrogative...

SPY TWO: ...requesting information...

SPY THREE: ...concerning the birth of the King of the Jews,

SPIES *(together)*: Your Highness.

HEROD: I know that! But I'M the king of the Jews!

SPIES *(together)*: Oh, yeah. We forgot.

HEROD: Well DON'T forget it! Or heads will roll! Well? What did they mean by that crack about king of the Jews?

SPY ONE: Perhaps they wish to know the date of your birth...

SPY TWO: ...to celebrate it with a great feast...

SPY THREE: ...and honor you with great riches,

SPIES *(together)*: Your Highness.

HEROD: Yeah! That's it. They do want to give me presents. No! That's not it! They didn't ask about MY birthday. They asked, "WHERE is He born King of the Jews?" They KNOW where I live. EVERYONE knows where I live. What other king could they be talking about? I must know! If there is somebody else claiming to be king, and if you're hiding him from me, heads will roll!

SPY ONE: Never in the world...

SPY TWO: ...would we do such a thing.

SPY THREE: That would be treason,

SPIES *(together)*: Your Highness.

HEROD: Then WHO is this king they're talking about?

SPIES *(softly, together)*: The Messiah.

HEROD: The who? Quit mumbling! Speak up, or heads will roll!

SPY ONE: There has been much talk lately...

SPY TWO: ...of one to be born from the family of David...

SPY THREE: ...to rule over Israel and save her from her enemies,

SPIES *(together)*: Your Highness.

HEROD: Well, nobody like that was born in THIS palace.

SPY ONE: Truer words...

SPY TWO: ...were never...

SPY THREE: ...spoken before,

SPIES *(together)*: Your Highness.

HEROD: Messiah, huh? Well, I'll show Him a thing or two about being king. I just have to find Him. If He wasn't born here, where was He born? Messiah—religion! Bring the chief priests and scribes to see me!

SPY ONE: With the greatest of haste.

SPY TWO: Never wasting a second.

SPY THREE: At the instant of your command,

SPIES *(together)*: Your Highness. *(Spies exit.)*

HEROD: That's why I'm king—because I'm smarter than anybody else. I'll tell those wisemen to search for the child so I can worship Him, too. And when they report back, I'll send my troops to find this King. And one head will roll.

The Big Book of Bible Skits ©1997 Gospel Light. Permission to photocopy granted.

TEMPTATION IN THE WILDERNESS

SCRIPTURE: Matthew 4:1-11; Luke 4:1-3

SUGGESTED TOPICS: Temptation; handling conflict; wisdom

BIBLE BACKGROUND

Near the age of thirty, Jesus was baptized by John, and was almost ready to start His ministry. First, the Holy Spirit led Him into the wilderness to be alone with His Father for forty days.

Jesus knew His ministry on Earth was to reconcile people to God. In order to have this happen, men and women had to listen to Him and then recognize their sin. How was He to accomplish this?

Satan had many suggestions. Recognizing Jesus' great hunger after forty days of fasting, Satan proposed that Jesus make bread to satisfy His need. But Jesus knew that "man does not live by bread alone." So Satan had another idea. Dazzle the populace with stunts like leaping from the Temple. But Jesus knew thrill-seekers would only follow so long as new thrills could be found. Then, Satan offered political power. Take over the world. Accept Satan's power over the affairs of this world. Jesus knew better. People must see themselves as lost sheep, needing to be redeemed through the only possible method, His death.

PERFORMANCE TIPS

1. Suggested props: several rocks.
2. Portraying Jesus may be difficult. To show righteous anger, Jesus should be firm and controlled, but not sarcastic.
3. Satan is a formidable adversary. Do not portray him as foolish.
4. Before the skit, briefly tell the story of Jesus' baptism (see Matthew 3:1-6,13-17). Then say, "After His baptism, Jesus went into the desert to pray for forty days. Here's what happened at the end of the forty days."

DISCUSSION QUESTIONS

1. Is being tempted the same as sinning? Why or why not?
2. In what ways are you tempted? What can you do when you are tempted?
3. Read 1 Corinthians 10:13. How would you say this verse in your own words? What advice does the verse give?

TEMPTATION IN THE WILDERNESS

CHARACTERS

SATAN

JESUS

SATAN: Hello there, young man. This desert is a pretty desolate place. At least there's no traffic. Have you been here very long?

JESUS: I've been here for forty days.

SATAN: My, my. Forty days. Say! Aren't You that fellow who thinks He's the Son of God?

JESUS: I don't think I'm the Son of God.

SATAN: That's strange. You look just like that Jesus of Nazareth fellow.

JESUS: There's a good reason for that. I am Jesus of Nazareth.

SATAN: Well then. You ARE the fellow who thinks He's the Son of God.

JESUS: No, I don't think that. I KNOW that I'm the Son of God.

SATAN: Oh, well, let's not quibble over words. But what are You doing out here in the wilderness? I thought You would be among the people You came to save.

JESUS: I have not yet begun my ministry. I came out to the wilderness to be alone with My Father before I begin.

SATAN: Funny. I don't see anybody else. Where's Your father? I would have thought he would be at home in the carpentry shop.

JESUS: I am referring to My Father in heaven.

SATAN: Forty days is a long time to be alone. You'd need lots of food to last that long out here. What did You carry it in?

JESUS: I didn't bring any food with Me. I have fasted for these forty days.

SATAN: You didn't bring any food? You must be very hungry by now. But I guess if You're the Son of God, You don't get hungry.

JESUS: You know very well that I am hungry.

SATAN: I do? Well then, look at those rocks. They almost look like loaves of bread. If You really are the Son of God, change the rocks to bread and feed Yourself. I bet that any bread God's Son personally made would be the best bread that anyone in the world ever tasted.

JESUS: It is written, "Man does not live on bread alone, but on every word that comes from the mouth of God."

SATAN: Yes, I've heard that. Wait! I want to show You something I think You will find very interesting. Don't move. I want to take You on a little trip. *(Pause, then SATAN stretches out his hand.)* Since You're the Son of God, You must recognize this place.

JESUS: Certainly. The Temple in Jerusalem.

SATAN: Prove that You are indeed the Son of God. Jump off the pinnacle of the Temple. For it is written, "He will command His angels concerning you, and they will lift you up in their hands, so that you will not strike your foot against a stone." *(Smiles.)* I believe that's Psalm 91:11 and 12.

JESUS: But it is also written, "Do not put the Lord your God to the test."

SATAN: Yes, I've heard that, too. *(Pause.)* Let me show You something else, up on that mountain over there. I know. You're hungry and don't feel like walking. You don't have to. I'll take You there. *(Pause, then SATAN stretches out his hand.)* What do You think?

JESUS: It's a very nice view of all the kingdoms of the world. If you have a point to make about them, then make it.

SATAN: Sometimes You can be very impatient. OK, the point is, I'm willing to give all of them to You. All You have to do is worship me. Then, I promise, everything I have in this world will be Yours.

JESUS: Get out of My sight, Satan! For it is written, "You shall worship the Lord, your God. Him only shall you serve."

SATAN: OK, Jesus. But I'm not finished with You. There'll be other times and places. You know me. I won't rest until You are destroyed.

NICODEMUS

SCRIPTURE: John 3:1-21

SUGGESTED TOPICS: Eternal life; God's plan of salvation

BIBLE BACKGROUND

Jesus created a stir wherever He went. He taught with authority, not as the scribes who would only quote what others had written about a topic. Jesus' teaching upset most of the religious hierarchy. But some Pharisees, such as Nicodemus, were deeply interested in what Jesus had to say.

The very quality in Jesus' teaching which attracted Nicodemus also made it hard for him to understand Jesus' words. Nicodemus was used to complicated, scholarly consideration in which the varying positions of respected rabbis were balanced one against the other. In contrast, Jesus spoke directly, even bluntly, causing Nicodemus to ask, "How can this be?"

Some people criticize Nicodemus for his lack of insight. However, Nicodemus deserves a great deal of credit for asking the questions that he did, for continuing to seek understanding. While many people of his day (and ours) reject what they do not immediately grasp, Nicodemus pursued his quest for insight. When other Pharisees were ready to pronounce a curse on anyone who believed in Jesus, Nicodemus courageously raised a question which shows deeper understanding. Then, at the Cross, unashamed of his Savior, Nicodemus accompanied Joseph of Arimathea, bringing enough burial spices for a royal funeral (see John 19:39).

PERFORMANCE TIPS

1. Suggested props: Bible-times costumes.

2. Introduce the skit by saying, "Nicodemus was a Pharisee who was interested in Jesus' teaching. The Bible tells us Nicodemus came by night to talk to Jesus. Nicodemus was puzzled by some of Jesus' words. This skit shows what might have happened if Nicodemus had talked to another Pharisee about Jesus' teachings."

DISCUSSION QUESTIONS

1. Read John 3:5-8,14,19,20 and discuss the other word pictures Jesus used when talking with Nicodemus.

2. Why was Nicodemus afraid to be seen visiting Jesus?

3. Read John 3:16,17. What is the main point of these verses?

3. God offers the gift of eternal life to everyone in the world. What happens if a person does not accept the gift?

4. Have you accepted God's gift of eternal life?

NICODEMUS

CHARACTERS

MATTHIAS (math-EYE-us)

NICODEMUS (nik-uh-DEE-mus)

MATTHIAS: Hey! Watch where you're going. Old men should get glasses if they can't see what's in front of— Oh, Nicodemus. Sorry. I didn't mean to yell at you.

NICODEMUS: I'm sorry I bumped into you, Matthias. But I'm glad I bumped into you, figuratively speaking.

MATTHIAS: You mean, you wanted to see me about something?

NICODEMUS: Yes. You've just graduated from seminary. Maybe some new things are being taught that I don't understand.

MATTHIAS: A man of your intellect? Not understanding something?

NICODEMUS: None of us are too old to have learned everything, I think.

MATTHIAS: Except possibly for yourself and Gamaliel. Not that you're so old, but that you have learned so much.

NICODEMUS: Sometimes a man of thirty can cause a much older man to think. But enough of my musings. The question: What would you say to the phrase, "You must be born again"?

MATTHIAS: A riddle?

NICODEMUS: Possibly.

MATTHIAS: I love riddles. Makes the old mind work a little harder. Now then, "You must be born again."

NICODEMUS: Is this anything new that is being discussed in theology?

MATTHIAS: Ah! A theological riddle. That makes it more interesting.

NICODEMUS: Why?

MATTHIAS: Well, if we were talking a question of nature, the thing is wholly impossible. I mean, really. You can't expect someone or something to be born twice, now can you?

NICODEMUS: Of course not. But you said it's more interesting as a theological riddle.

MATTHIAS: Certainly. Because now we can examine figures of speech, make parallel observations, really have some fun with this.

NICODEMUS: Then you believe it is understandable?

MATTHIAS: Well...maybe. Of course, we would all just be guessing, but that's half the fun. Let's see. Born again, born again. Hah! I've got it! It wasn't "born again." It was "borne again," spelled b-o-r-n-e.

NICODEMUS: That sounds like the same thing to me.

MATTHIAS: No, no, you don't understand. Born without the *e* means you have to be a baby for a second time. But that's obviously not the meaning. Borne with an *e* has to do with carrying something for a second time. Now let's see how this could be...

NICODEMUS: No, I think it means rebirth.

MATTHIAS: Don't interrupt. I think I've got a handle on this. Now, to bear again implies lifting and carrying. A burden. What could be a burden?

NICODEMUS: You weren't listening. The phrase was, "You must be born again," not "You must carry something again."

MATTHIAS: You're sure of that?

NICODEMUS: Positive.

MATTHIAS: Well, that is different. How can I reconcile the word "born," which obviously only happens once in a lifetime, with the word "again"? Wait! Wait! It's coming to me! Yes! I have it!

NICODEMUS: What? You can explain this clearly?

MATTHIAS: Of course. It's so simple that it's profound. "You must be born again" is some kind of comparison with change. So. You must change from the ways of the Gentiles and become a child of Judaism.

NICODEMUS: It's an interesting idea. But what if it was said to a devout Jew—a Pharisee? A rabbi?

MATTHIAS: You mean to somebody like you? Couldn't be. Wouldn't make sense. You already are a part of Judaism. You are just about as perfect as a man can be, as are all we Pharisees. I obviously don't need to change. I really don't see how any of this applies to you or to me, Nicodemus. See you around.

NICODEMUS: Well, I guess I'll just have to visit Jesus again. Maybe if I listen to Him again, He will help me understand what I need to know.

TO TRAP A TEACHER

SCRIPTURE: Matthew 6:5-15

SUGGESTED TOPICS: Prayer

BIBLE BACKGROUND

Jesus' teaching resulted in a variety of reactions. Some listened and believed, some were interested to hear more, others were jealous and listened only to trap Jesus.

Among those who opposed Jesus were men like Saul (later to become Paul), who saw His teaching as blasphemous and needing to be stopped. Others, motivated by nothing more than their possible loss of prestige, also wanted Jesus stopped. Still others who opposed Jesus did so because He came from Galilee—and not only from Galilee, but Nazareth. Nathaniel summed up the prevailing attitude toward Galilee in general and Nazareth in particular when he asked Philip, "Can anything good come out of Nazareth?" (see John 1:46).

The Pharisees were a highly learned group of men. They were not only religious leaders, but also political leaders. For dramatic interest, this skit assumes that at least one member would not have the same intellectual capacity and the same dedication to the Law and his duties as did the others. It also assumes that jokes about Galilee were told by those who considered themselves more educated than those from the north.

PERFORMANCE TIPS

1. Suggested props: notepads and pencils for Matthias and Lynas to use as they take notes about Jesus' teachings.

2. Thomas is portrayed as somewhat hard-of-hearing, not overly diligent and more interested in his comfort than his duty. During the skit Thomas looks around, shuffles his feet, etc. Have the other Pharisees, Matthias and Lynas, look at one spot in the room as though they are paying attention to Jesus.

3. Before the skit, have your group say the Lord's Prayer together or read it from Matthew 6:9-13.

DISCUSSION QUESTIONS

1. Why do you think most of the Pharisees did not believe Jesus' teaching?

2. From Matthew 6:9-13, what do you learn about prayer?

3. Why is it important to pray? When should you pray? What should we pray about?

4. Give an example of a time God answered your prayers.

TO TRAP A TEACHER

CHARACTERS

THOMAS

MATTHIAS

LYNAS

THOMAS: I still don't understand why we have to be here.

MATTHIAS: How many times do we have to tell you? It's part of the job.

LYNAS: Right! If you want to be a leader, then you have to accept responsibilities as well as privileges.

THOMAS: Well, I still don't see what's so important about coming up on this cold mountain first thing in the morning.

MATTHIAS: Weren't you listening at the meeting yesterday?

THOMAS: Well, of course...

LYNAS: He was probably sleeping again.

THOMAS: I was not...

MATTHIAS: Or daydreaming again.

THOMAS: I was not asleep or daydreaming! I just don't see what's so important.

LYNAS: Do you remember when the chief priest got up to speak?

MATTHIAS: Do you remember how he impressed upon us that we are the leaders of God's people?

LYNAS: Do you remember when he told us to make certain that Israel's religion remained pure?

MATTHIAS: Do you remember when he told us we had to set aside petty differences and have a common goal?

THOMAS: Please! I was at the meeting yesterday. It was long enough then. I don't need it rehashed again today.

LYNAS: Then you should remember why we are here today.

MATTHIAS: You know that it's our job to watch over this Jesus, to listen to every word He says.

THOMAS: That's the part I don't understand. Why is it so important to come all the way out to listen to some wandering teacher? Really! He's from Galilee. Nothing important has ever come from Galilee.

LYNAS: You really weren't listening, were you?

MATTHIAS: Haven't you noticed all these people out here this morning? They ARE listening to Him. They believe He's some kind of prophet. We have to be sure that He is not leading all of His listeners astray.

THOMAS: Why would people think He's a prophet? They can hear His Galilean accent. Surely they know that God wouldn't use a Galilean for a prophet.

LYNAS: Never underestimate people's ability to fall for anything. They're convinced that He's a prophet, and they listen to Him.

MATTHIAS: So we have to hear what He says if we're going to persuade people that He's telling lies.

THOMAS: But what if His teaching isn't false?

LYNAS: You not only don't listen at meetings, you don't even listen to yourself. Where does this man come from?

THOMAS: Galilee.

LYNAS: And has anything good ever come out of Galilee?

THOMAS: Well, there've been a few good jokes. You know, like how many Galileans does it take to start a fire?

MATTHIAS: Forget the jokes. Don't you understand?

LYNAS: Let me make it plain. He comes from Galilee. Therefore, He can't be a prophet or a teacher. Since He is not a prophet, He can't be telling the truth when He tries to teach about God. So, we have to catch Him in His lies and expose Him as a fraud.

MATTHIAS: Shh! He's starting to speak.

THOMAS: What's He talking about?

LYNAS: Don't tell me you not only can't remember, but you also can't hear?

MATTHIAS: Shh! Jesus is saying that people should pray.

THOMAS: If that's all He's saying, I don't think we'll catch Him in any lies.

LYNAS: Be quiet and listen. He's saying more than that.

MATTHIAS: He's saying that people shouldn't stand on street corners to pray but they should pray privately.

THOMAS: Then we've got Him! Everybody knows you're supposed to pray with a loud voice where lots of people can hear you.

LYNAS: Will you be quiet and let us listen? Everybody doesn't know that. Some may agree with Him. Give Him time to say more. The more He speaks, the more we'll hear and have a chance to prove Him false.

MATTHIAS: Did you hear that? He said that we Pharisees pray in public to impress people, and we will not have any other reward than that. This man could be dangerous if people believe Him.

THOMAS: But why would they believe Him? I can hear His accent quite plainly. Say, did you hear the one about the Galilean who was walking with his donkey—

LYNAS: Would you stop with the Galilean jokes already? We are supposed to be listening to HIM, not you. Now stop chattering and listen!

THOMAS: But I can't hear Him clearly.

MATTHIAS: Then be quiet and let us listen. We'll tell you what He says.

LYNAS: Listen to Him now. Telling people not to imitate the heathen who pray with vain repetitions. Sometimes this man makes sense.

MATTHIAS: There's no doubt how dangerous this man is. Listen to Him mixing truth and lies together. He will definitely confuse people if He's allowed to continue.

LYNAS: Now He's giving an example of how to pray. "Our Father who is in heaven..."

THOMAS: I thought we were supposed to pray to God?

MATTHIAS: We are.

THOMAS: Then we've got Him, because my father's not in heaven. He's in Jerusalem. In bed. Where I should be.

MATTHIAS: He doesn't mean pray to your father. He means God is your real Father. Your Father in heaven.

THOMAS: Oh, I get it.

LYNAS: Quiet, you two. I'm trying to listen to this guy's prayer. It's not a bad prayer, for a Galilean.

MATTHIAS: What's He been saying while I've been trying to explain things to our thickheaded friend?

LYNAS: First, He praises God for being holy.

MATTHIAS: That's a good beginning.

LYNAS: Then, He asks for God's commands to be obeyed on earth in the same way that they are in heaven.

MATTHIAS: That's a nice thought, but it sounds like wishful thinking.

LYNAS: Then He asks God to supply our needs for today.

MATTHIAS: I can't argue with that.

LYNAS: Next, He asks God to forgive us in the same manner that we forgive people who have sinned against us.

THOMAS: Say, did you hear about the Galilean who was asked if he could multiply—

LYNAS AND MATTHIAS: Cut it out!

MATTHIAS: What else did He say in His prayer?

LYNAS: He asks God not to let Him be tempted but instead to deliver Him from evil. Then, He closes with a little praise about power and glory being for God.

MATTHIAS: We had better get back to the Council to report on this Jesus. He could be a lot of trouble to us.

LYNAS: You're right. He's going to confuse people by mixing truth and lies the way He does. Let's go. *(LYNAS and MATTHIAS exit.)*

THOMAS: *(Yawns.)* Hey! Where did they go? Oh well. I think I'll go home and have a little more breakfast and maybe a little more sleep. Maybe I'll tell my wife the one about how many Galileans it takes to make a bed. If I can remember it....

DON'T WORRY

SCRIPTURE: Matthew 6:25-34; 7:7-11; Luke 12:6,7,22-31

SUGGESTED TOPICS: Worry; God's love and provision; our value to God; God's guidance

BIBLE BACKGROUND

Jesus chose twelve disciples to follow Him. These twelve left everything—jobs, homes, families—to follow. Along the way, Jesus gave them many lessons in God's love and care for His own.

Jesus wanted His disciples to understand the love of God to be like that of a loving father; and not just any father, but the perfect Father. Would a father on earth trick his child and give a rock instead of bread? Would he give his child something that appeared good but would bring harm, such as a snake or eel in place of a fish? Would a father deliberately give his child a white scorpion curled up and call it an egg? A father who cares for his children would not attempt to harm them, although we sometimes do inadvertently. The perfect Father never harms His children, even unintentionally.

However, not harming and disciplining are two different precepts. Jesus sometimes spoke sharply to His disciples and even more sharply to the Pharisees, who should have known God and His character. Jesus made it clear that we must expect God to correct us when we go astray, not out of vengeful or malicious intent, but out of His deep, abiding love for all who follow His Son.

PERFORMANCE TIPS

1. Suggested props: Bible-times costumes and/or walking sticks.
2. Introduce the skit by saying, "Jesus used stories and word pictures to teach people about God. Listen for the stories and word pictures in this skit."

DISCUSSION QUESTIONS

1. Some people do not feel love from their fathers. The word "father" may carry bad connotations for some people. In discussing the skit, comment, "Jesus said God was like a loving father. How would a perfect father act?"
2. Why do you think people worry? What do you know about God that will help you when you are worried or afraid?
3. How did God show His love for people in the Bible? How has He shown His love for you?
4. What can you do to thank God for His love?

Don't Worry

CHARACTERS
JAMES
JOHN
PETER
PHILIP
MATTHEW

JAMES (*whining*): We sure have to walk a long way. What happens if our sandals wear out? Where are we going to find the money to buy new ones?

JOHN: And what about our cloaks? Each of us has only one. What happens when a cloak gets a hole in it?

PETER: Weren't you Sons of Thunder listening to the Master today? Didn't He tell us not to worry about what we would wear? Didn't He remind us that the flowers of the field don't have to shear sheep or spin wool to weave their yarn into clothes?

PHILIP: That's right. Even Solomon, the richest king Israel has ever known, didn't have clothing as beautiful as the way God clothes the flowers.

PETER: Right. I wish you two would listen to what the Master says instead of always worrying. Besides, if you want to worry about something, worry about food. It's getting late and we're nowhere near any town. How are we going to fill our bellies tonight?

MATTHEW: That's you right to the core, Peter. Always worrying about your belly. When have we ever gone hungry since being with the Master? But you still worry about food. If you're going to be like that, go back to fishing.

PETER: At least I had an honorable profession before joining Jesus. I wasn't a lousy tax gatherer, working for the Romans...

PHILIP: Knock it off, Peter. You may not have been a tax gatherer before you met Jesus, but you weren't the best person in the country. How many fights did you get into over nothing?

JAMES: Besides, you aren't any better than John and me.

JOHN: That's right. You don't listen any better than we do to what the Master says. Didn't He tell us today not to worry about food?

PHILIP: They've got you there, Peter. Remember what He said about birds? God doesn't let them starve. He takes care of them.

MATTHEW: He even talked about how much more valuable we are than those birds. He said, "Five sparrows are sold for a few pennies..."

PETER: Trust a tax collector to know the price of everything.

MATTHEW: Better than only knowing about scaling fish and fixing nets.

PHILIP: Would you two stop bickering? How do you think Jesus would feel if He heard you two? Keep it up and you'll make the Pharisees look good.

PETER: What do you mean?

PHILIP: Don't they say one thing and do another? That makes them hypocrites. You two are acting exactly the same way, saying Jesus is your Master and then behaving the way you do. It's disgusting. Worrying and fighting over every little thing, when the only important thing to worry about is what's going to happen to us and our families—being separated for so long. How will everyone survive? Are we doing the right thing or not?

JAMES *(to John)*: Maybe Philip needs a taste of his own medicine.

JOHN: A little reminder of the Master's words.

PHILIP: What are you two going on about?

MATTHEW: Should we explain it to him, Peter?

PETER: Sure. You do it. You're the educated man. You know bigger words.

MATTHEW: Anybody could explain this. Remember Jesus asking, "If a child was hungry and asked his father for a piece of bread..."

PETER: "Would that father give the child a stone that looked like bread?"

JAMES: "And if the child asked for a piece of fish..."

JOHN: "Would the father give the child a snake that is not to be eaten?"

PETER: "And if earthly fathers, who sin, are kind to their children..."

MATTHEW: "How much more kind is our Father in heaven, who knows what we need even before we ask for it."

PHILIP: OK, so I'm not perfect either. I guess we all need to stick close to Jesus to understand what He says and put His words into practice.

OCEANFRONT PROPERTY

SCRIPTURE: Luke 6:46-49

SUGGESTED TOPICS: God's Word as foundation; putting it into practice

BIBLE BACKGROUND

Of all the questions Jesus asked—and He asked many—perhaps none is more penetrating and convicting than this one: "Why do you call me, 'Lord, Lord,' and do not do what I say?" Jesus' famous story about the wise and foolish builders was told to illustrate the crucial difference between the person who obeys the Word of God and the person who hears but does not obey. The story assumes that both types of person have the same information and ability; but one chooses to do what God says while the other chooses another path. Ignoring God's way seems to have gone satisfactorily for the foolish man until he hit a crisis. Then, his lack of a solid foundation for life was his undoing.

PERFORMANCE TIPS

1. Suggested props: several blueprints for Wise Mann to carry, a glass of lemonade for Don Key.

2. Before the skit, read Luke 6:46,47. Explain that these verses tell Jesus' introduction to the story in the skit.

3. After the skit, read Luke 6:48,49.

DISCUSSION QUESTIONS

1. In the skit, we are told that both men read the building code. Did reading the code help both men? Why or why not?

2. How do we build a strong foundation for our lives? What happens if we do not build a strong foundation?

OCEANFRONT PROPERTY

CHARACTERS
NARRATOR

WISE MANN

DON KEY

NARRATOR: Once upon a time, there were two men: Wisenthorpe Mann, known to his friends as Wise, and Donald Key. Both men decided to build a new house with an ocean view. Each man carefully studied the building codes and planned his new home.

WISE MANN: Hello. You must be my new neighbor. My name's Wisenthorpe Mann, but you can call me Wise, for short.

DON KEY: Donald Key. Don to my friends. You got your house all planned?

WISE MANN: I sure have. I'm going to lay the foundation next week. You see that spot back near those trees? Just in front. That way, I can save the trees, have a beautiful view out the back window, and have the ocean front view from the front window.

DON KEY: Are you crazy? Way back there? Why, you're going to have to walk forever to enjoy the water. Now me, I'm going to build my house right here. Big deck all around. I could practically dive off the deck into the ocean any time I want.

WISE MANN: Do you think that's a good idea? Look how high the tide comes in.

DON KEY: No sweat. I'm building it on stilts. That way, even if the tide comes in higher than expected, I'm still sitting high and dry.

WISE MANN: I have my doubts. But I guess you've read the charts and know what you're doing.

DON KEY: Darn tootin'. Got it planned to the last detail. How about you?

WISE MANN: Of course. First, I'm driving pylons way down deep into the bedrock.

DON KEY: Pylons into bedrock. Are you nuts? What a waste!

WISE MANN: What do you mean?

DON KEY: Look. You got about eight feet of sand before you get down to the rock, right? You plan to drill through a bunch of rock and plant pylons that deep? A waste of money. All you got to do is what I'm doing. Twelve stilts driven down six feet, connected with a series of triangles. Solid! Couldn't move it if you wanted to. Then, with the money you save, you can build an extra room or finish the walls with better materials. Put your money where it shows, I say.

WISE MANN *(slowly)*: I don't know. I read the building code and it suggests...

DON KEY: Code, schmode. Written by some guy who owns a lumber store. Just wants more business for himself. Take my word for it, my way's best.

WISE MANN: If you say so. But for me, I think I'll stick to what the code says and put in the pylons. Lay a firm foundation.

DON KEY: Suit yourself. Must be nice having money to throw away. I'm putting my money where it shows.

NARRATOR: So the two men went to work. While Wise Mann was still laying his foundation, Don Key had finished all the framing. While Wise Mann was putting up his exterior walls, Don Key had finished paneling his interior walls with the finest wood that money could buy. While Wise Mann was working to complete the interior—not as lavishly as Don Key's home, but stylishly and comfortably—Don Key was relaxing on his deck with a big glass of lemonade. One day, Wise Mann decided to take a short break from construction and go for a dip in the ocean.

DON KEY: Howdy, neighbor. How goes the house?

WISE MANN: Very well, thanks. Just a few more days and it'll be finished.

DON KEY: Now ain't that just hunky-dory. C'mon up and have some lemonade. I've been watching you, slaving away day and night, while my house was being enjoyed. Look at this deck. Know how much this wood cost? Probably nearly as much as your whole house. Finest material known to man. Specially treated to last a hundred years before it needs any work. Ah, yes. This is the life.

WISE MANN: Well, it sure is beautiful. But I'm happy with my home. When it's finished, it will suit me for the rest of my life.

DON KEY: Sure. When it's finished. Meantime, I've been enjoying my house for weeks while you've been slaving away.

WISE MANN: Well, to each his own. Thanks for the lemonade. I'm going for a quick swim and then, back to work.

DON KEY: Go ahead. I'm just going to sit here and relax.

NARRATOR: And so, Wise Mann finished his house, built to the specifications of the building code. Every morning he awoke, looked out his bedroom window to the trees behind the house, looked out the front window at the ocean and Don Key's house. Then, one morning, after a particularly heavy wind the night before...

WISE MANN: What a beautiful morning. Look at those gorgeous trees. And look at that beautiful beach and ocean. Nothing but sand and ocean as far as the eye can see. *(Pause.)* Wait a minute. Something's missing. Don's house. It's not there! I wonder what he did with it? I wonder where he moved it?

LOST AND FOUND

SCRIPTURE: Luke 15:1-10

SUGGESTED TOPICS: God's love; our worth to God

BIBLE BACKGROUND

The scribes and Pharisees criticized Jesus for associating with tax collectors and "sinners." Jesus, wanting them to understand God's care and concern for all people, told three parables concerning the lost: the lost sheep, the lost coin and the runaway son.

Jesus described God by using everyday situations people could easily understand. In a heavily agrarian society, everyone understood a shepherd's concern for each member of the flock. Everyone understood a woman's concern for a lost coin. Beyond the monetary value (the drachma was a silver coin worth about a full day's wage), it is likely that the ten coins Jesus' mentioned were part of this woman's headdress, which denoted her marital status and had been given as her dowry. And everyone understood the concern of a parent for a wayward child.

PERFORMANCE TIPS

1. Suggested props: walking stick for shepherd, broom and coin for woman.
2. Explain to the group that Jesus often told stories or parables about everyday situations in Israel. A single sheep or a coin were very valuable to Bible-times people.
3. To set the scene, read Luke 15:1,2. Then say, "Jesus told a story about two people who had lost something."

DISCUSSION QUESTIONS

1. What is something you have lost? What did you do to look for it? If you found it, how did you feel?
2. How is God like the shepherd and the woman in the story? What is God searching for?
3. When we are not members of God's family, we are lost from God. What did God do to show His love for lost people?
4. God loves us and doesn't want us to be lost from Him. That's why He sent Jesus to be our Savior. How can you respond to God's love?

LOST AND FOUND

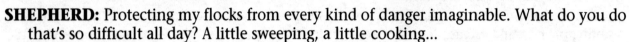

CHARACTERS
SHEPHERD
WOMAN

SHEPHERD: What a day I had yesterday! Nobody ever had a tougher day.

WOMAN: What do you know about hard days? Out in the fresh air, in the sun...

SHEPHERD: Protecting my flocks from every kind of danger imaginable. What do you do that's so difficult all day? A little sweeping, a little cooking...

WOMAN: Working to keep food on the table for ungrateful men like you. Watching every penny. Having to scrimp for myself so my children and husband can be fed. What do you know about such work?

SHEPHERD: I'll tell you about my day. Then you'll see how easy you have it. I was out in the fields all day. Finding good grass for my flock, finding some still waters so they would have something to drink. Keeping a sharp eye out for wolves, bears, lions. Do you know what a strain it is, never knowing if danger is near?

WOMAN: So you were outside on this nice warm day. Sounds rough.

SHEPHERD: Sweating under the hot sun. Chasing away flies. Lots of fun. But that was the easy part of the day. The hard part came when my day's work was supposed to be done.

WOMAN: Just like a man. *(Mocking.)* "The hard part of my day came when it was finished."

SHEPHERD: I didn't say it was finished. I said day was done. Just before dark, I brought my flock into the safety of the fold. I counted each one to be sure all were there. Sixty-seven, sixty-eight, sixty-nine, and so on.

WOMAN *(sarcastic)***:** Now I understand. Being a man, counting is hard for you.

SHEPHERD: Not the counting. The last few sheep were coming into the fold. Ninety-six, ninety-seven, ninety-eight, ninety-nine. Ninety-nine? But I have one hundred sheep in my flock!

WOMAN: So you counted wrong. Why worry about it?

SHEPHERD: Because they are my sheep. So I counted them again. And again, ninety-nine. Not one hundred—only ninety-nine.

WOMAN: It's only one out of one hundred. Why worry? You have lots in the fold.

SHEPHERD: Spoken like a woman. My sheep was out on the mountainside. Lost. In the dark. I had to find it. So, I got a torch and went back to the mountains to find my lost sheep. All night I searched. Over the rocks, in the valleys, everywhere I could think to look. Finally, just as dawn was breaking, I found him. Caught in some thorns. So I reached in, scratching my arm terribly as you can see, and freed him from the thorns. Poor thing was trembling and bleating. But I calmed him and petted him. Then I hoisted him onto my shoulders and carried him safely home.

The Big Book of Bible Skits ©1997 Gospel Light. Permission to photocopy granted.

WOMAN: So YOU'RE the fool who came into the village this morning shouting, "Rejoice, I have found my sheep which was lost!" Waking up everybody before they had to be out of their beds.

SHEPHERD: I was happy. I had found my sheep. Ah, how can I expect a woman to understand these things? But now you can see how difficult yesterday was. You maybe can understand how tiring a man's work is.

WOMAN: You call that tiring? Let me tell you about the day before yesterday. All day long, I cleaned the house, washed clothes, cooked meals for my husband and children. And one of the children was sick, so I had to spend extra time with that one. Which made my day much later than normal.

SHEPHERD: Inside. Out of the hot sun. Sounds difficult.

WOMAN: Children crying. Husband grumpy because things are late. Well, I didn't finish my cleaning until well into the evening, when you had already finished your supper and were getting ready for bed, no doubt.

SHEPHERD: Sleep. The well-earned reward of the just man.

WOMAN: Well, just as I was about finished, what do I see? One of my ten coins is missing! I say to myself, it's just the dim light. So I pick them all up and count them again. No. One is missing.

SHEPHERD: What are you worried about? Your husband has many coins...

WOMAN: But this is one from my headdress, from my wedding! I had to find the coin. I did not rest. I lit a candle and cleaned the entire house again. I looked in all the corners, under the beds, moved all the pots and pans, took everything from the cupboards. All this, searching for my silver coin by candlelight.

SHEPHERD: You would compare the ease of searching for a lost coin with that of searching for a lost sheep? You only had to search the inside of a house. I had to search the entire mountainside.

WOMAN: And when you called your sheep, it answered you. A coin cannot answer. I was frantic. I had to find my coin. Finally, after cleaning the entire house, I found the coin, right where it had fallen. I was so excited, I ran to my friends and told them.

SHEPHERD: YOU were the woman making that infernal racket in the night, waking men from their sleep? Such foolishness, over a lost coin!

WOMAN: You make such a fuss over a sheep and criticize me. Never will I understand men.

SHEPHERD: Nor will I ever understand women.

FORGIVE AND FORGET

SCRIPTURE: Matthew 18:21-35

SUGGESTED TOPICS: Forgiveness; gratitude; God's love

BIBLE BACKGROUND

Peter had a question for the Master: "How often should I forgive someone who sins against me?" Wanting to demonstrate his great patience, Peter suggested a very generous number—seven times.

Jesus' response to Peter was, "Not seven times but seventy-seven times." Jesus' words could also be translated as seventy times seven. In either case, the meaning is clear: keep on forgiving.

To show Peter what He meant, Jesus told the story of the unforgiving servant. Ten thousand talents was a great deal of money, the equivalent of millions of dollars. In the skit, the ten thousand talents has been assumed to be talents of gold, with gold priced at four hundred dollars an ounce. Obviously, Jesus intended to show that the man was hopelessly in debt. In contrast, the second servant owed the first one an insignificant debt in comparison. (The *denarius* was a Roman coin, equivalent to the Greek *drachma*, which was worth about a day's wages.)

Jesus' contrast of the debt the steward owed the king and the debt the other servant owed the steward showed Peter the magnitude of his debt to God compared to others' debts to him. The obvious point of Jesus' answer to Peter is that, if God forgives that which can never be repaid, we must forgive the comparatively tiny amount owed us.

PERFORMANCE TIPS

1. Suggested prop: a large book for use as an account book. (Or fold in half a large black sheet of construction paper.)
2. Before the skit, read Matthew 18:21,22.

DISCUSSION QUESTIONS

1. What does this story tell us about God? How is God like the king?
2. In Matthew 6:12, what does Jesus say about forgiveness?
3. When has someone done something wrong to you? How did you feel? What does God want you to do when this happens?
4. When have you done something wrong to somebody else? What does God want you to do when this happens?
5. How do you know God forgives our sins? How can you thank Him?

FORGIVE AND FORGET

CHARACTERS
KING

STEWARD

SERVANT

GUARD

KING: Steward! Bring me my account books.

STEWARD: Sire, it's late. Why look over the numbers now? Wait for tomorrow.

KING: No. I've decided to go over the accounts now.

STEWARD: Such tiring work. It really is best left until a new day dawns.

KING: No! I want to go over my accounts now. I must see what I owe everybody. And, better yet, what everybody owes me.

STEWARD: Very well. You're the king. Here are the books.

KING: They are very large. My subjects must owe me a great deal of money.

STEWARD: I'm sure you're right. Say, I have an idea. Why don't you go to bed now while I go through the books? And tomorrow, I'll tell you exactly who owes who how much.

KING: That's very kind of you. But I think I will check the accounts myself. *(Begins looking at books.)* My goodness, these books are much more complicated than I remember.

STEWARD: I made a few...improvements in the system. Really, Sire, these things are best left to the professionals. Let me decipher everything for you and let you know exactly where you stand in the morning.

KING: No, I think I'll be able to figure everything out.

STEWARD: Well, if you don't need me at the moment, I think I'll head out of the countr— I mean, off to bed. I'm rather tired...

KING: Wait here, Steward. I might need something explained.

STEWARD: Very well, Sire.

KING: Hmm. Good, good. Ah! Very good. Hmm. Not so good. What? STEWARD!

STEWARD: You bellowed, Sire?

KING: I'm having trouble with this one account.

STEWARD: Which one is that, Sire?

KING: YOUR account, Steward.

STEWARD: Oh. That one works out alright. I'm always careful about the household affairs and the money left in my trust. It's always in perfect balance.

KING: There seems to be a slight discrepancy in your account.

STEWARD: Impossible! Uh, how slight a discrepancy?

KING: TEN THOUSAND TALENTS!

STEWARD: T-t-t-ten....

KING: Just how do you explain that?

STEWARD: It's only ten, Sire. Not all that serious. Not as if it were a hundred thousand talents. It's only ten thousand talents.

KING: Or a few million dollars!

STEWARD: Give or take a few pennies here and there.

KING: It's time to settle the account. Give me my ten thousand talents.

STEWARD: Well, we have a slight problem. I've had a few bad investments in the past few weeks and don't have the money right now. But if you could give me a little time to recoup my losses...

KING: WE do not have a problem, YOU have a problem. If you cannot repay the debt, then all you own is forfeit. I hereby take your house, all your possessions, and your family. I will sell every last thing you have and cut my losses.

STEWARD: I beg you, Your Majesty, have mercy on me! Please be patient with me, and I will repay you every penny I owe.

KING: How will you repay me that much money?

STEWARD: I do not know, Your Highness. But please give me a little time. I will find a way.

KING: There is no way you could find to repay so great a debt. But I see you are in great distress for what you have done. So, I have an idea. Give me your pen.

STEWARD: At once, Sire. Here it is.

KING: There. One quick stroke of the pen and the debt is cancelled. Now, you owe me nothing.

STEWARD: Nothing?

KING: Nothing.

STEWARD: Oh, Your Majesty. May your great name be praised forever! May all your enemies fall before your mighty strength! May you live forever! Let all the nations sing your praise...

KING: Enough. We've been at this all night. I think I'll retire while you carry on with your duties.

STEWARD: Of course. Certainly. Good night, I mean, good day, Sire.

KING: Good day, Steward. *(Exits.)*

STEWARD: What luck! I can't believe my ears. I'm free. I still own all my possessions. My family has not been sold as slaves. *(Sees SERVANT.)* This IS my lucky day. Not only am I debt free, but there is that worthless servant who owes me money. Hey, you!

SERVANT: You called, steward of the house.

STEWARD: I sure did. I don't supposed you've forgotten that you owe me...

SERVANT: One hundred denarii. No. I've not forgotten. I certainly appreciate your loaning me the money. I've been saving carefully and have earned almost enough to pay you back...

STEWARD: Enough of that! You've been putting me off with that "I don't have the money right now" stuff. I want my money! I suppose you think that four months' pay is nothing! Well, you're wrong! It's a lot of money, and I want it paid now!

SERVANT: I know it's a lot of money. But I don't have it with me. If you could just wait until next payday, I'm sure I can find a way to pay you back all that I owe.

STEWARD: I've been too patient with you already! Guard! Take this worthless wretch and throw him into prison! *(GUARD and SERVANT exit.)* Let him sit there until he finds some way to pay me! I'll show these scoundrels they can't take advantage of me. *(GUARD enters.)* Well? Have you done what I told you to do?

GUARD: Certainly. But the king wishes to see you.

STEWARD: The king wants to see me? I wonder what he wants? On a lucky day like this one, he probably wants to give me a raise. *(KING enters.)* Your Majesty. You wanted to see me?

KING: I did. I understand you had a servant thrown into prison.

STEWARD: I certainly did. That scoundrel was giving me some kind of song and dance about not being able to pay me the one hundred denarii he owes me. So I decided to teach him a lesson. Let him rot in prison if he can't pay his debts.

KING: You ingrate! You despicable wretch! I forgave you a fortune merely because you begged me to give you a little time to pay. Could you not follow my example and treat your fellow servant with the same kindness? Well, as you have forgiven, so shall you be forgiven. Your debt has been reinstated. Guard! Take this worm and throw him into prison until he has paid me the full debt.

GUARD *(smiling)***:** With pleasure, Sire.

THE TALENTS

SCRIPTURE: Matthew 25:14-30

SUGGESTED TOPICS: Talents and abilities; responsibility; stewardship

BIBLE BACKGROUND

Jesus wanted His disciples to understand their responsibility to wisely use all they had been given by God, the great King. To make His point, Jesus told a parable which clearly indicates that God has given all of us something of real value. Along with the gift comes a responsibility—a responsibility which is measured, not in comparison with what others might do, but in proportion to what God has bestowed.

The talents which the man in the story entrusted to his servants were worth more than a thousand dollars each. The term "talent" was used originally to indicate weight (about sixty-five pounds) and gradually came to represent a monetary value.

PERFORMANCE TIPS

1. Suggested props: play money or coins.
2. Before the skit, explain that the word "talent" was a Bible-times word for money. (See Bible Back ground.)
3. Servants One and Two should speak confidently. Servant Three should whine.

DISCUSSION QUESTIONS

1. Think about the three servants. How did their attitudes affect their actions?
2. God has given abilities to everyone. What abilities or talents has He given to you?
3. How can you use your abilities or the things you enjoy doing to show your love for God?

THE TALENTS

CHARACTERS

MASTER
FIRST SERVANT
SECOND SERVANT
THIRD SERVANT

SCENE ONE

MASTER: Servants! Come here!

FIRST SERVANT: Here I am, Master.

SECOND SERVANT: And I.

THIRD SERVANT: Yo! Did you call?

MASTER: Yes, I did. Good, you're all here. I'm about to leave on a journey.

FIRST SERVANT: May the wind be at your back.

SECOND SERVANT: May all your roads be level.

THIRD SERVANT: Uh, good luck?

MASTER: Thank you. There are many things that need to be done while I'm gone.

FIRST SERVANT: The livestock. The sheep and camels must be watered and fed every day. I'll make certain all your livestock is well cared for.

SECOND SERVANT: Don't forget the crops. If the master is to be gone for a lengthy journey, the harvest might come before he returns. I'll see that the crops are watered and weeded and be sure that the harvesting is done on schedule.

FIRST SERVANT: Let's not forget the house. Think of all the things to be done inside.

SECOND SERVANT: You're right. There's the cleaning, and if something breaks, it will have to be repaired.

FIRST SERVANT: Not to mention general maintenance.

THIRD SERVANT: Uh, mmm, er...eat! We have to eat. Meals need to be prepared.

MASTER: Well, I can see I am leaving everything in capable hands.

FIRST SERVANT: You can count on us.

SECOND SERVANT: We'll look after everything.

THIRD SERVANT: Uh, yeah.

MASTER: However, I'm giving each of you an additional responsibility.

FIRST SERVANT: Anything you say, Master.

SECOND SERVANT: We're ready for any challenge.

THIRD SERVANT: Another one?

MASTER (*Pointing to FIRST SERVANT*): I'll begin with you. You have shown many abilities in the past. So I am entrusting five talents to you. Do whatever you think best with them. I'll ask for an accounting when I return.

FIRST SERVANT: Five thousand dollars! I've never seen so much money. I'll do my best, Master.

MASTER: I know you will. You always have in the past. (*Turns to SECOND SERVANT.*) And I'm trusting you with two talents.

SECOND SERVANT: Two thousand dollars! That's a lot of money. You can trust me, Master.

MASTER: I know I can. (*Turns to THIRD SERVANT.*) And you. Here is one talent.

THIRD SERVANT: One thousand dollars! But what am I supposed to do with it?

MASTER: Use it wisely. Remember, I will seek an accounting from all of you when I return. (*Exits.*)

FIRST SERVANT: Good-bye, Master. Have a pleasant journey.

SECOND SERVANT: Good-bye, Master. May everything go well.

THIRD SERVANT: Oh, woe is me. What am I going to do?

FIRST SERVANT: Well, what are you going to do with your money?

SECOND SERVANT: I'm not sure. I've got a few ideas to try out. Old Saul is trying to sell his business. Maybe I could buy it. I think I could do as well as he has, maybe even better. What are you planning to do?

FIRST SERVANT: I don't know, yet. I never planned on having so much money at one time. But I do remember seeing some good bargains in the marketplace. If I search out as many as I can, perhaps I could resell them at a profit. Or maybe land. There's always land available. I wonder if I could make a good real estate deal? I'll have to consider everything carefully. After all, it's not my money. It belongs to the Master.

SECOND SERVANT: True. So we will have to exercise care in our business deals.

FIRST SERVANT (*to THIRD SERVANT*): What about you? Have you thought about what you'll do with your talent?

THIRD SERVANT: Oh, woe is me. What will I do? What will I do?

SECOND SERVANT: Don't worry so much. You'll think of something. Well, I'm going to make sure the field hands are looking after the crops and then, off to see how much Saul wants for his business.

FIRST SERVANT: And I'll see that the stable boys are looking after the animals properly. Then I'm off to the market to see what bargains are waiting there.

THIRD SERVANT: Oh, woe is me. Woe is me.

SCENE TWO

MASTER: Servants! Come here!

FIRST SERVANT: Here I am.

SECOND SERVANT: And I.

THIRD SERVANT: Did you call?

MASTER: Yes, I called. I have returned from my journey.

FIRST SERVANT: And a long journey it was. I trust everything met with your approval.

SECOND SERVANT: I trust that all went in your favor.

THIRD SERVANT: Oh, me. It wasn't long enough.

MASTER: I had a marvelous journey. But I'm eager to see how you made out.

FIRST SERVANT: Well, it's kind of a long story. Here are all my records. You can examine them at your leisure in the next few days. The bottom line is, here are your original five thousand dollars. And here is the profit—five thousand more.

MASTER: Well done, good and faithful servant! You have been faithful over the few things I gave you, so I will make you ruler over many things.

FIRST SERVANT: You're too kind, Master. I was only doing my duty.

MASTER: Not at all. You are to be commended. Now, what about you?

SECOND SERVANT: Well, I tried my hand at a little of this and a little of that. Here are all the records of my dealings. But, to make a long story short, here are your original two thousand dollars. And here is your profit—two thousand more.

MASTER: Well done, good and faithful servant! You have been faithful over the little I have given you, so I will make you ruler over many things.

SECOND SERVANT: You're too kind, Master. I was only doing my duty.

MASTER: Not at all. You are to be commended. Now, what about you?

THIRD SERVANT: Me, Master?

MASTER: Yes, you. You're the only other one here. Give me an accounting. What did you do with your thousand dollars?

THIRD SERVANT: I knew you were a hard man, Master.

MASTER: Flattery will get you nowhere. What about the money?

THIRD SERVANT: I knew you take advantage of every opportunity.

MASTER: Sure. I'm a good businessman. The money?

THIRD SERVANT: I was afraid, Master. What if I lost your money? I knew you would be angry. So I kept it safe. I dug a hole and buried it. Here is your one thousand dollars.

MASTER: You did what?

THIRD SERVANT: I hid it. In the ground.

MASTER: You wicked and lazy servant! You knew that I expected some kind of profit! But you hid the money in the ground? You could have at least put it into the bank so it would have earned some interest. But no! You hid it! In the ground! Where it did no good! Give the one thousand dollars to the one who has ten. And then leave. You're fired for being lazy and worthless.

It's a Miracle

SCRIPTURE: Matthew 4:1-11; 8:14-17; 9:2-8; Luke 6:6-11; 18:31-34; John 6:1-59

SUGGESTED TOPICS: Jesus' fulfilling God's covenants; miracles; Jesus as God Incarnate

BIBLE BACKGROUND

"He was in the world, and though the world was made through him, the world did not recognize him. He came to that which was his own, but his own did not receive him" (John 1:10,11). God promised to send a Savior to redeem His people, and what a Savior! Not a person who could guide people back to God, not an angel who could tell people about being in God's presence, but God Himself in human flesh. The Creator of heaven and earth came to live among His people, but the very ones who should have been first to recognize Him, didn't.

Even the one who was sent to bear witness of the Light (see John 1:8) had his doubts. Locked in his prison cell, John sent two of his disciples to ask Jesus, "Are you the one who was to come, or should we expect someone else?" (Matthew 11:2,3). Jesus' answer made a clear reference to one of Isaiah's prophecies. "Go back and report to John what you hear and see: The blind receive sight, the lame walk, those who have leprosy are cured, the deaf hear, the dead are raised, and the good news is preached to the poor" (see Isaiah 35:4-6; 61:1 and Matthew 11:4,5). Jesus knew that John would recognize the report of Jesus' ministry as fulfillment of the promise.

PERFORMANCE TIPS

1. Suggested props: chairs, papers to represent reports to Caiaphas, notebook clearly titled "Robert's Rules of Order" or an actual copy of *Robert's Rules* if available.

2. Thomas is an annoyance to the other three. The others indicate this by shaking their heads when Thomas speaks, holding their heads in their hands, etc.

3. While the others are speaking, Thomas is deep in thought, consulting Robert's Rules of Order and planning his next motion.

4. Thomas limps; he has twisted his ankle and should act accordingly.

DISCUSSION QUESTIONS

1. Why do you think Jesus performed miracles?

2. Why do you think the Pharisees, priests and scribes did not recognize Jesus as the Messiah?

3. Jesus is sometimes called "God Incarnate." What do you think that means?

4. What are some reasons to accept Jesus as Savior?

It's a Miracle

CHARACTERS
CAIAPHAS (KYE-uh-fus)
ANNAS (ah-NAHS)
JOHN
THOMAS

PRONUNCIATION GUIDE
zealots (ZEL-uts)
blasphemy (BLAS-fuh-mee)

CAIAPHAS *(pacing)*: Where IS he?

ANNAS: Forget him. Let's start the meeting.

JOHN: He's always late, anyway. He can catch up with us.

ANNAS: Besides, it's not like he'll have anything to contribute.

JOHN: That's right. We always have to go over everything with him twice.

CAIAPHAS: But whenever we start before he gets here, we have to go over everything with him THREE times.

ANNAS: True.

JOHN: Why don't we just expel him from the Council?

CAIAPHAS: Because he is an honored and revered member of our group.

ANNAS: A highly respected man in the community.

CAIAPHAS: A shining light in the darkness.

ANNAS: A pillar of faith.

JOHN: And his father contributes more than anyone else to the Temple treasury?

CAIAPHAS and ANNAS: Exactly.

JOHN: OK. We'll wait. *(THOMAS enters, limping.)*

THOMAS: Hi, guys. Hope I didn't miss anything.

CAIAPHAS *(aside)*: Nothing you wouldn't have missed if you'd been here.

THOMAS: What?

ANNAS: We haven't started yet.

JOHN: What's wrong with you?

THOMAS: Nothing's wrong with me! I'm a good pharisee!

JOHN: I only meant...

THOMAS: You're always picking on me. And I don't know why.

JOHN: I was only asking...

THOMAS: I keep all the laws. Just as well as anybody. Well, almost as well.

JOHN: ...about your foot.

THOMAS: Is that some new kind of curse? About your foot! I don't get it.

ANNAS: He was inquiring about your foot.

CAIAPHAS: Showing a natural concern for his esteemed brother.

THOMAS: Is your brother here? John, I didn't know your brother Joseph was going to join us.

CAIAPHAS: Why are you LIMPING?

THOMAS: Oh. I twisted my ankle on the way here. There was a loose stone in the street. There should be a law against putting stones in the street.

JOHN: They help to keep the mud down when it rains.

ANNAS: They protect the road. They make it last longer.

THOMAS: Well, they should use different kinds. Ones that don't come loose.

CAIAPHAS: Gentlemen. We can leave the issue of public works to the Romans. They're the experts in building roads. We have more important matters at hand.

THOMAS: What could be more important than protecting our citizens?

CAIAPHAS: Nothing. That's why we're here.

(ALL turn to CAIAPHAS.)

ANNAS: Has something serious happened?

JOHN: Are the Romans planning to destroy Jerusalem? Are the zealots acting up again?

CAIAPHAS: No more than usual. The Romans are used to them. No man-made disaster is about to befall our city. It's philosophy we must worry about.

THOMAS: I move we tell the Romans to sharpen one edge of every stone. Is there a second?

ANNAS: What?

THOMAS: We need a second to the motion before we can vote. It's right here in Robert's Rules of Order.

JOHN: Why would we ask the Romans to sharpen stones?

THOMAS: We can't discuss the motion until it's seconded. It says so, right here. *(Points to his Robert's Rules of Order.)*

CAIAPHAS: Very well, I'll second it.

ANNAS and JOHN: What?

CAIAPHAS: It's easier to humor him than to argue with him.

JOHN: True. Thomas, why would we ask the Romans to sharpen stones?

THOMAS: Then they could pound the stones into the ground and there wouldn't be any loose stones in the street. Our citizens would be safe from the cruel and inhuman punishment of twisted ankles.

ANNAS: Can we vote on this and get it out of the way?

CAIAPHAS: Gladly. All in favor. *(THOMAS raises hand.)* Opposed. *(ANNAS and JOHN raise their hands.)* Defeated. Now, let's get on to important matters. There's a prophet going around the countryside.

JOHN: Jesus of Nazareth?

CAIAPHAS: You've heard of Him, then?

ANNAS: He's famous. Everyone's heard of Him. *(Looks at THOMAS.)* Well, maybe not everyone.

JOHN: What's the problem with Him? I've heard He's doing some wonderful things.

CAIAPHAS: That's precisely the problem.

ANNAS: What's wrong with helping people?

CAIAPHAS: Nothing, if He does it within the framework of the Law.

JOHN: He's been breaking the Law?

CAIAPHAS: Indeed He has! He's been healing the sick...

THOMAS: Of course He has. You don't heal the healthy. You heal the sick.

CAIAPHAS: He's been healing the sick on the Sabbath.

ANNAS: Blasphemy!

JOHN: I hadn't heard about this.

CAIAPHAS: Not only that—He's using His power of healing to claim to be God.

ANNAS: Double blasphemy!

CAIAPHAS: We have to get Jesus in here, away from the crowds...

THOMAS: That's a good idea. He could heal that ugly growth on you, John.

JOHN: What ugly growth?

THOMAS: That one. Right in the middle of your face.

JOHN: That's my nose!

THOMAS: It is? Well, maybe he could do something about it. A little plastic surgery would do wonders for your looks.

JOHN: MY looks? *(Shakes fist under THOMAS's nose.)* I'll do something about YOUR looks!

CAIAPHAS: Gentlemen! Bickering among ourselves won't help.

THOMAS: It might improve his personality, too. If you look good, you feel good.

ANNAS: Tell us what you've heard about Jesus, Caiaphas.

CAIAPHAS: First, there was all that healing over at Peter's house.

JOHN: We heard about that. I didn't hear of any problems there.

ANNAS: Didn't He just heal Peter's mother-in-law? And those who came to the house later in the evening?

CAIAPHAS: Yes. And if He'd been content to simply heal the sick, there would be no problem. But He's begun meddling with philosophy.

THOMAS: Well, I can't blame Him.

ANNAS: What?

THOMAS: Philip has always charged way too much for his legal advice.

JOHN: What are you talking about now?

THOMAS: Caiaphas just said Jesus was meddling with Phil's fees. And He should.

CAIAPHAS *(shaking his head)*: If his father weren't so rich...

THOMAS: I stopped to see Philip, right after I twisted my ankle. He wanted a full three talents to sue the Romans for personal damages. Well! That's way too much. It's highway robbery. He should be stopped.

CAIAPHAS (yelling)**:** Phil-o-so-phy!

THOMAS: That's what I said. Phil's law fees.

ANNAS (soothing CAIAPHAS)**:** Take it easy. It's only Thomas. John and I are here.

CAIAPHAS: Yes. You're right. Back to Jesus. He's forgiving sins.

JOHN: But He can't do that! Only God can forgive sin.

ANNAS: Of course. Anybody with an ounce of sense knows that.

CAIAPHAS: But He's using His healing powers to support His claim that He can forgive sin. He walked right up to a paralyzed man and said, "Your sins are forgiven." I told Him, "You can't do that. Only God can forgive sin."

JOHN: Of course. You did the right thing.

ANNAS: After all, a man cannot forgive another's sins.

CAIAPHAS: But this Jesus said, "Is it easier to say, 'Your sins are forgiven' or 'Get up and walk'?" Then He turned to the paralyzed man and said, "Get up. Take your mat and go home." And the man did.

JOHN: This could mean trouble.

CAIAPHAS: There are even rumors that He had a face-to-face confrontation with Satan and defeated him. Silly, of course. No man could do that.

ANNAS: The things people will believe. But if this is all He's done...

CAIAPHAS: It isn't. I have this report from Alexander. Last Sabbath, Jesus healed a man's hand. On the Sabbath!

JOHN: Blasphemy!

ANNAS: Double blasphemy!

THOMAS: I move we get Philip to bring an action against Jesus for practicing medicine without a license. He might do it for free if Jesus has been trying to make him reduce his fees.

JOHN: (Reaches for THOMAS's throat.) Why you...(THOMAS holds up Robert's Rules of Order.)

CAIAPHAS (restraining JOHN)**:** Seconded. In favor? (THOMAS holds up hand.) Against? (JOHN and ANNAS hold up hands.) Defeated.

ANNAS: (To JOHN.) He's right. It is faster to humor him than to argue.

CAIAPHAS: We must make plans to stop Jesus before His popularity gets out of hand.

JOHN: But if He's only healed a few people, we could counteract it.

ANNAS: How?

JOHN: Most of his popularity is from rumors of what He has done. We'll start rumors, blaming Him for evil. It shouldn't be too hard. The man's a blasphemer.

CAIAPHAS: I wish it were that easy! He's done other things.

ANNAS: Like what?

CAIAPHAS: He's been preaching. And huge crowds have been listening.

JOHN: That's nothing to worry about. We've been preaching for years.

ANNAS: The common man can't grasp important religious principles.

JOHN: He'll never persuade them. People don't listen to doctrine.

CAIAPHAS: No? Suppose you were one of a group of five thousand men. And some women and children.

ANNAS: Yes.

CAIAPHAS: Now suppose you were listening to Jesus when suppertime came.

JOHN: I'd go home for supper.

CAIAPHAS: But suppose you were a long way from home. You couldn't get home in time for supper.

THOMAS: I move...

CAIAPHAS: Seconded. In favor? Opposed? Defeated.

ANNAS: What does hunger have to do with doctrine?

CAIAPHAS: Now suppose a boy comes forward with his lunch. A few fish and a little bread. He offers to share it with the crowd.

JOHN: I'd laugh. What can so little do for so many?

CAIAPHAS: Jesus blessed it, broke it into pieces and had it passed around. It fed the whole crowd.

ANNAS *(stunned)***:** Are you certain?

CAIAPHAS: With enough to gather twelve baskets of leftovers.

JOHN: Impossible!

CAIAPHAS: It's all in Alexander's report.

ANNAS: Then, huge crowds could be following Him! Hoping to be fed.

CAIAPHAS: Fortunately, Jesus rebuked them. He told them they only followed Him for the food.

JOHN: Then where's the problem? They must have stopped.

CAIAPHAS: But those who DO follow have become fanatics. Jesus must be stopped. We must find an excuse to get Him in here. Some reason to have Him killed.

ANNAS: I agree.

JOHN: So do I. He must be stopped.

CAIAPHAS: Then we're agreed? Good. Let's go...

THOMAS: Wait a minute. *(Holds up Robert's Rules of Order.)* We don't have a motion.

CAIAPHAS *(irritated)***:** I move that we find an excuse to find Jesus guilty of a crime punishable by death. I further move that we have Him brought here before us for a trial.

THOMAS: I'll second the motion.

CAIAPHAS: In favor? *(ALL raise hands.)* Good. Then we're adjourned. *(ALL rise to leave, THOMAS limping.)*

THOMAS: I've got an idea. Let's not tell Him why we're bringing Him here. Then, before we find Him guilty, He could fix John's nose. And I wonder how He is with ankles? *(Looks around.)* And where is Joseph? I thought he was coming to this meeting.

WASTE NARD, WANT NARD

SCRIPTURE: Matthew 26:6-13; Mark 14:3-9; John 12:1-8

SUGGESTED TOPICS: Attitude in giving; stewardship

BIBLE BACKGROUND

Even being close to Jesus on a daily basis did not guarantee that the disciples instantly grasped the modeling they saw. Sometimes they must have seemed painfully slow to understand the life-changing truths unfolding before their eyes. Having lived with the very essence of selfless giving in their Master, Jesus' disciples were still blind to the message of the woman who gave the most precious thing she had to honor Him.

The apostle John is often pictured as a quiet man. After all, he was the beloved disciple. Most people tend to forget that he and his brother, James, were fishermen known as the "Sons of Thunder." This nickname suggests quick tempers and loud voices. This skit uses James and John to reflect the unthinking attitudes which occasionally trip up all Jesus' followers.

PERFORMANCE TIPS

1. Suggested props: Bible-times costumes.

2. James and John should speak in a scornful tone of voice.

3. Read Mark 14:6-9 after the skit and discuss Jesus' response.

DISCUSSION QUESTIONS

1. Compare the attitudes of James and John and the woman.

2. Who showed love for Jesus? How?

3. Read 2 Corinthians 9:7. What does the Bible say is the wrong way to give? What is the right way to give?

4. What can you give to show your love for God?

WASTE NARD, WANT NARD

CHARACTERS

JAMES

JOHN

JAMES: You know, following Jesus certainly does have its good points.

JOHN: You're right. Take this meal we're having, for example. Being invited to a prominent man's home. Being served the best food that money can buy. Nothing is too good when Jesus is visiting.

JAMES: Yes. It is good to have meat to eat. I was getting tired of fish.

JOHN: Say! What's that woman doing over near Jesus?

JAMES: She isn't one of the serving girls. What do you suppose she's planning to do with that box?

JOHN: I have no idea. She's holding it as if it's valuable.

JAMES: I wonder what's in it?

JOHN: Look at that! She broke the box! She's pouring the contents over Jesus!

JAMES: Well, now we know what was in the box. There's no mistaking the smell of spikenard! I wonder why she's being so wasteful. That stuff's very expensive.

JOHN: Somebody should reprimand her for this waste. In fact, I think I'll do it myself. Do you want to help?

JAMES: Gladly! I abhor waste.

JOHN: Hey! Woman! What's the matter with you?

JAMES: Yeah! That's expensive stuff you're pouring all over the floor!

JOHN: Do you know how much that stuff is worth?

JAMES: She probably does, since she bought it.

JOHN: Oh, yeah. That's right. Anyway, that would cost the average worker a whole year's wages! And you're pouring it out like it was cheap wine!

JAMES: You should have sold it and given the money to the poor. At least then somebody would have benefitted from the expense.

JOHN: Wait! Jesus is speaking. Oh, oh. We're in trouble again.

JAMES: Honest, Jesus. It wasn't my fault. *(Points to JOHN.)* It was all his idea.

SACRIFICE UNTIL IT KIND OF HURTS

SCRIPTURE: Mark 12:41-44; Luke 21:1-4; 22:20

SUGGESTED TOPICS: Giving; obeying God

BIBLE BACKGROUND

Sacrificial offerings began shortly after the Garden of Eden (see Genesis 4:3,4) and were extended by Noah (see Genesis 8:20), Abraham (see Genesis 22:13), Isaac (see Genesis 26:25) and Jacob (see Genesis 31:54). The system of sacrificial worship was fully instituted under Moses as part of the covenant (the old testament) between God and humanity. Recognizing that people are sinful, God provided a method by which they could approach Him. The people were instructed to bring their offerings to the priests to be offered as payment for their sins (see Leviticus 1—7). The sacrifice was to be an animal without blemish from one's herd. The poor could bring pigeons as a sacrifice instead; the very poor could offer flour (see Leviticus 5:11).

The Lord made it clear in the Old Testament that the sacrifice itself was not the redeeming factor. The spirit with which the sacrifice was given was the important thing. Saul was rebuked for offering a sacrifice rather than obeying God's instructions (see 1 Samuel 15:22). All of Judah was rebuked for offering sacrifices while taking advantage of other people (see Jeremiah 7:1-11). Jesus reiterated the importance of attitude when he commended a widow's small offering as being of greater value than the larger sums given by those of greater means (see Mark 12:41-44).

But the old covenant was flawed. Sin offerings had to be made over and over because the sacrifice was imperfect. God instituted a new covenant, one which was sealed by the Perfect Sacrifice, God Incarnate. By offering Himself for our sin, Jesus forgave all the sin ever committed and all that would be committed. This sacrifice does not need to be repeated (see Hebrews 7:27). By placing trust in this Perfect Sacrifice, our guilt is covered and the power of sin is destroyed (see Hebrews 10:10).

PERFORMANCE TIPS

1. Suggested props: toy lamb, two pennies for the widow, two bags of coins for the rich man, sack marked "flour" for the poor man's offering, small bowl, metal bowl for the Temple treasury.
2. The rich man speaks loudly (until he discovers his mistake). He wants everyone in the Temple to know how good he is.
3. The widow makes her offering with her head down. She does not look up until the poor man speaks to her.

DISCUSSION QUESTIONS

1. Which offering was most pleasing to God? Which was least pleasing? Why?
2. Does having material wealth show that God is pleased with us? Why or why not?
3. Jesus is often called "the Lamb of God." Why?
4. Why would Jesus allow Himself to be sacrificed on the cross?
5. What must we do to become part of God's family?

The Big Book of Bible Skits ©1997 Gospel Light. Permission to photocopy granted.

SACRIFICE UNTIL IT KIND OF HURTS

CHARACTERS

RICH MAN   **POOR MAN**   **WIDOW**

RICH MAN: *(Holds up lamb, speaks loudly toward sky.)* Oh, Lord God, see my noble sacrifice, a perfect lamb. Forgive my sins, few though they may be.

POOR MAN: *(Holds up small bowl of flour; sack is by his feet.)* I am but a poor man, Lord God. I have no wealth to present to You. Please accept this humble sacrifice. I have not even two pigeons. Accept this offering of flour, for it is all I can bring.

RICH MAN: *(To POOR MAN.)* You would offer THIS to God?

POOR MAN: It is all I have. Is it not lawful to offer such to God?

RICH MAN: It may be lawful, but it's also pitiful. See MY beautiful sacrifice. THIS is what the Lord wants. The best.

POOR MAN: But this IS my best!

RICH MAN: Well, then, your best just isn't good enough. *(Points to WIDOW.)* You're as pathetic as that woman over there by the treasury.

POOR MAN: She is a widow. I know her. She has even less than I do.

RICH MAN: Well, look at that offering. Two pennies! What's that to God?

POOR MAN: It is what she willingly gives. Isn't that enough?

RICH MAN: Look, we're supposed to be SACRIFICING. That means giving God something worthwhile. You see this lamb? THERE'S a sacrifice.

POOR MAN: It is indeed a fine lamb. *(To WIDOW who is walking by.)* How is it with you, sister?

WIDOW: Oh, hello, neighbor. I didn't see you.

RICH MAN: I don't wonder that you didn't see him, keeping your head down. Of course, if I only threw two pennies into the Temple treasury, I wouldn't hold my head up, either.

WIDOW: If I had more to give, I would give it. But I have none.

POOR MAN: You gave EVERYTHING?

WIDOW: It was what I had.

POOR MAN: Stop by my house on the way home. I have enough oil and flour for two days. You must take half.

WIDOW: No, I couldn't.

POOR MAN: But I insist. I won't take no for an answer!

RICH MAN: You two are so pathetic. Do you want to see how an offering should be made? *(Takes bag of money from belt and goes to treasury.)* Oh, God. You are so gracious to me. Look what I'm giving to You. This shows how good I am and why you bless me so. *(Pours money into treasury.)*

WIDOW: It must be wonderful to have so much to offer to God.

RICH MAN: He has blessed me because I don't sin. I'm not like tax gatherers or those others. You two must have done some really bad things.

POOR MAN *(sadly)*: Why do you say such a thing?

WIDOW: Is it a sin to be poor?

RICH MAN: Everyone knows God punishes sinners. And you two are being punished. I, on the other hand, keep all the laws. I am very nearly perfect. That's why God has blessed me with so much.

POOR MAN: I cannot believe this. Yes, I have sinned. We all have sinned.

WIDOW: That is true. I, too, have sinned. But God forgives sin.

RICH MAN: Not for a little flour and two pennies. You need good sheep and a bagful of cash to have forgiveness, even for MY paltry sins. Think what is required for YOUR great sins!

WIDOW: But doesn't God look at the heart?

POOR MAN: Doesn't He test the SPIRIT of the gift?

RICH MAN: Well, I suppose it counts a little. But it's the SIZE of the gift that really matters. Look at this sheep. Almost perfect.

POOR MAN: ALMOST perfect?

RICH MAN: She's lame. Not much good in my flock. But she makes a wonderful sacrifice. You don't think I'm going to waste the best of my flock by having it given to the Temple!

POOR MAN: But aren't we supposed to give our best? You said so yourself!

RICH MAN: What I have given is better than most. Better than yours, certainly. That makes it good.

WIDOW: I must be going.

POOR MAN: Remember to stop at my house. Get that flour and oil.

WIDOW: If you insist.

RICH MAN: You know, having my minor sins forgiven has made me feel generous. *(Takes a second bag of money from belt.)* Have a penny. *(Looks into bag.)* Oh, no!

WIDOW: What is wrong, sir?

RICH MAN: This bag is full of PENNIES.

WIDOW: It must be wonderful to have all that wealth.

RICH MAN: But...but—I brought two bags of money with me. One full of pennies, for the offering. The other had gold and silver in it. I put the wrong bag into the offering! Here, give me that. *(Takes penny back from WIDOW.)*

POOR MAN: It is not right to give and then to take away.

WIDOW: *(To POOR MAN.)* It doesn't matter, neighbor. I didn't expect to leave the Temple with any money. I have more than I expected with your kind offer of food.

POOR MAN: Come. We'll go and get it now.

RICH MAN: *(To himself.)* How can I get my money back? Maybe if I went to the priest and explained the problem. No. The priests are as greedy as everyone else. They wouldn't give it back.

POOR MAN: *(To RICH MAN.)* Good-bye, friend.

WIDOW: *(To RICH MAN.)* May the Lord bless you.

RICH MAN: He'd better, after all I gave Him today.

TRIALS, TRIALS, TRIALS

SCRIPTURE: Matthew 26:57-66; 27:11-14; Luke 22:66—23:11; John 18:12-37

SUGGESTED TOPICS: Events surrounding Jesus' death; Jesus' humility; God's love

BIBLE BACKGROUND

Jesus' earthly ministry was nearing completion. To fulfill all prophecy, He had to be betrayed and then killed. However, in order for an execution to be carried out, two trials had to be held—one under Jewish law and one under Roman law. It is interesting to note that, while both the Jewish and Roman trials of Jesus were conducted in highly irregular manners, the gospel accounts do not claim that the trial proceedings were illegal. The perspective of the writers was that of lay observers, not legal experts.

Caiaphas was a shrewd politician. With absolute cunning and disregard for the law he was sworn to uphold as high priest, he found a crime which required the death penalty and for which Jesus could be convicted: blasphemy. However, under Roman law, only a governor could sentence a man to death.

The Roman governor, Pilate, cared little for the Jews and their customs. Only the accusation that Jesus was guilty of treason against Rome held any interest for him. When he questioned Jesus, he quickly concluded that Jesus was no threat to Roman authority and sought to release Him. However, Caiaphas threatened Pilate that if he refused to sentence Jesus to death, Pilate could be found negligent in his duties by Rome. What was he to do? Simple. Pass the buck to Herod, the puppet king appointed by Rome.

Herod Antipas, one of the sons of Herod the Great, was tetrarch (ruler of one fourth of a region) of Galilee. He was in Jerusalem for Passover, even though he had no more interest in the Jews than did Pilate. He was, however, fascinated at the prospect of meeting Jesus, the miracle worker. When Jesus refused to answer Herod's questions or perform a miracle for him, Herod sent Jesus back to Pilate.

PERFORMANCE TIPS

1. Suggested props: gavel and/or black robe for Caiaphas.
2. If you have adequate space in your room, designate a separate area for each trial. March Jesus from place to place. If space is limited, march Jesus around the room each time Caiaphas, Pilate and Herod take their places.
3. Suggest that the person playing the part of Jesus act in a self-assured, calm manner. Since Jesus knew these events were part of God's plan, Jesus' attitude was not one of anger or rebellion.
4. Introduce the skit by asking the group to briefly summarize the events leading up to Jesus' arrest. Supplement their summary with information from John 18:1-12.

DISCUSSION QUESTIONS

1. What parts of Jesus' trials were illegal? Why do you think these illegal procedures were used?
2. Why did Jesus allow Himself to be arrested and tried?
3. How did Jesus' actions show God's love?

TRIALS, TRIALS, TRIALS

CHARACTERS
CAIAPHAS (KYE-ah-fus)
DAVID
JESUS
WITNESS ONE
WITNESS TWO
PILATE
HEROD
SERVANT

SCENE ONE

CAIAPHAS: OK. Let's begin this trial under duly appointed law...

DAVID: Excuse me, your High Priestliness.

CAIAPHAS: What is it?

DAVID: If we're operating under law, why is the trial at night?

CAIAPHAS: What are you babbling about?

DAVID: Under the law, a trial can't be held at night. Only during the day.

CAIAPHAS: Ahem. Yes. Well, sometimes one thing must bow to another. Because of Passover, we felt it was more important to resolve this matter quickly than to wait until tomorrow for the trial.

DAVID: And then, too, you wouldn't have to worry about too many of His friends showing up.

CAIAPHAS: Precisely. I mean, nonsense. Swift justice is what matters. Bring in the guilty party!

DAVID: You mean, the accused.

CAIAPHAS: Same difference. Now then, Jesus of Nazareth. You have been accused of blasphemy. How do You plead? What is it You have been teaching?

JESUS: I always spoke openly. I taught in the Temple and in the synagogues, where the Jews meet. I have said nothing in secret. Why ask what I have taught? Ask those who have heard. They know what I said.

CAIAPHAS: How dare you speak so to me? Very well, we shall assume this is a 'not guilty' plea. Bother. Bring in the first liar—I mean, witness.

WITNESS ONE: How d'you do, Your Honor.

CAIAPHAS: Now then, what did you hear this man say?

WITNESS ONE: Last Monday, I heard Him say that the Temple should be torn down.

CAIAPHAS: There you have it. Blasphemy. Is there any reason why sentence should not be passed immediately?

The Big Book of Bible Skits ©1997 Gospel Light. Permission to photocopy granted.

DAVID: Well...

CAIAPHAS: Well, what?

DAVID: Technically, He's not guilty until two witnesses agree in all aspects of their testimony.

CAIAPHAS: Very well. Call in the next li—ahem, witness.

WITNESS TWO: I'm here.

CAIAPHAS: Good. Now then, what did you hear this man say concerning tearing down the Temple on Monday?

DAVID: Isn't that leading the witness, Your High Priestliness?

CAIAPHAS: Nonsense! I'm just trying to speed up the judicial process. Answer the question.

WITNESS TWO: Oh, He said it, Your Worship. He said He could build up the walls in three days if somebody tore down the Temple. That's witchcraft, that is. And He said it.

CAIAPHAS: What about tearing down the Temple? Didn't He tell people to tear down the Temple? Think carefully.

WITNESS TWO: Uh, what is it you want me to say, Your Worship?

DAVID: Speak the truth. That's why you're here.

WITNESS TWO: Oh. Well, uh, He said He was a master builder or something like that and that He could build the Temple in three days and kind of that sort of thing.

CAIAPHAS: I'm calling a short recess. *(Calls offstage.)* Annas, check out the witnesses. See if you can find two in that crowd who can agree on a story. Now then, I think I will question the guilty party myself while we're waiting.

DAVID: You can't do that, Sir. You can't ask the accused to give evidence against Himself. It's against the law. You need two witnesses.

CAIAPHAS: Well, we'll find two witnesses if it takes all night. *(Calls offstage.)* Annas. Bring in the two witnesses that...What do you mean, you can't find two witnesses who agree in their testimony? I've had enough of this. You, Jesus! Are You the Christ?

DAVID: This is all highly irregular.

CAIAPHAS: What do I care about irregular? You heard the question. Well?

JESUS: If I tell you, you will not believe. And if I ask you, you will not answer Me nor let Me go. Hereafter, the Son of Man shall sit on the right hand of God.

CAIAPHAS: Are You, then, the Son of God?

JESUS: You say that I am.

CAIAPHAS: Hah! We have Him. What do we need witnesses for? He has accused Himself. Take Him to Pilate!

DAVID: This is all very irregular.

(Skit continues on next page.)

SCENE TWO

CAIAPHAS: This man has been perverting the nation. He has been saying that He is King. Being good, law-abiding citizens, we bring Him to you to get rid—I mean, to determine what to do about Him.

PILATE: Bring in the accused. Now then. Are you the King of the Jews?

JESUS: You say that I am. Do you say it of your own knowledge or did others tell it to you?

PILATE: I don't see that this man has done anything wrong. If He broke your Jewish laws, it's not my concern. I'm not a Jew. Try Him yourselves.

CAIAPHAS: We have done so. He is guilty. But you must pass sentence, for we cannot exact the death penalty.

PILATE: The death penalty? Surely that's a little harsh for a fellow who's only fault is maybe being a little bit crazy.

CAIAPHAS: He has been trying to incite riots for three years, beginning in Galilee and coming all the way to Jerusalem.

PILATE: Galilee? Is this man a Galilean?

CAIAPHAS: Of course. Just listening to Him, you can tell He's from Galilee.

PILATE: Wonderful! Then I don't have to make the decision. I mean, in the interests of justice, and following all the precepts of Roman law, I decide that this man should be sent to see Herod, because Galilee is part of Herod's jurisdiction.

CAIAPHAS: You're not sending Him all the way to Galilee to see Herod?

PILATE: Of course not. Herod happens to be in Jerusalem. Send Him to Herod.

SCENE THREE

HEROD: What a miserable little country. I wish I could be transferred to Rome. Nothing ever happens here.

SERVANT: Some men here to see you, my Lord. With a prisoner.

HEROD: What do I want with prisoners? Send Him to Pilate.

SERVANT: Pilate sent Him to you. Because He's a Galilean, my Lord.

HEROD: I don't care if He's a giraffe. Send Him back to Pilate.

SERVANT: Very good, my Lord. OK! Take Jesus back to Pilate.

HEROD: Wait a minute. Did you say Jesus?

SERVANT: Yes, my Lord.

HEROD: Jesus, the prophet from Galilee?

SERVANT: Yes, my Lord.

HEROD: The One who's done all the miracles? Raised people from the dead? Turned water into wine? Healed the sick? Or so I'm told.

SERVANT: That's the One, my Lord.

HEROD: Well, don't just stand there. Bring Him in! Maybe He'll perform a miracle. That would be fun.

CAIAPHAS: Here is the blasphemer, oh Herod. Sentence Him to death.

HEROD: Everything in good time. Now then. Jesus. What do You have to say for Yourself? Come on, man. Speak up. I'm the most powerful man in the country. *(JESUS is silent.)*

SERVANT: Standing mute won't help You. Speak to Herod.

HEROD: That's right. Now, it seems that the Jews accuse You of blasphemy. Well, show them they're wrong. Do a miracle. Look! Here's a glass of water. Turn it into wine.

SERVANT: It's still water, my Lord.

HEROD: I can see that. Wait a minute. *(To SERVANT.)* Does your wife still have that hideous boil on her face?

SERVANT: Yes, my Lord.

HEROD: *(To JESUS.)* You could heal her, couldn't You? I'd love to see that. Say that You'll heal her. Come on, man. Speak up!

CAIAPHAS: He has no respect for authority.

HEROD: How about walking on water? I heard You can do that. Let's go down to the river and You can walk across it. If You get to the other side, You're a free man. What do You say? Go ahead. Do it.

SERVANT: What's the matter with You? Don't You want to go free?

HEROD: I've had enough of this. Who cares if He comes from Galilee? His crimes were committed in Jerusalem. Send Him back to Pilate. Let Pilate make the decision.

HE AROSE

SCRIPTURE: Matthew 26:1-5,47-68; 27:11-66

SUGGESTED TOPICS: Jesus' resurrection

BIBLE BACKGROUND

Ghandi once said Christianity was exactly what India needed—if Christians truly believed what they said. His implication was that India could have her problems solved if Christians acted the way they said they believed; the central truth of Christianity was unimportant to him. The apostle Paul is not so charitable to Christians as Ghandi. To Paul, the importance of Christianity was not that people acted differently if they believed; the importance lay in its truth. "If there is not resurrection of the dead, then Christ is not risen. If Christ is not risen, our preaching and your faith are worthless. We would be false witnesses and you would still be lost in your sins" (see 1 Corinthians 15:13-17). To disprove Christianity, one must disprove the resurrection.

For centuries, people have tried to find reasonable explanations for the empty tomb. Various possibilities other than Jesus' resurrection have been proposed: "The disciples stole the body"; "He wasn't really dead, so the coolness of the tomb revived Him and He got up and left"; "He never really existed, it's all just a story." When examined closely, none of the alternative explanations hold water. Christians can rejoice in the confidence of a loving God who came to die so that our sins might be forgiven and rose, victorious over death.

PERFORMANCE TIPS

1. Suggested props: Bible-times costumes, table and chairs for Annas and Alexander.
2. These are shrewd men. Annas and Alexander are not as quick to catch on to things as Caiaphas, but they are not stupid.
3. Caiaphas paces throughout the skit. He is tense and eager to go.

DISCUSSION QUESTIONS

1. Why is Jesus' resurrection important?
2. Do you agree with this statement: "It's not important what you believe, only that you believe something." Why or why not?
3. What evidence do we have that the resurrection is a fact?
4. Some people believe Jesus' disciples stole the body and said Jesus rose. Why can we know this is not true?

HE AROSE

CHARACTERS
CAIAPHAS (KYE-uh-fus)
ANNAS
ALEXANDER

PRONUNCIATION GUIDE
Nicodemus (NICK-uh-DEE-mus)
Zebedee (ZEB-uh-dee)

CAIAPHAS: *(Rubs forehead.)* What a day!

ANNAS: *(Yawns.)* I've never been so tired in my life.

ALEXANDER: But at least it's over.

CAIAPHAS: Not yet, it isn't.

ANNAS: What do you mean?

ALEXANDER: The blasphemer, Jesus, has been crucified.

ANNAS: He's crucified and dead! You saw the blood and water spill from His side.

ALEXANDER: He'll be put into Joseph's tomb and that's the end of it.

CAIAPHAS: Not quite. We must go and see Pilate again.

ANNAS: Why? I don't like him.

ALEXANDER: And he doesn't like us. Look what he wrote on the charge sheet against Jesus. "This is Jesus, the King of the Jews."

ANNAS: And we couldn't get him to change it. It wouldn't have been so hard to have it say, "This is Jesus, who SAID He was the King of the Jews."

CAIAPHAS: Yes, he could have done that. *(Clenches fists.)* I'll never forgive him for it. I'll find a way to make him pay for that insult.

ALEXANDER: I still don't understand why Pilate had Jesus crucified.

ANNAS: Because He's a blasphemer. That requires death.

ALEXANDER: But PILATE doesn't care about blasphemy.

CAIAPHAS: But he cares about his own neck.

ANNAS: What do you mean?

CAIAPHAS: When we brought Jesus to Pilate for sentencing, did you think he would have Him killed because WE wanted it?

ANNAS: Why not? The man was guilty! He needed to be killed.

ALEXANDER: I WAS surprised. Pilate's never had any sensitivity to important religious matters in the past.

CAIAPHAS: I doubted he would pass sentence. That's why I had another plan waiting. Do you think I spoke to Pilate on the spur of the moment, without planning what I would say?

ANNAS: You mean you wrote out your speech beforehand?

ALEXANDER: You memorized it?

CAIAPHAS: Not exactly. But as we led Jesus to Pilate's court, I made preparations in case Pilate would not sentence Jesus to death.

ANNAS: I never quite understood that.

ALEXANDER: Neither did I. But it worked.

CAIAPHAS: Let me explain. Jesus claimed to be God. That's why WE sentenced Him to death.

ALEXANDER: Sure, but Pilate wouldn't care about that. Pilate doesn't care about religion.

ANNAS: He should!

CAIAPHAS: But he doesn't. But Pilate DOES care about politics. If Jesus claimed to be our God, He ALSO claimed to be our King! *(Gets blank stares from ANNAS and ALEXANDER.)* But only CAESAR can appoint a king.

ANNAS: Ah, now I see!

ALEXANDER: *(Strokes beard.)* By claiming to be King, Jesus committed treason against ROME!

CAIAPHAS: Precisely. Come, we must go and see Pilate.

ANNAS: He won't want to see us.

ALEXANDER: He was upset when you pressured him into crucifying Jesus.

CAIAPHAS: I don't care. We have more pressing issues.

ANNAS: Like what?

ALEXANDER: It's almost the Sabbath. Can't it wait for a few days?

CAIAPHAS: No. It must be done immediately!

ANNAS: What is so important that we must risk breaking the Sabbath?

CAIAPHAS: Do you remember the blasphemer claiming He would not remain in the grave?

ALEXANDER: A fool's boast. Dead is dead.

ANNAS: Those two traitors, Joseph and Nicodemus, will see to it that He's buried. They may not do a perfect job, but they'll use enough spices and linen to secure the body.

CAIAPHAS: But what if someone else decides to MOVE the body?

ALEXANDER: Who would disturb the body? Everyone knows who's buried there. Grave robbers aren't going to break into the tomb of a poor carpenter and preacher. There's nothing worth stealing.

CAIAPHAS: What about His disciples?

ANNAS: They all ran away. They're just a pack of cowards.

CAIAPHAS: I think I saw one near the Cross. John, the son of Zebedee.

ALEXANDER: He won't cause any trouble. He'll just go back to fishing.

CAIAPHAS: But suppose. What if the disciples suddenly find some courage? They might go and move the body and claim Jesus rose from the dead!

ANNAS: Why would they do that? There's no profit in it for them.

CAIAPHAS: They might do it in memory of their Master. Make people think He was more than just an ordinary man.

ALEXANDER: It sounds far-fetched to me. Not a chance in a hundred.

CAIAPHAS: But can we take that one chance?

ANNAS: What do you suggest we do? Sit by the tomb until Pentecost?

CAIAPHAS: No, but Pilate could assign a guard for the tomb.

ALEXANDER: The way he feels about us, right NOW? If we went and asked for a guard, he'd say, "Go peddle your papers!" or something like that.

CAIAPHAS: Of course he would.

ANNAS: So, you're saying we should go to Pilate so he can insult us?

CAIAPHAS: Not at all. We go in a position of strength. Remember, politics.

ANNAS: I'm a priest, not a politician.

ALEXANDER: These days, one must be both. How do we convince Pilate?

CAIAPHAS: We tell him that if Jesus' disciples steal the body, they will claim Jesus rose from the dead.

ANNAS: How will that convince Pilate? He'll say, "What utter nonsense!"

ALEXANDER: True. And probably have us thrown out.

CAIAPHAS: Pilate is smarter than that. He has studied our beliefs.

ANNAS: Not so you'd notice.

ALEXANDER: Hasn't changed him one bit. He's the same arrogant Roman dog he always was.

CAIAPHAS: Let me ask you, if Rome had crucified the REAL Messiah, what would the people of Israel do?

ANNAS: That's simple. They'd riot.

ALEXANDER: Ahh! Now I see.

CAIAPHAS: Pilate can't take that chance. A riot in Israel and he'll be back in Rome, facing a court-martial. He'd be disgraced, maybe even killed.

ANNAS: I have to hand it to you, Caiaphas. You think of everything.

CAIAPHAS: In this job, one must. That's what being high priest is all about.

ALEXANDER: Hey! If we can get a guard, maybe we can even have the tomb sealed.

CAIAPHAS: Sealed with a Roman seal. NOBODY'S going to touch THAT. Good thinking. Come! Let's go before it's too late. Jesus' body MUST stay in that tomb.

HE'S ALIVE!

SCRIPTURE: Matthew 28:1-10; Luke 24:1-12; John 20:1-18

SUGGESTED TOPICS: Jesus' resurrection; God's plan of salvation fulfilled

BIBLE BACKGROUND

Jesus was dead! His disciples, in fear for their own lives, were in hiding. Because Jesus' death had occurred so close to the beginning of the Sabbath, Joseph of Arimathea and Nicodemus had not had time to properly prepare His body for burial. Now, on the first day of the week, a small group of women made their way to the tomb to pay their last respects to the dead.

The Bible leaves no ambiguity with respect to Jesus' death and resurrection. This is the most important series of events in human history and the crux of Christianity (see 1 Corinthians 15:12-19). For centuries, people have tried to prove it false; for centuries, people have failed.

PERFORMANCE TIPS

1. Suggested props: Bible-times costumes.

2. In Scene One the three women should walk slowly towards one end of the room designated as the tomb. Designate another area of the room as the house where Peter and John are staying.

3. Peter and John should sound as if they are convinced that Mary is completely out of her mind. Because they saw Jesus die, they are certain He is dead.

DISCUSSION QUESTIONS

1. Suppose you saw a friend die and were later told he or she was alive again. How would you feel? What would make you believe the report?

2. Do you agree or disagree with the statement, "Jesus' resurrection is the most important event in history"? Why or why not?

3. How does the death and resurrection of Jesus affect your life now? What difference does it make today whether or not Jesus rose from the dead?

He's Alive!

CHARACTERS

MARY MAGDALENE

MARY (MOTHER OF JESUS)

JOANNA

PETER

JOHN

ANGEL

JESUS

SCENE ONE

MARY MAGDALENE: So? How are we going to do it?

MARY: I don't know.

JOANNA: It's a very heavy stone.

MARY MAGDALENE: Maybe if we all push together?

MARY: Don't be silly.

JOANNA: Maybe the guards will help us.

MARY: Maybe, maybe, maybe. We should go and get some of the men to help us. Four of the stronger ones should be enough to roll away the stone.

MARY MAGDALENE: No way! If the guards saw so many men coming, you know what would happen. They'd attack first and ask questions later. But maybe they'll help three women.

JOANNA: Why wouldn't they? We're only going to make sure that the body is properly buried. They'll be there the whole time. It's not like we're going to steal anything.

MARY MAGDALENE: Well, maybe they'll help.

MARY: It's the only hope we have.

JOANNA: Are we almost there?

MARY MAGDALENE: Of course. You know where the tomb is.

MARY: It's right over there.

JOANNA: But where are the guards?

MARY MAGDALENE: And why is the stone over on the side and not in front of the entrance?

MARY: There's something strange going on here.

JOANNA: The body's gone!

MARY MAGDALENE: I'd better go and tell Peter and John. *(She runs off.)*

MARY: Should we go in?

JOANNA: It's awfully dark.

MARY: But we must know what happened.

JOANNA: But it's awfully dark.

MARY: No it's not. It's light. Where did the light come from?

ANGEL: Who is it that you seek?

MARY AND JOANNA: Who are you, Sir? And why do you shine?

ANGEL: I am an angel of the Lord. Why do you seek for the living among the dead? Do you not remember that He said evil men would kill Him, but on the third day, He would rise again?

MARY: Are you telling us that He's alive?

JOANNA: Just as He said in Galilee. I remember.

ANGEL: Go to the disciples and tell them the good news. He's alive.

MARY AND JOANNA: We will! We will! *(They run off.)*

SCENE TWO

PETER: Who's banging on the door?

MARY MAGDALENE *(gasping for breath)***:** Mary.

PETER: Who?

JOHN: She said, "Mary."

PETER: It could be a trick. Mary who?

MARY MAGDALENE *(gasping for breath)***:** Mary...*(Gasps.)* Magdalene.

JOHN: It sounds like her. Let her in.

PETER: OK. You're in. What is it?

MARY MAGDALENE *(gasping for breath)***:** Jesus. Tomb. Stone. Gone. Body.

JOHN: Whoa. Whoa. Whoa.

PETER: Pull in your nets, woman. Take a deep breath and start over.

JOHN: You're not making any sense.

MARY MAGDALENE: We went to Jesus' tomb.

PETER: Why'd you do that?

MARY MAGDALENE: To anoint His body. To give it a proper burial.

JOHN: Well that was dumb. How are you women going to move that stone?

MARY MAGDALENE: We didn't have to. It was already moved.

PETER: Sure it was. With guards all around the tomb.

MARY MAGDALENE: I'm telling you. It was rolled away from the entrance.

JOHN: You must have gone to the wrong place.

MARY MAGDALENE: No we didn't. Go! See for yourselves.

PETER: We will! C'mon, John.

JOHN: Just far enough to see the guards.

PETER: Well, of course. No point in getting killed because some hysterical women can't find the right tomb.

The Big Book of Bible Skits ©1997 Gospel Light. Permission to photocopy granted.

MARY MAGDALENE: We were at the right place! Somebody's taken the body.

JOHN: Sure they did. Let's go and see, Peter. *(They run off to the tomb.)*

PETER *(puffing while jogging):* It looks peaceful enough so far.

JOHN *(also puffing):* Try to keep up! But be quiet. We don't want to alert the guards.

PETER: I am being quiet. Just over this hill, we'll see the tomb. Don't get so far ahead.

JOHN: I can see the tomb.

PETER: And?

JOHN: I can see the stone.

PETER: And?

JOHN: I can't see the guards.

PETER: What?

JOHN: I can't see the guards. They're not there.

PETER: What? Let me see. What's the stone doing way over there?

JOHN: I don't know.

PETER: Where are you going?

JOHN: To get a better look. C'mon.

PETER: Well, slow down. Don't go running into danger.

JOHN: What danger?

PETER: How do I know? But something strange is happening.

JOHN: C'mon. Maybe Mary was right.

PETER: Slow down. OK, you got here first and you're blocking the entrance. So what do ` you see?

JOHN: Nothing.

PETER: What do you mean, "nothing"? Get out of the way.

JOHN: Well, you don't have to push.

PETER: Look. Look at the burial cloths!

JOHN: What about them?

PETER: They're still completely wrapped. Just like the body floated out of them. Whoever did this was certainly neat.

JOHN: Something's wrong.

PETER: What do you mean?

JOHN: Where's the headpiece?

PETER: I don't know. Must have been taken with the body.

JOHN: But why? Why would anybody steal a body with the head piece and then rewrap the linen cloths?

PETER: They didn't.

JOHN: What?

PETER: They didn't take the head piece. It's wrapped up over here in the corner.

JOHN: What? Peter! He's alive! He must be.

PETER: What are you talking about?

JOHN: Jesus is alive! It's the only thing that makes sense!

PETER: He's dead. You saw Him crucified. You saw the spear in His side.

JOHN: But nobody would rob a grave this way. He's alive, I tell you!

PETER: Maybe. I want to study this some more. Let's go.

JOHN: But He's alive! We have to tell the others.

PETER: Just keep quiet. Dead people don't come back to life.

JOHN: What about Lazarus?

PETER: Just keep quiet and let me think. *(They leave for home.)*

SCENE THREE

MARY MAGDALENE *(sobbing softly)*: Why? Why? Why?

ANGEL: Why do you weep?

MARY MAGDALENE: Because somebody took away my Lord. And I don't know where they put Him. *(She sinks to her knees and covers her face with her hands.)*

JESUS: Woman, why do you weep?

MARY MAGDALENE *(sobbing)*: Sir?

JESUS: Whom do you seek?

MARY MAGDALENE: Sir, if you are the gardener and took away my Lord, please tell me where to find Him. Let me take Him to another place so that we can visit His grave.

JESUS: Mary.

MARY MAGDALENE: *(Looks up, amazed.)* Master?

JESUS: Go and tell My brothers that I am going back to My Father and your Father; to My God and your God.

MARY MAGDALENE: I will. I will. *(She gets up.)* He's alive! He's alive!

GOING FISHING

SCRIPTURE: John 13:1-17; 21:3-8

SUGGESTED TOPICS: Serving others; humility

BIBLE BACKGROUND

Jesus' disciples needed to learn the importance of being a servant. To teach this, He chose the worst imaginable task: washing feet.

In biblical times, feet were always dirty. The footwear of the day was sandals, the roads were dusty, and the most common mode of travel was walking. If a man, particularly a wealthy man, invited guests to dinner, he made certain his guests had their feet washed by one of his servants. Because washing people's feet was possibly the least desirable task in the household, it usually fell upon the servant of the lowest rank.

Jesus, the King of kings and Lord of lords, humbled Himself to the most lowly position imaginable to demonstrate the servant's heart to His disciples. It must have been a profoundly moving experience for them, particularly after His death a few days later.

PERFORMANCE TIPS

1. Suggested props: one or more large fish nets.
2. The skit indicates the presence of seven men on the boat. However, only three men have speaking parts. The other four can be invisible or can be played by four others who help to pantomime casting out the nets, pulling in the nets, rowing the boat, etc.
3. Have Peter and Thomas look at the shore while Nathanael pulls up the net. If your room is reasonably soundproof, Peter can yell to the man on shore. Or have Peter mimic shouting by placing his hands around his mouth.

DISCUSSION QUESTIONS

1. What are some jobs people do for you?
2. What are some things you could do to help others?
3. Read Jesus' words in Mark 10:43,44. What did Jesus say about the way to be a great person? Why do you think serving others is important?

Going Fishing

CHARACTERS

PETER

THOMAS

NATHANAEL

PETER: Thomas! Nathanael! I'm going fishing. Are you two coming or not?

THOMAS: Sounds good to me.

NATHANAEL: I'm in, Peter. Have you got a spot in mind?

PETER: What kind of dumb question is that, Nathanael? I always pick good spots.

THOMAS: James! John! And you other two! C'mon! Peter says he knows a good place to go fishing.

NATHANAEL: Looks like we're all coming, Peter. But level with me. You're not planning to go back to fishing, are you?

PETER: No, I don't think so. But I need a place to think. And the sea is as good a place as any. C'mon, Thomas! Hurry up!

THOMAS: We're here, Peter. Don't be so impatient. The fish aren't going anywhere.

NATHANAEL: Don't be too hard on him, Thomas. He says he wants to think. And you know how tough THAT is for him.

PETER: Some friend you are. C'mon! Let's move the boat out towards the east.

THOMAS: OK, Peter. We're underway. While we're heading towards your fishing spot, tell us what's on your mind. Sometimes it helps to think out loud.

PETER: I was thinking about the supper we had with Jesus.

THOMAS: Give us a break. Which one? We had lots of suppers with Him.

NATHANAEL: Don't pretend to be so dense, Thomas. The last one.

PETER: That's the one, Nathanael. And this is the best fishing spot in Galilee. Help me toss the net in, Nathanael. *(Pauses.)* Do you remember when Jesus washed our feet?

NATHANAEL: That would be pretty hard to forget.

THOMAS: Especially for you, Peter. Your quick tongue got you in trouble again.

PETER: Maybe it did, Thomas. But I had a reason for what I said and did. At least I didn't just sit there like a bump on a log and not understand what was happening.

NATHANAEL: Would you two stop arguing with each other? What's bothering you now, Peter?

PETER: Do you remember how you felt when Jesus got out the basin and the cloth and began washing our feet?

THOMAS: Of course. I was totally dumbfounded. I didn't know what to do or say. So I just sat there and let Him wash my feet.

NATHANAEL: So what do you need to think about now, Peter? Jesus explained that He was setting an example for us to follow. He washed our feet so that we should be willing to wash each other's feet.

THOMAS: Sure. It was a simple lesson. If the Master could humble Himself before His servants, then the servants can humble themselves before each other.

PETER: But here's the problem. Do you think He meant just us twelve—or eleven? Or do you think He meant we should be servants to anyone?

THOMAS: Peter, you surely do have a habit of complicating everything. We're to be the leaders of His Church on earth. Why would we be required to be servants of everyone who comes along?

PETER: That's what I thought, at first. But...do any of you doubt that He's the Messiah?

THOMAS: Not after I saw the nail holes in His hands and the gash in His side. Why do you ask?

PETER: Well, if He's the Messiah—and He is—then that means God Himself washed our feet. If He could stoop so low, how could we feel that we don't have to serve others in the same manner?

NATHANAEL: You've got a point there.

THOMAS: I think we should have a rule that Peter isn't allowed to think anymore. Every time he does, something I've just decided goes out the window. Besides, when he thinks, he loses his memory. I thought you said this was a good place to fish?

PETER: So excuse me for living. Didn't you ever have a day when you didn't catch anything before?

THOMAS: Not when somebody told me he had the best fishing spot in Israel.

NATHANAEL: Can't you two stop bickering?

PETER: I see we're not the only people out this early in the morning.

THOMAS: What do you mean?

PETER: Look. Over there on the shore. Some guy's out for a walk.

NATHANAEL: So what's he doing?

PETER: He's just standing there. Watching us.

NATHANAEL: So who is it? Do we know him?

THOMAS: It's hard to say. The light's not very good yet and it's mostly in our eyes.

PETER: Listen. The guy on the shore shouted something. He wants to know if we caught anything.

NATHANAEL: Well, isn't anyone going to answer him? We can still be civilized, even if we did have a bad night's fishing.

THOMAS: Let Peter do it. He has the biggest mouth.

PETER: Just to show how civilized I can be, I'm going to ignore that last crack. *(Shouts.)* No! We haven't caught anything. *(Speaks normally.)* Typical landlubber. He says we should try the other side of the boat. What's he think? That fish have a fence they can't cross over?

NATHANAEL: Well? What have we got to lose? The net's ready to cast again anyway. We can troll to shore and if we catch something, we won't have wasted a night. If we don't catch anything, we can teach the landlubber how to fold a net.

PETER: If you want to waste your time, go ahead. *(THOMAS and NATHANAEL cast net.)*

THOMAS: Hey! What's happening to the boat?

NATHANAEL: Well, I'll be! It's being pulled to one side by the weight of the fish in the net!

PETER: We'll have to row to shore. We'll never pull the nets in with this many fish in them!

THOMAS: Who is that guy on the shore?

NATHANAEL: I don't know. But he sure knows his fishing.

PETER: It's the Lord! It has to be!

THOMAS: Peter! What are you doing? Look at that! He jumps in the water to swim to shore and leaves the six of us to handle all these fish by ourselves. And he has the GALL to talk about being a servant!

Good News

SCRIPTURE: Matthew 28:16-20; Mark 6:7-13; Luke 10:1-20

SUGGESTED TOPICS: Spreading the gospel; trusting in God's guidance

BIBLE BACKGROUND

Jesus had been crucified and buried. His disciples were devastated. All their plans for a new world had been dashed. But on the third day, Jesus rose. During the next few weeks, He appeared to the disciples and hundreds of other people. Just prior to His ascension, Jesus gave the disciples specific instructions. "You will receive power when the Holy Spirit comes on you; and you will be my witnesses...to the ends of the earth" (Acts 1:8).

How would the disciples react to this final message? The Holy Spirit would come and fill them with power. What did that mean? How would they know? What exactly should they do and say? They must have had thousands of questions running through their minds while waiting to celebrate Pentecost.

PERFORMANCE TIPS

1. Suggested props: Bible-times costumes.
2. Toward the end of the skit, Philip and Andrew should show in their voices and facial expressions their increasing excitement at the prospect of telling the good news about Jesus.

DISCUSSION QUESTIONS

1. What is a witness?
2. Why did Jesus tell His disciples to wait before going out to be His witnesses?
3. How can you witness about Jesus?

Good News

Characters

ANDREW

PHILIP

ANDREW: Hi, Philip.

PHILIP: Hi, Andrew. What are you doing?

ANDREW: Just thinking about the events of the past few weeks.

PHILIP: It really has been amazing, hasn't it? Are you thinking about anything special or just things in general?

ANDREW: Mostly, I've been thinking about the last thing Jesus said to us. You know, about going into the world, baptizing people and teaching them the things that He taught us.

PHILIP: Yeah. That's quite a responsibility He's given us. What are you planning to do?

ANDREW: I don't know. I just sometimes wonder if I'm up to the task.

PHILIP: Well, Jesus must have thought that we are capable of doing the job. If He didn't, then He wouldn't have left us with the responsibility. He would have given it to somebody else.

ANDREW: I guess that's true. Do you remember the first time He sent us out to preach and teach?

PHILIP: How could I forget? Just between you and me, I was scared witless. If I hadn't been so afraid, I probably would have told Jesus that I couldn't speak to people. But I was more afraid to say that than to go.

ANDREW: I didn't know you felt that way. I thought I was the only frightened one out of the twelve of us.

PHILIP: You sure weren't! And I bet if you spoke to the others, you'd find that all of us were scared and felt the same way.

ANDREW: Well, that helps some. Anyway, to get back to your original question, I was wondering what I was going to do about this latest assignment we've been given. Am I supposed to go out now? Do I sit and wait for further instructions? When I go, do I go alone? I guess you get the picture.

PHILIP: It really is nice to know I'm not the only one who doesn't seem to know what's happening. Maybe if we go over the first two preaching missions again, it will help us decide what to do now.

ANDREW: That sounds good to me. I remember that first mission. The twelve of us were sent out two by two.

PHILIP: Right. And when the seventy were sent out, we went two by two again.

ANDREW: I think we've maybe hit on the answer to one of our questions already.

PHILIP: Go with somebody, not alone.

ANDREW: Remember when we were first sent out? All those sick people healed. And Jesus gave us power over the unclean spirits. He told us, even before we went, that we had more authority than they did.

PHILIP: We learned that again on the second journey. All the spirits obeyed us because we spoke with the authority given to us by Jesus. It was so exciting! We were nearly bubbling over.

ANDREW: He also gave us authority over serpents and scorpions—in fact, all the power of the enemy. We didn't have to be afraid of anything.

PHILIP: I think we've just hit on something else.

ANDREW: Right. If Jesus is sending us, we have authority and we don't need to be afraid. Just knowing that helps. But what are we going to eat? How will we earn a living if we're teaching and preaching?

PHILIP: I think that concern was answered on our first two journeys, also. What did we take with us then?

ANDREW: Other than the clothes on our backs and a staff, nothing.

PHILIP: Well, it doesn't appear to me that you starved to death.

ANDREW: That's true. We always did have enough to eat.

PHILIP: So what's different now?

ANDREW: For one thing, those were just short trips. This is now a lifetime career.

PHILIP: True. But maybe those short trips were just for practice. So we would know when we were told to do something more difficult, we would be able to.

ANDREW: That's possible.

PHILIP: What sort of things do you think we should be teaching?

ANDREW: Well, if the other times were for practice, then I think we have a pretty good idea. We were always supposed to greet whoever agreed to be our host and wish peace upon his house.

PHILIP: I don't see any reason for changing that practice. We were also to call people to repentance.

ANDREW: We might as well continue doing that. I don't see that the world has improved significantly yet.

PHILIP: And if the city won't receive us, do you think we should shake off its very dust, the way we did before?

ANDREW: Well, Jesus hasn't changed that rule, so I guess it still stands. Do you think there will be those who won't want to listen to us?

PHILIP: They crucified Jesus. I would say there's a very good chance that some will not want to hear us.

ANDREW: You know, I think you've just hit on what the main thrust of our preaching should be.

PHILIP: You mean that Jesus was crucified?

ANDREW: Yes, but not to stop there. Also, that He is risen.

PHILIP: And that He is the Lord of all creation.

ANDREW: That He's the Messiah, promised since the fall of man.

PHILIP: This is getting more exciting all the time. Should we start now? We could go out together, the two of us, and tell all that we've seen and heard.

ANDREW: No. Not yet. Remember? Jesus said He would send the Holy Spirit. I'm not sure what it feels like, to be filled with the Holy Spirit, but I am sure that when I am, I will know that it has happened. I think we're supposed to wait before we go.

PHILIP: But what do we do while we're waiting? I'm too excited to do any of the ordinary things that I used to do.

ANDREW: Maybe we should find the others. We could go some place together. And wait and pray.

PHILIP: That sounds perfect. Let's go now.

ANDREW: I'm with you. Let's go.

ACTS

SCRIPTURE: Acts 1; 2

SUGGESTED TOPICS: Early church; arrival of the Holy Spirit/Pentecost; witnessing

BIBLE BACKGROUND

Jesus had risen! For the next few weeks, He appeared to hundreds of people. All had the same exciting message to tell their friends. "He's alive! Jesus is risen!" But Jesus knew His earthly ministry had ended. He would not remain on earth forever. He would ascend to take His rightful place as the King of Kings and Lord of Lords. He would not, however, leave His followers defenseless. He promised to send the Holy Spirit.

Luke, writer of the Gospel which bears his name and the book of Acts, was a medical doctor. Most of Acts was written from firsthand experience as he traveled with Paul. Being a doctor, he would be trained to observe. Surely, his firsthand accounts, however incredible some of the events may seem, can be considered reliable.

As a confidant of Paul, Luke had opportunity to meet most of the apostles and many other witnesses of Jesus' life and the life of the early church. His history is a record of the period in which he lived. No other work of history refutes his. The Church of Jesus Christ did spread throughout the Roman Empire in spite of severe persecution. If his writing were false, where are the arguments which could have corrected his errors? The record says his book must be accepted as an accurate account of the time.

PERFORMANCE TIPS

1. Suggested props: table, chair, pad of paper and pen.
2. After the skit, read Acts 2:42-47 to find out ways the Holy Spirit helped the believers as they began the early church.

DISCUSSION QUESTIONS

1. Read John 18:15-18,25-27 and Acts 2:38-41. How did Peter act when Jesus was on trial? How did he act after Pentecost? Why do you think he changed so much in 50 days?
2. According to John 14:26 and Acts 1:8, why do people need the Holy Spirit?
3. What is one way the Holy Spirit can help you?

Acts

CHARACTERS

MARK

LUKE

MARK: Who are you writing to, Luke?

LUKE: To Theophilus again.

MARK: Is this one going to be as long as the first?

LUKE: Hard to say. I have a lot to tell him.

MARK: You told him all about Jesus in the first letter. Why do you need to write another?

LUKE: It's important that he hear everything that's happened since then.

MARK: C'mon. There's not enough paper and ink to tell everything that's happened since Jesus rose. You're going to have to pick and choose.

LUKE: I meant the important things. I think I should begin with Jesus' ascension into heaven. And the angels.

MARK: Maybe you should leave the angels out.

LUKE: Why should I do that?

MARK: Most people have never seen angels. They'll think you made it up.

LUKE: I've talked personally to most of those who were there. You know what everyone says happened. Were there angels?

MARK: Well, yes.

LUKE: And was their message important?

MARK: That Jesus was taken up into heaven and would return again? Yes.

LUKE: Then I must include it. It should be written accurately.

MARK: Then you'll probably write about Peter's sermon.

LUKE: All in good time. He should know about the waiting period.

MARK: Why? Nothing exciting happened until the Feast of Pentecost.

LUKE: I'm not trying to write a thriller. I'm writing history.

MARK: What's so important about waiting?

LUKE: Have you learned so little? People need to know that God has a time for all things. It's important not to rush off and try to do things on our own. It's also important to tell that Matthias was chosen to be an apostle in Judas' place.

MARK: Why is that important?

LUKE: To show that the apostles are people of God. People who seek His will.

MARK: OK. Then, of course, the tongues of fire.

LUKE: Naturally. But I need some help. I have, of course, heard it described. But I need an eyewitness to be certain that I have all the details correctly recorded.

MARK: Well, we were all in the same place...

LUKE: About one hundred twenty of you?

MARK: Yes. Suddenly, there was a sound like a strong wind blowing. The noise filled the whole house. But there was no breeze.

LUKE: I wish I had been there. And then, the fire.

MARK: I remember looking at Peter. And above his head was what looked like a small flame. And I thought, "Wow! God chose Peter to be someone extra special." Then I looked around. And the same kind of flame was over everyone's head.

LUKE: And then?

MARK: Everybody began to speak in different languages.

LUKE: That must have been very confusing.

MARK: Yes and no. It should have been, but everyone sensed the presence of the Holy Spirit, and there was peace in the noise.

LUKE: You see why I included the angels. Many will find this hard to believe, also. But since it is the truth and it's important, it must be included.

MARK: Yes, I see what you mean. Then, Peter's sermon.

LUKE: That's right. Everything in good order. Peter's sermon on that day.

MARK: Nobody will have trouble believing that. Lots of people who heard it are still living, even those who didn't believe.

LUKE: I still have trouble believing that some people thought the apostles were drunk.

MARK: Why is that so hard to believe?

LUKE: How many people, when they are drunk, can speak another language perfectly? To call the men drunk! Why, that's crazy.

MARK: Some would rather believe anything than to believe in Jesus.

LUKE: True. And sad. But back to that day.

MARK: Peter's sermon was really something. Just think—this was the same Peter who, only a few short weeks before, had denied that he even knew Jesus. And now he was standing in front of a huge crowd, telling them that Jesus, who had been crucified, is the Messiah, the Son of God.

LUKE: God used that sermon to touch many lives. More than three thousand. Incredible!

MARK: So what else are you going to write about?

LUKE: Many things. Baptism of the Gentiles. Preaching missions.

MARK: You're not planning to mention that little homesickness episode of mine, are you?

LUKE: Now that you mention it, I think I shall.

MARK: *(Groans.)* Why?

LUKE: Everyone knows the solid friend you've become. It's good for people to know that you don't have to be perfect in order for God to use you.

MARK: Well, OK. But go a little easy on me, will you? After all, I was pretty young then.

LUKE: And now, you're a strong man of God. Don't worry. People will remember your faith more than your failings. But I'm getting a cramp in my writing hand. I wish there were a faster way to get all this down on paper. I'll write some more tomorrow.

CRIPPLED

SCRIPTURE: Acts 3:1—4:22

SUGGESTED TOPICS: Acts of the Holy Spirit; opposition to the early church; witnessing

BIBLE BACKGROUND

The Sanhedrin, the highest Jewish court of justice during the Greek and Roman periods, thought they had solved the problem of Jesus. He was dead. His body, however, had disappeared. Pulling all the political strings possible, they spread the rumor that the apostles had stolen the body. Surely now their problems were over.

However, fifty days later, during the Feast of Pentecost, new problems arose. Peter preached a sermon convincing three thousand people that Jesus is the Christ. As if that was not bad enough, while going to the Temple to pray, Peter and John had healed a lame man and credited Jesus with the healing. In order to preserve their prestige and power, the Sanhedrin had to act quickly. The Sanhedrin had a great deal of power with which to threaten the disciples. Jesus had been crucified; the disciples had to face the possibility that they would meet the same fate. Did this deter them, weaken their resolve, slow them down? No. Because they knew whom they believed and that what they believed was true.

PERFORMANCE TIPS

1. Suggested props: table and three chairs.
2. Caiaphas and Annas should show by their forceful mannerisms and voices that they are the leaders of the group. Alexander should sound as if he doesn't quite understand what is happening.
3. After the skit, read or briefly summarize Acts 4:18-20 to find how the disciples reacted to the Sanhedrin's threats.

DISCUSSION QUESTIONS

1. What did the Jewish leaders threaten to do to Peter and John if they kept preaching about Jesus? Why did the Jewish leaders think their threats would be successful?
2. How might Peter and John have felt when they first heard these threats? How would you have felt?
3. Why did Peter and John keep on preaching about Jesus? Why were the threats ineffective?
4. When have you been reluctant or afraid to tell someone about Jesus? Who helped Peter and John have courage? Who can help you?

CRIPPLED

CHARACTERS
ANNAS (ah-NAHS)

ALEXANDER

CAIAPHAS (KYE-uh-fus)

ANNAS: Gentlemen, we have a problem. The cripple who's usually outside the Temple gate isn't there.

ALEXANDER: You mean the one always begging?

CAIAPHAS: Precisely.

ALEXANDER: That's no problem. He always annoyed me when I came to the Temple to pray. If he's missing, good riddance.

ANNAS: He's not missing. He's running and jumping INSIDE the Temple courts.

ALEXANDER *(confused)***:** The cripple?

CAIAPHAS: Right.

ALEXANDER: Do all you priests and scribes know the meaning of the word "cripple"?

CAIAPHAS: Of course we do!

ALEXANDER: Then how can he be running and leaping? He's a cripple!

ANNAS: Obviously, he's been healed.

ALEXANDER: Then he's no longer a cripple?

CAIAPHAS: Right.

ALEXANDER: So he can make his own living and won't be begging anymore?

CAIAPHAS: I suppose so.

ALEXANDER: Then what's the problem? He's gone. I can come to pray in peace.

ANNAS: If you'll be quiet and listen, you'll know what the problem is. At three o'clock this afternoon the cripple was sitting at the Temple gate, as usual...

CAIAPHAS: Begging, as usual...

ANNAS: When two men came up to him and spoke to him.

CAIAPHAS: But instead of giving him money, one of them reached out...

ANNAS: Took his hand...

CAIAPHAS: And pulled him to his feet.

ANNAS: Now he's leaping all around the Temple.

ALEXANDER: I still don't see a problem.

CAIAPHAS: The man's a fool.

ALEXANDER: Just because he's leaping and running is no reason to call him a fool.

CAIAPHAS: Not him! You!

ALEXANDER: Me? Did you hear that? He called me a fool.

ANNAS: With good reason. Don't you ever think?

ALEXANDER: Well, let's see. About noon, I thought I was hungry.

CAIAPHAS: A fool. A complete fool.

ANNAS: Sit down. Try not to speak. Just listen.

CAIAPHAS: A lame man was suddenly healed this afternoon.

ANNAS: Everybody in the Temple heard about it.

CAIAPHAS: There was a great uproar.

ANNAS: Everybody wanted to see the healed man.

CAIAPHAS: AND the men who had healed him.

ANNAS: Now do you see the problem?

ALEXANDER: I sure do. Why, everybody in Jerusalem will be flocking to these two doctors. All the other doctors will go broke.

CAIAPHAS: A fool. The man's a fool.

ANNAS: Alexander. Try to understand. The two men are not doctors.

ALEXANDER: And you call me a fool. Only doctors can heal the sick.

CAIAPHAS: How long has that man been lame?

ALEXANDER: I don't know. I've been coming to the Temple for thirty years and he's always been begging at the door.

ANNAS: Precisely. And he was lame before that. He was born lame.

CAIAPHAS: Maybe forty years ago.

ANNAS: No doctor has ever been able to help him.

CAIAPHAS: Suddenly, he's healed.

ANNAS: What do you think happens?

ALEXANDER: He signs up for dancing lessons?

CAIAPHAS: NO! Everybody in the Temple runs to see what happened.

ANNAS: They want to see this miracle.

CAIAPHAS: And they want to see the men who did it.

ALEXANDER: Well, I should think so. What's the big deal?

ANNAS: Those two men are preaching right now. Here in the Temple.

CAIAPHAS: About Jesus.

ALEXANDER: So? Jesus is dead. What's the big deal?

ANNAS: Those men claim He's no longer dead...

CAIAPHAS: That it was Jesus' power that healed the lame man...

ANNAS: And that everyone must believe in Jesus as the Son of God.

ALEXANDER: Well, that's just plain crazy. Jesus is dead. We saw to that.

ANNAS: But they're saying that He rose from the dead.

ALEXANDER: Nobody believes that.

CAIAPHAS: Many do. Remember—there's no body. The tomb is empty.

ALEXANDER: Sure. But His disciples stole the body. Remember?

CAIAPHAS: A fool. An utter, complete fool.

ANNAS: Alexander, do you remember how that story was started?

ALEXANDER: Sure. We paid the guards to say they fell asleep on duty.

CAIAPHAS: So, do you really believe the disciples stole the body?

ALEXANDER: Well, sure. What else could have happened?

ANNAS: We don't know. But we don't want people going around teaching that Jesus came back to life. If people believe Jesus is the Son of God, what happens to us?

ALEXANDER: Why should anything happen to us?

ANNAS: Because He was crucified.

ALEXANDER: Sure. But the Romans did that.

CAIAPHAS: Because we demanded it.

ALEXANDER: Oh.

ANNAS: So you see what that means?

ALEXANDER: People might not like us much.

CAIAPHAS: Who cares about liking us? They might stop respecting us.

ANNAS: They might refuse to listen to us anymore.

CAIAPHAS: We'd lose much of our power over the people.

ALEXANDER: We have to stop these radicals.

ANNAS: Finally, he begins to understand.

CAIAPHAS: Now that we've agreed there is a problem, we must decide what to do.

ALEXANDER: We can pretend the miracle didn't happen.

ANNAS: How can we do that?

ALEXANDER: We can say the healed man is an imposter.

CAIAPHAS: Who's going to believe that?

ALEXANDER: They believed that the guards fell asleep.

ANNAS: True. Maybe...no. Too many people know this man. That lie wouldn't work.

CAIAPHAS: I have it! We simply have to stop the story from spreading.

ALEXANDER: How can we do that?

CAIAPHAS: We order those two to stop talking about Jesus.

ALEXANDER: How much are we going to have to pay them? Bribing those guards cost our treasury most of its ready cash.

ANNAS: He has a point, Caiaphas. Even if we had cash, I doubt we could bribe them.

CAIAPHAS: Of course not. Money wouldn't silence them. But threats...

ANNAS: Ah...

CAIAPHAS: Beatings.

ANNAS: Long-term imprisonment.

CAIAPHAS: That's the trick. Nobody will keep telling lies if they have to suffer for it. If we can just make them suffer, they'll be silent.

ANNAS: I like it. OK, bring the Temple guards along and we'll lock these men up for the night. That should put a stop to all this nonsense.

OPEN DOORS

SCRIPTURE: Acts 5:12-26

SUGGESTED TOPICS: Acts of the Holy Spirit; early church; witnessing; response to injustice; courage under persecution

BIBLE BACKGROUND

The disciples, having been filled with the Holy Spirit, were actively preaching the gospel throughout Jerusalem. Many people accepted the apostles' teaching and were converted to "The Way." The Jewish council, comprised of Pharisees and Sadducees, finally agreed that teaching about Jesus had to be stopped. In the past, they had called in Peter and John and ordered them to cease their preaching. But no punishment had yet been meted out, for they could find no law which had been broken and were wary of the general population which was excited about the miracles that they had seen performed. However, warnings alone could not stop the apostles and the Council decided that more drastic action must be taken.

What were the motives of these religious leaders in trying to stop the preaching of the disciples? Were they jealous of the attention that this new teaching was bringing to the apostles? Were they afraid that this new teaching would lead Israel astray and that God's displeasure would erupt into the destruction of the nation? Were they afraid of a potential uprising against the Roman government and the resulting martial law that would be imposed? Were they afraid if Rome had to intervene directly that they could lose their political power?

Any of the above could be true. But whatever their motives, their actions were wrong. God called them to account for their behavior because, as religious leaders, they should have been the most receptive to Jesus the Messiah. They should have been ready to lead Israel to God, when in fact they did the opposite.

PERFORMANCE TIPS

1. Suggested props: Bible-times costumes.
2. Before the skit, explain to the group that we tend to think of prisons as modern facilities where prisoners are treated well. However, in Roman times, prisoners often died from neglect and mistreatment. The threat of imprisonment was powerful.
3. After the skit, read or summarize the conclusion of the story as found in Acts 5:27-42.

DISCUSSION QUESTIONS

1. What words would you use to describe Peter's actions?
2. Do you think Peter and the other believers were afraid? Why or why not?
3. What does God promise His followers in Hebrews 13:5,6?
4. When is a time you need to remember these promises?

OPEN DOORS

CHARACTERS
CAPTAIN
ANNAS (ah-NAHS)
CAIAPHAS (KYE-uh-fus)
ALEXANDER
JOHN
OTHERS
PHARISEES
MESSENGER

SCENE ONE

CAPTAIN: O Your Holinesses, we have a problem.

ANNAS: What kind of problem, Captain?

CAPTAIN: Well, you remember those apostle characters?

CAIAPHAS: You mean those blasphemers who tried to make people believe that Jesus of Nazareth is the Messiah?

CAPTAIN: The very same, Your High Priestliness.

ANNAS: What about them?

CAPTAIN: They're doing it again, Your Most Worthiness.

CAIAPHAS: Cut the fancy titles! What are they doing?

CAPTAIN: All kinds of terrible things.

ANNAS: Such as?

CAPTAIN: They're healing the sick.

CAIAPHAS: Didn't we tell them to stop doing that?

ANNAS: We certainly did! We have doctors to heal the sick. What else?

CAPTAIN: They're casting out demons again.

CAIAPHAS: Oh, infamy!

ANNAS: Disgraceful!

CAPTAIN: And...

CAIAPHAS and ANNAS: AND?

CAPTAIN: And they're saying that Jesus gives them the power to do these things.

CAIAPHAS: Blasphemy!

ANNAS: Double blasphemy!

CAIAPHAS: Call the council!

CAPTAIN: Council!

ANNAS: Not you. Me. Council! Convene immediately.

ALEXANDER: What is it, Annas? I was just settling down to a refreshing study of the law.

JOHN: And I was trying to decide if we've been too lax about the Sabbath. Maybe we should add some more regulations.

CAIAPHAS: That can wait. This can't.

ALEXANDER: Then it must be important.

ANNAS: More than important.

JOHN: Then we're all ears. What happened?

CAIAPHAS: You remember those blasphemers.

JOHN: Which ones? So many fail to keep the Sabbath anymore.

ANNAS: Not mild offenders. Blasphemers!

ALEXANDER: Well, I don't think that those who fail to keep each minor regulation can be described only as minor offenders. After all, our tradition...

ANNAS and CAIAPHAS: Be quiet and listen!

JOHN: You don't need to yell.

ALEXANDER: We're listening.

ANNAS: We're talking about the blasphemers.

CAIAPHAS: The ones who claim to have seen the Messiah.

JOHN: Oh, those blasphemers.

ALEXANDER: What's the big deal about them?

CAIAPHAS: They're out healing.

ANNAS: And casting out demons.

CAIAPHAS and ANNAS: And preaching!

ALEXANDER: Oh, infamy!

JOHN: Disgraceful!

ALEXANDER: Blasphemy!

JOHN: Double blasphemy!

ANNAS: Our feelings precisely.

CAIAPHAS: So what do we do?

ALEXANDER: This requires thought.

JOHN: We need time.

ANNAS: They must be stopped.

CAIAPHAS: Aha!

ALEXANDER, JOHN and ANNAS: What?

CAIAPHAS: An idea. Captain!

CAPTAIN: Present and accounted for, Your High Priestliness.

CAIAPHAS: Go and arrest those men.

CAPTAIN: Which men?

ANNAS: The blasphemers!

CAPTAIN: Which ones? There are so many these days.

CAIAPHAS: The ones who call themselves apostles.

CAPTAIN: Oh, them. Where should I take them?

CAIAPHAS: To prison!

ANNAS: Throw them into a cell.

ALEXANDER: A small cell.

CAPTAIN: But there are twelve of them. Shouldn't I use a large cell?

ALEXANDER: A small, dark cell.

CAIAPHAS: While they're cooling their heels, we'll have a good night's sleep.

ANNAS: And awake to consider the matter with cool heads.

CAPTAIN: That's a good one. Cool heels and cool heads.

ALEXANDER: Are you still here?

JOHN: Go and arrest those men.

CAIAPHAS: Good night, gentlemen. We'll meet here tomorrow morning.

ANNAS: And throw the book at those blasphemers.

JOHN: After giving them a fair trial, of course.

CAIAPHAS, ANNAS and ALEXANDER: Of course.

(Skit continues on next page.)

SCENE TWO

CAIAPHAS: Good morning, gentlemen.

OTHERS: Good morning.

CAIAPHAS: I see some of you who were not here yesterday. Guard, go get the prisoners.

CAPTAIN: At once, Your High Priestliness.

ANNAS: You? I thought you were a captain. Why isn't one of your men doing this job?

CAPTAIN: I wanted to see this trial.

ALEXANDER: Well, go and get the prisoners.

JOHN: We can't start the trial until they arrive.

CAPTAIN: At once, with the greatest of haste, I obey your every command...

PHARISEES: Go already!

CAIAPHAS: While he's bringing the prisoners, I'll explain the situation to those who were not here yesterday. Those blasphemers have started up, again.

OTHERS: Hmm.

ANNAS: And you'll remember how we specifically warned them to stop.

ALEXANDER: With words of unmistakable meaning.

JOHN: And yet with kindness.

CAIAPHAS: And how has our consideration been repaid?

ANNAS: With treachery.

ALEXANDER: Yesterday, they were healing.

JOHN: And casting out demons.

CAIAPHAS: And preaching that Jesus is the Messiah.

OTHERS: Oh, infamy! Disgraceful! Blasphemy! Double blasphemy!

CAIAPHAS: Our feelings precisely.

CAPTAIN: Excuse me, Your High Priestliness.

CAIAPHAS: Oh, you. Well, speak up. What is it?

CAPTAIN: If we could have a word in private...

CAIAPHAS: Nonsense! We're ready to start the trial. Bring the prisoners.

CAPTAIN: There may be a slight delay.

ANNAS: What do you mean, a slight delay?

ALEXANDER: We're busy men. We have important things to do.

JOHN: Bring the prisoners. Let the trial begin.

CAPTAIN: That's the reason for the delay.

CAIAPHAS: What reason?

CAPTAIN: The prisoners.

CAIAPHAS: What about the prisoners?

CAPTAIN: We, uh, well, uh...it's kind of, uh...

ANNAS: Stop humming and hawing. Where are the prisoners?

CAPTAIN: Well, we're not sure.

PHARISEES: What?

ALEXANDER: You put them in prison last night, didn't you?

CAPTAIN: I sure did.

JOHN: And you let them escape.

CAPTAIN: Not exactly.

ANNAS: Then you have them in custody.

CAPTAIN: Not exactly.

ALEXANDER: Then where, exactly, are they?

CAPTAIN: We're not sure.

CAIAPHAS: Explain yourself, Captain, or you will soon be a former captain!

CAPTAIN: Well, I went to the Temple with my men yesterday and did just what you told me to do. I found those men healing and casting out demons and preaching...

PHARISEES: Infamy! Disgraceful! Blasphemy! Double blasphemy!

CAPTAIN: And I arrested them. I said, "In the name of the Most Holy Council and by the authority of His Great High Priestliness..."

CAIAPHAS: Get on with it!

CAPTAIN: Yes, Sir. So I took them to jail.

ALEXANDER: And...

CAPTAIN: And I found a cell just like you described.

JOHN: To the letter?

CAPTAIN: Exactly. And I threw all twelve of them in.

ALEXANDER: And...

CAPTAIN: I got to thinking—that many in one cell, maybe they'll break down the door.

ANNAS: And so you took precautions.

CAPTAIN: No, Sir! If any precautions are missing, I didn't take them.

CAIAPHAS: Please, just finish your story.

CAPTAIN: Yes, Sir. Well, I put extra guards at the door all night.

CAIAPHAS: Excellent. So what is the problem?

CAPTAIN: I went down this morning, unlocked the door and ordered the prisoners out of the cell. When they didn't come out, I went in after them. But they weren't there. The bars were all firmly in place, the door was securely locked, the guards were all on duty, but the jail cell was empty. The prisoners were gone.

ANNAS: You expect us to believe this fairy tale?

MESSENGER: Pardon me, gentlemen. But those men you arrested yesterday are back in the Temple. They're teaching the people again.

CAIAPHAS: What?

ANNAS: You! Go and arrest them and bring them here.

CAPTAIN: I will! I'll take my men and we'll beat them and whip them and...

CAIAPHAS: No! Who can tell what that might do to a crowd. We don't want a riot. Go and bring them quietly. We can deal with them here. Oh, my head. How it aches!

SAMARIA TODAY

SCRIPTURE: Acts 8:1-25

SUGGESTED TOPICS: Witness of the early church; acts of the Holy Spirit; free gift of eternal life

BIBLE BACKGROUND

Having been filled with the Holy Spirit, the disciples preached in Jerusalem and thousands embraced the new faith. However, Jesus' command to the disciples had been to preach the good news in Jerusalem, in Judea, in Samaria and to the farthest parts of the world.

The religious leaders in Jerusalem were angered by the preaching of the apostles. To quell the preaching, these leaders began to persecute the believers. They tried everything from arresting entire families to the murder of Stephen (only a Roman governor was permitted to sentence anyone to death under Roman law).

In response to the persecution, many believers fled Jerusalem. They went to Judea, to Samaria and to faraway parts of the world. Wherever they went, they shared the gospel, fulfilling the Great Commission.

The Samaritans were a mixture of Jews and Gentiles. During and after the years of the captivity, Samaria had perverted the true faith, Judaism. As a result, Jews looked down upon Samaritans perhaps even more than they did on any other group. Centuries of animosity existed between these closely related ethnic and religious groups.

All cultures have some form of ethnic joke. Most of these "jokes" are not worth the breath expended to tell them. However, they persist because some people find them humorous. The Samaritans and the Jews were bitter enemies and it is reasonable to assume there would be Samaritan jokes told in Israel and vice versa. Although the "Jewish jokes" told in Perez' monologue are not funny, they might be to a certain mentality of Samaritan, simply because they are "Jewish."

PERFORMANCE TIPS

1. Suggested props: table and chairs set up as for a TV talk show; large APPLAUSE, LAUGH and CHEER signs to direct audience response at the appropriate times.
2. Introduce the skit by discussing the hatred between the Jews and Samaritans. (The Jews looked down on the Samaritans because the Jews believed the Samaritans had distorted their religion. It was not likely that a Samaritan would even want to hear about a new Jewish religion, much less believe in it.)

DISCUSSION QUESTIONS

1. This skit uses several ethnic jokes which make fun of Jews. Read Matthew 5:43,44. How does Jesus tell us to treat others?
2. Why must it have been hard for Simon to become a Christian?
3. What changes did Simon make in his life after he believed in Jesus?
4. What changes might a person today make in his or her life after becoming a Christian? Would these changes be hard or easy?

280   *The Big Book of Bible Skits* ©1997 Gospel Light. Permission to photocopy granted.

SAMARIA TODAY

CHARACTERS

AZARIAH (aa-zuh-RYE-uh)
AUDIENCE
PEREZ (peh-REZ)
SIMON

AZARIAH: Welcome to Samaria Today! Tonight, an all-star magic show, featuring none other than Samaria's own—Simon, the Sorcerer! And now, a big Samaritan welcome to the star of the show, the man who makes all others fear to show their faces, Perez!

> *(AUDIENCE cheers loudly.)*

PEREZ: Thank you, thank you, thank you. Well, let's see what's happening in the news. There's been lots brewing in Jerusalem, and it's not just coffee.

> *(AZARIAH chuckles.)*

PEREZ: The followers of that Galilean upstart, Jesus, are trying to turn the city upside down. I guess that's an extension of Jesus' claim that He could rebuild the Temple in three days.

> *(AUDIENCE sits silently. AZARIAH laughs.)*

PEREZ: See, it's an even bigger miracle—the streets up in the air, the houses pointing down...OK, so there are no miracle lovers here today. Well, how 'bout those Israelites. There are SO MANY Israelites spread throughout the Empire...

AUDIENCE *(shouting)*: How many are there?

PEREZ: There are so many Israelites spread throughout the Empire that every other woman's name is JEW-dy.

> *(AUDIENCE laughs.)*

PEREZ: And she sells JEW-elery.

> *(AUDIENCE laughs louder.)*

PEREZ: And her birthday is in JEW-ly.

> *(AUDIENCE laughs louder.)*

PEREZ: And last but not least, how 'bout Saul?

AUDIENCE *(shouting)*: How 'BOUT Saul?

PEREZ: He's out arresting all those Christians. I guess he's discovered an eleventh commandment—Thou shalt not think.

> *(AUDIENCE laughs loudly.)*

PEREZ: Thank you. We'll be right back with the rest of the show, including the truly amazing magical wizardry of Simon, the Sorcerer! Stay tuned.

AZARIAH: And now, a special word from our new sponsor, Sylvan's Water. Are you tired of having to travel every day to Jacob's Well to draw fresh water? Well, you're about to receive the best news you've heard since Babylon took Israel into captivity. Sylvan's special caravan will travel to the well, draw the water and deliver it right to your door. Don't wait! Call Sylvan today! And now, back to the show.

(AUDIENCE cheers.)

PEREZ: Thank you. Thank you. We've got a great show today, so let's get right to it. Here's a man we've all seen before. He's wowed you in the streets! He's dazzled you in the high places! The man known far and wide as "The Great Power of God!"—Simon, the Sorcerer!

(AUDIENCE cheers as SIMON enters.)

PEREZ: Welcome to the show.

SIMON: Thank you. It's a pleasure to be here.

PEREZ: I know you've got lots of magic to show us, but first, let's talk a bit.

SIMON: Actually, I don't have any magic to show.

PEREZ: Always the kidder. So, what's happening in the life of the sorcerer?

SIMON: I don't call myself a sorcerer any more.

PEREZ: OK, then. What's happening in the life of "The Great Power of God?"

SIMON: I don't use that title any more, either.

PEREZ: OK, then. What do you call yourself?

SIMON: A believer.

AZARIAH: Not very catchy. "Simon, the Believer!" If I were you, I'd change back.

SIMON: But I don't want to change back. I prefer being a believer.

PEREZ: Tell us about this believer bit. What kind of believer?

SIMON: A believer in the Lord Jesus Christ.

PEREZ: That Israelite heresy?

SIMON: It's not Israelite and it's not heresy. It's truth for all people.

PEREZ: How does an intelligent magician like yourself allow himself to be fooled by something that comes out of Judea? Or Galilee, of all places.

SIMON: Because this isn't something foolish.

PEREZ: How can you say that? If you're a believer living in Jerusalem, you could be killed. It sounds foolish to believe something that could get you killed.

SIMON: It is foolish to believe lies. Intelligence believes the truth.

PEREZ: But you're a magician. A great man.

SIMON: I WAS a fraud. A fake. All of my magic was nothing more than tricks. But I heard about a man named Philip, one who performed miracles. So I went to see what the competition was doing.

PEREZ: And what was this Philip doing?

SIMON: Real miracles. Healing the sick. Casting out unclean spirits.

PEREZ: If he's doing all that, why haven't I heard about him?

AZARIAH: We tried to get him on the show, but he wouldn't come and perform his magic for us.

SIMON: He doesn't perform magic. He works miracles by the power of the Lord Jesus Christ. Not for applause. Not for fame. But for the glory and honor of God.

PEREZ: Why would someone waste great talents like that?

The Big Book of Bible Skits ©1997 Gospel Light. Permission to photocopy granted.

SIMON: That's what I wanted to know. So I went to see what he did and how he did it. That's when I discovered he doesn't do tricks. He uses the power of the true God to perform miracles. That made me a believer and I was baptized.

PEREZ: This is great! I thought we were going to see some of your magic tricks. But, if you've been baptized and believe, then you can actually do miracles here for us! What do you say, audience? Do you want to see a miracle?

AUDIENCE (cheering loudly)**:** Yes! Yes!

SIMON: We don't do miracles so that people will be entertained. Only so that God will be glorified.

PEREZ: C'mon. Show us a miracle. We'll double your fee.

SIMON (shaking his head)**:** You're just the same as I used to be. I thought that money could buy everything. But I was wrong.

AZARIAH: For a real miracle, we'll triple your fee.

SIMON: You don't understand. God's power is not for sale. I thought it was. But I was wrong.

PEREZ: We'll quadruple your fee. But that's our last offer.

SIMON: But you can't buy God's power. I learned that from Peter.

PEREZ: Who's Peter?

AZARIAH: A rabbit, isn't he?

SIMON: No, the apostle Peter.

PEREZ: I've never heard of him.

SIMON: He was one of the twelve who followed Jesus. When he heard that people in Samaria were being baptized and believing in Jesus, he and John came to help. I saw them pray that the new believers would be filled with the Holy Spirit.

PEREZ: What's so special about that?

SIMON: It's more proof that this is real. Magicians never tell anybody how they do a trick. They guard their secrets. But the apostles want all believers to have the power of the Holy Spirit to help them in their faith. I watched as Peter and John prayed for the new believers, and I saw them filled with the Holy Spirit!

PEREZ: Wait a minute. These apostles are Jews. The Jews hate Samaritans. Why would they want Samaritans to have anything good? Maybe it's some kind of a trick.

SIMON: It's no trick. I lived with tricks all my life. This is real. This is the gospel, the good news for all people. I saw the power that Peter and John had, and I knew it was far more than my own. So I asked them, how much? How much to give people the Holy Spirit?

PEREZ: And how much was it?

SIMON: That's when I learned that God is not for sale. Peter told me, "You can't purchase God's gift! You're still in sin and can't be a part of the believers because you treasure money more than God."

PEREZ: Then how can you call yourself a believer?

SIMON: Because Peter told me to pray, to ask God to forgive my greed. And he helped me. He prayed with me. And God forgave my sin. That's the good news of Jesus Christ—that God loves us and wants to forgive our sins. Not just the Jews' sins, but everybody's.

PEREZ: Interesting story. But we're almost out of time. We do have enough left for one bit of magic. How about it, Simon? Show us one of your old tricks—a bit of the old Simon, "The Great Power of God."

SIMON: You haven't heard a word I said. I am not the great power of God. I never was. The great power of God is His love for us, a love that would surrender His only Son, Jesus Christ, to die for us on the cross...

PEREZ: Well, that's the show for tonight, folks. Sorry that there wasn't any magic, but tomorrow's show will more than make up for it: singers, dancers and jugglers. See you tomorrow, same time, same place.

TRIPLE P TRIAL

SCRIPTURE: Acts 8:26-38; 10; 11:15-18; 13:13-49

SUGGESTED TOPICS: Baptism; the good news; salvation for everyone

BIBLE BACKGROUND

Jesus' death and resurrection achieved the fulfillment of God's plan of salvation. The only job remaining was to spread the good news. Just before His ascension, Jesus instructed His disciples to "Go and make disciples of all nations, baptizing them in the name of the Father and of the Son and of the Holy Spirit" (Matthew 28:19). On the Day of Pentecost, the disciples began to carry out this commission, and as they spoke in Jerusalem, thousands of Jews became converts. However, the gospel was not yet preached to the Gentiles. Religious and cultural barriers remained intact. The disciples were good Jewish men who had been taught from their infancy to avoid contact with the Gentiles.

The persecution of the Christians in Jerusalem gradually drove them to escape their homeland. Philip found the people of Samaria were amazingly open to the message of Jesus. But they were half Jewish, so it was almost the same as preaching to Jews. The good news spread easily into Samaria. Philip was called out of his ministry in Samaria to the Desert of Gaza. There, he met an Ethiopian reading Isaiah. As the man was a Jewish proselyte, Philip saw no problem in sharing the gospel with him. But the Gentiles remained unreached until God sent Peter to a Roman centurian's home and Paul found himself invited to teach the word of God to Sergius Paulus, the proconsul of Cyprus. Finally, the door was opening so Gentiles could join the family of God.

PERFORMANCE TIPS

1. Suggested props: gavel and robe for the judge, table and chair for the judge, two tables for the prosecution and defense, chairs, files for the prosecutor.
2. After a judgment is handed down, the defendant and lawyers should return to their chairs and wait for the next case to be called.
3. After calling the case, the bailiff should stand at attention to the side.

DISCUSSION QUESTIONS

1. What made it difficult for the Jewish believers to tell Gentiles about the good news?
2. Who doesn't deserve to hear God's plan of salvation? Why?
3. Describe God's plan of salvation in your own words.
4. How can you share God's plan with others?

TRIPLE P TRIAL

CHARACTERS
PHIL
PETE
PAUL
PROSECUTOR
BAILIFF
JUDGE
DEFENSE LAWYER

PRONUNCIATION GUIDE
Cornelius (kor-NEEL-yus)

BAILIFF: Criminal court is now in session, the honorable Judge Blind Justice presiding. All rise.

JUDGE: *(Enters and sits.)* Be seated. *(Bangs gavel. To audience.)* I love that. *(To LAWYER.)* Defense counsel. Why are so many people seated over there?

LAWYER: They are all my clients, Your Honor. The cases are all interrelated.

JUDGE: That's a little unusual, isn't it? One lawyer for three defendants?

LAWYER: Yes, Your Honor. But we feel there's no conflict of interest.

JUDGE: Mr. Prosecutor?

PROSECUTOR: The prosecution has no objection, Your Honor.

JUDGE: Okey, dokey. First case. *(Bangs gavel. To audience.)* I love that.

BAILIFF: Phil versus The People. Attempted Murder.

 (PHIL, DEFENSE LAWYER and PROSECUTOR stand before JUDGE.)

JUDGE: How do you plead?

LAWYER: Not guilty, Your Honor.

JUDGE: Mr. Prosecutor?

PROSECUTOR *(consulting file)***:** Yes, Your Honor. It seems the guilty scum...

LAWYER: Objection.

JUDGE: You were referring to the defendant, Mr. Prosecutor.

PROSECUTOR: Yes, Your Honor.

JUDGE: It's up to the court to decide if he's guilty scum. Objection sustained. Strike the word "guilty" from the record. Now, Mr. Prosecutor, what did the scum do?

    The Big Book of Bible Skits ©1997 Gospel Light. Permission to photocopy granted.

PROSECUTOR: On or about noon, on the second of the month, in the Desert of Gaza, this scumbag was seen holding an Ethiopian man under water.

JUDGE: Is the man in court?

LAWYER: No, Your Honor.

JUDGE: Why not? Shouldn't he be here as a witness, Mr. Prosecutor?

PROSECUTOR: We couldn't insist on his testimony, Your Honor.

JUDGE: Why not?

PROSECUTOR: It seems he's an official in the court of Queen Candace of Ethiopia. He has diplomatic immunity. You know how these political types don't want to be involved in scandal.

JUDGE: That makes it difficult to throw the book at this one.

PROSECUTOR: Unfortunately true, Your Honor. However, we have a stipulation from the defense that the allegations are correct as to their substance.

JUDGE: Defense?

LAWYER: Yes, Your Honor. We stipulated that Phil was holding a man under water.

JUDGE: Seems open and shut, then.

LAWYER: If we may present our defense?

PROSECUTOR: *(Sighs.)* Are we required to waste the court's time this way?

JUDGE: Unfortunately, Mr. Prosecutor, each defendant is allowed a defense. Continue.

LAWYER: My client was holding a man under water, Your Honor. But it was not an act of violence; it was an act of compassion!

PROSECUTOR *(sarcastically)***:** Right! And he pulls legs off grasshoppers so they won't get tired.

JUDGE: No interrupting, Mr. Prosecutor. *(To LAWYER.)* What about this grasshopper thing?

LAWYER: Nothing more than the prosecution's imagination, Your Honor. Not a part of the proceedings.

JUDGE: Okey, dokey. You want to explain this compassionate drowning, Phil?

PHIL: I was in the villages of Samaria, Your Honor...

JUDGE: I thought you said Gaza. Mr. Prosecutor?

PROSECUTOR: *(Looks at file.)* That's how the complaint reads, Your Honor.

PHIL: Yes, Your Honor. I was called by an angel of the Lord to go to Gaza.

JUDGE: OK. So now you're in Gaza?

PHIL: As I was walking along, I saw a chariot and heard a man reading from the prophet Isaiah.

JUDGE: Continue.

PHIL: I ran alongside the chariot and asked the man if he understood what he was reading. He said, "How can I, if I have no one to explain it to me?"

JUDGE: So you're saying this man was semiliterate?

PHIL: No, Your Honor. He was a very intelligent and influential man in Ethiopia. But some of the passages in the prophets are difficult to understand if you haven't grown up with the Scriptures.

JUDGE: Continue.

PHIL: He invited me to sit with him in the chariot and we went through the passage together. I explained how the prophet was speaking of Jesus.

PROSECUTOR *(sarcastically)*: Right! Isaiah lived CENTURIES before Jesus. He didn't even KNOW Jesus. How could he talk about Jesus?

JUDGE: Good point. How about it, Phil?

PHIL: Isaiah was given the information about the Messiah by God. That's why Isaiah is called a prophet.

JUDGE: *(Nods.)* Seems to cover it. What about the drowning?

PHIL: As we continued along, we came to some water. The Ethiopian said, "Here's some water. Is there anything to stop me from being baptized?" I said, "Nothing at all, if you believe with all your heart. The good news of Jesus Christ is for you, too." So we went down to the water and I baptized him.

JUDGE: So you're saying it was a BAPTISM, not a drowning?

PHIL: Yes, Your Honor.

JUDGE: Anything to add, Mr. Prosecutor?

PROSECUTOR: No, Your Honor. The facts speak for themselves.

JUDGE: After careful consideration, I can't see that there is anything to show it wasn't a baptism. Case dismissed. *(Bangs gavel. To audience.)* I love that. Next case.

BAILIFF: Pete versus The People. Attempted Bribery of a Peace Officer.

(PETE, DEFENSE LAWYER and PROSECUTOR stand before JUDGE.)

JUDGE: How do you plead?

LAWYER: Not guilty, Your Honor.

JUDGE: Mr. Prosecutor?

PROSECUTOR *(consulting file)*: Yes, Your Honor. It seems the slime-sucking...

LAWYER: Objection.

JUDGE: Sustained. Mr. Prosecutor, there is nothing in evidence to show the defendant sucks slime.

PROSECUTOR: On or about ten o'clock on the morning of the fifteenth of the month, the defendant was seen entering the premises of Cornelius, leader of the Italian Band.

JUDGE: Are they the ones who made that record, "Roma, Roma, Wherefore Art Thou, Roma?" That was a terrific song!

PROSECUTOR: No, Your Honor. That was the Italian Jug Band.

JUDGE: Too bad. I really like that song. What did this Italian Band record?

PROSECUTOR: Nothing, Your Honor. The Italian Band is one of the special squads of the Roman Army. Cornelius is one of its centurions.

JUDGE: I knew that. Continue with the complaint.

PROSECUTOR: As I said, the defendant was seen slinking into the premises of Cornelius. As Cornelius is a Roman officer and the defendant is Jewish, the obvious conclusion is bribery.

JUDGE: I think I smell something fishy here, alright.

LAWYER: Probably from my client's clothing, Your Honor. Left over from his previous profession.

JUDGE: That could be it. Defense?

LAWYER: My client was there on a social visit, Your Honor, at Cornelius' request.

PROSECUTOR *(sarcastically)*: Oh, right! As if a Jew would enter the house of a Gentile.

JUDGE: Very good point, Counselor. The Jews are well known for their reluctance to associate with Gentiles. What about it, Pete?

PETE: It is well known, Your Honor. I used to be the same way.

PROSECUTOR: See? He admits it. Throw the book at him!

JUDGE: In due time. In due time. So you don't like Gentiles?

PETE: It wasn't that I hated Gentiles. Like all Jews, I believed that God only loved the Jews. But I learned that I was wrong. Now, many Gentiles are my brothers and sisters in Christ.

PROSECUTOR *(sarcastically)*: And I'm the King of Siam.

JUDGE: Really? I hadn't heard. Congratulations.

PROSECUTOR: Thank you, Your Honor.

JUDGE: *(To PETE.)* Continue.

PETE: I was in Joppa...

JUDGE: Doesn't Cornelius live in Caesarea?

PROSECUTOR: *(Looks at file.)* So the record shows, Your Honor.

PETE: He does. But I was visiting my friend, Simon, the tanner. About noon, I was on the roof, praying. I was hungry, but lunch wasn't ready.

JUDGE: I hate having to wait for lunch. How about you, Mr. Prosecutor?

PROSECUTOR: I hate waiting for anything. Especially convictions. Can we get on with this fairy tale?

JUDGE: That's MY job. Continue with your fairy tale, Pete.

PETE: It's no fairy tale! While I was waiting, I saw a vision. A large sheet containing various animals, birds and reptiles came down from heaven. A voice said, "Take. Kill and eat."

JUDGE: I bet they looked good, what with lunch being late.

PETE: No, Your Honor. Because they were all unclean.

JUDGE: Well, haven't you heard of WATER? My goodness, if they were dirty, you could have washed them before you cooked them. And boiling kills germs, you know.

LAWYER: My client refers to the well-known Jewish custom of determining ceremonial cleanliness of some animals and uncleanliness of others.

JUDGE: Mr. Prosecutor?

PROSECUTOR: It is a known fact, Your Honor.

JUDGE: I knew that. Continue.

PETE: So I protested to the voice. I said, "I would never eat anything unclean." Then the voice said, "Don't call unclean the things I have made clean." This happened three times.

JUDGE: You take a lot of convincing. So you ate something?

PETE: No, Your Honor. The animals weren't real. It was just a vision. But I didn't understand it. While I was meditating on it...

JUDGE: Meditating? Are you into T.M.? Do you have a mantra?

PETE: Of course not! That's not from God. Meditating means to think hard about something. So I was thinking about the vision, trying to understand it...

PROSECUTOR: *(To the ceiling.)* He can't understand that it's OK to eat frogs' legs?

PETE: I knew it was more than that. But I didn't know what. Then the Holy Spirit told me there were men waiting for me in the house. The Holy Spirit said, "Don't be afraid to go with these men. I have sent them."

JUDGE: And these men were...?

PETE: Servants of Cornelius. They told me Cornelius wanted to speak with me. Suddenly, I understood the vision. God was telling me that Gentiles are not unclean! So the next day, I went with them to Caesarea.

JUDGE: And that's when you tried to bribe Cornelius?

PETE: I never tried to bribe him! I went and spoke to him about Jesus! I told him how I had thought God's saving grace was only for the Jews, but God had shown me differently. Then the Holy Spirit came upon everyone there. So I baptized Cornelius' household.

JUDGE: Good thing we don't have a water shortage, with all this baptizing.

PROSECUTOR: He really expects us to fall for that sad story. If the Jews have changed their attitude toward Gentiles, how come Gentiles aren't welcome in the homes of Jews?

PETE: I didn't say ALL Jews had changed their attitude. I had to defend my position with my Jewish Christian brothers. But now we know God's plan of salvation is for everyone.

LAWYER: We submit that there is no evidence of bribery and ask for dismissal of all charges, Your Honor.

PROSECUTOR *(outraged)*: No evidence? A Jew in a Gentile home and you say no EVIDENCE?

JUDGE: I have to agree with defense. Case dismissed. *(Bangs gavel. To audience.)* Love that. Next case.

BAILIFF: Paul versus The People. Conspiring to Start a Riot.

> *(PAUL, DEFENSE LAWYER and PROSECUTOR stand before JUDGE.)*

JUDGE: How do you plead?

LAWYER: Not guilty, Your Honor.

JUDGE: Mr. Prosecutor?

PROSECUTOR *(consulting file)*: Yes, Your Honor. It seems the snake...

LAWYER: Objection.

JUDGE: Sustained. Nothing in evidence about reptiles. What are the facts?

PROSECUTOR: On numerous occasions, the defendant went into synagogues to preach.

JUDGE: Happens all the time, Mr. Prosecutor.

PROSECUTOR: But when they don't listen to him, he tells them he will preach to the Gentiles. He tells them God's Word is for the Gentiles.

JUDGE: No big deal, Mr. Prosecutor. Lots of Romans say the Jews don't know what they're talking about. Hasn't caused a riot yet.

PROSECUTOR: But, HE'S a Jew, Your Honor. And a PHARISEE.

JUDGE: Whoo! THAT could ruffle a few feathers. How about it, Paul?

PAUL: What he says is true. I preach to the Jews because they are God's chosen people. But if they refuse to listen, I preach to the Gentiles. God's Word is for them also.

JUDGE: Hmm. But you didn't know it would upset the Jews?

PAUL: Of course I knew it. I used to be the same way. But God's truth must be spoken!

PROSECUTOR: See? He admits it! You gotta give me this one, Your Honor. Totally premeditated. He's guilty!

JUDGE: There's certainly enough evidence to hold this one over. We'll pass it along to the Grand Jury. Defendant remanded to house custody to await trial in Rome. Have you anything else to say?

PAUL: Have you heard of God's love for you? How He wants you to have eternal life?

JUDGE: Whoa! Trying to convert me, Paul? *(Chuckles. To BAILIFF.)* That's a wrap, folks. *(Bangs gavel and mouths, "I love that.")*

BAILIFF: All rise. *(EVERYONE rises as JUDGE exits.)*

THE GENTILES, TOO?

SCRIPTURE: Acts 10

SUGGESTED TOPICS: Salvation for all people; prejudice; witnessing; obedience in trust

BIBLE BACKGROUND

Jesus' last command to His disciples, the Great Commission, was to go into all the world and preach the good news. How could the disciples truly understand the commission? All their lives they had been taught how God loved His chosen people, Israel, and hated all others.

Between Philip (see Acts 8) and Peter, the process had begun. Philip needed a message from an angel and the prompting of the Spirit to nudge him to approach the Ethiopian. Still, Philip saw that the man was heading south from Jerusalem and was reading from the prophet, Isaiah. Likely, the man was a proselyte, one whose nationality was not Hebrew but who had converted to the Jewish faith.

Peter also needed encouragement from God to go to Cornelius. Here was a man who was not only a Gentile but a Roman centurion. Although he was a devout and generous man, there were massive cultural barriers which would keep Peter from entering this man's house. To prepare Peter for the invitation from Cornelius, God had to tell Peter three times not to call unclean that which God has cleansed. Lest we judge Peter too harshly for needing to hear this message three times, we should recognize that he had already shown acceptance of Gentiles. A tanner treated the skins of dead animals and was thus rendered "unclean" according to Jewish law. By staying with Simon the tanner, Peter stretched the narrow limits of traditional Jewish practice.

PERFORMANCE TIPS

1. Suggested props: Bible-times costumes.

2. Before the skit, be certain the group understands how much the Jews hated the Gentiles. Ask your group to think of contemporary examples of prejudice toward others.

3. Introduce the skit by saying, "This skit refers to Jewish food laws given in Leviticus 11. Certain foods, such as meat from pigs, were considered unclean. The Jews were not to eat these foods. Other foods, such as meat from cows, were considered clean. The Jews were allowed to eat these foods. Many of these regulations made good sense for maintaining health. But, mainly, they taught God's people obedience and reminded them that they belonged to God. Listen to the skit to find how God used the examples of clean and unclean foods to teach Peter about God's love for all people."

4. Members of your group may enjoy writing and acting out an additional scene for this skit. Read the story of Peter's defense of his actions in Acts 11:1-18. Several members in the group may play the part of prosecutors, questioning Peter about his actions.

DISCUSSION QUESTIONS

1. Why do you think God gave food laws in the Old Testament?

2. What should our attitudes be toward people who are different from us?

3. In what ways can you show God's love to people who are not like you?

The Big Book of Bible Skits ©1997 Gospel Light. Permission to photocopy granted.

THE GENTILES, TOO?

CHARACTERS
PETER

SIMON

CORNELIUS

SCENE ONE

PETER: Simon, I thank you for your hospitality. But I must leave now. I have to go to Caesarea to the house of a Gentile.

SIMON: Is that wise, Peter?

PETER: Of course. Do I look like the type who would do something foolish?

SIMON: Sorry, Peter. But you know that some people do not understand how you have stayed at my house.

PETER: How so?

SIMON: I'm a tanner. I make my living tanning and preserving the hides of animals. That makes me ceremonially unclean and many people will have nothing to do with me except when they have to.

PETER: I realize that.

SIMON: Still, you accepted my invitation to stay at my home and have been with me for many days.

PETER: Why not? You are a follower of Jesus, just as I am. And I believe the Gentile I am going to visit also wants to learn of Jesus.

SIMON: But, Peter! To enter a Gentile's house is forbidden by law.

PETER: Whose law forbids it?

SIMON: You know very well, Peter. Our law.

PETER: An hour ago, I would have agreed with you. But something strange happened upstairs.

SIMON: Tell me.

PETER: It was just about noon. I was feeling a bit hungry and thinking about coming down for a bite to eat when, suddenly, I saw a vision.

SIMON: You're sure it was a vision. Not a hallucination from hunger?

PETER: It was definitely a vision. I saw a sheet, coming down from heaven, filled with all kinds of unclean animals, reptiles and birds.

SIMON: You're sure this is a vision?

PETER: Yes. And I heard a voice saying, "Rise, Peter, kill and eat."

SIMON: What did you make of it?

PETER: I knew that God was testing my faithfulness. I knew the answer and I gave it. I replied, "No, Lord. For I have never eaten any unclean thing."

SIMON: Good answer. I knew you knew the law.

PETER: But the voice answered me. It said, "Do not call anything unclean that God has cleaned." This happened a second time, and I protested again that the animals were unclean. And again the voice said, "Do not call anything unclean that God has cleaned." And it happened a third time. After the third time, the sheet was pulled up into heaven again.

SIMON: What can be the meaning of this vision?

PETER: That's what I wondered. I sat, thinking about the vision, when the Holy Spirit told me three men were looking for me and I was to go with them. The Holy Spirit said He had sent them to me.

SIMON: The Holy Spirit told you about three men? The three men who came to the house? The Roman soldier and two servants.

PETER: Right.

SIMON: They are servants of a Gentile.

PETER: Right.

SIMON: Not only a Gentile, but a Roman centurion. The enemy.

PETER: Right.

SIMON: But he is a Gentile. He is unclean.

PETER: Simon, do not call unclean that which God has cleaned.

SIMON: I see. The vision was talking about people, not animals.

PETER: Now you understand, also. That is what God was telling me with the sheet from heaven. So I must leave you now and go to see what this man, Cornelius, wants.

SIMON: But suppose some of the others come to ask for you. What shall I tell them?

PETER: The truth. Tell them I have gone to visit a Gentile.

SIMON: But, Peter! They won't understand.

PETER: Perhaps not. But I must obey God, not men. Farewell, my friend. I'll see you on my return. Thank you again for all your hospitality.

SCENE TWO

PETER: So this is the house of Cornelius. I wonder what he wants.

CORNELIUS: *(Falls on his knees.)* My Lord and Master.

PETER: Please get up. I am only a man.

CORNELIUS: Thank you for coming.

PETER: You're welcome. But why did you send for me?

CORNELIUS: I'm not sure.

PETER: What? You, a centurion, a leader of men—you don't know your own actions and thoughts?

CORNELIUS: Let me explain.

PETER: Please do.

CORNELIUS: I was praying...

PETER: To which of the Roman gods?

CORNELIUS: To the God of Israel. I have been here many years and I know that He is the only true God.

PETER: You speak wisely. What happened while you were praying?

CORNELIUS: I had a vision!

PETER: You, too?

CORNELIUS: What?

PETER: Nothing. Please continue.

CORNELIUS: In the vision, I saw an angel of God. The angel told me God had heard my prayers and had seen my charitable works. Then, he told me to send men to Joppa to find a man named Peter. He told me this man would be at the house of Simon, the tanner. You are this man? Peter?

PETER: I am he.

CORNELIUS: Then tell me what to do. The angel said you would.

PETER: For years, I believed God only loved the Israelites. Now I see how wrong I was. I see that God accepts people of all nations who believe in Him. You truly believe?

CORNELIUS: You know I do.

PETER: Yes. I have eyes. You know a little of the love and power of God. God has sent me here to tell you the rest.

CORNELIUS: Please, tell us more. We must hear the rest.

PETER: God anointed Jesus of Nazareth with the Holy Spirit to do good and to heal those who were oppressed by the devil. I am a witness of all that He did and said.

CORNELIUS: I have heard of this man. He was executed.

PETER: He was wrongly judged and executed. He died the death of a criminal. But He is no longer dead. God has raised Him to life. He appeared openly to myself and many others.

CORNELIUS: How can this be? Surely, when a man is dead, he is dead?

PETER: Jesus is no ordinary man. He is God in human flesh. He is the One of whom all the prophets spoke, the One who forgives all sins of those who believe in Him.

CORNELIUS: I believe. And all my household. We all believe.

PETER: Can this be? The Holy Spirit has descended upon this household in the same way He came to us in the Upper Room at Pentecost. You who have come with me, you see these Gentiles have received the Holy Spirit. Can we refuse to baptize with water those whom God has baptized with the Holy Spirit? Come, Cornelius, be baptized in the name of the Lord.

CORNELIUS: We shall. And you must stay. Tell us more about Jesus.

PETER: I will. But what will I tell those in Jerusalem when they ask about this thing? The truth. I shall tell them what has happened. If they don't believe me, God will have to give them a vision, also.

The Big Book of Bible Skits ©1997 Gospel Light. Permission to photocopy granted.

FREE!

SCRIPTURE: Acts 12:1-17

SUGGESTED TOPICS: God answers prayer; early church

BIBLE BACKGROUND

The Church continued to grow, much to the annoyance of the Jewish leaders. Fortunately for them, they had an ally in the latest Herod. Herod Agrippa I, grandson of Herod the Great, seemed to believe the best way to rule was to appease the Jewish leaders. Many believers were arrested on his orders and he even had James, the brother of John, executed by the sword. His next step was to have Peter imprisoned, intending to have Peter brought to a public trial in the near future.

Peter would have been not long for this world, if Herod had his way. Long-term imprisonment was not a normal practice under Roman law. There were better forms of punishment: execution, scourging, sentencing to the galleys. In Peter's case, judging from Herod's actions in dealing with James, execution was the most likely outcome.

Not only Peter, but all the other believers, must have realized this. Hence, prayer was made for Peter without ceasing (see Acts 12:5). On the very eve of Peter's intended trial, God intervened. Somewhat humorously, we find that those who faithfully gathered to pray were unprepared to accept the answer to those prayers.

PERFORMANCE TIPS

1. Before the skit, read or summarize Acts 12:1-11 which tells the story of Peter's arrest and miraculous escape from prison. Also read Acts 12:19 to find out what happened in Roman times to soldiers who allowed a prisoner to escape.

2. Arrange the skit performers so that a door is nearby. The skit should begin with the sound of Peter knocking on the closed door.

DISCUSSION QUESTIONS

1. Why is it important for Christians to pray?

2. When have you felt that God didn't hear your prayers? What could you do if you become discouraged in praying?

3. We are told in 1 Thessalonians 5:17 to "pray continually." What does it mean to pray continually? How would you say this verse in your own words?

4. What are some things you can talk to God about?

FREE!

CHARACTERS
MARY

RHODA

PETER

MARY: Who's knocking at the door? We're trying to pray. Rhoda, go and see who it is. But be careful. If it's Roman soldiers, don't let them in. We don't want to be arrested.

RHODA: Yes, ma'am.

MARY: Now then, let's continue. Oh Lord, grant our request to keep Peter safe. Preserve him from Herod and from the evil...

RHODA: Mary, Mary, Mary...

MARY: What is the matter with you, girl? Can't you see we're praying? Be quiet.

RHODA: But, but, but...

MARY: Stop stuttering and either join us in praying for Peter or go about your chores.

RHODA: But it's Peter.

MARY: Yes. We're all sad about Peter. But we'll continue to pray...

RHODA: No! At the door! It's Peter!

MARY: What are you talking about? Peter's in prison. We've been praying for his safety all evening.

RHODA: No! He's at the door. He spoke to me. I recognized his voice.

MARY: Nonsense! You're a silly girl. If he were here, he would come in. And why is someone still knocking at the door?

RHODA: Oh! I forgot to open the door. *(Runs out.)*

MARY: I don't know why I put up with the girl. She's always imagining things...

PETER: Friends!

MARY: Peter! You're here! But you're in prison! I mean, you're supposed to be in prison. No, no. I don't mean you're supposed to be there. I mean, you are there. Herod arrested you.

PETER: I was in jail. God heard your prayers and sent an angel who brought me out. I'll tell you what happened, but then, I'll have to leave. It wouldn't be safe for you if I stayed here. After I've gone, send someone to tell James and the other believers.

Paphos by Night

SCRIPTURE: Acts 13:1-12

SUGGESTED TOPICS: Respect; acts of the early church; spreading the gospel

BIBLE BACKGROUND

Much had happened since the ascension of the Lord. The believers began preaching in Jerusalem, converting thousands to faith in Jesus Christ as the Jewish Messiah and Savior of all. Vexed by the success of this preaching, the religious leaders began persecuting the new church, culminating in the death of Stephen. This persecution drove many believers from Jerusalem to the surrounding countryside of Judea and into Samaria. From Samaria, Philip was led by the Lord into the desert where he met an influential Ethiopian on his way home. Philip proclaimed the gospel to the Ethiopian, helping to spread the good news into Africa.

Completely angered by the spread of this message, Saul, a devout Pharisee from Tarsus, received permission from the high priest to pursue his persecution of the Church to Damascus. On the way, however, Saul met the Lord and was converted. Although the message of Christ had spread widely, it was still being preached only to Jews and Samaritans, who were half-Jewish. Peter changed that when he journeyed to Caesarea to present the good news to Cornelius, a Roman centurion.

Herod Agrippa, Herod the Great's grandson, seeking the favor of the Jews, began persecuting the Church with renewed vigor in Jerusalem. In response, the Church began to expand its missionary vision through Barnabas and Saul who were sent from the church in Antioch to Cyprus, Barnabas's original home.

A crucial encounter occurred on the island of Cyprus. Saul confronted a sorcerer in the presence of the Roman governor, Sergius Paulus. This dramatic moment was Saul's first declaration of the good news before a Gentile. As a result, the governor believed, and from this point on, Saul is referred to by his Roman, Hellenistic name, Paul, indicating the beginning of Paul's great ministry beyond the confines of Judaism.

As a Roman governor, Sergius Paulus's job was not filled with security. Should a rumor of his infidelity to the emperor (Claudius) reach the ears of Rome and be believed, the governor would be recalled immediately, possibly at the cost of his life. How would Rome respond to the news that one of its proconsuls had embraced the Christian faith? Certainly, he would now refuse to join in the worship of the emperor as a god. That could be considered disloyalty and ultimately treason.

PERFORMANCE TIPS

1. Suggested props: table and chairs arranged for a talk show.

2. Marcus Hamus is an intelligent individual who sees the danger of Sergius Paulus' words about his conversion to Christianity. As the skit progresses, Marcus should show increasing concern for Sergius Paulus by his facial expression and gestures.

3. Flavius should be portrayed as dense, but eager to hear about new ideas.

4. Paul and Barnabas do not insult anyone. Rather, they show respect to all persons when they speak.

5. Introduce the skit by reading Acts 13:1,2 aloud. After the skit, briefly summarize Acts 13:13-52 telling of Paul and Barnabas' journey into Pisidian Antioch and the results of their preaching to the Jews in that city.

DISCUSSION QUESTIONS

1. Why do you think Elymas didn't appear on the talk show? Read Acts 13:6-12 to find the answer.

2. How would you describe the attitudes of Paul and Barnabas towards Sergius Paulus and the talk show hosts? Why did they act respectfully?

3. Would Sergius Paulus have listened to Paul and Barnabas if they began their conversation with him by saying, "Proconsul, the religion of Rome is false and you are stupid to believe it?" Why or why not?

4. Read Acts 13:14,15. What did Paul and Barnabas do when they first went into the Jewish synagogue? What might have happened if they had interrupted the worship service without being invited to speak?

5. Throughout their journey, Paul and Barnabas showed respect to the people they met. How can you show respect to the people you meet?

PAPHOS BY NIGHT

CHARACTERS
FLAVIUS (FLAY-vee-us)
MARCUS
SERGIUS (SER-jee-us)
PAUL
BARNABAS
AUDIENCE

PRONUNCIATION GUIDE
Antioch (AN-tee-ahk)
Elymas (EEL-ih-mus)
Iliad (IH-lee-ad)
Paphos (PAY-fos)
synagogue (SIN-a-gog)

FLAVIUS: Welcome to "Paphos by Night," the nighttime talk show that brings you interesting people from all over the world. Tonight's guest host is the well-known actor who has just finished a worldwide tour performing *The Iliad* to sellout crowds, Marcus Hamus! Marcus' guests tonight include sorcerer and prophet, Elymas; governor of the island of Cyprus, Sergius Paulus. Also two traveling preachers who caused quite a stir today: Paul and Barnabas! And now, here's Marcus! *(AUDIENCE applauds.)*

MARCUS: Thank you. What a terrific audience. It's great to be here in Paphos. Even though the audience response has been terrific wherever we've been, the best audience in the world is always right here in Paphos. *(AUDIENCE applauds.)* But we have a really packed show tonight, so let's get right to our first guest. I think it's safe to say that everyone here has heard of this man. He's the governor of Cyprus. Well known as a man of courage and great intelligence, here's Sergius Paulus! Welcome to the show. *(AUDIENCE applauds.)*

SERGIUS: Thank you, Marcus. It's good to be here. By the way, I caught your play when you were in Antioch, and I must say, you were brilliant.

MARCUS: Thank you, Sergius, that is indeed a compliment.

SERGIUS: It's not flattery, Marcus. I really mean it.

MARCUS: OK, any more of this and I'll think you're trying to borrow money from me. Anyway, I want to ask a few questions that I think will be interesting to everybody.

SERGIUS: Fire away, Marcus.

MARCUS: Sergius, how have you managed to gain such a reputation as an intelligent man?

SERGIUS: I'm not sure what you mean, Marcus. By being intelligent, perhaps?

MARCUS: Well, we all know that many people are given political appointments because of their family connections or to repay favors. You actually seem to be qualified to be a governor.

SERGIUS: I hope so. All I can say is I just try to do the best job I can each day.

MARCUS: C'mon! Level with us. Have you done something special to please the gods so they keep you looking smart?

SERGIUS: No, nothing at all. Particularly now.

MARCUS: What do you mean by that?

SERGIUS: By what?

MARCUS: You said, "Particularly now." Why particularly now?

SERGIUS: Well, until yesterday, I thought much the same as you. I believed there were many gods and you had to be sure not to get the wrong god upset on the wrong day or you were in big trouble. But I don't believe that anymore.

MARCUS: What? You don't believe—I haven't heard...I mean, I'm no theologian. I don't have any divinity degrees. But I would think that those who do would have made some kind of an announcement about such a major change, and I haven't heard anything. Have you, Flavius?

FLAVIUS: No, I sure haven't! Of course, I WAS out of town for a few days.

MARCUS: When did this big change come about, Sergius? And why didn't anyone tell me about it?

SERGIUS: I didn't say there was an official change in Roman religious policy, Marcus. I said that I no longer believe there are many gods. I no longer believe that I must appease many gods in order to have a good day and a prosperous life.

FLAVIUS: Excuse me for interrupting, Marcus. I know you're the host but I just want to be sure I understand what Sergius is saying. Are you speaking against official Roman religious policy?

SERGIUS: Well, I guess I am, Flavius.

MARCUS: Wow! This is something! I've never heard an important official disagree with official Roman policy before.

SERGIUS: Religious freedom is allowed in the Roman Empire, Marcus. I thought you traveled throughout the world. Surely you've seen various religious practices in your travels.

MARCUS: Sure I have. But never by a governor or a deputy or any other important official before. Maybe we'd better stop right now before we get you removed from office. This would be a good time to bring out Elymas to show us some of his astounding magic.

SERGIUS: Thank you for your consideration, Marcus, but I don't think that Elymas is going to be able to make it tonight.

FLAVIUS: I think he's right, Marcus. I just checked with the director, and Elymas isn't here yet.

MARCUS: You are truly amazing, Sergius. Have you gone into the prophecy business, too?

SERGIUS: No. But Elymas was partly responsible for my change of heart regarding my religious practices.

MARCUS: Enough said, Sergius. We're trying to save your job, remember? Well, we still have the two wandering preachers waiting to come out. They're still here, aren't they, Flavius?

FLAVIUS: Oh, yes, they're here.

MARCUS: Good. OK, let's welcome these preachers, Paul and Barnabas!

PAUL: Hello, Marcus.

BARNABAS: And thanks for inviting us.

MARCUS: Paul and Barnabas? Those are unusual names to be linked together. Roman and Jewish, aren't they? I thought Roman and Jewish religion were miles apart in their doctrine.

PAUL: Absolutely. As far as the heavens are from the ocean depths.

BARNABAS: As far as the East is from the West.

MARCUS: Then how is it that you, Paul, are traveling with a Jew?

PAUL: There's really nothing unusual about it. You see, I'm Jewish. I just go by my Roman name.

MARCUS: Then you and Barnabas are actually two Jews, going around preaching together. You ARE Jewish I hope, Barnabas? You're not an Egyptian going by his Jewish name?

BARNABAS: No, I'm Jewish. Although I was born here in Cyprus.

MARCUS: Good! Then we've got that straight. Oh, I'm sorry. I don't know what has happened to my manners. I forgot to introduce you to Sergius Paulus.

PAUL: That's perfectly alright. We've met before.

BARNABAS: We sure have. How are you doing, sir?

SERGIUS: Very well, thank you.

MARCUS: Now this is perplexing. How is it that two Jewish preachers know a Roman governor?

SERGIUS: They were preaching in Paphos. They're the reason I no longer believe in many Roman gods.

MARCUS: Everything I hear confuses me more and more. What were you doing in a Jewish synagogue, Sergius? How could that possibly relate to your job as governor of Cyprus?

SERGIUS: I didn't hear them in a synagogue.

MARCUS: But I thought Jewish preachers spoke in synagogues. Isn't that right?

BARNABAS: We did speak in the synagogue. We always speak in the synagogue.

PAUL: But Sergius Paulus wanted to hear us and asked us to visit him.

MARCUS: I don't understand this. Sergius, why would you want to hear these itinerant preachers?

SERGIUS: Part of my job as governor is to keep the peace. If there is any new idea being spoken in my country, I should know what it is.

FLAVIUS: I hate to keep butting in, but since Marcus has his head in his hands and looks like he has a splitting headache, maybe I could ask the obvious question. Why did you have to ask Jewish preachers to come to see you? Jews haven't changed their teachings in all of recorded history. Didn't you already know what Jews believe?

SERGIUS: Certainly. I studied Jewish history and religion at Rome when I was learning how to be a governor. But these men were preaching something new.

PAUL: Actually, it's nothing new at all.

BARNABAS: In fact, it's the very foundation of Jewish faith.

PAUL: It's actually the fulfillment of all that was spoken by the prophets and written in the Scriptures.

BARNABAS: A fact that we try to point out to the worshipers in the synagogue when we speak to them.

SERGIUS: I was so impressed with what they said and did that I now believe in their God as the one and only true God, and in His Son, Jesus Christ. The One who is responsible for all prophecy and its fulfillment.

MARCUS: Oh, yes, I really do wish that Elymas could have been with us tonight. His act is truly worth seeing, but we're out of time. I want to thank my guests tonight—Sergius Paulus, Paul and Barnabas—for taking time out of their busy schedules to come and speak with us. Tune in tomorrow for another...uh, interesting show. Good night.

TROUBLEMAKERS

SCRIPTURE: Acts 17

SUGGESTED TOPICS: Respect; acts of the early church; spreading the gospel

BIBLE BACKGROUND

On his first missionary journey, Paul was accompanied by Barnabas and, for a short time, Barnabas' nephew, John Mark. Paul and Barnabas prepared to set out on a second journey, but they had a disagreement over whether or not to have John Mark accompany them a second time. So great was the disagreement that Paul and Barnabas went their separate ways; Barnabas took John Mark with him and set sail for Cyprus. Paul chose Silas and headed north through Cilicia. Apparently, they were also accompanied by Luke and Timothy.

The second missionary journey was filled with ups and downs. In Macedonia Paul and Silas were beaten and imprisoned for casting a demon out of a young girl (see Acts 16:16-24). Through a miracle of God, they were released from prison but were told to leave the city. The journey continued on to Thessalonica.

This skit assumes that, even though they were not alone, Paul and Silas were the two who created most of the uproar in Thessalonica. Timothy was still a young man and Luke seems to be more of a chronicler than a preacher.

PERFORMANCE TIPS

1. Suggested props: microphones, video camera.
2. Bring a map showing Paul's missionary journeys. Ask group members to locate the cities of Thessalonica, Berea and Athens and check the distances between these cities. Compare the distances to cities with which your group is familiar. Emphasize the great distances Paul walked in order to preach the gospel.
3. Carpus and Fortunatus have slightly longer passages than the other characters. If you are using these skits with children, ask two better readers to play these parts.

DISCUSSION QUESTIONS

1. Why might some of the Jews in Thessalonica have hated Paul and Silas? Read Acts 17:5 to check your answer. Why did Paul and Silas keep preaching in spite of the trouble they encountered?
2. Acts 17:16 says Paul was greatly upset when he saw Athens was full of idols. How does Paul begin his speech to the people of Athens? (Refer to Acts 17:22,23.) Why did Paul choose to preach that way?
3. What do you learn about witnessing to others from Paul's actions?

TROUBLEMAKERS

CHARACTERS
FORTUNATUS (for-choon-AH-tus)
CARPUS (KAR-pus)
TEMAN (TAY-mun)
OMAR
SOPETER
DIONYSIUS (dye-uh-NIH-see-us)

PRONUNCIATION GUIDE
Babylon (BAB-ih-lon)
Berea (buh-REE-uh)
blasphemers (BLAS-fee-murs)
blasphemy (BLAS-fuh-mee)
synagogue (SIN-uh-gog)
Thessalonica (THESS-uh-low-NYE-kuh)

FORTUNATUS: Good evening. I'm Fortunatus and this is Athens Radio News. Today's top story: "Have We Learned the Identity of the Unknown God?" With more from Mars' Hill, here's our roving reporter, Carpus.

CARPUS: Thank you, Fortunatus. Mars' Hill has been in an uproar today. A Roman citizen by the name of Paul claims to know the identity of "The Unknown God." As you all know, Athens contains magnificent temples to many gods. Just in case we might miss one, and, not wanting his wrath poured out on us, we've also erected a monument to an unknown god.

FORTUNATUS: A fact known by all our listeners, Carpus. But you say that a Roman claims to know the identity of the unknown god?

CARPUS: That's right. This man, Paul, spoke with the wise men of Athens today. I'm gathering firsthand reports from those who were there and I'll update you later in the broadcast.

FORTUNATUS: Thank you, Carpus. We'll be looking forward to that update. In other news, all is not well in Athens. We have information that a group of troublemakers may be on their way here. For more on this story, we go via satellite feed to Thessalonica. Teman and Omar, are you there?

TEMAN: We sure are.

OMAR: Ready and waiting.

FORTUNATUS: Gentlemen, I understand there has been some trouble for the Jewish community in Thessalonica.

TEMAN: Trouble? Four hundred years of slavery in Egypt was trouble.

OMAR: Being dragged off into captivity by Babylon was trouble.

TEMAN: The attempted wipeout of the Jews by Haman was trouble.

TEMAN and OMAR: This is SERIOUS.

FORTUNATUS: Please, tell us about it.

OMAR: It all started with these two blasphemers, Silas and Paul.

TEMAN: Paul is really the one to blame.

OMAR: He was just more vocal. Silas backed him up at every turn.

FORTUNATUS: Gentlemen...

TEMAN (*ignoring Fortunatus*)**:** And let's not forget Jason.

OMAR: True! He should have known better.

FORTUNATUS: Gentlemen...

TEMAN (*ignoring Fortunatus*)**:** But we sure showed him.

OMAR: We sure did. He won't help troublemakers again.

FORTUNATUS: GENTLEMEN!

TEMAN and OMAR: Yes?

FORTUNATUS: We seem to have lost track of the story. Perhaps if I ask a few questions, we can get this straightened out.

TEMAN: Ask away.

OMAR: Anything you want to know.

TEMAN: We've got nothing to hide.

OMAR: Always ready to help the press. That's us.

FORTUNATUS: Good. Now then, you mentioned two men by name. Troublemakers.

OMAR: Silas!

TEMAN: Paul!

FORTUNATUS: Those are the two. Just who are they?

OMAR: They claim to be Jews.

TEMAN: But they can't be.

OMAR: They've got no respect for our tradition.

TEMAN: Or the Torah.

FORTUNATUS: What exactly did they do?

OMAR: Oh, they were clever.

TEMAN: They came slinking into town.

OMAR: No they didn't.

TEMAN: Of course they did.

OMAR: No. They just walked straight in. They didn't slide down any stairs.

TEMAN: Not slinky. Slink-ING. Sneaking in.

OMAR: Oh. Right. Slinking in. That's how they came, alright.

FORTUNATUS: But what did they do?

TEMAN: What did they do? They nearly burned the city to the ground.

OMAR: They nearly turned our streets into piles of rubble.

FORTUNATUS: And how did two men do all this?

TEMAN: First, they came sneaking into the synagogue.

OMAR: And they pretended to know the Scriptures.

TEMAN: But they didn't.

OMAR: They just misquoted everything they could.

FORTUNATUS: I'm afraid I don't understand. How can talking in a synagogue create all this trouble?

TEMAN: It's all Paul's fault.

OMAR: And Silas, too.

TEMAN and OMAR: And Jason!

TEMAN: They said that Jesus is the Christ.

OMAR: They said the Christ had to suffer.

TEMAN: They said the Christ was killed.

OMAR: And that He was raised from the dead.

TEMAN and OMAR: Blasphemy!

FORTUNATUS: And how did this blasphemy nearly burn the city to the ground and turn the streets into piles of rubble?

TEMAN: Some of the Jews in the synagogue believed these blasphemers.

OMAR: This sort of thing cannot be tolerated.

TEMAN: So we got a mob—I mean, a group of concerned citizens together.

OMAR: And we stormed—I mean, we went to Jason's house.

TEMAN: And we kicked—I mean, we knocked on the door.

OMAR: And we dragged—I mean, we escorted Jason to the city officials.

TEMAN: And we yelled—I mean, we explained to the officials how Jason had harbored these criminal types in his house.

OMAR: And we screamed—I mean, we calmly showed the officials how these men were breaking the laws of Rome by claiming there was another king other than Caesar.

FORTUNATUS: So these men nearly caused a riot.

TEMAN: Nearly?

OMAR: Why, they would have destroyed the city had we not stopped them.

TEMAN: In fact, we chased them right out of the city.

OMAR: And made sure that Jason had to pay a large fine for his part in this sordid affair.

FORTUNATUS: But they're gone now. So all's well that ends well.

TEMAN: It's not all over.

OMAR: They went to Berea and tried to destroy that city, too.

TEMAN: But we heard about it.

OMAR: And marched in and stirred up trouble—I mean, we showed those ignorant Bereans the error of Paul and Silas' preaching.

TEMAN: But what can you expect from Bereans? You wouldn't believe how many of them believed these upstarts.

FORTUNATUS: Thank you for taking time out of your busy schedules to talk with us. Our satellite feed now takes us to Berea, where Sopeter can give us a firsthand account of the happenings in that city. Sopeter, welcome to Athens Radio News.

SOPETER: Thank you, Fortunatus.

FORTUNATUS: We've received reports about some troublemakers invading your city.

SOPETER: They sure have, and for no reason at all.

FORTUNATUS: Can you tell us what happened?

SOPETER: Certainly. Paul and Silas came to town...

FORTUNATUS: And tried to burn it to the ground?

SOPETER: No. Of course not. They came to visit, to come to the synagogue and speak with us. Together, we searched the Scriptures with them and learned many marvelous things about the law and the prophets and how they relate to Jesus the Christ.

FORTUNATUS: But you said they were troublemakers.

SOPETER: Not them. Some hotheads from Thessalonica were the troublemakers.

FORTUNATUS: I'm afraid I don't understand.

SOPETER: There was no trouble in Berea until some men from Thessalonica came into town and tried to convince us to lynch Paul and Silas. They caused so much trouble, we thought it best to send Paul away for his own safety.

FORTUNATUS: And where is Paul now?

SOPETER: Last I heard, he was headed your way.

FORTUNATUS: There you have it listeners, the probability that some Jewish troublemaker might be headed our way. I understand that Carpus has his update from Mars' Hill ready. Carpus?

CARPUS: Fortunatus, I'm here with Dionysius, the well-known philosopher. He was one of the men on Mars' Hill when this Roman, Paul, spoke about the unknown god.

DIONYSIUS: Actually, Paul is Jewish.

CARPUS: He is? Then why does he have a Roman name?

DIONYSIUS: Because he's a Roman citizen. But he's Jewish.

CARPUS: Can you tell us what Paul said on Mars' Hill today?

DIONYSIUS: Certainly. He spoke to us by saying that he noticed we were very devout men because we had so many monuments to the gods.

CARPUS: Perceptive enough.

DIONYSIUS: Yes. Then, he spoke to us about the unknown god. He told us that this was the God who made all things, the God who does not live in temples made with human hands.

CARPUS: Then this god would live on Mount Olympus.

DIONYSIUS: No. This God is not like other gods.

CARPUS: All gods are the same. Mostly.

DIONYSIUS: Not this one. His likeness cannot be made from gold or silver.

CARPUS: So this is a god of stone?

DIONYSIUS: No. This God's image cannot be fashioned from anything. This God creates; He cannot be created from men's work. He is the giver of all life and wants people to worship Him, not the idols we vainly set up.

CARPUS: This is all very strange. I don't understand any of it.

DIONYSIUS: The best is yet to come. He sent His Son to call people back to Him, but some people would not listen and put His Son to death.

CARPUS: And now He seeks revenge and will destroy us?

DIONYSIUS: No. This God is a loving God. He raised His Son from the dead.

CARPUS (*laughing*)**:** Wait! He raised Him from the dead?

DIONYSIUS: Many believe Paul. Others are interested. Others mock, as you do.

CARPUS: There you have it, Fortunatus. Some crazy Jew was on Mars' Hill trying to convince the wise men of Athens that there is a god who cares about people. And that the dead can come back to life. From Mars' Hill, this is Carpus.

FORTUNATUS: Sounds like some of those wise men have been out in the sun too long. That's the news for tonight. Next news, tomorrow at sunrise. For Athens Radio News, this is Fortunatus, saying good-night.

FAREWELL

SCRIPTURE: Acts 20

SUGGESTED TOPICS: Early church; God's guidance

BIBLE BACKGROUND

Paul, persecutor of the Church, had become its greatest champion. He preached the Word from Palestine to Greece. He preached to Jews and Gentiles alike. Acts 20 records the latter part of his third missionary journey. For about three years, Paul had made Ephesus a center for evangelism into all of Asia Minor. He then traveled again through Macedonia and Greece. Paul was determined to return to Jerusalem, even though he had been warned repeatedly that imprisonment and other hardships awaited him there. Likely, he discussed the situation in Jerusalem with his friends and companions. Paul probably asked his friends to pray, to be certain that all were in agreement in the Spirit.

Knowing that he would not have another opportunity to minister in Ephesus, Paul wanted to meet with the Ephesian church leaders one more time. Paul wanted to prepare them for the trials he knew would come. He warned the Ephesian elders to be on the lookout for wolves that would prey among their flock.

PERFORMANCE TIPS

1. Suggested props: Bible-time costumes.
2. The skit does not include the story of Eutychus (Acts 20:7-12). You may ask a member of your group to act the part of Luke and describe the event. Or, a group member may act the part of Eutychus and tell the story in the first person. In either case, allow the person time to prepare a script.

DISCUSSION QUESTIONS

1. Why was it so important to Paul to meet with the Ephesian church leaders again?
2. How did Paul show respect for the Ephesian leaders? (Read Acts 20:17-20,29-31,35.)
3. Romans 12:10 tells us to honor or respect others more highly than ourselves. What does it mean to honor someone? How can you honor a friend? A parent? A teammate?

FAREWELL

CHARACTERS
PAUL
LUKE
SILVANUS (SIL-vuh-nus)
DEMAS (DEE-mus)

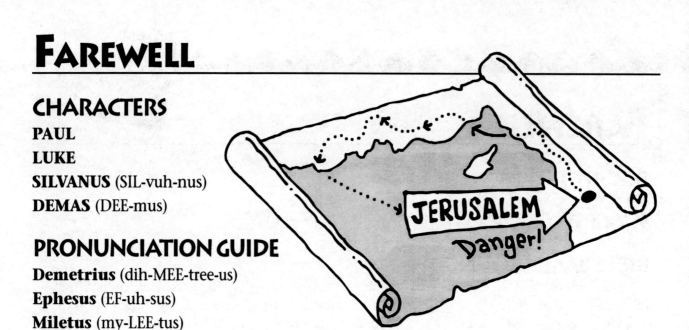

PRONUNCIATION GUIDE
Demetrius (dih-MEE-tree-us)
Ephesus (EF-uh-sus)
Miletus (my-LEE-tus)
Troas (TROH-az)

SCENE ONE

PAUL: Luke, we need to change our plans.

LUKE: Why's that, Paul? Everything's ready for our return to Antioch. I've made all the arrangements with the ship's captain.

PAUL: I know, Luke. But our enemies have plotted to jump us as we board the ship.

LUKE: Don't those guys ever give up? What are we going to do instead?

PAUL: We'll go back through Macedonia. It'll take longer, but it will give us another chance to see the believers there.

LUKE: Imagine how those fellows who've been plotting will feel when they realize we're not getting on that boat.

PAUL: I wish I could be there to see it, but we'd better get started right away. I really want to get to Jerusalem before Pentecost.

LUKE: I don't get it, Paul. We change our plans here in Greece to avoid our enemies, but then we go back to Jerusalem where the city is full of even more people who hate you?

PAUL: But I must. The church in Jerusalem needs the offering we're carrying and I want to encourage the leaders there.

LUKE: How will it help the church in Jerusalem if you get arrested?

PAUL: You have a point. But I really feel God's Spirit is compelling me to go there. So let's hit the road before our enemies come looking for us.

(Skit continues on next page.)

SCENE TWO

LUKE: Paul. I thought you were in a hurry to get to Jerusalem.

PAUL: I am.

LUKE: So why did we stay in Philippi for a week?

PAUL: I just couldn't leave during the feast, Luke. Passover and the week of celebration afterwards are so important, I really wanted to spend it with the believers there.

LUKE: Fine, but why did we stay in Troas for a week?

PAUL: The believers here asked me to meet with them on the first day of the week to share the Lord's Supper. I couldn't say no.

LUKE: Paul, you're an old softie.

PAUL: I know, I know, but we still have time to get to Jerusalem by Pentecost. I just wish we had time to stop in Ephesus.

LUKE: Oh, right. And start another riot?

PAUL: Well, maybe there'll be time at Miletus to meet with the leaders from Ephesus. I've checked the boat schedules, and it just might work.

LUKE: If you don't preach any more all-night sermons.

PAUL: OK, I went on a little long. I'll keep it shorter next time.

SCENE THREE

PAUL: My good friends, thank you for coming. I trust the trip was pleasant.

SILVANUS: The sea was perfectly calm.

DEMAS: And the ship was trustworthy.

PAUL: I'm glad you arrived so quickly. Tomorrow I sail towards Jerusalem. I hope to be there in time for Pentecost.

SILVANUS: You can't!

DEMAS: You must not!

PAUL: I can and I must.

SILVANUS: But your enemies will be waiting for you.

DEMAS: You know how quickly news travels. You won't be safe in Jerusalem.

PAUL: Well, I wasn't too safe in Ephesus or Greece, or anywhere else. And, since the Holy Spirit has called me to Jerusalem, I must go.

SILVANUS: Is there nothing we can say...

DEMAS: Nothing we can do...

SILVANUS and DEMAS: ...to convince you to stay?

PAUL: Do you remember how I lived with you? I lived humbly and did nothing to cause you any shame.

SILVANUS: That's true.

PAUL: I always served the Lord, in spite of dangers and temptations around me.

DEMAS: You did indeed.

PAUL: I never held back anything from you. I taught the things of our Lord Jesus Christ, both on the street corners and in your homes.

SILVANUS: You certainly did. We are so grateful to you for that.

DEMAS: Before you came, some of us believed in the God of Abraham, but we had never heard of Jesus.

SILVANUS: And many others of us only believed in the goddess Artemis. A belief that couldn't help us at all.

DEMAS: But you came and showed us the truth—life, through Jesus Christ.

SILVANUS: And forgiveness through Him.

PAUL: I did not fear for myself then, and I am not afraid now. I must go to Jerusalem and finish the course laid out for me by the Lord Jesus.

DEMAS: But when will we see you again?

PAUL: To tell you the truth, you will never see me again. Prison and other trials await me in Jerusalem. But difficult trials await you, also.

SILVANUS: Trials? We're going to be arrested?

PAUL: Not that kind of trial. Listen! Danger will come to the flock.

DEMAS: Flock? Where did the sheep come from?

PAUL: Not sheep. The Holy Spirit has made you shepherds to feed the Church of God. That is the flock which Jesus Christ purchased with His own blood.

DEMAS: Oh! The Church.

PAUL: Be warned that after I leave, wolves shall enter among you.

DEMAS: I'm pretty good with a bow and arrow.

PAUL: Not four-legged wolves. I'm talking about people! Enemies of the Church!

SILVANUS: We'll be ready for them.

PAUL: Remember my warnings in the years to come.

DEMAS: But how can we shoulder such a responsibility?

PAUL: I entrust you to God. His grace will give you the strength to do all these things. Through His power, you will build up the Church.

SILVANUS: But what shall we do?

PAUL: Follow my example. Do not long for things owned by others, but earn your own living, as I did. Support those who are weak, remembering the words of our Lord Jesus Christ, "It's better to give than to receive."

DEMAS: All these things, we shall do.

SILVANUS: We'll protect the Church with our own lives.

PAUL: I know you will. But time grows short. We have time to pray, then I must be off to Jerusalem.

DEMAS: Farewell, Paul.

SILVANUS: We'll always remember what you've done for us.

THE SCOURGE OF JERUSALEM

SCRIPTURE: Acts 21:27—22:30

SUGGESTED TOPICS: Responsibility for choices; wisdom; early church

BIBLE BACKGROUND

Rome's system of world domination differed from that of other conquerors. Instead of bringing in new rulers, the conquered leaders were often permitted to retain their leadership roles. Rome alone was permitted to sentence a man to death, but most other criminal matters could be settled before a local court overseen by local judges. However, Rome's presence in major cities was represented by a local garrison whose main purpose was to keep order. Under no circumstances was civil disobedience tolerated.

Paul returned to Jerusalem, during Roman rule, for the Feast of Pentecost. While in Jerusalem, he was spotted walking with a Gentile, Trophimus, by some of the Jews from the province of Asia. Apparently, they had not forgotten Paul and his preaching in their land. Seizing on the fact that Paul had been seen with a Gentile and that Paul was now in the Temple, they quickly spread the rumor that Paul had brought a Gentile into the Temple, thereby defiling the holy place.

Nothing more was required to stir the crowd into a frenzy and to change a peaceful group of worshipers into a murderous mob. Without the intervention of the Roman guard, Paul would have been murdered just outside of the Temple. To keep him safe from the mob, the commander of the Jerusalem garrison took soldiers and centurions (at least two hundred soldiers) to quell the riot and remove Paul to the adjacent Roman fortress for questioning. Considering Rome's high regard for order, the ruthlessness of the army in dealing with civil disobedience is understandable. Being in the army was considered one of the better jobs in Rome, offering excitement, adventure and many fringe benefits for the loyal soldier. Although the Roman army was one of the finest fighting machines the world has known, there must have been an occasional sadist or fool who made his way into its ranks. However, no matter what his rank or disposition, each soldier knew there were two sets of laws; one for Roman citizens and one for non-citizens.

PERFORMANCE TIPS

1. Suggested props: chair for the commander to sit in, rope or chain to tie Paul's hands.

2. Introduce the skit by saying, "The apostle Paul wanted to celebrate the Jewish Feast of Pentecost in Jerusalem. Many people warned him against traveling to Jerusalem because of his enemies. However, Paul was determined to meet with the Christians in Jerusalem. When he went to the Temple, a riot broke out. Roman soldiers were called and their commander questioned him. Listen to what happened."

3. After the skit, ask a member of your group to read Acts 21:27-29 to find out what caused the riot.

DISCUSSION QUESTIONS

1. Acts 22:29 tells us the commander was frightened when he learned Paul was a Roman citizen. Why was he frightened? (Roman citizens had special rights and privileges.)

2. As Christians, we are called by God to act responsibly. How did Paul act responsibly?

3. What are some ways someone your age can act responsibly?

THE SCOURGE OF JERUSALEM

CHARACTERS
COMMANDER

PAUL

SOLDIER

CENTURION (sen-CHUR-ee-un)

PRONUNCIATION GUIDE
Gamaliel (gah-MAY-lee-el)

scourge (SKURJ)

COMMANDER: Now then. You're no longer in danger of being torn apart by the mob. What started the riot?

PAUL: The hardness of the people's hearts, sir.

COMMANDER: A typical criminal response. Guard!

SOLDIER: Present and accounted for, O Supreme Commander!

COMMANDER: I need more information about this riot. Go down and find out what you can. Report back to me.

SOLDIER: But you were there. You heard it all.

COMMANDER: I heard shouting and screaming. But I heard nothing that made any sense. Maybe the mob has cooled down enough to give us some facts.

SOLDIER: With the speed of chariot and steed, I fly to obey your command. *(Exits.)*

COMMANDER: Now then, prisoner. Why are you in Jerusalem?

PAUL: I came to celebrate the Feast of Pentecost with my people.

COMMANDER: Another excuse for trouble. That's all these feasts are.

SOLDIER: *(Enters.)* Ahem.

COMMANDER: What did you learn?

SOLDIER: The people are still yelling a lot.

COMMANDER: I can hear that from here. What did you learn about the prisoner?

SOLDIER: As near as I can figure, he's some sort of Egyptian radical.

COMMANDER: Fool! Listen to the man. He spoke perfect Greek and Hebrew out there. And you think he's an Egyptian?

SOLDIER: Is that what he was speaking? I'm not a language specialist, myself. I only speak Latin.

COMMANDER: Well, go back and question the crowd.

SOLDIER: Your pleasure is my strictest order, my liege.

The Big Book of Bible Skits ©1997 Gospel Light. Permission to photocopy granted.

COMMANDER: I know that. Go! *(SOLDIER exits.)* Now then, prisoner, who are you?

PAUL: As I told you outside, my name is Paul. I am a citizen of Tarsus.

COMMANDER: Don't be insolent with me! Your fate is in my hands.

PAUL: Forgive me, sir. I meant no insult to you.

COMMANDER: Well, don't let it happen again.

SOLDIER: *(Enters.)* Ahem.

COMMANDER: Ah! You've returned. What did you learn this time?

SOLDIER: I've discovered this man's crime, Chief of Chiefs. It's so horrible as to be almost unmentionable.

COMMANDER: Well, what is it? We haven't got all day.

SOLDIER: This man, O Supreme One, is a...

COMMANDER: What?

SOLDIER: He's a...teacher.

COMMANDER: What?

SOLDIER: Well, you can understand why the crowd doesn't like him. He's a teacher.

COMMANDER: I find it difficult to believe that a riot started because the man is a teacher.

SOLDIER: Then you must not have gone to school.

COMMANDER: Insolent dog! Do you dare to criticize me?

SOLDIER: No, no, I just meant that every student hates teachers.

COMMANDER: Well in the future, watch your tongue. Riots don't start because men are teachers. What are you doing?

SOLDIER *(speaking with tongue sticking out)*: I'm trying to watch my tongue.

COMMANDER: I understand why you didn't get along with teachers. Put your tongue back into your mouth! Now, then. What did this teacher do?

SOLDIER: The most terrible of crimes. He tried to make people go to school on a holiday.

COMMANDER: Fool!

SOLDIER: Yes, he certainly is.

COMMANDER: Not him! You! Did that crowd look like a bunch of school children to you?

SOLDIER: Well, maybe they're all slow learners. I remember in my ancient history class...

COMMANDER: Go find out what happened or you will BE history!

SOLDIER: I leave with the greatest of haste. *(Exits.)*

COMMANDER: What's this army coming to? We used to be the best in the world. Now then, prisoner, are you a teacher?

PAUL: I am a Jew, born in Tarsus but raised in Jerusalem at the feet of the great scholar, Gamaliel. As such, I learned the Law and am well versed in the Prophets. I have gone to the Temple and discussed Scripture with the men gathered there.

COMMANDER: Another teacher of Jewish law. You claim they tried to kill you for teaching their own law?

SOLDIER: *(Enters.)* Ahem.

COMMANDER: Ah! You must know the reason for the riot now.

SOLDIER: I have learned all there is to know, O Mighty Commander.

COMMANDER: Good. What is this man's crime?

SOLDIER: He invited someone to the Temple.

COMMANDER: What?

SOLDIER: I know it sounds impossible that this man could be such a villain, but that's what he did. I got it straight from the horse's mouth.

COMMANDER: You talk to animals, do you? That's the first thing you've said that I find believable. Apparently we'll learn nothing from this buffoon.

SOLDIER: Dragoon, Commander, Sir. I'm a dragoon, not a buffoon. Sounds like someone in charge of shining sandals.

COMMANDER: He's in charge of driving his commander crazy! Leave!

SOLDIER: Oh, thank you, Commander.

COMMANDER: What?

SOLDIER: I've only been on the job two days and already you're giving me leave. I told my mother I'd be the best soldier she's ever seen. How much leave are you giving me, Sir?

COMMANDER: *(Hides his face in his hands.)* The rest of your life. Which, if I have my way, will not be long. Now go.

SOLDIER: With haste, before you change your mind, I go.

COMMANDER: Has he gone?

PAUL: Yes.

COMMANDER: Good. *(Looks up.)* Now then, we can't seem to learn anything from the crowd. We'll have to examine you more thoroughly. Centurion!

CENTURION: Yes, Commander.

COMMANDER: Take this man away and question him.

CENTURION: Come along. *(Leads Paul away.)*

PAUL: What's going to happen next?

CENTURION: Nothing too bad. You see these leather thongs? We use them to bind your hands. You see that whip? We use it to scourge you until you tell us the truth. Don't worry. A year from now, your wounds will be healed.

PAUL: Is it lawful to scourge an uncondemned Roman?

CENTURION: Of course not. But...you're Jewish, right?

PAUL: Yes.

CENTURION: Good.

PAUL: And a Roman citizen.

CENTURION: Not good. Come with me. Commander!

COMMANDER: What? Has he confessed already?

CENTURION: We must be careful. This man is a Roman citizen.

COMMANDER: What? Are you a Roman citizen?

PAUL: I am.

COMMANDER: I am, too. My freedom cost me a great deal of money. How much did you pay?

PAUL: I am a Roman citizen from birth. Free born in the city of Tarsus.

COMMANDER: Centurion! Why is this man bound? Release him! Citizen.

PAUL: Commander?

COMMANDER: Citizen, come. We'll have a little supper, a little wine. We can discuss this unfortunate incident. I don't think we need report it to Rome, do you?

PAUL: It's up to you.

COMMANDER: Good. Then, after a good night's sleep, we'll bring in the high priest and the Jewish council tomorrow and hear what they have to say.

THE PLOT THICKENS

SCRIPTURE: Acts 22:30—23:15

SUGGESTED TOPICS: Responsibility; courage; early church

BIBLE BACKGROUND

Paul had been accused of one of the most serious crimes under Roman law, civil disobedience. The Roman government was not concerned about defiling holy places (the charge brought against Paul by the Jewish leaders), but they were concerned about the consequences that could arise from this action. Paul had to stand trial. However, he had all the benefits available under two legal systems. At least, he should have.

Jewish law could not find a man guilty of any crime unless two witnesses would agree upon every element of their testimony. However, given the experience of the Lord at His trial, and Stephen at his, Paul could not expect the Jewish council to follow the letter of the law. But Paul had an ace in the hole. The Roman government might not care very much about what happened to the local residents in disputes, but it cared very much that justice should be properly meted out to Roman citizens. Paul was not only a Roman citizen—he had been born a free man.

The Jewish council was the civil ruling body in Judea, having been permitted to retain its position by the Roman governor. But it would only be allowed to keep its authority if it could keep the peace. The council also had to oversee the religious affairs of the Jewish people. Balancing these two duties— civil authority and religious authority—was not easy in a country which hated its Roman overseers and believed that God wanted Rome to be destroyed. The zealots were forever hatching plots to throw off Rome's yoke and, because the council was the religious authority, it had to secretly, though not overtly, approve of any action which would give Judea its independence.

Jesus had not criticized the religious leaders for their lack of courage in not standing up to the Roman government. He attacked them for their lack of spiritual leadership. Fearing that His criticism could damage their standing with the people and ultimately with Rome, the council conspired to have Him crucified, thereby preserving their secular and religious authority and position. Unfortunately, for them, Jesus' followers were not daunted by the threat of beatings and death. Not only were the original apostles preaching, but the council's staunchest ally, Saul of Tarsus, had become one of the leading proponents of the teachings of Jesus.

PERFORMANCE TIPS

1. Prior to the skit, introduce the class to the differences between the Pharisees and Sadducees. Briefly tell the class about the Jewish council and its diversity of religious opinion before the skit begins.

2. Give the class a brief synopsis of last week's adventure. "Last week, Paul was almost killed by a mob in Jerusalem." Have the class quickly update Paul's current location (in a Roman jail, awaiting his appearance before the council).

3. Depending on the maturity of your class, either tell the story of the trial and then begin the skit or, do the skit and ask your class to tell you what happened at the trial. Read Acts 23:1-5 and Acts 23:11 with the class.

4. After the skit, have the class tell what they think happened to Paul the next day. Then, finish the story with Paul's appearance before Felix.

DISCUSSION QUESTIONS

1. Paul acted responsibly during his trials. In what ways did he act responsibly?

2. Does acting responsibly always make you comfortable? Why or why not?

3. What would have happened if Paul told the council he would never talk about Jesus again?

4. Sometimes it feels easier to lie than to tell the truth. What should you do when you are tempted to lie?

5. If you tell the truth, will everybody like you? Why or why not?

THE PLOT THICKENS

CHARACTERS

TERTULLUS (tur-TUL-us)

ANNAS (ah-NAHS)

ALEXANDER

PRONUNCIATION GUIDE

Pharisee (FARE-uh-see)

Sadducee (SAD-you-see)

TERTULLUS: OK. We all know why we're here. It's time to stop Paul for good.

ANNAS: Have you got a plan?

TERTULLUS: I have.

ANNAS: Well? Tell us.

TERTULLUS: Come closer. We'll need as many men as possible.

ANNAS: That should be no problem. We already have forty men here.

ALEXANDER: Correction. Forty-one. I'm here.

TERTULLUS: Where have you been? You should have been here an hour ago.

ALEXANDER: Well, it was supper time. So I went to see that old guy with the white beard and hair. You know, he wears a white suit. He makes the best chicken...

ANNAS: We don't want to hear about it.

ALEXANDER: I think it must be the combination of herbs and spices...

ANNAS: We don't want to hear about it.

ALEXANDER: Or maybe it's the oil he cooks it in...

ANNAS (yelling)**:** We don't want to hear about it!

ALEXANDER: You don't have to yell. I'm not deaf, you know.

TERTULLUS: If you two have finished...

ANNAS: We're listening.

TERTULLUS: Now then, here's what we do about Paul.

ALEXANDER: Why do we have to do anything about Paul?

TERTULLUS: Are you insane? The man's a menace to society.

ANNAS: A wreaker of havoc among honest people.

ALEXANDER: Well of course he is. Everyone knows that.

TERTULLUS: That's why we have to get rid of him.

ALEXANDER: But he's a prisoner of the Romans. Nobody lives too long in a Roman prison. Let THEM get rid of him.

ANNAS: They may not kill him.

ALEXANDER: I don't see why not. The Romans don't like Jews.

TERTULLUS: But he's more than a Jew.

ALEXANDER: OK, so he's a member of the Pharisees. They don't like Pharisees very much, either.

ANNAS: He's more than a Jew and a Pharisee. He's a Roman citizen.

ALEXANDER: So they'll speak to him nicely when they torture and kill him.

TERTULLUS: No, they'll give him a fair trial.

ALEXANDER: You mean...

ANNAS: That's right. They might acquit him.

ALEXANDER: We can't have that! What's the plan?

TERTULLUS: Come close. We don't want this overheard by any curious ears.

(ALEXANDER covers his ears.)

ANNAS: Why are you covering your ears?

ALEXANDER: Because I'm curious about the plan. And Tertullus doesn't want it over heard by any curious ears.

ANNAS: He doesn't mean people here. He means anyone who might be sympathetic to Paul.

ALEXANDER: Well, he should make himself clear. Go ahead, Tertullus.

TERTULLUS: We must stand together to fight this common enemy. You know what happened this morning?

ALEXANDER: Yeah. That sure was funny.

TERTULLUS: Funny?

ALEXANDER: Yeah, the way he got the Pharisees and the Sadducees fighting among themselves. *(Imitating Sadducee.)* "There is no resurrection. The man's a blasphemer." *(Imitating Pharisee.)* "Of course there's a resurrection. You Sadducees are just too stupid for words."

TERTULLUS: You thought that was funny?

ALEXANDER: Well sure. All those holier-than-thou types just about punching each others' lights out.

ANNAS: That's why Paul is so dangerous. He encourages disputes among good people. Even so, we almost got to him during the minor disagreement between the Pharisees and Sadducees.

TERTULLUS: Yes, but the Roman captain interfered before we could dispose of Paul during the riot—I mean, discussion. But here's how we get rid of him for good.

ANNAS: Go ahead. We're all ears.

ALEXANDER: No we're not. We have eyes and mouths and fingers and...

ANNAS: We're all listening attentively.

ALEXANDER: Oh.

TERTULLUS: We will have the council tell the Roman captain that they wish to question Paul more about certain aspects of his testimony.

ALEXANDER: I thought he made himself very clear this morning.

TERTULLUS: Of course he did. This is just an excuse to get him away from his Roman guards. We will position ourselves throughout the council hall. When Paul is brought down, he will have to pass one of us. When he comes near, we strike. Paul is dead, no problems.

ANNAS: Brilliant! It can't fail.

ALEXANDER: Unless the Pharisees and Sadducees start fighting again.

TERTULLUS: I've thought of that. For the plan to succeed, we must be of one mind. We must put aside our petty differences for the common good.

ANNAS: How will we do that?

TERTULLUS: We swear a common oath. Now. All of us.

ALEXANDER: How exciting. What kind of an oath? Like, "If Paul lives, may maggots eat me when I die." Something like that?

TERTULLUS: Something a little more forceful. Repeat after me. I hereby swear...

ANNAS and ALEXANDER: I hereby swear...

TERTULLUS: ...that until Paul is dead...

ANNAS and ALEXANDER: ...that until Paul is dead...

TERTULLUS: ...I shall neither...

ANNAS and ALEXANDER: ...I shall neither...

TERTULLUS: ...eat nor drink anything.

ANNAS: ...eat nor drink anything.

ALEXANDER: Time out! Time out!

TERTULLUS: What?

ALEXANDER: Let me get this straight. We're going to kill Paul...

TERTULLUS: Of course.

ALEXANDER: On an empty stomach? Is that wise? I mean, what happens if Paul comes down to the council hall and just as I'm ready to strike, I faint from hunger.

ANNAS: Paul will be brought down to the council hall tomorrow morning. You're only going to miss breakfast.

ALEXANDER: But breakfast is the most important meal of the day.

TERTULLUS: Are you with us or against us, Alexander?

ALEXANDER: I'm in complete sympathy with your cause. It's your oath that concerns me. But wait—I'll go home and have breakfast tonight. Then I'll make the vow in the morning. Am I brilliant or what?

TERTULLUS and ANNAS: You're what.

TERTULLUS: The oath is made now. From this moment, none of us will eat or drink until Paul is dead.

ALEXANDER: Of course, a small snack wouldn't count as a meal...

ANNAS: None of us will eat ANYTHING...

ALEXANDER: A nice big glass of goat's milk. That wouldn't be eating...

TERTULLUS: Or DRINK anything...

ALEXANDER: Maybe a...

ANNAS: Nothing.

TERTULLUS: Until Paul is dead.

ALEXANDER: Which will be...

ANNAS: Tomorrow morning.

ALEXANDER: Oh, all right. I swear not to eat or drink anything until Paul is dead.

TERTULLUS: Good. I'll go see the council and have them get in touch with the Roman captain. Annas!

ANNAS: Yes?

TERTULLUS: Tomorrow, make certain you're stationed beside Alexander. We don't want any slipups.

EMERGENCY

SCRIPTURE: Acts 27

SUGGESTED TOPICS: Choices; responsibility; wisdom; courage; trust; early church

BIBLE BACKGROUND

Paul had been placed on trial before the governor, Felix. Although Felix found no reason to keep Paul in custody, Paul was kept under a loose house arrest for two years. Paul was in the custody of a centurion, but the centurion had orders not to deny any visit to Paul by any of his friends. Apparently, Felix was hoping for some monetary gain from Paul (see Acts 24:26). However, then as now, political appointments are not for life, and Felix's place as governor was taken over by Porcius Festus.

The Jewish leaders tried again to have Paul assassinated by requesting that Festus send Paul to trial in Jerusalem. Instead, Festus arranged the trial in Caesarea. During the trial, Paul, being a Roman citizen, exercised his right to have his case heard before Caesar. He also pled his case before King Herod Agrippa II, who, although he found Paul innocent of wrongdoing, could not release him because of the appeal to Rome. On the trip to Rome, disaster struck.

What sort of people did Paul meet along the way? Julius, the centurion, was courteous to Paul from the start (see Acts 27:3). Was this a result of Paul impressing Julius, or merely the courtesy that Julius would have shown to any citizen who had not yet been convicted of a crime? Whatever the centurion's attitude at the beginning, it was definitely one of great respect by the time of the shipwreck (see Acts 27:31,32,43). On the other hand, the hardened sailors had no trust in Paul, preferring to risk their lives in a lifeboat rather than stay with the ship.

PERFORMANCE TIPS

1. Suggested props: sailor hats, binoculars.

2. Introduce the skit by explaining, "Because Paul was a Roman citizen, he had the right to appeal his case before Caesar in Rome. Julius, a Roman centurion, was assigned to escort Paul to Rome. Their trip was anything but smooth. Listen to what happened."

3. Display a map which traces Paul's trip to Rome. Locate these places on the map: Caesarea, Antioch, Tarsus, Myra, Cnidus, Fair Havens, Phoenix, Malta.

4. The captain obviously does not respect Paul. Suggest the person playing this role speak sarcastically whenever he addresses Paul.

DISCUSSION QUESTIONS

1. Who acted in a responsible way during the storm? How?

2. What sort of emergencies might you face in your life? How could you act responsibly in the midst of an emergency?

3. How can you prepare yourself ahead of time to handle those emergencies?

EMERGENCY

CHARACTERS

JULIUS

CAPTAIN

PAUL

SCENE ONE

JULIUS: Will we soon be ready to sail, Captain?

CAPTAIN: Aye, soon enough. Ship's nearly loaded.

PAUL: If I may speak freely, Julius, I think it would be best to wait.

CAPTAIN: Oh? And would you be a sailor, laddie?

PAUL: No, I am a tentmaker by trade. But I have traveled a great deal.

CAPTAIN: No doubt you have, laddie. No doubt you have great wisdom of the ways of the sea. Forbid it that I, a mere sea captain, should know as much as yourself.

JULIUS: Why do you think it unwise to sail, Paul?

PAUL: This voyage will be perilous. I see danger and damage, not only to the ship and cargo, but also to everyone aboard.

JULIUS: What do you say, Captain?

CAPTAIN: Oh, would you stoop to seek the unworthy opinion of your humble seagoing servant? Late in the season it might be, but I've sailed worse seas and am alive to tell my adventures. Of course, I can understand how one having to face trial in Rome might want to wait.

PAUL: I am not afraid of what might await me in Rome. But this voyage is ill-advised.

CAPTAIN: Is the poor tentmaker not afraid of Rome? Then he's a fool. But, sail we must. This is no place to winter a ship. If you be afraid to sail for Rome, then we must sail to Phoenix and lay over there.

JULIUS: Paul, you know I respect your opinion. But I must believe that the captain knows his business. We'll sail to Phoenix and from there we'll decide whether or not to continue to Rome.

CAPTAIN: There's a man who knows how to be a leader. That's why he's a centurion. Tentmakers! Pah!

JULIUS: Alright, men! Load the prisoners on board! We set sail.

(Skit continues on next page.)

SCENE TWO

CAPTAIN: Oh, they let tentmakers have their free roam of the ship, do they?

PAUL: Julius knows I have no intention of attempting an escape.

CAPTAIN: Truly, you are the strangest man I've met. But no sailor.

PAUL: What do you mean?

CAPTAIN: Oh, you haven't noticed the gentle south breeze under which we're sailing, have you? Makes you fear for your life, don't it? A few more days, we'll be in Phoenix, safe and sound.

PAUL: I don't want to alarm you, but hasn't the wind shifted direction? And isn't it blowing stronger?

CAPTAIN: Oh, I'm so frightened. Ha! Haven't you seen the wind change before? Sometimes it swirls a bit. Sometimes it changes speed. But then, being a tentmaker, you must live all your life indoors. Wouldn't know about the wind inside, would you?

PAUL: I know you don't believe me. But the wind is considerably stronger and has shifted direction.

CAPTAIN: You needn't tell me my job, laddie. C'mon sailors. Look alive. Let's show these landlubbers how real men face the weather.

SCENE THREE

JULIUS: Captain, we've been tossed about in this storm for days without seeing the sun or the stars. Have you any idea where we are?

CAPTAIN: Aye. We're in the middle of the Great Sea in a tempest. And we're headed for Sheol, every man jack of us. Make your peace with your god.

PAUL: Gentlemen, I hate to say I told you so...

JULIUS: But you told us so. Paul, before we all perish, let me say it has truly been a pleasure to know you.

PAUL: Thank you, Julius. But do not fear. Even though we should have stayed at Crete, all is not lost. True, the ship and its cargo have been damaged, but no man aboard shall lose his life.

CAPTAIN: So you're a fortune-teller now, are you?

PAUL: No. But this very night, an angel of the God I serve stood before me and told me not to be afraid. He told me I must go to Rome to face Caesar and that God will spare all who are with me on this ship. I believe God. However, before we're through, we'll be cast ashore on an island.

CAPTAIN: Well excuse me for livin', but I'll believe the wisdom of the sea. Not your angels.

JULIUS: Paul, you've shown much wisdom in the past. I believe you.

CAPTAIN: Look alive men! What's over starboard? Land ho!

JULIUS: Can we make it to the island?

CAPTAIN: We're sounding fifteen fathoms. There's rocks all about and it's the middle of the night. Throw four anchors from the stern! We'll have to weather the night here and sail tomorrow in daylight!

JULIUS: Whatever you say. You're the captain.

CAPTAIN: Aye. And we'll want to be setting anchors in the fore. Let down the boat!

PAUL: Julius, the captain is not planning to use the small boat to set anchors in the fore of the ship. He and the crew are planning to abandon the ship. But if they do not stay with the ship, we'll all perish.

JULIUS: Paul, I failed to listen to you in the past and I regret it. I won't ask you how you know the crew's intentions, I'll just believe you do. Soldiers, cut the ropes and let that boat fall into the sea.

CAPTAIN: Think you're smart, don't you, tentmaker! See you in Sheol.

PAUL: Not likely, Captain. Not likely. Certainly not this night. Men! All of you, soldiers, sailors, prisoners—for fourteen days we've battled the storm, and we haven't had time or stomach to eat. Take food now and eat. You'll need all your strength in the morning.

CAPTAIN: Now that's the first decent idea you've had this trip.

PAUL: But first, let's give thanks to God.

JULIUS: Would you lead us in prayer to your God, Paul?

SCENE FOUR

CAPTAIN: Well, tentmaker, we've lightened the ship as best we could, but the storm still blows.

PAUL: But at least it's day, and we can see a little better.

CAPTAIN: Wonderful. We'll be able to see the wave that drowns us all.

JULIUS: Look! Up ahead! A beach!

CAPTAIN: We just might be able to sail onto it. Look lively, lads! We're headed for shore! If that's alright with you, tentmaker.

PAUL: You're the captain.

CAPTAIN: Weigh the anchors! Look lively, lads! You know what to do!

(All stagger from the jolt.)

JULIUS: What was that?

CAPTAIN: We've run aground! Must be a sandbar. We're stuck fast.

JULIUS: Will we be safe here?

CAPTAIN: Not likely! The aft is breaking up!

JULIUS: We'll have to swim for it. Spare the prisoners! Paul said we would all land safely! Those who can swim, dive in and make for land. Those who can't, find a board or a piece of the ship. Don't be afraid. We'll all make it.

TAKE A LETTER

SCRIPTURE: Selected Epistles; Philemon

SUGGESTED TOPICS: Encouragement toward obedience; guidance through God's Word

BIBLE BACKGROUND

Paul's missionary journeys were instrumental in founding the early churches throughout the Mediterranean region. However, the time Paul could spend with these fledgling churches was not enough. Each church had its own problems which needed to be addressed. In order to instruct, edify, and correct the churches and the church leaders, Paul wrote letters which were often shared among those early churches.

Let's consider a few of the problems which beset the New Testament churches and which Paul addressed in his letters:

1. Misunderstanding the relationship between the Law and the grace of God (see Romans, Galatians, Philippians);

2. Divisions and immorality within the church (see 1 Corinthians);

3. Distrust of church authority (see 2 Corinthians);

4. Lack of knowledge about God's purpose for the church (see Ephesians);

5. Threat of new and curious teaching (see Colossians);

6. Questions about the Lord's return (see 1 and 2 Thessalonians);

Obviously, two thousand years have not improved mankind to any noticeable degree. Imperfect people run the church, therefore, the church is not perfect. How gracious of our Lord to provide us with a mirror in which we can see our faults and discover the guidance we need to help us correct those faults.

PERFORMANCE TIPS

1. After Paul tells Stephen to "take a letter," read 1 Corinthians 10:1,2,6,7,11,12. Point out that Paul used a familiar story from the Old Testament to show that we need to learn from the past.

2. Consider reading the whole letter to Philemon. If there are sufficient Bibles for your group, have each person read a verse. Stop from time to time to explain what is happening in case anyone in the group has difficulty understanding the letter.

DISCUSSION QUESTIONS

1. Why do you think Paul wrote letters to the churches and the church leaders?

2. How did Paul use the letters to help the early Christians?

3. How can Paul's letters help us today?

4. What other ways can we receive help to obey God? How can we help others to obey God?

TAKE A LETTER

CHARACTERS
TIMOTHY
PAUL
ONESIMUS (oh-NEH-sih-mus)

SCENE ONE

TIMOTHY: Paul, I think we have a problem.

PAUL: What seems to be the trouble, Timothy?

TIMOTHY: It's the Romans.

PAUL: We always knew we would have trouble from the authorities.

TIMOTHY: Not THOSE Romans. I mean the CHRISTIANS in Rome. They don't seem to understand the basics of what it means to be a Christian. And what can we do for them when we're here, in Corinth?

PAUL: No problem. *(Calls offstage.)* Tertius, take a letter. "Paul, a servant of Christ Jesus, called to be an apostle..."

SCENE TWO

TIMOTHY: Paul, I think we have a problem.

PAUL: What seems to be the trouble, Timothy?

TIMOTHY: It's the Corinthians.

PAUL: Well, we always knew that those who work evil in Corinth would attack our work there.

TIMOTHY: Not THOSE Corinthians. The CHRISTIANS in Corinth. They seem to have forgotten Jesus' love. Instead of showing love for each other, they are showing all the evil traits of that ungodly city. For example, the rich don't give to the poor—it's terrible. But what can we do when we're here, in Ephesus?

PAUL: No problem. *(Calls offstage.)* Stephen, take a letter. "Paul, called to be an apostle of Jesus Christ by the will of God..."

SCENE THREE

TIMOTHY: Paul, I think we have a problem.

PAUL: What seems to be the trouble, Timothy?

TIMOTHY: It's the Corinthians again.

PAUL: What's happening this time?

TIMOTHY: Same as always. But now, some even question your authority.

PAUL: No problem. *(Calls offstage.)* Titus, take a letter. "Paul, an apostle of Jesus Christ by the will of God, and Timothy our brother, to the church of God in Corinth..."

SCENE FOUR

TIMOTHY: Paul, I think we have a problem.

PAUL: What seems to be the trouble, Timothy?

TIMOTHY: It's the Galatians.

PAUL: What are the unbelievers in Galatia doing to the church?

TIMOTHY: It's not that. It's the believers. The Jewish believers are fighting with the Gentile believers. And what can we do about it when we're hundreds of miles away?

PAUL: No problem. Timothy, take a letter. On second thought, I'll write this one myself. Let's see, "Paul, an apostle—sent not from men, nor by man, but by Jesus Christ and God the Father, who raised Him from the dead—"

SCENE FIVE

TIMOTHY: Paul, I think we have a problem.

PAUL: What seems to be the trouble, Timothy?

TIMOTHY: It's the Ephesians.

PAUL: What seems to be their problem?

TIMOTHY: What ISN'T their problem? They seem to have forgotten the great love of Christ, that they were saved by His grace. They're no longer unified, but are fighting amongst themselves—you name it, they're doing it. And here we are, stuck in Rome.

PAUL: No problem. *(Calls offstage.)* Tychicus, take a letter. "Paul, an apostle of Christ Jesus by the will of God, to the saints in Ephesus, the faithful in Christ Jesus..."

SCENE SIX

PAUL: Onesimus, we have a problem.

ONESIMUS: What is the problem, my teacher?

PAUL: The problem is that you are not where you belong.

ONESIMUS: My teacher, you know that I would return to my owner, but I cannot. You know the punishment for a runaway slave. If I could return, I would. But I fear for my life.

PAUL: No problem. Onesimus, take a letter. And I mean, not only write it down but take it to Philemon, personally. "Paul, a prisoner of Christ Jesus, and Timothy our brother, to Philemon our dear friend and fellow worker...."

BROTHERS UNDER THE SKIN

SCRIPTURE: Genesis 17:7

SUGGESTED TOPICS: Covenant; friendship

BIBLE BACKGROUND

Covenants are made in every society in the world. Many ancient cultures used the passing of blood to mark the solemnity of the agreement. In the Old Testament, many covenants were made; some of them were between people (David and Jonathan, see 1 Samuel 20:42; Ruth and Naomi, see Ruth 1:16,17); some between God and a person or persons (Noah, see Genesis 9:12-17; Abram, see Genesis 12:1-3; all of Israel, see Deuteronomy 28:1—29:1). All of the covenants between God and people broke down, but never because God was unfaithful. The problem was always that a covenant requires fulfillment of the agreement by both parties, and people continue to struggle with sin. Time after time, people were unable to fulfill the human part of the covenant.

But God, in His mercy, instituted a new covenant to replace the old ones (see Luke 22:20). This new covenant was sealed by the blood of Jesus and could never fail, for the only party who promised to do something was God. All that is necessary for any person to receive eternal life with God is to accept the gift of forgiveness which has already been bought with Jesus' blood (see Ephesians 2:8,9).

PERFORMANCE TIPS

1. Suggested props: card lettered "applause" to hold up before audience at appropriate times, rumpled western clothing for the Ranger, headband for Toronto, bowl of dry cereal, rubber knife, blanket.

2. If possible, partially darken the room for performance.

3. Theme music (opening bars of the "William Tell Overture") may be played on cassette player or kazoos (or anything in between).

DISCUSSION QUESTIONS

1. What is the meaning of the word "covenant"?

2. At the end of the skit, the Single Ranger and Toronto have forgotten their covenant. Why?

3. Why is it important to keep covenants?

4. Another word for covenant is "testament." We call part of the Bible the Old Testament and part of it the New Testament. What is the old testament? What is the new testament?

5. How can you become part of the new testament?

Brothers Under the Skin

CHARACTERS

NARRATOR   **TORONTO**   **THE SINGLE RANGER**

NARRATOR *(grandly)*: Out of the west he came, riding a white horse, carrying twin pearl-handled revolvers and wearing...rumpled clothes. Looking like a man who needed to visit a laundromat, he rode across rivers over hill and plain (loud crash) and cliffs... Heigh-ho, Platinum! It's the SINGLE RANGER! (Hold up applause card.) Return with us now to those thrilling days of yesteryear! As our story opens, we find our hero lying in a dark cave, not knowing how he got there, recovering from his latest over-the-cliff ADVENTURE!

> *(RANGER is lying on blanket, recovering from unspecified wounds.)*

RANGER *(moaning)*: Ohh...

TORONTO: Hmm. The paleface awakes.

RANGER *(moaning)*: Ohh. *(Tries to sit up but lies down again.)* Where am I?

TORONTO: In the dark.

RANGER: I know I'm in the dark. That's why I asked where I am.

TORONTO: In a cave. In the mountains. Safe.

RANGER: How did I get here?

TORONTO: Toronto.

RANGER: Funny. I didn't think I was that far north. I thought I was in Texas!

TORONTO: I'M Toronto. I brought you to the cave.

RANGER: *(Tries to sit up. TORONTO comes and helps.)* Thanks, Toronto. Strange name.

TORONTO: It means, "Eastern Canadian who thinks he's the entire world."

RANGER: An INDIAN NAME? You don't sound like an Indian.

TORONTO: That's because I'm not an Indian. One white guy gets lost, thinks he's in India, and all of you keep making the same mistake. I'm Native American. You know, the people who were here first.

RANGER: But I thought you Native Americans talked funny. I thought you said things like "heap big trouble" and "white man speaks with forked tongue!"

TORONTO: Only in the movies. But I like that "forked tongue" bit. I'll have to remember to use it.

RANGER: Well, I'm sure glad you're here! What happened to me?

TORONTO: I don't know. Found you lying on the road. Looks like you jumped over a cliff. *(Hands RANGER a bowl.)* Here. Better eat something.

RANGER: What is it?

TORONTO: Food. Why else would I say "eat"?

RANGER: I mean, what kind of food?

TORONTO: Dry cereal. Not exciting, but easy to carry. The healthy kind. High protein. No added sugar or fat.

RANGER: *(Eats a little.)* That's good! Why are you being so kind to me?

TORONTO: It's the ancient custom of my people. We feed people when they're hungry. Novel concept, eh?

RANGER: And to think how we've repaid you. *(Sees snake near TORONTO's feet. Jumps up, waving arms.)* Hey! Look out! Shoo! Shoo!

TORONTO: *(Looks down.)* Something wrong with my moccasins?

RANGER: No. There was a snake there! He was ready to strike!

TORONTO: And you chased it away. You saved my life! But why didn't you shoot it?

RANGER: I couldn't! It's an endangered species.

TORONTO: Ah. One smart ranger! Protect that wildlife!

RANGER: *(Rubs chin thoughtfully.)* How about that. Now we've each saved the other's life.

TORONTO: Well then, it's time for another ancient custom of my people. We must make a pact. *(Draws knife, runs blade across his palm. Gives knife to RANGER.)* Now, you do the same.

RANGER: Sounds strange, but if you say so. *(Takes TORONTO's hand to cut it.)*

TORONTO: Not MY hand. YOUR hand.

RANGER: *(Gulps.)* But, I'll BLEED!

TORONTO: That the idea.

RANGER: Oh. You don't have any anesthesia, do you?

TORONTO: No.

RANGER: A bullet to bite on?

TORONTO: No.

RANGER: Oh, well. Here goes. *(Grimaces and draws knife across palm.)*

TORONTO: Now, give me your hand.

RANGER *(alarmed)***:** Oh, no. It stays on my arm where it belongs!

TORONTO: Reach your hand to mine.

RANGER: Oh, I see. Yes, alright.

TORONTO: *(Joins his hand with that of RANGER.)* There. OUR blood mingles.

RANGER: Yes. So what?

TORONTO: Now, we are blood brothers, you and me. Your blood is mine; my blood is yours.

RANGER: Oh. I get it. Very poetic. You don't have any diseases, do you?

TORONTO: No. No diseases. But I'll give you something else. A new name, a name of my people. From now on, you are "Keemo Slobby."

RANGER: I thought that was supposed to be "Keemosabe"?

TORONTO: *(Looks him up and down.)* No. Definitely "Keemo Slobby."

RANGER: Alright. But what does this "brothers" thing mean?

TORONTO: *(Holds up right hand.)* We promise to protect each other and love each other, the same as brothers.

RANGER: *(Holds up right hand.)* I see. So, if we're in town and some white men start pushing you around, I'll go up to them and say, "Leave him alone!"

TORONTO: Something like that. And if we are surrounded by many angry braves who want to kill us, you'll say, "Looks like we die now, Toronto."

RANGER: Yes? Yes?

TORONTO: I say, "What do you mean 'we' white man?"

RANGER: What?

TORONTO: *(Chuckles.)* Pretty good joke, eh?

RANGER: Oh, a joke! Now I get it.

TORONTO: Don't worry, Keemo Slobby. I'll always protect you, too. We're brothers now. So. Is Keemo Slobby ready to ride? It's time for me to go.

RANGER: Say, I've got an idea. We make a pretty good team. Why don't we ride together?

TORONTO: Together?

RANGER: Sure. We could go around the wild west, saving people from danger.

TORONTO: Could be fun.

RANGER: We might become famous. Somebody might write about us, we'll get a series, the works!

TORONTO: Famous? That sounds good.

RANGER: They could call it, "The Saga of the Single Ranger!"

TORONTO: Single Ranger? Hey, brother. What about Toronto?

RANGER: *(Ignores TORONTO.)* I'll need some music. Heroes should always have music. Something from the classics.

TORONTO: Native American music's good.

RANGER: *(Continues to ignore TORONTO.)* Something that appeals to the average consumer. Beethoven's Fifth? Dum, dum, dum, dum! No. Too slow. "The Flight of the Bumblebee"? No. Too fast. Something with shooting in it.

TORONTO: You could use the "William Tell Overture." He used to shoot arrows. A civilized weapon.

RANGER: *(Still ignoring TORONTO.)* Well, I'll figure out the music later.

TORONTO: You do that. *(Takes out newspaper want ads.)* I think we should go to Denver. To the mint. *(Reads aloud.)* "Wanted. Native American with rugged profile to appear on nickel."

RANGER: *(Still in his own world.)* Where should I begin to clean up the west? Arizona's pretty tough. That's a good spot to start. And I should give away some kind of token. Then when I ride off, people will ask, "Who is that mussed man?"

TORONTO: How about laundromat tokens? Then you could really clean up the west. But save a few for yourself. *(Strikes a stiff pose, turns profile to audience.)* I'll be perfect for the nickel.

RANGER: *(Continuing deep in thought.)* Well, I'll figure that out later, too. *(To TORONTO.)* Let's ride!

> *(RANGER and TORONTO point in different directions. RANGER says, "To Arizona!" at the same time as TORONTO says, "To Denver!" Hold up applause card. Theme music comes up as they gallop offstage in different directions.)*

THE BULLY

SCRIPTURE: Acts 9:1-31

SUGGESTED TOPICS: Trust; Christian life; prejudice; courage under persecution

BIBLE BACKGROUND

Everyone has met a bully. Everyone has known an enemy, someone who was tougher and meaner than everybody else. How would you react to meeting that person years later? If that person claimed to have changed, would you believe it?

That was the dilemma that faced the followers of Jesus in Damascus and then in Jerusalem. Saul was a notorious enemy of the believers. He had been instrumental in the murder of Stephen and was threatening a similar fate for any other followers of the Lord. Who could believe that such a man could change? Who could believe that this specific man had changed?

PERFORMANCE TIPS

1. Suggested props: baseball hats and gloves, baseball, chewing gum.
2. Doug and Joe chew gum and play catch during the skit.

DISCUSSION QUESTIONS

1. If you were Doug or Joe, would you believe Tough Tony had changed? Why or why not?
2. When Saul became a Christian, the believers in Jerusalem were afraid of him because of his past hatred of Jesus' followers. What does Acts 9:26-28 say about the way Barnabas helped Saul?
3. What does Galatians 6:10 say about the way we should treat others?

THE BULLY

CHARACTERS

DOUG

JOE

BARNEY

TONY

DOUG: Did you hear the news?

JOE: What news?

DOUG: Tough Tony.

JOE: What about him? He moved away. We don't have to worry about him.

DOUG: Oh, yeah? He's back.

JOE: He CAN'T be back!

DOUG: Well, he is.

JOE: And just when things were starting to settle down.

DOUG: I heard that he changed. He's not a bully anymore.

JOE: Sure. Like cows fly.

DOUG: Maybe he did change.

JOE: No way. People like Tony don't change.

DOUG: You're right. Now his gang has a leader again.

JOE: And I was just getting used to not looking over my shoulder all the time.

DOUG: They'll be stealing everything we have.

JOE: Maybe we can avoid him.

DOUG: Yeah, right.

(BARNEY enters with TOUGH TONY.)

BARNEY: Hi, guys.

JOE: Hi, Barn—

DOUG: Barney! What are you doing with him?

BARNEY: Guys, meet my friend, Tony.

TONY: Hi, guys.

JOE: Barney! Are you crazy? Why'd you bring Tough Tony here?

BARNEY: His name's not Tough Tony.

TONY: It's just Tony, now.

DOUG: Right. Well, we don't want him here. You know what he did to us before.

BARNEY: But that was before. He's different now.

JOE: Oh, yeah! How? Is he only going to beat us up every other day instead of every day?

TONY: Honest, guys—I've changed. I'm not the same as I was before.

338   *The Big Book of Bible Skits* ©1997 Gospel Light. Permission to photocopy granted.

BARNEY: Listen, guys. Tony has changed. And he wants to be friends with us.

DOUG: Well, we don't want to be friends with him.

JOE: Yeah. How do we know he's changed?

TONY: I really have changed.

JOE: No way. Once a bully, always a bully.

BARNEY: But he has changed. When he moved to the other side of town, he met some new friends. And they invited him to Sunday School with them. Now, he's different.

DOUG: Come off it, Barney! Sunday School doesn't change people.

BARNEY: Sure it does.

TONY: No, he's right, Barney. Sunday School doesn't change people.

BARNEY: What?

JOE: See, I told you. He's just pretending.

TONY: Sunday School doesn't change people. But Jesus does.

DOUG: What are you talking about?

TONY: I met Jesus.

JOE: Right! Jesus died a long time ago. He's history.

BARNEY: Joe, I thought you were a Christian.

DOUG: Sure he is. We both are.

BARNEY: Well, you don't talk like you are.

JOE: What do you mean?

BARNEY: Jesus is alive.

DOUG: Well, yeah. But you don't meet Him.

BARNEY: Maybe you don't. But you can—you can pray.

DOUG: Maybe. But Jesus doesn't talk to people today.

TONY: You're wrong, Doug. Jesus spoke to me.

JOE: Prove it. How did Jesus speak to you?

TONY: He used a Sunday School teacher—a man who used to be a gang leader.

BARNEY: And now, Tony knows Jesus. And he's changed.

TONY: Please, guys. I'm sorry for all the stuff I did before. Please forgive me and let me be your friend.

JOE: We'll think about it.

DOUG: But don't hold your breath.

JOE: Yeah! We're not sure about you. *(JOE and DOUG exit.)*

TONY: How can I make them believe me?

BARNEY: It may take awhile, but together, we'll convince them. I'll tell them what you've done. You'll have to show them by the way you live. Hey! I'll ask Mom if you can come for supper tonight.

TONY: Great!

CAN I?

SCRIPTURE: 1 Samuel 8; Psalm 103:8,10

SUGGESTED TOPICS: Obedience; honoring parents; making wise choices

BIBLE BACKGROUND

The Israelites were called to be holy—different from those around them—because their God was holy. Their early history differed from that of other nations in that they had no king. Instead, every man did that which was right in his own eyes (see Judges 21:25) and any disputes which arose were settled by the judges who were appointed.

The period of the judges can best be described as a vicious circle. The circle began with things going well in the country. The people worshiped the true God, the God who had delivered them from Egypt and led them to victory in the Promised Land. But because they had not fully obeyed God and driven out all the inhabitants of the land, pagan practices surrounded them and the Israelites fell into the worship of idols.

The spiritual decay of idolatry led to a serious decline in all areas of Israelite life and God raised up a people to chastise Israel. When things were at their blackest, the Israelites remembered the God of Abraham, Isaac and Jacob and cried out to Him. In His mercy, God raised up a judge who would lead them back to the worship of the true God. However, when peace and prosperity returned, the circle would begin anew with the people turning from God to follow the practices of their neighbors.

This vicious circle continued throughout the book of Judges until the time of Samuel. Unfortunately, evil judges turned the people of Israel away from God's system. Samuel's sons judged Israel so unfairly that the people demanded a king like the other nations had. In spite of Samuel's warnings of the consequences of having a king (see 1 Samuel 8:11-18), Israel became a kingdom.

PERFORMANCE TIPS

1. Suggested props: chair or sofa, magazine for Mom, cookies and milk, backpack or school bag and papers.

2. If you are in a place that will not permit food and drink, Calvin can pretend to have a mouth full of cookies. Give him an opaque glass for his milk.

3. For humor, consider having Calvin played by an adult and Mom by a student.

DISCUSSION QUESTIONS

1. Sometimes people around us can influence us to do the wrong things. Who influences you? What sort of things are you tempted to do by their example?

2. What are some things you can do to avoid doing the wrong things?

3. Why does God give us His commands in the Bible? How can you use the Bible to help you make decisions?

4. If everyone believes something, does that mean it is true? Why or why not?

CAN I?

CHARACTERS

CALVIN
MOM

(MOM sits on sofa, reading a magazine.)

CALVIN: *(Enters with backpack.)* Hi, Mom! I'm home.

MOM: Hi, dear. How was school?

CALVIN: Oh, it was OK. Math wasn't so good.

MOM: Oh? Why not?

CALVIN: Almost all the answers on my assignment were WRONG.

MOM: The ones I helped you with last night?

CALVIN: Yup.

MOM: I'm sorry, dear! I thought I remembered how to solve simultaneous equations.

CALVIN: Well, it wasn't too bad. I got full marks for the work. Only the answers were wrong.

MOM: That's strange. Can I see the paper?

CALVIN: *(Backs away.)* No. That's OK, Mom. You can't always be right.

MOM: But I want to see how I was wrong. Let me see the paper, please.

CALVIN: *(Gets paper out of pack, hands to MOM. Sighs.)* Here.

MOM: But I don't understand. These aren't the same answers you had last night!

CALVIN: Well, see, when I got to school, Jimmy and me compared papers and his answers were all different from mine. I didn't have time to change all the work part so I just changed the answers.

MOM: Calvin, when will you learn? Other people's answers aren't always right!

CALVIN: I know that now, Mom. Have we got anything...

MOM: ...to eat for a snack? There are some cookies on the table and milk in the fridge.

CALVIN: Thanks.

> *(Exits.)*

MOM: What a kid.

> *(CALVIN enters with mouth full of cookie and drinking glass of milk.)*

CALVIN *(talking with mouth full)***:** Know what, Mom?

MOM: How many times must I remind you, Calvin? Not with your mouth full.

CALVIN: *(Makes exaggerated chewing and swallowing motion.)* Know what, Mom?

MOM: What?

CALVIN: You're the best Mom in the whole world.

MOM: Well, thank you. But I didn't make the cookies. Your Dad woke up this morning in one of his baking moods. And since he's on the afternoon shift, he had time to do something about it. So we have cookies.

CALVIN: I wasn't just talking about cookies. It's everything.

MOM *(warily)*: Uh-huh?

CALVIN: I mean, you're just the best mom anyone could have.

MOM *(more warily)*: Uh-huh?

CALVIN: I was just saying to Jimmy, this morning, "My mom's the greatest mom in the whole wide world."

MOM: Was that before or AFTER you changed your math?

CALVIN: Oh, Mom. I just wanted to tell you how great I think you are.

MOM: OK, what do you want?

CALVIN: Me? Mom, I don't want anything. Well, maybe another cookie?

MOM *(laughing)*: Go help yourself.

> *(CALVIN starts to exit but stops.)*

CALVIN: But since you mentioned it...

MOM: What do you want, Calvin?

CALVIN: Can I go down to the river after supper?

MOM: Will you have your homework finished before you go?

CALVIN: Of course, I will! When have I ever...

MOM: Three weeks ago on Wednesday and Thursday. Two weeks ago on Monday, Tuesday and Friday. Last week Wednesday, Thursday and Friday. The day before yesterday.

CALVIN: I'll do it right now.

MOM: OK. If your homework's done, you may go to the river. But remember the rules. Only as far as Three Mile Bend.

CALVIN: But, Mom, the other guys want to go up near the dam. I want to go with them. Can I, Mom? Please. Can I?

MOM: No! Absolutely not!

CALVIN: But, Mom. Jimmy's going to be there. And Billy and Juan. PLEASE, let me go, too?

MOM: No! That's final!

CALVIN: But, Mom, it's no fun down near Three Mile Bend. There's more to do near the dam.

MOM: How do YOU know? Have you been there?

CALVIN: No. But everyone says so. Pierre says it's really neat up there.

MOM: Calvin. Your father and I have talked to you about this before. It isn't safe up near the dam. The ground is too unpredictable.

CALVIN: But I'd be careful, Mom. We'd all be careful. Can I go? Please.

MOM: How did you manage to get so wet on Saturday?

CALVIN: I slipped and fell in the river. But that was just an accident.

MOM: That's my point. If you have an accident near Three Mile Bend, you get wet. If you have an accident near the dam, you could be killed.

CALVIN: But I wouldn't have an accident. I'd be really careful if you'd let me go. Please. Can I?

MOM: No, Calvin! My patience is wearing thin. Stop asking. The answer won't change.

CALVIN: You never let me do anything fun! All the other guys will laugh at me.

MOM: I doubt it very much. Only the ones whose parents let them do things that could easily hurt them. What about Paul? I didn't hear his name mentioned. Is he going up to the dam, too?

CALVIN: No. But he's no fun.

MOM: That's not what you said when you came back from his birthday party.

CALVIN: His birthday party wasn't any fun.

MOM: But you were bubbling over when you came home from it.

CALVIN: But when I told Jimmy about it the next day, he said it was stupid.

MOM: This is the same Jimmy who helped you with your math?

CALVIN: Yeah, but math and life are different.

MOM: I thought you solved problems in math.

CALVIN: So?

MOM: That's what you do in life, too. You solve problems.

CALVIN (pouting)**:** Not me. I just get told what to do.

MOM: No, you don't. You make lots of choices every day. The trick is to make the right choice. That's where parents come in.

CALVIN: To keep kids from having fun.

MOM: No. To help them grow up learning how to make the right choices. In the process, we sometimes have to say no. If we never said no, you'd never learn how to decide between right and wrong.

CALVIN: I KNOW how to decide.

MOM: I know you do. Sometimes. And as you grow older and more mature, you'll make more and more choices for yourself.

CALVIN: That means I still can't go up to the dam?

MOM: That means you still can't go up to the dam.

CALVIN: Then there's no point in going ANYwhere.

MOM: I hear there's a big gathering down at the rec center. Something about radio-controlled car races.

CALVIN: So?

MOM: I just heard that Paul's going to win tonight. I've heard his new Jaguar XKE is faster than anything in town.

CALVIN: Who says?

MOM: I was talking to his mom today. I guess he thinks he's got the hottest thing on four wheels.

CALVIN: Well, he's nuts. My Corvette can run circles around his XKE.

MOM: That's what I said. But Paul doesn't think so.

CALVIN: Well, I'll show him. Look out, Paul. The "Vette Viper" will show the whole town that your Jaguar's nothing more than a kitten. I'll be there. Can I go, Mom? Can I show him his Jaguar's nothing?

MOM: After your homework's done, of course.

CALVIN: Of course. I'll do it right now.

(CALVIN exits running. MOM watches him go, turns to AUDIENCE, makes a "victory" gesture and smiles.)

DEMONSTRATION

SCRIPTURE: Selections from 1 John

SUGGESTED TOPICS: Showing love; sharing; giving

BIBLE BACKGROUND

How easy is it to say, "I love you"? Every day, countless people utter these three words, fully believing they mean what they say. The Bible repeatedly talks about a kind of love which requires more than uttering trite phrases under the influence of soft lights, quiet music and the presence of one who currently stimulates our better nature. "God so *loved* the world that he gave his one and only Son" (John 3:16, italics added) to pay the price we owed for our sin. "Greater *love* has no one than this, that one lay down his life for his friends" (John 15:13, italics added). "Do you *love* me?...Feed my sheep" (said three times by Jesus to Peter in John 21:15-17).

First Corinthians 13 describes a love that is both action *and* the attitude behind the action. If a "loving" action is done to puff up one's ego, it is not really love—but neither is a warm feeling which is not demonstrated in actively seeking the highest good for the other person. The first letter of John calls all Christians to realize that accepting the great gift offered by our Redeemer must result in showing God's love to those around us. God's great love enables us to act in love towards those to whom we may not feel attracted. And as we share God's love with the lovely and the unlovely alike, God's love lives within us.

PERFORMANCE TIPS

1. Suggested props: masks to suggest a pig and a hen—perhaps merely a snout and a beak.
2. Farmer Brown might throw an old boot in the general direction of the pig and hen when he tells them to be quiet.
3. As the two exit, they should be muttering about ways to show their affection for Pastor Jones.
4. For the sake of humor, your pastor's name may be substituted.

DISCUSSION QUESTIONS

1. The hen claims you must show affection, not just talk about it. Is she right? Why or why not?
2. Read 1 John 3:1. What does the writer mean when he says "How great is the love the Father has lavished on us"?
3. What is love? (See 1 Corinthians 13:4-7.)
4. What are some ways we can demonstrate our love for God?
5. Read 1 John 4:10,11. Who should we love? Why?

DEMONSTRATION

CHARACTERS
PIG
HEN
FARMER BROWN (voice offstage)

PRONUNCIATION GUIDE

voila (vwa-LA)

(PIG enters. HEN is pecking at ground.)

PIG: Hello there, Mrs. Hen.

HEN: *(Straightens up.)* Why, Mr. Pig, as I live and breathe! How do you do?

PIG: I'm doing fine. In fact, I am doing most excellently well.

HEN: Gracious! Whatever has put you in such good spirits?

PIG: I've just heard some wonderful news. Pastor Jones is coming for a visit. In fact, he's staying overnight.

HEN: Pastor Jones? That IS good news! He's such a nice man.

PIG: That he is. Wonderful man.

HEN: Always smiling.

PIG: Never says an unkind word. Not like Farmer Brown. Do you know what HE said about me?

HEN: Farmer Brown said something unkind about you?

PIG: He did. He was talking with his boy, pointed at me and called me a boar.

HEN: He didn't!

PIG: He did! He said, "Look at that old bore." Now I ask you, am I an uninteresting animal?

HEN: Why, of course not! You are one of the most interesting animals on the farm! But that Farmer Brown will say unkind things! Why, he even called me a coward!

PIG: No!

HEN: He did! He was talking to Mrs. Farmer Brown. He pointed at me and said, "We should be feeding that chicken more." Have I ever struck you as being a coward?

PIG: I should say not! You have always shown remarkable courage when someone comes near your young ones. To call you a chicken! The man has no shame.

HEN: But Pastor Jones always speaks well of folks.

PIG: And always does such nice things for everyone. Do you know, when he stays for supper and the family serves corn on the cob, he always leaves a little corn on the end of the cob. Just for me.

HEN: I declare! I thought he was only kind to ME in that way.

PIG: Why, what do you mean?

HEN: Well, when the family has watermelon, Pastor Jones always spits the seeds out on the ground. Right in the open where they're easy to find. Best part of the watermelon, and he leaves it for me.

PIG: Such a nice man.

HEN: So kind.

PIG and HEN *(sighing)*: Ah.

HEN: You know what, Mr. Pig?

PIG: What, Mrs. Hen?

HEN: We need a demonstration.

PIG: Is that wise? Do you think we should be marching around the farmyard with picket signs reading, "Farmer Brown Unfair to Farm Animals" when Pastor Jones is coming to visit?

HEN: Not that kind of demonstration. We need to demonstrate our feelings about Pastor Jones.

PIG: So we walk around with picket signs saying, "We Love Pastor Jones"?

HEN: I declare, you are difficult at times. No, we don't need signs. We need to do something nice for Pastor Jones. To SHOW him that we care, not just SAY we care.

PIG: That is an excellent suggestion. But what can we do?

HEN: What indeed? That is the problem. Wait!

PIG: You've thought of something?

HEN: You said Pastor Jones was staying the night? Are you sure about that? He's never stayed all night before!

PIG: Well, he's staying tonight. I heard Farmer Brown talking to his boy. And he distinctly said, "Pastor Jones is coming tonight. I reckon he'll put us all to sleep with another one of his stories."

HEN: Now isn't that nice. Just like Pastor Jones.

PIG: Yes! Not only is he a guest, but he's the one who tells the bedtime story.

HEN: Then I have the perfect way of showing him how much we admire him.

PIG: Then tell me! I'm all ears! *(Pause.)* Well, a little snout, too.

HEN: You know how city folks come out to the country and say, "It's too quiet. I can't get to sleep because it's too quiet."

PIG: I have heard them say that very thing. Strange thing to say. So?

HEN: Pastor Jones may have a hard time getting to sleep. Well, we'll sing him a lullaby!

PIG: Wonderful! We could sing "Old MacDonald Had a Farm." We've always done that one well.

HEN: No! That's not a lullaby. We need a soft, soothing song. I know! We'll sing "Brahms' Lullaby."

PIG: I always knew the bull was strong, but I had no idea he was a musician.

HEN: Not "BRAHMA'S Lullaby!" "BRAHMS' Lullaby." You know it.

PIG: No, I don't believe I do.

HEN: Well, I'll sing a little of it and you join in. *(Clucks "Brahms' Lullaby.")*

PIG: Oh! That one. *(Joins in grunting "Brahms' Lullaby" with HEN.)*

FARMER BROWN *(voice from offstage)*: Would you two stop that racket?

PIG: Listen to that! He's also a music critic.

HEN: Well, I don't care. Pastor Jones will like it. We'll sing it for him anyway!

PIG: But what if Farmer Brown yells again? He'd wake up Pastor Jones!

HEN: You're right. We'll have to think of something else.

PIG: I've got it! Do you think you can scratch up some worms?

HEN: Well, of course! I'm the best scratcher in the world.

PIG: Good, because in the garbage there's an old tin can.

HEN: I don't think Pastor Jones would appreciate worms and a can.

PIG: Of course he would! He's an avid fisherman. You get the worms, I'll get the can. We put the worms in the can. Voila—bait! Then he can go fishing in the stream first thing tomorrow morning.

HEN: It would be a good present—if he's a fisherman.

PIG: He is. Last time he was here, I heard him talking to Farmer Brown. "There's nothing I like better than fishing for soles." That's exactly what he said to Farmer Brown. I heard it from his own lips.

HEN: But there's no sole in the stream. Only perch. What if he doesn't like perch?

PIG: What's not to like? They're delicious. Especially the heads. Yum!

HEN: But perch and sole are different kinds of fish. If he goes fishing for sole and only catches perch, he would be disappointed. We wouldn't demonstrate our true feelings if that happened!

PIG: True. But what else can we do?

HEN: I have it! I have the perfect gift!

PIG: Tell me.

HEN: Tomorrow morning when Pastor Jones wakes up, he'll be hungry.

PIG: If he's anything like me, he certainly will be.

HEN: We could serve him bacon and eggs for breakfast.

PIG: Well, I don't know....

HEN: Of course, we can! ALL pastors like bacon and eggs for breakfast. It will be the perfect gift to show Pastor Jones we care. A PERFECT demonstration.

PIG: I don't know.

HEN: It's perfect. We'll each make a contribution and he'll love it.

PIG: No, YOU'LL make a contribution. But you're asking ME for total commitment!

HEN: Oh, yes, I see. Well, what else can we do?

PIG: I don't know. But bacon's out. *(HEN and PIG exit, discussing what to do.)*

The Big Book of Bible Skits ©1997 Gospel Light. Permission to photocopy granted.

DOT YOUR I'S AND CROSS YOUR T'S

SUGGESTED TOPICS:

History of the Bible; reverence for God's Word; trusting God's Word

BIBLE BACKGROUND

The Bible is the written record of how God has interacted with His creation. It is not a science textbook, a history textbook or a sociology textbook, although it contains elements of virtually every science. Historians use it to test the accuracy of other histories; archaeologists consult it to help them determine what to look for and where to look. But its unique value lies in its helping people to see God so they may respond to what His Word teaches (see James 1:22). When Peter urged his readers to "crave pure spiritual milk" (1 Peter 2:2), it is obvious from the verses immediately preceding that he is referring to God's Word as the source of spiritual nourishment.

The care with which the Scriptures were passed down through the ages has been unmatched in the annals of literature. No other book from antiquity had so much care in its recopying. Scribes counted pen strokes to be certain not one had been missed or added to their copies. Thousands of scholars have worked over the centuries to ensure that God's Word has come to us as accurately as it did to the prophets of old. They took seriously the warning of John in the Revelation, "If anyone adds anything to them, God will add to him the plagues described in this book. And if anyone takes words away from this book of prophecy, God will take away from him his share in the tree of life and in the holy city, which are described in this book" (Revelation 22:18,19).

PERFORMANCE TIPS

1. Suggested props: two scrolls, table and two chairs, Bible, box to represent a printing press, wrench for Gutenberg.
2. The younger scribe talks and moves quickly. When the older scribe is proofreading the scrolls, the younger one should pace, fidget, etc. to show his impatience.
3. The second priest has no convictions. He wavers from argument to argument until he learns his financial well-being rests in the argument of the first priest.

DISCUSSION QUESTIONS

1. Why did the scribes take so much care in copying the Scriptures?
2. Why was the Bible translated into Latin from its original languages?
3. Why are there so many English translations of the Bible today?
4. How can we be sure that the Bible is accurate?
5. Why is it important to read the Bible?

DOT YOUR I'S AND CROSS YOUR T'S

CHARACTERS

YOUNG SCRIBE
OLDER SCRIBE
PRIEST ONE
PRIEST TWO
PRIEST THREE
GUTENBERG (GOO-tn-berg)
ASSISTANT

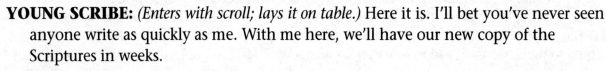

PRONUNCIATION GUIDE

Wycliffe (WEYE-klif)

SCENE ONE

> *(OLDER SCRIBE seated at table.*
> *ASSISTANT stands nearby.)*

YOUNG SCRIBE: *(Enters with scroll; lays it on table.)* Here it is. I'll bet you've never seen anyone write as quickly as me. With me here, we'll have our new copy of the Scriptures in weeks.

OLDER SCRIBE: Very impressive. Very clear writing.

YOUNG SCRIBE: Of course. I'm the best. Where's another scroll? Time's a-wasting.

OLDER SCRIBE: Patience, my young friend.

YOUNG SCRIBE: Patience? I've got things to do, places to go, people to see.

OLDER SCRIBE: Every time you completed a line, did you count each pen stroke and then compare it to the original?

YOUNG SCRIBE: Sure. *(Pauses.)* Sort of.

OLDER SCRIBE: Sort of? Either you did or you didn't.

YOUNG SCRIBE: Look, here's how I figure it. I write a paragraph, then I go back and read the paragraph from the first scroll. If the meaning's the same, I'm done. So what if I missed one dot over an *i* or didn't cross a *t*? Even if I missed a word, the meaning's there. And I'm done a lot faster than anyone else!

OLDER SCRIBE: Oh, dear. I'm afraid you don't appreciate the gravity of the situation.

YOUNG SCRIBE: Sure I do. Without gravity, I'd float right off the earth.

OLDER SCRIBE: Not THAT kind of gravity. The importance of what you're doing.

YOUNG SCRIBE: Hey, I'm copying some old scrolls. That's all.

OLDER SCRIBE: No, you are preserving God's Word to His people. I'd better proofread this very carefully. *(Looks at new scroll.)* Let's see, "In." *(Consults old scroll.)* In the original, "In." Good! It's the same. Now then, "the." In the original, "the." No. Different. The *t* is not crossed. Carefully, we must cross the *t*. There. Done.

YOUNG SCRIBE *(impatiently)***:** This is going to take all month!

OLDER SCRIBE: It's what you should have been doing, all along. Check every letter as you write it down.

> *(YOUNG SCRIBE exits, then returns to show passage of time.)*

YOUNG SCRIBE: You've been poring over that manuscript for HOURS. All you've done is cross a couple of *t*'s, dot a few *i*'s and add a couple of commas. None of that stuff matters.

OLDER SCRIBE: Oh, oh. It is as I feared.

YOUNG SCRIBE: What is?

OLDER SCRIBE: You have missed an entire WORD.

YOUNG SCRIBE: So? It's only one word.

OLDER SCRIBE: Listen, you have written, "I will leave thee, until I have done that which I have spoken to you of."

YOUNG SCRIBE: And very neatly, too. See how easy it is to read?

OLDER SCRIBE: But the original says, "I will NOT leave thee, until I have done that which I have spoken to you of."

YOUNG SCRIBE: Hey! No problemo. We can fix that.

OLDER SCRIBE: We do not FIX! We copy ACCURATELY the first time! This scroll is flawed. It will have to be destroyed.

YOUNG SCRIBE: You can't do that. I spent WEEKS on it!

OLDER SCRIBE: To the profit of no one. I'm afraid this job is not for you. You're just not careful enough.

YOUNG SCRIBE: You just nitpick. But you're right. It's not for me. I need something to stimulate my creative talents. Maybe I should write history. Nobody cares how accurate THAT is. Or political speeches. That's even better. Everybody EXPECTS them to be filled with errors!

OLDER SCRIBE *(rolling scroll)***:** Do that. It will be perfect for you. *(To ASSISTANT.)* Please take this scroll and destroy it. It is filled with errors.

SCENE TWO

> *(PRIEST ONE stands; PRIESTS TWO and THREE are seated.)*

PRIEST ONE: You're probably wondering why I've called you all here.

OTHER PRIESTS: Yes, we are.

PRIEST ONE: We have a major problem. Heresy, in fact.

PRIEST TWO: Heresy?

PRIEST THREE: That is serious.

PRIEST ONE: John Wycliffe is at it.

PRIEST TWO: But he seems like such a nice man!

PRIEST THREE: Are you certain he is committing heresy?

PRIEST ONE: Positively. Look what I have found. *(Holds up Bible.)*

PRIEST TWO: He had this in his possession? Heresy!

PRIEST THREE: It's a BIBLE. That's not heresy.

PRIEST ONE: You're both wrong. He DIDN'T have it in his possession and it IS heresy.

PRIEST THREE: How can you say that?

PRIEST TWO: It's easy. You just have to force a lot of air out when you pronounce the *h*. Heresy. If you don't, it sounds like "air-eh-see."

PRIEST THREE: Not how to pronounce it. Why would you call having a Bible heresy?

PRIEST ONE: I TOLD you. He didn't have it. He WROTE it. In ENGLISH!

PRIEST TWO: *(Gasps.)* Heresy!

PRIEST THREE: And it's filled with errors?

PRIEST ONE: How should I know? I didn't read it.

PRIEST THREE: Then how do you know it's heresy?

PRIEST ONE: It's written in English, not Latin! Therefore, it's heresy.

PRIEST TWO: Yeah, heresy!

PRIEST THREE: But is having the Scriptures in another language heresy?

PRIEST ONE: Of course it is.

PRIEST TWO: I always say, if Latin was good enough for Jesus and the disciples, it's good enough for me.

PRIEST THREE: They did not read the Scriptures in Latin. The Old Testament was mostly written in Hebrew; the New Testament, mostly in Greek. It was not translated into Latin, the language people understood at that time, until about A.D. 400. Don't you read history?

PRIEST TWO: Only if it's written creatively. There's one Jewish historian I particularly enjoy. He doesn't seem to agree with anyone else, but his manuscripts are always written clearly.

PRIEST ONE: All this arguing is pointless. The people must NOT have the Bible in their own language.

PRIEST THREE: I think it would be a good idea. Then people could read God's Word for themselves. So few people really understand Latin any more.

PRIEST TWO: Sure. Where's the harm in that?

PRIEST ONE: If they can read it themselves, they might no longer need us! We might be out of a job!

PRIEST THREE: You mean, they might discover that some priests have perverted God's Word and are using it for their own evil purposes.

PRIEST ONE: Either way you look at it, we're out good money.

PRIEST TWO: This heresy must be stopped! I'm making a good living.

PRIEST THREE: *(Picks up Bible.)* May I take this? I want to compare it to my Latin Bible. If it has errors, I will join with you in denouncing Wycliffe. But if it's accurate....*(Shrugs.)*

PRIEST ONE: Take it with you. Study it all you want. Whether you support us or not doesn't matter. We'll stop Wycliffe. He can only make a few copies. All that writing takes time. Before long, they'll all be burned.

SCENE THREE

(GUTENBERG and ASSISTANT are bent over machine, tinkering.)

GUTENBERG: One more bolt to tighten and—there—I have finished.

ASSISTANT: It's beautiful, sir. What are you going to name it?

GUTENBERG: I think I shall call it the "printing press."

ASSISTANT: Why not call it, the "book cranker-outer"? Because that's what it does.

GUTENBERG: It does, indeed. But "printing press" is more scientifically accurate.

ASSISTANT: OK. But people won't understand the name.

GUTENBERG: I'll take that chance. Now then, what shall we print first?

ASSISTANT: Something easy to read. *(Holds up scroll.)* How about this old scroll?

GUTENBERG: Are you still reading that Jewish historian? The one who disagrees with everyone else?

ASSISTANT: He has an interesting style. And look how neat his handwriting is.

GUTENBERG: Legibility and style are not as important as content. This machine will help people for centuries to come. The first book must be one of extreme importance.

ASSISTANT: I've got it. We can write a new comic book. The first edition would be priceless in a few years. We could make a fortune.

GUTENBERG: No! Something valuable. Something truly priceless. There can only be one book to print. The Bible. It must be the first.

ASSISTANT: Why the Bible?

GUTENBERG: Just think. We very carefully make a printing plate. We check it, double check and triple check. When we are certain it is accurate, we can print thousands of Bibles in the time ONE was copied in the past!

ASSISTANT: I think comics would be better. Who's going to buy Bibles?

GUTENBERG: We shall see. We shall see.

ENCOURAGE ONE ANOTHER

SCRIPTURE: Acts 2:42-47; 4:32-37

SUGGESTED TOPICS: Encouragement; conflict; Christian life; responsibility to body of believers

BIBLE BACKGROUND

The Church had been growing at a tremendous rate as the apostles continued preaching with courage and conviction. As it grew, many problems should have driven wedges between various believers. Although this threatened to happen, the love and encouragement of the believers to one another overcame the danger of separation.

This skit explores the challenge of encouraging others to use their abilities for the good of the group. The skit takes a look at the biggest problem facing every coach of a sports team: getting the team to play together as a team rather than a group of individuals. Nothing breaks down a team more quickly than bickering among the players. And nothing hinders the work of the gospel more than lack of cooperation and mutual support.

PERFORMANCE TIPS

1. Suggested props: hat, whistle and clipboard for coach; soccer shirts and ball for players.

2. If you are not familiar with coaching techniques, invite a coach to come to your group. Ask the coach to describe ways of encouraging a team to work together.

3. Soccer players in your group will be familiar with the terms used in the skit. Ask them to play the parts of the players. They may also explain terms to group members who are unfamiliar with the game of soccer.

DISCUSSION QUESTIONS

1. What was the coach trying to accomplish in his half-time pep talk?

2. What might have happened if the players had kept arguing with each other? Why?

3. What does it mean to encourage someone? How did the team members encourage each other? What are some benefits of encouraging others?

4. Who are some people you spend time with? What are specific ways you may encourage them?

5. Read Hebrews 10:24,25. How do these verses say Christians should encourage each other? How do the people in your church encourage each other? What can you do to encourage another Christian?

ENCOURAGE ONE ANOTHER

CHARACTERS

COACH
PETE
JIM
TOM
JOHN

COACH: OK, guys! Off the field! C'mon over here. We need a half-time chat.

PETE: I'll say! These turkeys can't do anything right!

JIM: Oh yeah? Well, if you'd pass the ball...

PETE: I would, if anyone could shoot.

COACH: Enough! Settle down and listen.

PETE and JIM: OK.

COACH: Good. Now, we're not out of the game. We're only down two goals and we have a full half to play. We can come back, if we play as a team.

JIM: What good would it do? Didn't you see those two soft goals Tom let in?

TOM: What do you mean, soft? If I had any kind of defensive help...

JOHN: What do you think we've been doing out there? Playing checkers? We've been working a lot harder than you.

COACH: Enough! I mean it.

TOM and JOHN: OK.

COACH: Listen, guys. Soccer is a team sport. It's played by a team of eleven people. No one person wins a game and no one person loses a game. It's won or lost by a team.

PETE: Yeah, but some of these guys...

COACH: Let's try something. Everyone who has played a perfect game, step over here.

JIM: Well, maybe not perfect but better than...

COACH: I didn't say better than. I said perfect. Has anybody here played a perfect game today?

PETE, JIM, TOM and JOHN: No.

COACH: Alright. The only person who is in a position to criticize is the person who played a perfect game. If you haven't been perfect, the only person you should criticize is yourself.

PETE, JIM, TOM and JOHN: OK.

COACH: Now, we have the kickoff in the second half. I think we can catch these guys napping, if we play as a team. On the kickoff, tap the ball back to Bart.

PETE: Why?

COACH: Who's the best passer on the team?

PETE: Bart is.

COACH: That's why the ball goes to him, first. Bart, lead Andy with a pass down the right sideline.

JIM: Why Andy? I score more goals than he does.

COACH: Who's the fastest man on the team?

JIM: Well, Andy. But...

COACH: That's why the pass goes to Andy. We can beat their left side with speed. Andy, once you've passed the left fullback, break for the goal. When you get to the penalty area, shoot. Any shot not directly at the goaltender should score.

JOHN: But even if it does work, it'll only work once.

COACH: True. But if it works once, they may overcorrect for fear it'll work again. That will open up other areas of the field.

PETE: But what if they score again?

COACH: They shouldn't. We have a good goaltender and a good defense. We're just not playing together as well as we can. Tom, remember—you can see the whole field from the goal. Talk to your fullbacks. If you want them to move, tell them. They can't read your mind.

TOM: OK. Hey, John. You see that number eleven? If you and Matt double team him every time he gets the ball, we should be able to rattle him.

JOHN: You got it. Nobody gets a decent shot against us this half.

COACH: OK, the half's about to begin. Remember the plan. There's the whistle! Let's go!

PETE: It's all yours, Bart.

JOHN: Beautiful pass, Bart! Nobody's gonna beat Andy to it!

TOM: C'mon Andy! Run. Use your speed. That's the way! You've got him beat!

JIM: You're clear, Andy! Hit it! Hit it!

PETE: Yes! Goal! Good shot, Andy! Way to go!

COACH: Great play, team! We're only down one, now!

JOHN: No problem. We'll get it back.

JIM: And they won't beat our defense again.

COACH: Let's go, guys. Lots of time to win this one.

FAITH AND BEGORRA

SCRIPTURE: James 2:17

SUGGESTED TOPICS: Faith; honesty

BIBLE BACKGROUND

"Now faith is being sure of what we hope for and certain of what we do not see" (Hebrews 11:1). So the writer to the Hebrews began the chapter honoring the heroes of the faith. Biblical faith is more than just idly believing something; Biblical faith requires some sort of action, some sort of response. Belief in the saving grace of Jesus Christ requires a response from the believer. "What good is it," James writes, "...if a man claims to have faith but has no deeds? Suppose a brother or sister is without clothes and daily food. If one of you says, 'Go, I wish you well; keep warm and well fed,' but does nothing about his physical needs, what good is it? In the same way, faith by itself, if it is not accompanied by action, is dead" (see James 2:14-17). James continued a discussion of faith, indicating that if it does not affect our actions toward others, we have no faith. "I will show you my faith by what I do" (v. 18).

James chapter 1 tells us to treat all equally and to share with the needy. Chapter 2 discusses the importance of showing faith in times of hardship and temptation. Chapter 3 shows that true wisdom comes from God but we must trust Him to grant it to us. Chapters 4 and 5 further discuss human relationships and the need to pray for each other. Through the entire book, James tells us our conduct proves our faith. One without the other is dead.

PERFORMANCE TIPS

1. Suggested props: table and chairs.

2. The man has obviously told tall tales in the past. The wife and neighbor should sound skeptical, even sarcastic when speaking.

3. The "little people" can be played by students walking on their knees. For humor, attach shoes to the knees with rubber bands. Also, any attempt at Irish brogue will add to the appeal.

4. Consider arranging with the kindergarten teacher to bring her class in to be the "little people." If so, have milk and cookies available for a snack.

5. If choosing the above, begin with discussion of faith. Do the skit near the end of the class and have your class serve the little ones. This can give the older students a sense of their responsibility for the welfare of the younger ones.

DISCUSSION QUESTIONS

1. Why were the wife and neighbor reluctant to believe (have faith in) the man?

2. What effect does making up stories have on people around us?

3. Why can we have faith in the promises of God—even the ones we've never seen?

4. God promises us salvation and eternal life through Jesus. What effect should believing this have on our lives? our attitudes and behavior?

5. How can we demonstrate our faith in God to others?

FAITH AND BEGORRA

CHARACTERS
MAN

WIFE

NEIGHBOR

THE LITTLE PEOPLE

PRONUNCIATION GUIDE
begorra (beh-GOR-ah)

banshee (BAN-shee)

leprechaun (LEP-ra-kon)

(WIFE and NEIGHBOR are in yards, pulling weeds. NEIGHBOR stands a little away.)

MAN : *(Enters running, breathless.)* Wife! Wife! They're coming! They're coming!

WIFE: Faith and begorra, slow yourself down. Who're coming?

NEIGHBOR *(walking nearer)***:** Would it be the soldiers? I've heard they're back from the war.

MAN: No! Not the soldiers!

WIFE: Aye, and that's a fact. We'd have heard the pipers.

NEIGHBOR: Well then, who? What's the cause of all your commotion?

MAN: It's the little people.

WIFE: The little people? *(Rolls eyes.)*

NEIGHBOR: We're not having more of your dreams, are we?

MAN: No! It's true! I saw them.

WIFE: And were they dancing around a pot o' gold?

MAN: Aye, they're dancing. Not around a pot o' gold. Kind of skipping, like.

NEIGHBOR: *(Elbows WIFE. Enjoys mocking MAN.)* Would they be singing, then? Funny little songs?

MAN: Oh, right enough. Singing, they are. Most happy songs.

WIFE: *(Elbows NEIGHBOR. Plays along.)* And were they wearing funny little hats and green leotards?

MAN: No. They're wearing ordinary clothing. Like you and me.

NEIGHBOR: Well, then. Be they smoking funny little pipes?

MAN: No. They're not smoking pipes.

WIFE: *(To NEIGHBOR.)* Ah, the little people have suddenly become concerned about ruining their health.

NEIGHBOR: Sure and that would explain why they've stopped smoking!

MAN: Now you're making fun o' me, and that's the truth.

WIFE: Well, really man. You come in telling us of the little people!

NEIGHBOR: And the strangest little people they sound.

WIFE: They have no gold.

NEIGHBOR: They smoke no pipes.

MAN: I'm telling you for truth. I saw the little people!

WIFE: I think you'd best be sure you wear your hat from now on.

NEIGHBOR: And take nothing stronger than water.

MAN: I haven't the sunstroke. And I've not been drinking. I'm telling you what I saw. Have you no faith in my eyes?

WIFE: Sure, and I've faith in your eyes.

NEIGHBOR: Just as we've faith in your ears. Do you remember the banshee?

WIFE: Oh, true. HOWLING, he was.

NEIGHBOR: The devil himself, come to take you.

MAN: It was an honest mistake.

WIFE: Waking up the house with your moaning!

NEIGHBOR: And there was the banshee—Mrs. O'Finley's cat. Caught up in the tree.

WIFE: Crying his heart out, the poor dear thing.

NEIGHBOR: But hardly likely to take a man off to his doom.

WIFE: A mouse, perhaps.

NEIGHBOR: Or even a small bird.

WIFE: But a man should be quite safe.

MAN: That's different. I was wakened from a sound sleep by the unearthly moanings of the beast. It could have tricked anyone!

NEIGHBOR: But it didn't trick anyone, excepting of course for your own self.

MAN: I tell you, it's different! I've not just awakened from a sound sleep. I've been wide awake for hours. And I saw them coming.

WIFE: And supposing we BELIEVE you saw the little people? What would you have us do?

MAN: We must prepare for them. Make them welcome.

NEIGHBOR *(sarcastically)***:** Oh! We must prepare for the little people.

WIFE *(sarcastically)***:** We mustn't offend the wee creatures.

NEIGHBOR: Think what they might do to us!

WIFE: Why, they might turn us into toads!

NEIGHBOR: Or they might wait until night. And turn us into bats!

MAN: Will you two stop jabbering and help me get ready? They'll be here any time.

WIFE: *(To NEIGHBOR.)* What do you suppose the little people will be wanting?

NEIGHBOR: *(To WIFE.)* I haven't an idea. Shall we ask the expert?

MAN: Have we no milk and cookies?

WIFE: Milk and cookies?

NEIGHBOR: Sure and the little people certainly are a reformed lot.

WIFE: Do you not think they might be wanting something a little stronger?

MAN: Possibly some ginger ale, should we have it.

NEIGHBOR: Ho! Ginger ale. Milk and cookies.

WIFE: Not only have you been dreaming, you've been kissing the blarney stone, too, if you'd have us believe this fantastic tale.

MAN: *(Looks offstage.)* They're here! They're here! They're coming in the yard!

WIFE: Oh, my heart trembles with fear.

NEIGHBOR: *(Hides face.)* I cannot bear to look.

WIFE: *(Hides face.)* We'd best be covering our eyes.

NEIGHBOR: But shut them tight, too. Just in case.

MAN: They're here! Come in! Come in!

    (LITTLE PEOPLE [children] enter. WIFE and NEIGHBOR look.)

WIFE: THESE are the little people?

MAN: Aye. The wee ones, from the village.

NEIGHBOR: You mean, you were talking of CHILDREN?

MAN: Who ELSE would I call "little people"?

WIFE: We thought you were talking about...the little people!

NEIGHBOR: The little people. The ones who dance in the forest.

MAN: You're not talking about leprechauns?

WIFE: Well, of course.

NEIGHBOR: Who else would we be thinking of?

MAN: Leprechauns?

WIFE: Aye, the little people.

NEIGHBOR: Wee, little men.

MAN: Well, that's just plain daft. There's no such thing as leprechauns.

WIFE: But you said...

NEIGHBOR: And you talked about...

MAN: But leprechauns don't exist. Don't you know that?

WIFE: But we thought...

NEIGHBOR: It's only natural...

MAN: And what kind of hosts do we be? Here's our guests, standing and starving after their long walk. *(To LITTLE PEOPLE, bowing.)* Come. Be seated. *(LITTLE PEOPLE sit.)*

WIFE: Sure. Sit. Rest.

NEIGHBOR: And we'll be finding some refreshments.

WIFE: Some milk and cookies. *(Exits.)*

NEIGHBOR: And perhaps a little ginger ale. *(Exits.)*

MAN: Now then, while we're waiting, did I ever tell you how I won the war? Sure and I did. I was out in no man's land, all alone. Suddenly, the entire enemy army jumped out from the trenches and surrounded me. Did I panic? Did I cry out? No! I took my flute from under my coat. And I played the sweetest melody you've ever heard. To a man, they threw down their guns. "Never could we harm a man who plays such music!" That's what they said. So I took them all prisoner. The generals wanted to decorate me with medals. But I said, "Leave them for the lesser men, who need symbols of glory..."

I AM CONTENT

SCRIPTURE: Philippians 4:12

SUGGESTED TOPIC: Contentment

BIBLE BACKGROUND

Paul criticized the Corinthian church for timidity, lack of contentment and selfishness, among other failings evident in that early group of Christians. Similar shortcomings continue to be prevalent within the Church.

Rodeo is one of the strangest sports and attracts some of the most unusual competitors. Making one's living by trying to stay on the back of a raging bull for eight seconds, risking life and limb, is not for the faint-hearted. Huge monetary rewards are not their guiding principle. The few elite make large dollars, but most barely make enough to pay their travel expenses. And yet, they are among the most contented athletes in the world. Rarely does one hear complaints from them about any aspect of the life they have chosen.

PERFORMANCE TIPS

1. Suggested props: western clothes and hats.
2. Suggest that Johnny Jay speak loudly and excitedly. Jim Bob should show calmness by his relaxed tone of voice.
3. Just for fun, announce the rodeo to your group ahead of time. Ask group members to wear western clothes. Provide popcorn, peanuts and other snacks for a group party.

DISCUSSION QUESTIONS

1. How would you describe Jim Bob's attitude? Why was he so calm even in the middle of a difficult situation?
2. What might make someone discontent or unhappy with his or her life circumstances? When are some times you feel discontent? Why?
3. Read Philippians 4:11,12. How would you describe Paul's attitude? What key to Paul's contentment do you find in verse 13?
4. What is a difficult situation you are in? If you can't change the situation, what can you do to be contented?

I AM CONTENT

CHARACTERS
GABBY

JIM BOB

JOHNNY

GABBY: Hello, rodeo fans! This is Gabby Day welcoming you to another edition of all-pro rodeo. We've got lots of excitement lined up for you today, all the events you know and love. And today, we have a special guest. Last year's world champion bull rider, Jim Bob James. Jim Bob, welcome to the show.

JIM BOB: Thank you, Gabby. Always a pleasure.

GABBY: Jim Bob, you've drawn a tough ride for tonight. Your old nemesis, Twisted Mister.

JIM BOB: Beg pardon there, Gabby?

GABBY: A bull that's given you lots of trouble in the past. Your nemesis.

JIM BOB: Yeah. Well now, Twisted Mister is one rank bull, that's for certain. Don't hardly never get rode by nobody.

GABBY: How do you feel about drawing such a tough bull?

JIM BOB: Well, that's just the way things happen. Sometimes you draw a rockin' chair that won't give no trouble at all, and other times you get a bad one that's liable to kick you clear to Oklahoma. Ain't no use frettin' about it.

GABBY: So, how are you planning to ride him tonight?

JIM BOB: Well now, I been ponderin' this for some time. He tends to go left, so I gotta ride him outta the chute and plan on a tough left spin. Ride that boy right tonight, could be I'll be at the pay window before the night's out.

GABBY: Last year, you had your best year ever. World Champion at the National Finals Rodeo.

JIM BOB: Well now, feller couldn't hardly plan on having a better year than I had last. Won lots of cash. Traveled the country, meetin' lots of fine folks. Enjoyed that year mighty well.

GABBY: This year has been something of a disappointment, however.

JIM BOB: Ain't been as fine as others. But can't say as I got anything particular to complain about.

GABBY: But it started out with a broken leg in your first rodeo of the year.

JIM BOB: That's true, yeah. But broken legs heal up and I'm ridin' again, so I guess it ain't all bad.

GABBY: Speaking of injuries, you also had three concussions, two broken ribs and a broken jaw.

JIM BOB: I suppose it ain't been the best season a cowboy could hope for, but everything's healing up just fine. And I'm sure glad I'm riding these days. Few years back, some of them little nicks coulda put you out of action for a whole year. Now, things is different.

GABBY: In what way?

JIM BOB: Oh, they's got these new braces and mouth shield things. Shucks, a fella's pretty near indestructible with all this here equipment.

GABBY: It's been great talking to you, Jim Bob. We'll be looking forward to seeing your ride tonight.

JIM BOB: Always a pleasure. See you at the pay window.

GABBY: We're ready for the first section of bull riders. This is always an exciting event, a crowd favorite. Joining me now is former bull riding great, Johnny Jay.

JOHNNY: Hey there, Gabby! We got us some excitement here tonight! Ol' Jim Bob, he's got his hands full with that big Brahma, Twisted Mister. But that bull's capable of getting a cowboy to the pay window, that's for sure.

GABBY: Speaking of Jim Bob, he'll be the first rider tonight.

JOHNNY: He sure will be. Get ready! The clowns are coming out! Old Ray Coutts, the grand old man of bull fighters, is rolling out the barrel, and Billy Ayers and Mickey Jones will be protecting those riders who get thrown.

GABBY: The clowns are ready, the judges are ready. Looking into chute number six, we see Jim Bob wrapping the bull rope around his right hand. Looks like he's ready. He nods his head.

JOHNNY: Whoowee! Look at that bull come outta that chute! Oh, oh! Looks like Jim Bob's in trouble! Bail outta there, boy! He's down! Come on, Billy Ayers! Get in there! Protect that cowboy!

GABBY: Ouch! Looks like Twisted Mister stepped right on old Jim Bob.

JOHNNY: Let's check out that replay. You can see how Jim Bob figured Twisted Mister was gonna spin left. But that ol' bull outright fooled him, that's for sure. Jim Bob was leaning and the big Brahma went the other way. He was out of there right from the start.

GABBY: Right here, at the end. Look at that. Twisted Mister stepped right on Jim Bob's boot. Looks like he got him right on the ankle.

JOHNNY: He sure did. That boy's in a lotta pain. But he's a tough old boy. You know he'll be back.

GABBY: They're helping him out of the arena now. I'm going back to try to get a word with him, see how he is.

JOHNNY: While Gabby's gettin' down there, let's take one last look at the replay. Yeah, he definitely didn't have a chance of staying with that bull, right from the get-go.

GABBY: Jim Bob. Tough break on the ride. Tell us what happened.

JIM BOB: Well, he just downright kinda fooled me. I was expecting the left spin, but he went right.

GABBY: Right at the end, just before Billy Ayers got in there, it looked like Twisted Mister stepped on you.

JIM BOB: Well, he did that, right enough.

GABBY: What's the condition of your leg?

JIM BOB: Oh, she's hurtin' a mite. But she's been hurt before. Can't waste time complainin' about what's happened in the past. Feels like she might be broke, but we won't know for sure 'til the X rays get took.

GABBY: It looked like Billy Ayers may have been a bit late getting in to distract the bull. What can you tell us about that?

JIM BOB: Oh, Billy's a good ol' boy. Does a fine job. Couldn't have done much better than he did. Hadn't been for him, I mighta been hurt a lot worse. Plumb thankful he was quick as he was.

GABBY: I see the ambulance is ready to leave...

JIM BOB: It's been right nice talking to you again. And all you folks out there, I wanna thank you for all them prayers you been saying for me and all them cards you been sending. Don't you worry. Ol' Jim Bob'll be back soon.

GABBY: An amazing display of courage. Back to you, Johnny, for the next ride.

I WILL RETURN

SCRIPTURE: John 14:3

SUGGESTED TOPICS: Jesus' return; faithfulness; obeying God

BIBLE BACKGROUND

Jesus' earthly ministry lasted only three-and-a-half short years. In that time, He gathered twelve men to walk with Him and learn His commandments. Many others became followers of Jesus' example and teaching. However, God's full plan of salvation required a sacrifice: a pure Lamb without blemish to take away the sin of the world. To fulfill God's promise, Jesus had to die.

Even though Jesus had carefully prepared His disciples for the events of Passion Week, they were devastated. They went into hiding, afraid that they, too, might suffer Jesus' fate. Unable to connect Jesus' death with the explanations He had given them, they simply did not grasp that God had planned these circumstances. Then, on their third day of cowering, the greatest miracle of all time occurred. Jesus rose from the dead and began a series of remarkable appearances to His followers. For forty days, He was with them. Then His time came to ascend and take His place at the right hand of the Father. His followers were left to await the coming of the Holy Spirit and to ponder the great promise Jesus had made to them during the Last Supper when He said, "I will return" (see John 14:3).

PERFORMANCE TIPS

1. Suggested props: soldiers' uniforms; duffle bag or backpack for captain; notebook and pencil for one soldier.

2. The captain is decisive. To completely win the battle, he must go.

3. The soldiers are unswerving in their loyalty to their captain. They want to go with him but, if he says, "Stay," they will stay.

DISCUSSION QUESTIONS

1. Why did the captain leave his faithful soldiers behind? What things were they to do while he was gone?

2. What feelings do you think they had as they watched him leave?

3. You are a soldier in a spiritual war. What kinds of things does your captain ask you to do in your battles?

4. Read Matthew 24. What are some things that will happen before Jesus returns?

5. Read John 14:1-4. Why did Jesus leave the earth?

6. Jesus sent the Holy Spirit to help us while we wait for His return. In what ways does the Holy Spirit help us? How can we learn to use His power?

I WILL RETURN

CHARACTERS

CAPTAIN
SOLDIERS

CAPTAIN (*closing up duffle bag*)**:** Well, men, the time has come. I'll be leaving shortly.

SOLDIER ONE: Don't go, sir.

SOLDIER TWO: We need you here.

SOLDIER THREE: It just won't seem like home without you.

CAPTAIN: It's not SUPPOSED to seem like home—It ISN'T home!

SOLDIER THREE: Oh, yeah. I forgot. We've been here for so long.

SOLDIER ONE: Can't we come with you, sir?

SOLDIER TWO: Yeah, please take us with you.

CAPTAIN: I can't. There's still a lot to do here. I'm counting on you to do it.

SOLDIER ONE: Yes, sir.

SOLDIER TWO: Whatever you say, sir.

SOLDIER THREE: We'll do our duty, sir.

CAPTAIN: Good men. I knew when I chose you that you would be faithful.

SOLDIERS (*saluting*)**:** Yes, sir!

CAPTAIN: Now, here's the plan. I'll be leaving as soon as the chopper gets here.

SOLDIER ONE: You need someone to clear away the undergrowth for you, sir?

SOLDIER TWO: Someone with a machete?

SOLDIER THREE: Choose me, sir. I can do it.

CAPTAIN: Chopper. Helicopter.

SOLDIERS (*to each other*)**:** I knew that.

CAPTAIN: There is one important thing to remember. I'm leaving now, but I will return.

SOLDIER ONE: You will?

SOLDIER TWO: When?

SOLDIER THREE: Will there be some kind of special signal?

CAPTAIN: Many things will happen before I return.

SOLDIER ONE: What kind of things, sir?

CAPTAIN: You will hear rumors of battles around you.

SOLDIER TWO: Check.

CAPTAIN: You will see battles happening around you.

SOLDIER THREE: Check.

CAPTAIN: There will be hardships—hunger, disease, earthquakes.

SOLDIER ONE: Check.

CAPTAIN: But I'm counting on you to remain true to your allegiance.

SOLDIERS: Check!

CAPTAIN: Before my return, many will be disheartened.

SOLDIER ONE: Not us.

CAPTAIN: No, not you three.

SOLDIER TWO: What do we do about the others?

CAPTAIN: Encourage them. Support them in their times of weakness.

SOLDIER THREE: But, sir, how will we have the strength?

CAPTAIN: I'm not leaving you alone. You'll have the radio.

SOLDIER ONE: Begging your pardon, sir, but how will that help us?

CAPTAIN: Good question. A lieutenant will be monitoring the radio day and night. He will be in contact with me. If you ever need help, call.

SOLDIER TWO: We will, sir.

CAPTAIN: When I return, I'll be coming by air.

SOLDIER THREE: We'll watch for you every day, sir.

CAPTAIN: No, you won't.

SOLDIERS: We won't?

CAPTAIN: No. You'll be busy. I expect you to do the things we've been doing.

SOLDIER ONE: You mean like helping the sick?

SOLDIER TWO: Feeding the hungry?

SOLDIER THREE: Saving the nation from its oppressors?

CAPTAIN: That's right. *(Lifts backpack to shoulder.)* Carry on.

SOLDIER ONE: But, Captain. Before you go—WHY must you go?

CAPTAIN: I'm heading out to prepare the new headquarters. When your tour of duty is finished, there'll be a place for you there.

SOLDIER TWO: But how do we know that for sure?

CAPTAIN: Because I'm telling you. Would I say it if it were false?

The Big Book of Bible Skits ©1997 Gospel Light. Permission to photocopy granted.

SOLDIER THREE: No, sir. You've never lied to us. But can't you give us some idea of when you'll be back?

CAPTAIN: No, because I don't know myself. One last warning...

SOLDIERS: Yes, sir?

CAPTAIN: The enemy will send many false signals, telling you they're from me. They may even send an impersonator.

SOLDIER ONE: How will we know if a message is from you, sir?

CAPTAIN: Have I ever wavered in my orders?

SOLDIER TWO: No, sir. You've always been the same.

CAPTAIN: Test any new orders against my old ones. If they're in conflict, I did not send them.

SOLDIER THREE: How will we know if you've come back or if it's an impersonator?

CAPTAIN: You will all see me. If anyone comes and says he's seen me, don't believe him. I will show myself to all of you when I return. There's my ride. I have to go now.

SOLDIER ONE: Good-bye, sir.

SOLDIER TWO: We'll be waiting for you.

SOLDIER THREE: But while we wait, we'll be obeying your orders, sir. *(SOLDIERS salute, CAPTAIN returns salute.)*

CAPTAIN: As you were. *(CAPTAIN exits. SOLDIERS slowly raise their heads as they watch helicopter take off. ALL salute.)*

KNIGHT WITHOUT ARMOR

SCRIPTURE: Ephesians 6:10-18

SUGGESTED TOPICS: Armor of God; choosing wisely; Christian life

BIBLE BACKGROUND

Paul wanted the early church to realize that it was engaged in warfare. To accomplish this end, he illustrated God's protection for His warriors by describing a common sight in the Roman Empire—a Roman soldier's armor.

PERFORMANCE TIPS

1. Suggested props: camouflage jackets.

2. Most of your group members will probably not be familiar with the armor referred to in Ephesians 6:10-18. This skit can help your group understand how each piece of armor was used by soldiers in the first century. Introduce the skit by asking, "What kinds of weapons do soldiers use today?" After group suggests answers say, "In Bible times a soldier's armor was very different. Listen to find out what he used."

DISCUSSION QUESTIONS

1. In Ephesians 6 Paul talks about Christians fighting battles. Who is the enemy we fight against? (See Ephesians 6:11-12.) What evidence of this enemy do you see in our world?

2. What might happen to an army that is not prepared for battle? What armor has God given His followers so they may be prepared for battle?

3. For each part of God's armor, what specific action can you take to put on or use the armor?

4. Satan is an intelligent enemy who will attack our weak points—the places in our lives where we have difficulty obeying God. What are your weak points? How can putting on God's armor protect you against this attack? Prepare yourself for battle. Put on God's armor everyday and ask for His protection.

Knight Without Armor

Characters

SERGEANT

SOLDIER

SERGEANT: Alright, men. I have a dangerous mission and need a volunteer.

SOLDIER: I'm ready, Sarge! What do you want me to do?

SERGEANT: As you know, the main attack will come from the north side. I need you to approach from the south and allow yourself to be seen.

SOLDIER: But if they see me, they're going to shoot at me.

SERGEANT: That's the idea. While you're diverting their fire, we'll catch them unawares.

SOLDIER: I don't want to seem squeamish, Sarge, but I could be killed.

SERGEANT: I said it was a dangerous mission. What did you think that meant?

SOLDIER: Oh, yeah. I forgot. OK! I'm ready! When do we start?

SERGEANT: As soon as you're ready.

SOLDIER: I'm ready now, Sarge! I'm off.

SERGEANT: Hold it!

SOLDIER: Changed your mind, Sarge? Decided I was too important to risk?

SERGEANT: No. I have a question.

SOLDIER: Fire away, Sarge!

SERGEANT: You've got a lot of equipment to carry. You'll be on your own. How will you carry your equipment?

SOLDIER: No problem! All my equipment fits onto my belt. Not only that, my belt protects the old stomach. Didn't you take basic training, Sarge?

SERGEANT: I taught it. Where's your belt?

SOLDIER: It's here, around my—oh. No it isn't...oh, I remember. I took it off in the tent while I was resting. Half a minute. I'll just run and get it.

SERGEANT: And he wonders if he's expendable. OK, men. Listen up. When he comes back, he'll be heading south. Now, we'll split up into three sections...

SOLDIER: Ready now, Sarge! I'm off! Wish me luck?

SERGEANT: Wait a minute! I have another question.

SOLDIER: Questions, questions, questions. I thought we were supposed to fight.

SERGEANT: We are. But we're also supposed to be prepared. Now. What's going to happen when the enemy spots you?

SOLDIER: They'll be so overcome with fear, they'll all run away?

SERGEANT: Guess again.

SOLDIER: They'll shoot at me?

SERGEANT: Right! And what will happen if an arrow strikes you on the chest?

SOLDIER: Nothing, Sarge.

SERGEANT: Why not?

SOLDIER: Because it will bounce harmlessly off of my breastplate.

SERGEANT: What breastplate?

SOLDIER: The one that I'm wearing. *(Looks.)* The one I'm not wearing. Where did I leave it? I remember. When we stopped to make camp, I saw some blueberries and decided they would be good for dessert. But I didn't have a bucket to collect them, so I used my breastplate. It's over at the mess hall. Wait here. I'll be right back.

SERGEANT: OK, men. Let's go over the plan one more time. James and John, you'll command the other two sections. If anything happens to me, Peter, you'll take over the third section...

SOLDIER: I'm back. And I'm off.

SERGEANT: I was afraid of that. But before you go...

SOLDIER: Yes, Sarge?

SERGEANT: What sort of terrain will you be going through?

SOLDIER: Train? I'm not taking the train. I'm walking. Besides, trains haven't been invented yet.

SERGEANT: Not "train." I said terrain. That's the territory, the ground, the land. What will it be like?

SOLDIER: Didn't you read the reconnaissance reports, Sarge?

SERGEANT: Yes, I did. Did you?

SOLDIER: Of course I did. There's rocks and thistles and thorns...

SERGEANT: And how will you get across that terrain without hurting your feet?

SOLDIER: Are you kidding? These army sandals are the finest made. Nothing can penetrate their soles. Made to withstand all the rigors of battle and hiking.

SERGEANT: Which sandals are you talking about?

SOLDIER: The ones I have...where? What did I do with my sandals? Wait! I remember! When we stopped, my feet were tired and sore. So I took off my sandals and swished my feet in the river. I must have left them by the river. Don't go away. I'll be back.

SERGEANT: That's what I'm afraid of. OK, men. Now, James and John, you'll have to select an alternate from your section to replace you as leader in case something happens...

SOLDIER: Ta da! I found them. Right there by the river, just like I said.

SERGEANT: So now you're ready to go?

SOLDIER: You got that right!

SERGEANT: One question about basic combat. Suppose you stumble on an enemy sentry and he strikes at you with his sword? What will you do?

SOLDIER: Easy. I ward off his blow with my...

SERGEANT: Bare arm?

SOLDIER: Shield. I know I had one when I left. What did I do with it?

SERGEANT: Why me? What did I do to deserve him?

SOLDIER: Umbrella!

SERGEANT: What?

SOLDIER: My tent doesn't have any shade around it. So I took two poles and stuck them in the ground. Then, I strung a rope between the two poles and through my shield. Pretty clever, huh? I made my own shade tree. I'll just run, quick like a bunny, and get it.

SERGEANT: I don't think this attack will ever happen.

SOLDIER: OK, Sarge. Ready for inspection.

SERGEANT: Another basic element of combat. You'll be traveling through the trees. Suppose you're fighting and your head strikes a large tree branch?

SOLDIER: Bwonggggg! Right off the old helmet. No damage...

SERGEANT: If you're wearing a helmet. Where's your helmet, soldier?

SOLDIER: Heh, heh, heh. You're not going to believe this, Sarge...

SERGEANT: Try me. I'm ready to believe anything.

SOLDIER: When I was down at the river, I got to thinking...

SERGEANT: Thinking? You're right. I don't believe it.

SOLDIER: I'm going to need hot water in the morning. To shave with. So I took my helmet and filled it with water. Then I took it to my tent. See. I'm prepared.

SERGEANT: Go and get it! He's driving me crazy. Two more like him and we'll lose the war.

SOLDIER: Okey-dokey, Sarge. Ready when you are.

SERGEANT: You can't believe how relieved I am to hear that. Now, is your sword sharp?

SOLDIER: You bet. See...what do you suppose happened to my sword?

SERGEANT: I couldn't even hazard a guess.

SOLDIER: Ohhhhh! Sure! When I tried to push the poles into the ground, they wouldn't go. So I used my sword to sharpen their ends. You wouldn't believe how much simpler it is to push pointed sticks into the ground than rounded ones.

SERGEANT: I believe it.

SOLDIER: I've got it. Now I'm ready to go.

SERGEANT: I don't think there's any need.

SOLDIER: You just realized how important I am to this army, right?

SERGEANT: No. While we were waiting for you, the enemy snuck up and surrounded us. Don't shoot. We surrender.

LOVE, LOVE, LOVE

SCRIPTURE: 1 Corinthians 13

SUGGESTED TOPICS: Love; Christian life

BIBLE BACKGROUND

Love is easily the most misunderstood word in the English language. Most people hear the word and associate it with tender feelings, soft music and soft lights, walks on warm summer nights, moods and situations that change. It has been used to mean so many different things that it now means almost nothing. Paul's letter to the Corinthians gives the correct perception of love as an active verb, not a passive noun.

Children and teenagers—and many adults—tend to view the world around them on an emotional level. If something feels right, it is right. Stopping to analyze a situation intellectually does not come naturally. One way to break through the emotional barrier is to present a situation as a caricature, to make it so obvious and ludicrous that it is laughable. Although learners may not see themselves clearly, they do catch a glimpse of themselves.

PERFORMANCE TIPS

1. Suggested props: backpacks for girls to wear.

2. Ask group members to suggest a popular singer and a favorite store for the script.

3. In preparing to use this skit, explain that you need two people to pretend to be silly teenagers. If you are using the skit with young people, they may be reluctant to play these parts for fear of being laughed at. Consider playing one part yourself, even if you are male. Your participation will encourage a student's willingness to participate.

DISCUSSION QUESTIONS

1. The two girls in the skit used the word love many times. How would you define love?

2. Does your definition include feelings, actions, or both?

3. Read 1 Corinthians 13:4-7. Compare your definition with Paul's definition. Does his definition of love include feelings or actions?

4. In Matthew 5:44 Jesus tells us to "love your enemies." How can you show love to an enemy?

5. If you show love to your enemies, will they always show love to you? Why does Jesus tell us to show love to them?

6. Paul's letter to the Romans explains that God loved us when we were His enemies (see Romans 5:6-11). How can we respond to God's love?

LOVE, LOVE, LOVE

CHARACTERS
BUFFY
MUFFY

BUFFY: Hi, Muffy. Where are you going in such a hurry?

MUFFY: Hi, Buffy. I have to get down to the record store, like NOW.

BUFFY: Why?

MUFFY: Why? Are you kidding? *(Insert name)*'s new CD comes out today, and I just HAVE to be the first to get it.

BUFFY: Today! I thought it came out tomorrow. I'll go with you. I just LOVE him so much. I'll just DIE if I don't get ALL his CDs.

MUFFY: What's your favorite song?

BUFFY: Favorite? How can anyone have a favorite? ALL of his songs are just SO-O-O wonderful. I love them all!

MUFFY: Me, too! But I especially love his love songs. They're SO romantic, they send goose bumps up my arms. I LOVE it when he sings about how much he loves me.

BUFFY: I love that, too. I just KNOW he's singing to me. Oh, I love him!

MUFFY: Are you going to his concert next month?

BUFFY: How can you even ask? When the tickets go on sale, I'll be first in line.

MUFFY: Right behind me. He's so wonderful on CD, I just know I'll love him a HUNDRED times more in person.

BUFFY: Me, too. But I have to decide what to wear. It has to be special, to show him how much I love him.

MUFFY: I already have my outfit picked out.

BUFFY: No! What? Tell me.

MUFFY: I just bought these electric blue pants at *(insert store name)*.

BUFFY: Oh, I've seen them—I LOVE those. They're so cool. I'd love to have some just like them.

MUFFY: Well, they'll be absolutely perfect with a T-shirt I saw yesterday. I'm buying it right after the CD.

BUFFY: Wait a minute. Don't tell me. It's white.

MUFFY: That's right.

BUFFY: With blue lettering on the back?

MUFFY: Right again.

BUFFY: And on the front...

MUFFY and BUFFY: His picture!

BUFFY: Oh, I LOVE that shirt!

MUFFY: Me, too. I fell in love with it as soon as I saw it.

BUFFY: We're here. I've got an idea. We'll buy the CDs, then we'll go to my house. We'll play them over and over and over, and you can help me pick out what I'll wear to the concert.

MUFFY: I LOVE it. What a great idea! We'll have such a wonderful afternoon.

MINE, MINE, MINE

SCRIPTURE: 2 Corinthians 8; 9

SUGGESTED TOPICS: Serving others; stewardship; responsibility to body of believers

BIBLE BACKGROUND

Paul's second letter to the Corinthian church has a great deal to say about giving. The church at Corinth was materially well-to-do, but suffered from spiritual poverty. Those who had wealth were reluctant to share with those less fortunate (see 1 Corinthians 11:17-34). Paul, seeing their lack of charity, commended the Macedonian church to the Corinthians and recommended that they examine their ways.

"Our desire is not that others might be relieved while you are hard pressed, but that there might be equality. At the present time your plenty will supply what they need, so that in turn their plenty will supply what you need" (2 Corinthians 8:13,14). Some condemn the above statement as communism. Indeed, it sounds similar to the writings of Karl Marx. But there is a major difference. Communism uses the power of government to force people to share with those around them. Christianity commends charity toward one another on the basis of Christ's gift to us (see 2 Corinthians 8:9).

PERFORMANCE TIPS

1. Suggested props: real or pretend money.
2. After the skit, present opportunities for group members to respond by donating time or money to someone in need.

DISCUSSION QUESTIONS

1. Compare the two attitudes described in 2 Corinthians 9:6. Which is better? To give a lot, grudgingly, or to give a little, cheerfully? Why? (In your discussion emphasize that the Bible does not teach that the purpose of giving is to gain more money. The Bible teaches that our generous giving is a response to the generous love God has shown us.)

2. What does 2 Corinthians 8:14 say will be the result when people give as they are able?

3. Some people are not able to give money. What are examples of other ways to share with people in need?

4. What can you give this week?

MINE, MINE, MINE

CHARACTERS

VINNIE

ZACK

VINNIE: *(Counting money.)* Nineteen, nineteen twenty-five, nineteen fifty, sixty, seventy, eighty, ninety, twenty dollars. Alright!

ZACK: Hi, Vinnie. What are you doing?

VINNIE: *(Quickly hides money.)* Nothing, nothing, nothing. What about you?

ZACK: I'm going over to Mrs. Green's.

VINNIE: Why? She's an old woman.

ZACK: That's one reason why I'm going.

VINNIE: Sometimes you don't make much sense, Zack.

ZACK: Well, she lives in that old house. And you've seen her fence.

VINNIE: Yeah. The thing's an eyesore. The city should make her tear it down.

ZACK: There's nothing wrong with her fence that a little paint won't cure. I looked at it yesterday. The wood's all OK. Only the paint is flaking off.

VINNIE: Well, she should do something about it. It's a disgrace to the whole neighborhood!

ZACK: Something is being done about it. I'm going over to paint it today.

VINNIE: That explains the can of paint you're carrying. Hey! That's a good idea. Painting a fence. How long would that take?

ZACK: Well, there's more than just painting. First, you have to scrape off the old paint. Then you prime the wood, because it's awfully dry right now. Then, you can paint it. It should take most of the day. Maybe even longer. I might have to finish tomorrow.

VINNIE: OK. Let's see now. All of today...say, eight hours?

ZACK: At least.

VINNIE: At five dollars an hour, that would be forty dollars. But that's pretty cheap, because you're supplying materials as well as labor. And you want to make a decent profit so, say, sixty dollars. Hey, you're going to do alright out of this.

ZACK: What do you mean?

VINNIE: Money! You know, the thing that makes the world go around.

ZACK: I thought love made the world go around.

VINNIE: Boy, have you got a lot to learn. Now, about that paint.

ZACK: What about it?

VINNIE: It's too good. Use cheaper paint. Less money spent, more profit.

ZACK: You don't understand at all. Mrs. Green hasn't painted her fence herself because of her arthritis. And she hasn't hired someone to do it because she can't afford it. I'm going over to paint it for free.

The Big Book of Bible Skits ©1997 Gospel Light. Permission to photocopy granted.

VINNIE: You've been out in the sun without a hat for too long. You've lost your marbles.

ZACK: No I haven't. They're on top of my dresser.

VINNIE: Think, boy. If you ain't got money, you ain't got nothin'. Don't do things for free. It's...it's un-American.

ZACK: No wonder you failed history. It's a hundred percent American. Not only that, it's Christian. People have always helped each other.

VINNIE: Yeah, right. Nobody does anything for nothing anymore.

ZACK: You don't believe that.

VINNIE: I sure do. Everybody looks out for Number One. You have to look out for yourself, because nobody else will.

ZACK: You not only don't know history, you don't even remember your own life.

VINNIE: What are you talking about?

ZACK: Five years ago.

VINNIE: What about it? I was a kid.

ZACK: Do you remember when your Mom was sick in the hospital?

VINNIE: Yeah, vaguely. She was there for a few days.

ZACK: And then?

VINNIE: She had to stay in bed for a few more days. What a drag. We all had to be quiet so we wouldn't disturb her.

ZACK: So who looked after your family?

VINNIE: Dad did. He went to work and then came home. Every day.

ZACK: So, who made lunch for you?

VINNIE: I don't know. I guess Dad must have.

ZACK: But he was at work.

VINNIE: Well, maybe it just materialized out of nowhere. What does it matter?

ZACK: I'll tell you who did it. Mrs. Green. And Mrs. Alverez. And Mrs. Vincetti. The older ladies in the church. They all got together and made sure your house was cleaned and all you kids had lunches.

VINNIE: So they made a few extra bucks helping us out. What's the big deal?

ZACK: They didn't make a few bucks. They did it out of love. For free.

VINNIE: Ah, who cares? That's ancient history.

ZACK: No it isn't. It's everyday life. People need other people. That's why all those ladies helped your family, and that's why I'm going to paint Mrs. Green's fence. Everybody needs help sometime. That's one reason people get together to be the church. To help other people. It's called giving.

VINNIE: I thought giving is when you put money in the offering plate.

ZACK: That's a part of giving. But even when you have no money, you can give. You can give your time and your talents.

VINNIE: It still doesn't make sense. Why should I give anything to anybody? I work hard to make what I do.

ZACK: Why are you able to work hard?

VINNIE: What is this? Some kind of game show? Answer the question and win a hundred bucks?

ZACK: No. I'm serious. Why can you work hard?

VINNIE: Because I'm healthy.

ZACK: And who made you healthy?

VINNIE: Nobody. I just am.

ZACK: Wrong. God made you healthy. He's given you good health. Not everybody is as fortunate. So what do we do with our good health? We thank God for it by using it to help others.

VINNIE: Why should we?

ZACK: Because it's right.

VINNIE (pauses)**:** And what do I get out of it?

ZACK: Maybe nothing. That is, nothing you can see. But it makes you a better person, and that's something you can't buy with all the money in the world.

VINNIE: Look, I'm not doing anything right now anyway. If we stop at my house, I could change into some old clothes and maybe come and help you.

ZACK: Great! I could use the help.

VINNIE: Not that I'm saying you're right. But Mrs. Green did help us....

ONE RIGHT ROAD

SCRIPTURE: 2 Samuel 6:1-8

SUGGESTED TOPICS: Making wise choices; ignoring God's instructions; courage

BIBLE BACKGROUND

Throughout human history, God has given people the ability and the responsibility to make choices. Eve had to choose between obedience to God or following the advice of the serpent; Adam, between God and Eve. The Israelites, after arriving at the Promised Land, had to choose between accepting the advice of Joshua and Caleb or the other ten spies. Joshua, in his final exhortation to the people of Israel, told them to choose between the gods they left behind in Egypt, the gods of the Amorites or the Lord. Ruth had to choose between going with Naomi or returning to her own country. The disciples had to choose between obeying Jesus' command to preach the good news or the command of the Jewish religious leaders to keep silent.

We do not always choose the best path. Even a man after God's own heart could make mistakes and follow his own understanding instead of God's. David knew the rules for the movement of the Ark of the Covenant. We will never know why he chose to move it by cart instead of having it carried by the priests as God had commanded. The consequences of his wrong choice were disastrous. But God, in His mercy, is quick to forgive anyone who humbly turns back to Him.

PERFORMANCE TIPS

1. Suggested props: pith helmets and safari jackets for the explorers, a map, a ruler, newspapers and chairs for the club.
2. The explorers should speak with a thick British accent and walk with a military bearing. They mistake posture for ability.
3. After the skit, tell the story of David moving the Ark of the Covenant to Jerusalem. Tell the class to listen for good and bad choices David made.

DISCUSSION QUESTIONS

1. What are some of the choices the explorers tried to make? What might have been the consequences of those choices?
2. How valuable is a map if you do not read it correctly? What can happen if you don't believe what the map tells you?
3. Why do you think the explorers wouldn't listen to their guide?
4. The Bible is a map for our lives. What are some of the ways it tells us to go?
5. Who are some of the guides in your life who can show you the correct path to follow?

ONE RIGHT ROAD

CHARACTERS

EXPLORER ONE

EXPLORER TWO

GUIDE

SCENE ONE

EXPLORER ONE *(consulting map)*: Here we are, right here.

EXPLORER TWO *(pointing on map)*: And the lost city of Beluba should be over there.

EXPLORER ONE: So we must go from here to there.

EXPLORER TWO *(measuring with a ruler)*: Shouldn't take long. It's only a few inches.

EXPLORER ONE: Now then, what would be the best way to get from here to there?

EXPLORER TWO *(tracing on map)*: We could go south, over this river. *(Scans the horizon.)* The south looks like an easy route.

EXPLORER ONE: But we might get our feet wet. I promised Mother not to get my feet wet. *(Traces on map.)* What about this northern route? Absolutely no rivers or lakes of any kind. No chance of getting my feet wet.

EXPLORER TWO: Capital! *(Scans horizon in other direction.)* It also appears to be easy going.

EXPLORER ONE: Good! Then it's decided. Where's that guide chappie?

GUIDE: *(Steps from behind explorers.)* Here.

EXPLORER TWO: Capital. We've decided upon our route.

EXPLORER ONE: *(Shows map to guide.)* We've decided to follow this northern route.

EXPLORER TWO: Why bother showing the map to him?

EXPLORER ONE: Quite. It's not as if he would know how to read it.

GUIDE: *(Studies map and turns map one-quarter turn.)* Eastern route not good.

EXPLORER TWO: I say! Were we looking at the map incorrectly?

EXPLORER ONE: By jove! So we were.

GUIDE *(pointing to map)*: Beluba city here.

EXPLORER TWO: It is NOT here. We're here. The city is THERE. *(To EXPLORER ONE.)* Chap doesn't even speak the Queen's English properly.

EXPLORER ONE: Quite! Good help is so hard to come by.

GUIDE: Go now. Toward setting sun.

EXPLORER TWO: Go west? I hardly think so, young man.

The Big Book of Bible Skits ©1997 Gospel Light. Permission to photocopy granted.

EXPLORER ONE: Quite. There are mountains to the west.

EXPLORER TWO: Don't relish the idea of crossing mountains.

GUIDE: Best route.

EXPLORER ONE: Nonsense! Look here! If we go a little to the north, we miss the mountains completely.

EXPLORER TWO: Capital!

GUIDE: Route no good. No water.

EXPLORER ONE: Excellent! Then I shan't get my feet wet. Mummy will be pleased.

EXPLORER TWO *(pointing)***:** Onward!

GUIDE: Route no good. No water.

EXPLORER ONE: You've said that before.

GUIDE: Route no good. No water.

EXPLORER TWO: What is the matter with you, chap? We don't wish to go where our feet might get wet.

EXPLORER ONE: We could catch a cold. Be the death of us.

EXPLORER TWO: And our boots could get muddy.

EXPLORER ONE: And the tent could get all mildewy in the damp.

EXPLORER TWO: Best to go the dry route.

GUIDE: Need water to drink.

EXPLORER ONE: Oh. Yes. Hadn't thought of that.

EXPLORER TWO: Should be a consideration, I suppose.

EXPLORER ONE: See here, chap. Other routes would have water without mountains.

EXPLORER TWO: Yes. What about a bit to the south? No mountains there.

GUIDE: Go toward setting sun. Best route.

EXPLORER ONE: There's no reasoning with these people.

GUIDE: Go toward setting sun. Best route.

EXPLORER TWO: But if we go a bit to the south, we miss the mountains.

EXPLORER ONE: Saves all the hard work of climbing.

EXPLORER TWO: And the vegetation is lush. Should be plenty of water.

GUIDE: Too much water. Go toward setting sun.

EXPLORER ONE: There is just no pleasing this chap. First, no water. Now, too much.

EXPLORER TWO: Sounds just like a farmer.

EXPLORER ONE: Quite! Now then, guide chappie. We've decided. Southwest.

EXPLORER TWO: So lead on.

GUIDE: Swamps. Quicksand. Mosquitos.

EXPLORERS ONE and TWO: Mosquitos? Eeeww!

GUIDE: Go toward setting sun. Best route.

EXPLORER ONE: I hadn't realized this exploring would be so difficult. Wait!

EXPLORER TWO: What? Have you an idea?

EXPLORER ONE: Yes. Let's go back the way we came.

EXPLORER TWO: Capital! That was a very pleasant route.

GUIDE: But, Beluba city other direction.

EXPLORER ONE: But the club is this way.

EXPLORER TWO: Capital! I could use a soda right now.

EXPLORER ONE: Onward.

EXPLORER TWO: We'll find the lost city next year.

(ALL exit.)

SCENE TWO

(EXPLORERS enter club, sit in chairs and open newspapers.)

EXPLORER ONE: Good to be back in civilization.

EXPLORER TWO: Indeed it is.

EXPLORER ONE: I say! Did you read this bit about Hadley?

EXPLORER TWO: Saw his name, stopped reading. Insufferable chap, Hadley.

EXPLORER ONE: Made a bit of a splash, though.

EXPLORER TWO: Fell into the Thames, did he?

EXPLORER ONE: No. Listen. "Ronald Hadley, noted explorer..."

EXPLORER TWO: Noted? Hadley? Hardly. Nothing more than an amateur.

EXPLORER ONE: "...announced major archaeological find."

EXPLORER TWO: Chap couldn't find archaeology if he looked in a dictionary.

EXPLORER ONE: "...discovered lost city of Beluba."

EXPLORER TWO: He did what?

EXPLORER ONE: "...discovered lost city of Beluba. Donating treasures to British Museum in London."

EXPLORER TWO: Horned in on our expedition. Told you the chap was insufferable.

EXPLORER ONE: Quite.

PRAY, TELL ME

SCRIPTURE: Psalm 27:7,8

SUGGESTED TOPICS: Prayer; patience

BIBLE BACKGROUND

One of the evidences of David as "a man after God's own heart" is his readiness to pray. We see him dancing in praise, repenting of his sin, pleading with God for the life of his child, asking that his long-time advisor's counsel will not aid Absalom's rebellion against him. The glimpses we see of David's life and the many psalms he wrote provide a rich tapestry of communion with God in a wide variety of situations. For David, prayer was not an activity relegated to periodic visits to the Tabernacle, nor was it a device to fall back on when nothing else worked. Instead, prayer was woven into the fabric of his life, a life filled with awareness of God's constant presence.

PERFORMANCE TIPS

1. Suggested props: a Bible for Jenny.

2. Consider having others read portions of the applicable Scripture (e.g., 2 Samuel 12:16,17,22; Psalm 3; 51:1-4,9-13; 92:1-5) during or after the skit.

3. Read Matthew 6:5-13 with the class.

DISCUSSION QUESTIONS

1. Why do you think Jamie's prayer wasn't answered?

2. What other kinds of prayer are there? Give an example of that kind of prayer.

3. Does God promise to give us everything we want? Why might He not give us something?

4. If your prayer doesn't seem to be answered, does that mean you're doing something wrong? What else might it mean?

5. Why should we pray?

PRAY, TELL ME

CHARACTERS
JAMIE

JENNY

PRONUNCIATION GUIDE
Bathsheba (bath-SHEE-buh)

Uriah (yoo-REYE-uh)

(JENNY enters, JAMIE is seated on the floor in a contorted position.)

JENNY: Hi, Jamie. What are you doing? Some new kind of exercise?

JAMIE: Nope. I'm trying to figure out this prayer thing.

JENNY: What's to figure out?

JAMIE: Well, I didn't get what I asked for, so I figure I did something wrong. Maybe I was praying in the wrong position. So, I'm experimenting.

JENNY: That's just plain silly.

JAMIE: I'm not so sure. But this is uncomfortable. Just a minute. *(Changes to a normal position.)* Whew! That's better.

JENNY: Now, explain what that was all about.

JAMIE: I told you. I've been doing something wrong when I pray. So, I'm trying new positions.

JENNY: What makes you think you've been doing something wrong?

JAMIE: Well, three days ago, I was lying in bed and I prayed, "Lord, give me a new bicycle." Next day, nothing. So that night, I sat in a chair and prayed, "Lord, give me a new bicycle." The next day, nothing. So last night, I knelt and prayed, "Lord, give me a new bicycle." This morning, nothing. I've used up all the positions I know. I have to find some new ones.

JENNY: Do you really believe that your physical position when you pray makes a difference?

JAMIE: Well, it must. Those yoga guys have all kinds of special positions.

JENNY: But it doesn't mean they know God!

JAMIE: You're right. I'll bet it's the words! I need to use different words. Let's see. How about this? "O, Lord, granteth this Thy servant whateth he wisheth. Showeth Thine great giving power and giveth to me a new bicycle."

JENNY: Oh, brother.

JAMIE: You don't think it sounded spiritual enough?

JENNY: I think it sounded stupid. You can't impress God with the way you stand or the words you say.

JAMIE: Well, I've got to impress Him somehow. I really want a new bike.

JENNY: I think you need to learn a little something about prayer.

JAMIE: Yeah, like how to get God to give me the stuff I want.

JENNY: No. You need to learn what prayer IS.

JAMIE: That's easy. Prayer is asking God to give you stuff.

JENNY: No it isn't. It's talking with God. And it's not just asking for stuff.

JAMIE: It isn't? What else could it be?

JENNY: First, it's praise.

JAMIE: You mean, I should say, "Good job, God!" Like that?

JENNY: Not exactly. *(Opens Bible.)* Here, look at Psalm 92. That's one of David's prayers of praise to God.

JAMIE: I thought psalms were poems.

JENNY: They are, but poems can be prayers. See how David says to praise God? He says you can sing or play a musical instrument. And when David brought the Ark of the Covenant to Jerusalem, people praised by shouting and dancing. Praise is thanking God for who He is and the wonderful things He has done. *(Closes Bible.)*

JAMIE: But how is that going to get me a new bicycle?

JENNY: FORGET the bicycle for a minute! Prayer is important.

JAMIE: I don't see what this praise stuff does for me.

JENNY: It helps to remind you of who GOD is. And who YOU are.

JAMIE: If you say so. What else is prayer?

JENNY: Another kind of prayer is confession.

JAMIE: Con-fes-sion. Hmm. I don't like the sound of that.

JENNY: Why not? Confession is only telling God you've sinned.

JAMIE: Yeah. But if I tell Him, maybe He won't give me my new bicycle.

JENNY: The bike, again! Do you think God doesn't KNOW you've sinned?

JAMIE: Well, no. But if He already knows, why should I tell Him again?

JENNY: Confession isn't for GOD to know what's going on. It helps us to see how we need God's help. *(Opens Bible.)* Look at Psalm 51. Most people think David wrote this after he sinned with Bathsheba.

JAMIE: You mean after he stole that guy's wife away and killed the guy?

JENNY: Uriah.

JAMIE: I'm what?

JENNY: The dead guy's name was Uriah.

JAMIE: Oh.

JENNY: David's prayer here shows God's love. Confession helps us, because it reminds us that if we are sorry for our sins, God is willing to forgive. It also helps us to remember that we're not perfect but that God's strength is there to help us. *(Closes Bible.)*

JAMIE: And THEN God will give me my new bicycle.

JENNY: Bicycles! Aagh!

JAMIE: What's wrong with bicycles?

JENNY: Nothing. But you're supposed to be learning about prayer! Another type of prayer is intercession.

JAMIE: That's when you go to the snack bar and get a drink. Kind of a break between prayers.

JENNY: Not interMISSION. InterCESSION. Praying for someone ELSE besides yourself!

JAMIE: No way! If Joey wants a bike, let HIM pray for it. There's not enough to go around. I'm praying for my OWN bike.

JENNY: I'm not talking about bikes! I'm talking about people! Aren't people more important than bikes?

JAMIE: Not if you want to get to the park in a hurry.

JENNY: AAGH!

JAMIE: Well, I guess most of the time people are more important. But everyone can pray for themselves, can't they?

JENNY: What about in 2 Samuel 12? David prayed for his little baby. Could a baby pray for itself?

JAMIE: Well, I guess not.

JENNY: And what about people in comas? Can they pray for themselves?

JAMIE: Well, I guess not.

JENNY: And what about people who don't know God? Can they pray for themselves?

JAMIE: Well, maybe not. But God doesn't care about them.

JENNY: Of COURSE He does! He loves ALL people enough to die on a cross for them.

JAMIE: Oh. Yeah.

JENNY: And other Christians need prayer. Nobody can pray perfectly. So we help each other by praying for each other.

JAMIE: Great! *(Punches JENNY playfully.)* So you can help me pray for a new bike!

JENNY: Which leads us to another type of prayer. Petition.

JAMIE: What's that? Are we finally getting around to asking for stuff?

JENNY: That's one way to describe it.

JAMIE: Good! This is the one I need. How do I get my new bike?

JENNY: Maybe you don't.

JAMIE: Don't tell me God doesn't give stuff to people. I've heard people thanking God for giving them stuff. Right in church, I've heard it.

JENNY: I didn't say God doesn't give. But He gives what's best for us, and He gives it in His time. *(Opens Bible.)* Look in 2 Samuel 15:31. One of David's prayers was for God to have Absalom's counselor give him bad advice. And God answered David's petition. And in Psalm 3, David tells how he feels about God's answer.

JAMIE: I TOLD you God gives people stuff. So how come I don't get my bike?

JENNY: I didn't say you won't get a bike. I said, maybe you won't get it. Look at Matthew 26:39. Jesus didn't want to suffer pain on the cross. He asked His Father to be spared that pain. But Jesus also said, "You make the decision, Father. Do whatever is best."

JAMIE: But I don't WANT whatever is best. I want a BIKE. Maybe if I stand on my head and hold my breath...

REMEMBER

SCRIPTURE: Matthew 26:26-29; Luke 22:14-20

SUGGESTED TOPICS: Lord's Supper; Christian heritage

BIBLE BACKGROUND

Throughout Scripture, God gave His people symbols to help them remember important events and concepts. The Passover dinner is a reminder of how God rescued Israel from slavery (see Exodus 12:26,27). The Ark of the Covenant was a tangible reminder of God's presence with His people. Joshua's altars (see Joshua 4:5,6,20) stood as reminders of God's power shown in the conquest of Canaan.

In the New Testament, the Lord's Supper is the symbolic reminder of Jesus' death, the single most important event in history (see Matthew 26:26-28). The connection between this observance and the Passover meal is more than superficial. Not only was the original Lord's Supper celebrated at Passover, it also is a reminder of deliverance brought by God. Echoing Passover, blood is shed and a body is broken. This time the Lamb is the very Son of God, offered as a sacrifice to secure our freedom.

PERFORMANCE TIPS

1. Suggested props: several photo albums.

2. Ask group members to bring special mementos or souvenirs and describe the significance of the objects. Bring something yourself to share with the group. Comment, "Objects such as these help us remember special times in our lives."

DISCUSSION QUESTIONS

1. What things do you have at home to help you remember special people or places?

2. Where do you see symbols in our church building? What are they? Of what do the symbols remind you?

3. What symbols did Jesus talk about in Luke 22:19,20? Of what were these symbols supposed to remind people?

4. Why did Jesus want people to remember Him and His death and resurrection?

REMEMBER

CHARACTERS

JOHN

JOAN

MOTHER

JOHN: What a lousy day!

JOAN: What's wrong?

JOHN: Everything! We had a game planned for today.

JOAN: So?

JOHN: So it's raining. The game's cancelled. There's nothing to do.

JOAN: Well, you can sit here and be miserable, like you're doing, or you can find something else to do.

JOHN: Yeah, like what?

JOAN: Well, on a cold, rainy day like today, we could have some hot chocolate and look at our old photographs.

JOHN: Well...I guess so.

JOAN: Good. You go get the albums while I make the hot chocolate.

JOHN: What's the matter? My hot chocolate's not good enough for you?

JOAN: OK. You make the hot chocolate and I'll get the pictures.

JOHN: *(Pause.)* No. You make the hot chocolate. I just remembered how bad mine is.

JOAN: Right. Meet you in the kitchen.

(Pause while JOAN and JOHN move to kitchen.)

JOHN: Look. Here's a baby picture of me. I sure was bald.

JOAN: Wow! That must be almost the first picture of you that Mom and Dad took.

JOHN: Couldn't tell you. I don't remember back that far.

JOAN: I do. I remember when Mom went to the hospital. I was kind of upset.

JOHN: Why?

JOAN: I guess I felt like Mom and Dad wanted another kid because maybe I wasn't good enough.

JOHN: That's silly! Girls can sure be dumb sometimes.

JOAN: But I remember when Mom was at the hospital, Dad took me into your room and told me how I was now a big sister and how important that job was. And he asked me where we should put things so the baby's room would look really nice.

JOHN: But Dad would know where to put things. He wouldn't need your advice.

JOAN: I know that, now. But back then, that was really important to me. It told me that Mom and Dad still loved me, too.

JOHN: Look! Here's a picture of you in that dress you got for the school Christmas concert.

JOAN: How could you remember that? You weren't even five years old then.

JOHN: But I remember. I remember you almost fell off the stage.

JOAN: I didn't fall. Sharon pushed me.

JOHN: That's what you said. But I think you tripped. I remember.

JOAN: No you don't. I was pushed!

JOHN: Look at this old picture. Remember when we went on vacation to that Lake Minnewackamucka...I never could remember how to pronounce it.

JOAN: Winne...I don't remember either. But I remember how much fun we had.

JOHN: Me, too. Remember when I fell off the pier?

JOAN: I sure do. And I was the only one around to save you.

JOHN: I knew I was a goner. My head was sinking under water for the third time.

JOAN: So I jumped off the pier after you. With all my clothes on.

JOHN: Into about three feet of water. It was so shallow, nobody could have drowned. I sure tricked you, that time.

JOAN: And Mom and Dad laughed at us when we got back to the tent.

JOHN: I remember. Hey! Look at this old picture that fell out. Who's this old guy?

JOAN: I don't know. He can't be anybody important. I never saw him before. *(Holds up another photo.)* Look! Remember that party we had? Where we played that game where everybody tried to get as dirty as they could?

JOHN: How could I forget it? I was sure that I would win....

MOTHER: *(Enters.)* Hi, kids. Can you help me bring in the groceries, please?

JOHN: Did you get ice cream?

MOTHER: Among other things.

JOHN: I'll get the ice cream bag. *(Exits.)*

JOAN: I'll get the other things. *(Exits.)*

JOHN *(from offstage)*: Mom! Which is the bag with the ice cream in it? Mom! Mom!

JOAN: *(Enters.)* Mom. Didn't you hear John? What are you looking at?

MOTHER: This old photo of Uncle Ethan.

JOAN: Who?

JOHN: *(Enters.)* I found it...What's going on?

JOAN: Mom knows the old guy in the picture.

MOTHER: It's my Uncle Ethan. This is the only picture anybody ever took of him.

JOHN: Why? Didn't anybody like him?

MOTHER: Everybody adored him. But, way back then, most people didn't have cameras. I thought I had lost this one. Where did you find it?

JOAN: It just fell out of one of the albums.

JOHN: If he was such a great guy, how come I never heard of him?

MOTHER: Probably because when all the family gets together, the adults tell their favorite stories about Uncle Ethan while you kids are hanging out with your cousins. But almost every family has one of his carvings.

JOAN: You mean like that old wood thing in the living room?

MOTHER: Yes. That was one of Uncle Ethan's.

JOHN: It's not very good. I never knew why you had it there. I thought maybe you did it when you were a little girl.

MOTHER: It's true—he was never a great craftsman. He carved just because he enjoyed it. And everyone asked him for one of his carvings.

JOAN: But why? Why would anyone want something that wasn't very good?

MOTHER: It's a symbol. It's something to help you remember.

JOHN: Huh?

MOTHER: Look at those pictures.

JOAN: We have been. All afternoon.

MOTHER: How good are those pictures?

JOHN: They're the best pictures in the world.

MOTHER: No, they're not. Most are out of focus or overexposed. If you took them to a photo display, people would laugh at them. But they're special to you and so you see them differently than other people do. They're symbols of your lives. That's the same with Uncle Ethan's carvings. They're special because they help us to remember.

(JOHN gets up to exit.)

JOAN: Where are you going, John?

JOHN: To the living room.

JOAN: Why?

JOHN: To look at that old wood thing. The next time the family gets together, I'm going to ask about this guy.

MOTHER: Children! The grocer—never mind. Some things are more important than food. Go. Learn. And remember.

RESPECT

SCRIPTURE: Ezra 1—3; Zechariah 7

SUGGESTED TOPICS: Respect; courtesy

BIBLE BACKGROUND

Judah had been carried into exile by Babylon. Years later, Babylon was overthrown by the Medes and Persians. However, Judah was still in captivity. With the permission of King Cyrus (as prophesied in Isaiah 44:28 before Judah was exiled), approximately fifty thousand Jews were allowed to return to their homeland to begin the rebuilding process. Under the capable leadership of Zerubbabel, the work began.

Throughout the lengthy rebuilding process, Zerubbabel and the prophets Haggai and Zechariah encouraged the people in Jerusalem to remember the God of Israel and to honor Him by being obedient to His word and commandments. Their actions and their words demonstrated the respect due to God.

PERFORMANCE TIPS

1. Suggested props: various goods for sale, a table to represent the counter, cash register, maps, oil containers, etc.
2. The customer is in a hurry. All of his actions should indicate impatience.
3. The old man moves and speaks slowly. Everything he does is deliberate.
4. The old man always speaks respectfully to the customer; the customer rarely speaks respectfully to the old man.

DISCUSSION QUESTIONS

1. What does the word "respect" mean?
2. In what ways did the old man show respect to his customer?
3. In what ways did the customer show lack of respect for the old man?
4. The old man also showed respect for his country. How?
5. Suppose certain people in powerful positions don't earn our respect (e.g., policemen, politicians, judges, parents, teachers). Should we show respect to them anyway? Why or why not?

RESPECT

CHARACTERS

OLD MAN
CUSTOMER

(CUSTOMER comes running into service station.)

CUSTOMER: Hey! Hey! Hey! Hop to it! Car's outside, needs a fill. I'm in a hurry. Move it, old fellow.

OLD MAN: On my way, sir. *(Slowly shuffles offstage.)*

CUSTOMER: *(To himself.)* Doddering old fool. *(To OLD MAN.)* C'mon, c'mon, c'mon. I got things to do, places to go, people to see. Move it! *(OLD MAN slowly shuffles onstage.)*

OLD MAN: Want the oil checked, sir?

CUSTOMER: No, no, no! Fill it with gas. Move it, move it, move it! *(OLD MAN slowly shuffles to oil rack, picks up container.)*

OLD MAN: It's on special today, sir.

CUSTOMER: How many times do I have to tell you? No! N-O! Fill the car! Go, go, go!

OLD MAN *(saluting CUSTOMER)***:** Right away, sir. *(Slowly shuffles offstage.)*

CUSTOMER *(looking at merchandise)***:** Everything here but speed. *(Looks at watch.)* Hurry up, old fellow. I don't have all day. *(OLD MAN slowly shuffles onstage.)*

OLD MAN: You've got a broken headlight, sir. Could be dangerous driving at night. Want I should fix it for you? *(Shuffles over to counter, picks up box.)* Got some real good ones. On special.

CUSTOMER: No! I'm not planning to drive at night, old-timer. Gas?

OLD MAN: Filling up now, sir. Help yourself to coffee. *(Points.)* On the house. *(Shuffles offstage.)*

CUSTOMER: What a place! TURTLES move faster! C'mon, c'mon, c'mon. *(Paces around. OLD MAN shuffles onstage.)*

OLD MAN: There. The windshield's nice and clean. But there's a problem, sir.

CUSTOMER: What, what, what, what, WHAT?

The Big Book of Bible Skits ©1997 Gospel Light. Permission to photocopy granted.

OLD MAN: You got a star. Right up near the roof line where it's hard to see. Should take care of it, sir. Could turn into a crack if you don't.

CUSTOMER: And you've got a special to take care of it?

OLD MAN: Nope.

CUSTOMER: Well, that's a surprise.

OLD MAN (*pointing*): Harry's Glass. One block down. Special this week, sir.

CUSTOMER: Look! I came in for GAS! Hurry, hurry, hurry. I don't WANT other things. If the glass cracks, it cracks. Now get out there and finish filling my tank!

OLD MAN: Almost finished, sir. (*Shuffles offstage.*)

CUSTOMER: That's what I get for stopping at a small town. Geezerville. What's taking him so long? (*OLD MAN shuffles in, goes behind counter.*)

OLD MAN: All filled, sir. Will that be cash or credit card?

CUSTOMER: There's no difference. It doesn't matter, Pops.

OLD MAN: Discount for cash, sir.

CUSTOMER: Yeah, OK. Cash.

OLD MAN: Figure that discount for you, sir. (*Takes pencil and slowly writes. CUSTOMER throws up hands in despair, looks around, sees picture on wall.*)

CUSTOMER: I see you're a (name of political party currently in power).

OLD MAN: No, sir. Been a (name of alternate political party) all my life.

CUSTOMER: But you've got a picture of (name of current president) on the wall.

OLD MAN: No, sir.

CUSTOMER: Sure you do. Are you blind as well as lame? Right there. (*Points.*)

OLD MAN: No, sir. That's a picture of the president of the United States on the wall. That'll be nine dollars and twenty-five cents.

CUSTOMER: Here! (*Throws money on counter, turns to leave.*)

OLD MAN: Thank you, sir. You from around these parts?

CUSTOMER: (*Turns.*) No! Why?

OLD MAN: Might need a map, sir. Wouldn't want to get lost on a back road. (*Shuffles over to map stand, picks up map and holds it out.*) On the house. (*CUSTOMER looks at OLD MAN, gestures disdainfully and leaves.*)

OLD MAN (*looking off stage, saluting*): Happy motoring, sir.

RIOT

SCRIPTURE: Acts 19:23-41

SUGGESTED TOPICS: Peer pressure; injustice; respect; gossip

BIBLE BACKGROUND

As Paul's preaching convinced more and more to follow the Way, jealousies were kindled in various people. Certain Jewish leaders saw their importance being diminished in the eyes of the Jews who believed. But some of Paul's fiercest enemies were those who saw their livelihoods slipping away before their eyes. The owners of the slave girl in Acts 16 accused Paul of breaking Roman law. The silversmith, Demetrius, in chapter 19, was more honest about his motives in wanting Paul stopped, and he started a riot in an attempt to achieve his ends. The mob scene which resulted is a typical display of mass hysteria in which people become incapable of rational, individual thought and become absorbed in the emotion of the crowd.

PERFORMANCE TIPS

1. Suggested props: video game cartridges or packages.
2. The entire group may participate in this skit as part of the mob. Point out the appropriate time in the script when the mob quiets down.
3. When the script calls for the mob to mutter, several lines are suggested. However, the mob may use other appropriate dialogue.

DISCUSSION QUESTIONS

1. Danny decided to use a mob to stop his business from failing. If you were Danny, would you have done the same thing? How else could you have handled the situation?
2. Danny wanted to stop the sale of computer games in order to increase the profits of his own business. But that's not what he told the crowd. Why not? What would have happened if he had told the crowd the truth?
3. Have there been any riots reported on the news recently? What was the cause of the riot? Were there any other reasons that may not have been obvious?
4. Read Acts 19:23-41. How are the characters of the skit and the people in this Bible event similar? When might someone like Demetrius exist in your school or community? What makes a mob so dangerous?

RIOT

CHARACTERS

DANNY

SHAWNA

MOB

AL

JOHN

DANNY: I can't understand it.

SHAWNA: What's wrong, Danny?

DANNY: I can't understand why business is so bad.

SHAWNA: I would have thought the reason was obvious.

DANNY: Well it's not obvious to me, Shawna. Explain it.

SHAWNA: What exactly do you sell?

DANNY: Video games. The best games in the world. Action-packed adventure. Excitement. All the thrills you can imagine.

SHAWNA: But sales are down.

DANNY: Yes. But why?

SHAWNA: Paul.

DANNY: Who's Paul?

SHAWNA: He's a computer game salesman. He's been going up and down the mall showing off his computer games.

DANNY: So what? Video games have been around a long time. What do I care about computer games?

SHAWNA: You had better care. He's selling them to all the computer outlets in the mall. He says they have better graphics, they're more intelligent. In short, he says they're better games.

DANNY: Nobody's going to believe that hype.

SHAWNA: Yeah? What's been happening to your sales?

DANNY: They've been dropping.

SHAWNA: But look at the crowds around the computer stores where the new computer games are being demonstrated.

DANNY: You're right! Paul's the cause of this. He has to be stopped.

SHAWNA: But how?

DANNY: How? How...how...I've GOT it. Watch genius at work.

SHAWNA: I'm almost afraid to look.

DANNY: People! People! People! Gather 'round!

MOB *(muttering)*: What's going on? What's happening?

DANNY: People! We face a crisis and you're ignoring it!

MOB *(muttering):* What's he talking about?

DANNY: There's an evil in our midst! The computer game!

MOB *(muttering):* What?

DANNY: Don't you see the danger? Your children are out squandering your hard-earned money on expensive nonsense! Did you buy your child a computer to use as nothing more than a toy?

MOB *(muttering):* No. Not me. Did you?

DANNY: Of course you didn't! You're good parents! You bought your computer to help your child's education, so your children could learn how to compete in today's high-tech world!

MOB *(muttering):* He's right. That's why we bought ours.

DANNY: But what's happening? Not behind your backs but right out in the open! Paul has invaded your home through the computer stores! He's turning your good intentions into garbage! If he is allowed to continue, your computers will be nothing more than high-tech game boards.

MOB *(slightly louder):* He makes sense.

DANNY: Do you want your children to waste their minds and your computers?

MOB *(louder):* No!

DANNY: Well, it's happening! What are you going to do about it?

MOB *(confused):* I don't know. Do you? What do you think?

DANNY: I'll tell you what we'll do! We'll stop the computer game plot!

MOB *(shouting):* Right on!

DANNY: We'll end this travesty! Stop selling computer games!

MOB *(shouting):* Stop selling computer games! Stop selling computer games!

DANNY: March on the stores!

MOB: Stop selling computer games!

DANNY: Find Paul! Throw him out of the mall!

MOB: Stop selling computer games!

DANNY: Rid the mall of Paul! Rid the mall of Paul!

MOB: Stop selling computer games! Rid the mall of Paul!

AL: Ladies and gentlemen! Please! Control yourselves.

MOB *(quietly muttering):* Who's he? I don't know. Do you?

AL: We must behave in a civilized manner.

DANNY: Wait! He owns a computer store! He just wants your children's money! Stop selling computer games! Rid the mall of Paul!

MOB *(shouting):* Stop selling computer games! Rid the mall of Paul!

SHAWNA: What are you doing, Danny?

DANNY: I'm saving my business.

MOB: Stop selling computer games! Rid the mall of Paul!

SHAWNA: But you've started a riot! They'll tear the computer stores to pieces.

DANNY: I don't care. Let them look after their own businesses.

MOB: Stop selling computer games! Rid the mall of Paul!

JOHN: Ladies and gentlemen! Stop this noise right now!

MOB: Stop selling computer games! Rid the mall of Paul!

JOHN: People! Citizens! Silence, I beg of you!

MOB (*muttering*)**:** Who's he? I don't know? Does he sell computers, too?

JOHN: I am the manager of the mall! I must have your attention!

MOB: (*Mutters.*)

JOHN: Ladies and gentlemen. Everyone knows that you are good citizens, caring mothers and fathers. Since you are, you should not be reckless.

MOB (*muttering*)**:** He's right. Yes. He's right.

JOHN: You are marching against honest shopkeepers. And for what reason? If you don't like the merchandise they sell, then don't buy it. We have laws to protect everyone— not just the store owners, but you and your children. If these men are injuring Danny, let him bring a lawsuit against them.

MOB (*muttering*)**:** He makes sense.

JOHN: If you want to express yourselves, do it in a lawful assembly. A mob like this will only hurt people, the innocent and the guilty alike. If you persist, you will leave yourselves open to criminal charges.

MOB (*muttering*)**:** Why were we behaving that way? Do you know?

JOHN: Please. Go about your business and let this incident be a thing of the past. Help your fellow human beings, don't hurt them.

DANNY: Rats! He ruined my plan. Oh well, I'll just have to think of another.

THE ROBOT

SCRIPTURE: Psalm 19:7,8

SUGGESTED TOPICS: Following instructions; obedience to God's Word; living according to God's plan

BIBLE BACKGROUND

The Bible is far more than a record of past events. While filled with intriguing stories of many people, it is also a living blueprint for each of our lives, the instruction manual for how to live as God's people in this world. If we only study the Bible to discover insights about the ancient world, we miss the real purpose for which it was given. The psalmist celebrated the exciting realization that "Your word is a lamp to my feet and a light for my path" (Psalm 119:105).

PERFORMANCE TIPS

1. Suggested props: a large cardboard box; an assortment of nuts, bolts, screws and tools; a remote control unit for Lee to use as he tries to start the robot.

2. Ask one person to play the robot. He or she should stand completely still during the skit.

DISCUSSION QUESTIONS

1. Have you ever used a kit to build a model? Was it hard or easy? How did the model turn out?

2. If you planned to build something complicated, what's the first thing you would do? Why?

3. Sometimes it's hard to know the right choices to make. When do you read God's instructions for your life? What are some instructions from the Bible you remember?

THE ROBOT

CHARACTERS

KIM

LEE

KIM: Hi, Lee. What are you doing?

LEE: Hi, Kim. I'm building a robot.

KIM: A robot! Where did you learn how to build a robot?

LEE: Oh, it's easy. I bought a kit. Everything's in it.

KIM: That's a neat robot. What will it do?

LEE: I'm not sure yet. But I think that it'll do almost anything I want it to.

KIM: Wow! It sure looks great! How soon will you be finished?

LEE: I'm just putting on the final touches now. One more screw to tighten. There! Finito!

KIM: Great! How about a demo?

LEE: Sure. What do you want it to do?

KIM: I don't know. Surprise me. Make it do anything.

LEE: OK. Watch this! *(Pushes button.)*

KIM: I'm watching. What's happening?

LEE: Nothing! Must be a malfunction in this remote control. Just let me check it a minute. Aha! The red wire is where the green wire should be. There! Now watch!

KIM: I'm watching. I don't see anything.

LEE: Why doesn't this stupid thing work? People shouldn't be allowed to sell defective merchandise like this. I worked so hard on this thing and all for nothing. They didn't put the right things in the package.

KIM: Are you sure you put it together right?

LEE: Of course I'm sure! What do you think I am? A two-year-old who can't build things?

KIM: Well, no. But there sure are a lot of parts lying around outside of the robot. Maybe you didn't put something in that you should have.

LEE: Those are just extra parts. Whenever you have a model, there's always extra parts so you can build it different ways if you want to. Boy, when I get my hands on the guy who sold me this piece of junk, I'll hit him so hard he won't know up from down.

KIM: I think before you punch somebody's lights out, you should check your work first. You know, go over the instructions one more time and be absolutely certain that you didn't make a mistake.

LEE: What do you mean, "Go over the instructions one more time?" I didn't read them the first time.

KIM: Are you telling me that you tried to build something as complicated as a robot without reading the instructions so you would know what you were doing?

LEE: Of course not! I've built lots of things before, and I didn't have time to waste. I wanted to get this thing built so I could have fun with it. Get it to do things, like cleaning up my room, taking out the garbage—things I don't like to do myself. But now I can't. All because somebody at the factory was too lazy to make sure that all the right parts were in the box.

KIM *(softly)*: Or because somebody was too lazy to read instructions.

LEE: What's that? Did you say something?

KIM: No. Nothing.

LEE: Well, I'm going to take this tin man back to the store and give that salesperson a piece of my mind.

KIM *(softly)*: Are you sure you have any to spare?

LEE: Huh? Did you say something?

KIM: Nothing important.

LEE: Help me pack up this box again, would you? I don't want them telling me the store can't take it back because I kept some of the extra parts. Boy, when I get through with them....

RULE THE WORLD

SCRIPTURE: 1 Kings 16:29-34; Proverbs 20:11

SUGGESTED TOPICS: Using one's influence

BIBLE BACKGROUND

Throughout the history of Israel's divided kingdom, most of the rulers seemed intent to wipe out any memory of the God of Abraham, Isaac and Jacob. Idol worship seemed so much easier than devotion to the true God. Although many kings and queens led Israel astray, none so epitomizes evil as does Jezebel. The name still conjures up visions of a vicious, scheming woman, one who is unworthy of trust. Using her influence over King Ahab, Jezebel turned the nation of Israel into a nation of idol worshipers. The prophets of Baal dined at her table. Against the power of this decadent royal couple stood a man of God, Elijah.

PERFORMANCE TIPS

1. Suggested props: lab coat, test tube and other laboratory equipment, white jelly beans for "eye of newt."

2. The mad scientist should alternate between periods of calmness and raving lunacy.

3. The assistant fawns over the scientist. The scientist is his god.

DISCUSSION QUESTIONS

1. What influence does the mad scientist have? What influence does he want to have?

2. What people influence the world today?

3. Who influences your personal life? In what ways?

4. How can you recognize how other people are influencing you?

5. Read Proverbs 20:11. What kind of influence can a kid your age have?

6. Who do you influence? In what ways?

7. Name a good way you can influence others.

RULE THE WORLD

CHARACTERS

MAD SCIENTIST
ASSISTANT

SCIENTIST: Have you got it?

ASSISTANT: Yes, Master.

SCIENTIST: Just as I ordered?

ASSISTANT: To the smallest detail, Master.

SCIENTIST: At last. My dream shall be achieved!

ASSISTANT: Oh, Master. This is so exciting!

SCIENTIST: Yes. With this last ingredient, my invention will be complete. And with its completion, I shall—dare I say it?

ASSISTANT: Please, Master, say it! It's so exciting.

SCIENTIST: With its completion, I shall...rule the world.

ASSISTANT: Oh, Master. When you rule the world, can I be prime minister?

SCIENTIST: Of course not. There will only be room for one ruler. Me.

ASSISTANT: Forgive me, Master. I lost my head.

SCIENTIST: If you keep up these ideas of grandeur, that can be arranged.

ASSISTANT: I would rather it stay where it is.

SCIENTIST: Then forget ruling and follow.

ASSISTANT: Of course, Master. You lead, I follow.

SCIENTIST: Good. Now, give me the final ingredient. Then I shall rule the world.

ASSISTANT: Here it is, Master. But how can this let you rule the world?

SCIENTIST: By adding this last ingredient, I shall have a solution that is absolutely potent. So I shall be an absolute potentate!

ASSISTANT: Oh, Master, you are so brilliant.

SCIENTIST: Yes, I am.

ASSISTANT: Please explain it to me again.

SCIENTIST: Very well. First, I take ten milligrams of sodium hydroxide.

ASSISTANT: This is so exciting.

SCIENTIST: Then, I take one hundred milligrams of auric sulphate.

ASSISTANT: You are so brilliant. You are my idol.

SCIENTIST: As well I should be. Then, a pinch of potassium pentothal...

ASSISTANT: How alliterative.

SCIENTIST: Now, I shall add the final ingredient, eye of newt, and I shall, dare I say it?

ASSISTANT: Say it! Say it!

SCIENTIST: I shall...rule the world.

ASSISTANT: But, Master. What will this invention do?

SCIENTIST: What will it DO? Why, it will dissolve anything it touches!

ASSISTANT: Oh!

SCIENTIST: Does China have nuclear missiles? Hah! I laugh at nuclear missiles.

ASSISTANT: But, Master...

SCIENTIST: Does Turkey have an atomic bomb? Hah! I laugh at atomic bombs.

ASSISTANT: But, Master...

SCIENTIST: Does (name of your country) have (name of current leader)? Hmm. That is scary. No matter. I laugh. Hah!

ASSISTANT: But, Master...

SCIENTIST: Why must you interrupt my brilliant speech? With this invention, all nations must bow to me. Whatever *I* say, THEY must do. I shall...rule the world.

ASSISTANT: But, Master...

SCIENTIST: What?

ASSISTANT: If it will dissolve ANYthing, how will you store it?

SCIENTIST: Hmm. That is a tricky question. Store it. *(Pauses.)* I have it! I will invent a material that will never dissolve! And with an invention such as that, I shall...rule the world.

ASSISTANT: That's my master. He always has an answer. What shall I do with the newt's eyes?

SCIENTIST: *(Takes one from jar and eats it.)* Keep them. They'll make a marvelous casserole for supper tonight.

ASSISTANT: Oh, Master.

THE SACRIFICE

SCRIPTURE: Matthew 27:15-66; Luke 23:18-56; John 19

SUGGESTED TOPICS: Death of the Savior; God's plan of salvation fulfilled; God's love

BIBLE BACKGROUND

The fullness of time had finally come. For centuries, Satan had challenged God's control. When the long-promised Messiah was born, Satan, through Herod, had attempted to murder Jesus while He was still a child. Finally, the Savior was about to be crucified. Satan was sure he had finally won.

Sacrifice is never easy, not even for the One who is perfect (see Matthew 26:39-44). Jesus, the perfect Son, knew the pain He must endure for His Father's plan to be completed. Willingly, He took the sin of the entire world upon Himself, giving all mankind the only hope of being reconciled to God.

PERFORMANCE TIPS

1. Suggested props: chalk and chalkboard for coach to use in sketching the trick play.
2. By the end of the skit, Josh's voice and gestures must show that he is certain of his actions. He should show his determination to do whatever is needed for his team to win. The other players on the team are still questioning the wisdom of the trick play.

DISCUSSION QUESTIONS

1. Why was it necessary for Jesus to die on the cross?
2. When Jesus died, what did most people who knew Him think about Him?
3. Instead of ending God's plan, the Bible tells us that Jesus' death was the fulfillment of God's plan. Because He followed God's plan, Jesus is able to offer us the gift of eternal life. What do you need to do to accept this gift?

The Big Book of Bible Skits ©1997 Gospel Light. Permission to photocopy granted.

THE SACRIFICE

CHARACTERS

COACH
PLAYERS
PETE
JIM
JOHNNY
JOSH

COACH: OK, guys. Listen up. The big game's almost here.

PLAYERS: Yeah! Let's get 'em! We're number one!

COACH: Hold it down! Hold it down!

PLAYERS *(softly)***:** We're number one!

COACH: That's better. Now, you all know that this is the most important game of our lives. We've GOTTA win this game!

PLAYERS: No problem! Beat 'em! Crush 'em! We're number one!

COACH: Hold it down!

PLAYERS *(softly)***:** We're number one!

COACH: OK. What we need is a trick play. Something we can count on if we need to score a last-minute touchdown. Something the opposition won't expect.

PLAYERS: Trick play! Trick play! We're number one!

COACH: Hold...

PLAYERS *(softly)***:** We're number one!

COACH: Now, then. I don't have to tell you what our best play has been this season.

PETE: I seal the defensive end!

JIM: I kick out the outside linebacker!

JOHNNY: I cut the middle linebacker!

JOSH: And I run for daylight! Touchdown!

PLAYERS: Yeah, Josh! Score, score, score! We're number one!

COACH: Now, the trick play is a variation of this.

JOSH: So where do I run?

PETE, JIM AND JOHNNY: And who do we hit?

COACH: First, Pete. When you seal the end, don't block him as well as normal.

PETE: You mean, miss him?

COACH: No, but just a brush block. Not your usual crushing blow.

PETE: I don't know...

COACH: Jim. Pretend to block the outside backer, but let him get inside of you.

JIM: I don't know...

COACH: Johnny. Make a show of cutting the middle linebacker, but let him jump over you.

JOHNNY: I don't know...

COACH: In the meantime, Pete, you miss three more blocks.

PETE: Three blocks! I'd never miss three blocks. I'm too good!

JOSH: Wait a minute, Coach. If they do that, I'm going to get creamed.

COACH: Yes, Josh. You will.

JOSH: But I'm your best player! I'm your son! Don't you love me any more or what?

COACH: Of course I do. It's because I love you that I want you to win this game.

JOSH: Sure. But if I'm buried, how will the play ever work?

COACH: Simple. You won't have the ball.

PETE, JIM AND JOHNNY: But they'll kill him!

COACH: No they won't. They'll think they have. But Josh will rise to play again.

JOSH: So what happens to the ball?

COACH: Before you're hit, you hand the ball to Bart. He runs the opposite direction. You pretend you still have the ball, and while the enemy is concentrating on you, Bart gains big yardage.

JOSH: Will it work?

COACH: Guaranteed.

JOSH: If I sacrifice myself, we'll win?

COACH: Absolutely.

JOSH: Then I'll do it. Let's go through it once again so I've got everything straight. We don't want to mess this up.

SILENCE IS GOLDEN

SCRIPTURE: Proverbs 12:18

SUGGESTED TOPICS: Controlling speech; humility; pride; influence on others

BIBLE BACKGROUND

The Bible repeatedly presents examples which show us the consequences of our actions and attitudes toward others. The book of Proverbs is filled with advice concerning controlling one's tongue, thoughts and actions. Proverbs 12:18 tells us that foolish, rash words are as dangerous and as wounding as the thrusts of a sword. We've all experienced the painful consequences of those kinds of words. And we've all felt remorse for cruel and slanderous words that came from our mouths.

God's Word teaches us to "watch our language," for what we say and how we say it provides windows to our hearts and is an important part of our relationship with Him and others. It's a life's work to learn to put aside all words that do not guard and advance the reputation and well-being of others.

PERFORMANCE TIPS

1. Suggested props: sign that says "TALENT AGENCY," table and chair for Ed, notepad and pencil.
2. Ted is loud and brash. He is theatrical and punctuates his words with sweeping gestures. He constantly tries to step between Ed and Fred.
3. Fred always speaks only when spoken to. He does not brag, but is quietly confident.

DISCUSSION QUESTIONS

1. Would you rather know Ted or Fred? Why?
2. In what ways were Ted's words harmful? to himself? to others?
3. Read Proverbs 12:18. What does it mean?
4. When are you tempted to speak unkindly about others? What can you do when this happens?
5. What are some ways your words can heal?

SILENCE IS GOLDEN

CHARACTERS

TED

FRED

EDWARD GAD

TED: Hi there! It's your lucky day!
Allow me to introduce myself:
"THE AMAZING TED TUNER!"
(To audience.) No applause! Just throw money!

EDWARD *(holding out hand to shake)*: E. Gad.

TED: *(Jumps back.)* What's wrong?

EDWARD: Nothing. Why do you ask?

TED: You just said, "Egad!"

EDWARD: Sorry. A bit confusing. That's my name.
Edward Gad. *(Slowly.)* E. Gad.

TED: Ah! OK. Well, enough about YOU. We're here to talk about ME. No doubt you've heard of me. Amazing Ted Tuner, the greatest guitarist since, well, since guitars were invented! And to think, I've only been playing for six months! I'm a legend in my own mind, er, time!

EDWARD: No, I HAVEN'T heard of you. But I have HEARD you. Who's your friend?

TED: Huh? Oh, Fred. Take a bow, Fred. Amateur keyboard player of sorts. But nothing to compare to the AMAZING TED TUNER! *(To audience.)* That's me, you know.

EDWARD: Yes. I've heard. How can I help you?

TED: Simple. You're a talent AGENT. I'm a TALENT. You agent, I'll talent, and we'll make a million bucks! See? I told you this was your lucky day!

EDWARD: I see. And Fred, tell me about your keyboard work. What's your background?

FRED *(quietly)*: I have a degree from the Chicago Conservatory. I've been playing keyboard instruments since I was seven. I've organized and led classical and jazz groups.

TED: *(Steps in front of FRED.)* Hey! That's old Fred for you. He's just full of education, kind of a stuffed shirt, so to speak. Not me. I'm fresh. I'm a prodigy! Just six months ago I was watching TV and I realized, *Hey! I can do this!* And here I am, THE AMAZING TED TUNER!

EDWARD *(writing)*: Yes. You are. Fresh, that is. *(To himself.)* Fred. *(Flips page and continues writing.)* Ted.

TED: Hey! It's THE AMAZ—

EDWARD *(writing)*: Yes. The Amazing Ted Tuner.

TED: And don't you forget it, little buddy! Amazing's the name; amazing's my game!

EDWARD: I beg your pardon.

TED: That's my slogan, man! "THE AMAZING TED TUNER—Amazing's my name; amazing's my game!" Write that down. We'll want to use it. But then, once you've seen my act, you'll never forget THE AMAZ—

EDWARD: Yes. Quite. And Fred?

TED: *(Steps in front of FRED.)* Does some simple, folksy stuff. I brought him along because I'm gonna give him a BIG BREAK! He can open for me. Wait till you see MY stuff!

EDWARD: I imagine it's AMAZING.

TED: Egad, but you catch on fast, E. Gad! *(To audience.)* See how quick I am to turn a phrase?

EDWARD *(bored)*: Amazing.

TED: Amazing? Why it's STUPENDOUS! COLOSSAL! *(Announcing.)* I AM THE AMAZING TED—

EDWARD: *(Cuts TED off.)* What sort of act do you do?

TED: I TOLD you. What I do is TOTALLY fresh! That's what makes me so AMAZING!

EDWARD: *(Looks past TED.)* Not you. Him. Fred, what do you prefer to play? It seems that you're experienced in many styles.

FRED: Well, I enjoy playing my own work the most. But I enjoy anything I play.

TED: *(Steps in front of FRED.)* BORING! ANYBODY can be VERSATILE! But MY act's the stuff you gotta see. I run onto a completely dark stage. The audience only hears footsteps. Then the lights come up and, ta da! There I am! THE AMAZING TED TUNER starts wailing on his guitar! WOW!

EDWARD: What styles do you prefer?

TED: You lost me, Eddie, baby. I wasn't talking about styles. I DEFINE style!

EDWARD: I was talking to Fred. Again. I have someone who might be interested in your own compositions. She's looking for something...fresh.

FRED: I'd be glad for the chance. Thank you very much!

TED: *(Steps in front of FRED.)* We've heard ORIGINAL work a thousand, billion, trillion, zillion times before. But I'M unique. THE AMAZING TED has no equal!

EDWARD *(looking skyward)*: We can only hope so.

TED: *(Leans over EDWARD.)* Prepare to be amazed! I have big plans for this show! MY show won't be like anything you've ever seen!

EDWARD: Anything else?

TED: Are you kidding? I've only just begun.

EDWARD: I was speaking to Fred. Do you play anything else?

FRED: I have been playing guitar for a few years. I've been giving Ted lessons.

TED: *(Jumps in front of FRED.)* Hey! Did I tell you that my act is not only music but COMEDY? Listen! I'm a musical magician. I can turn one thing into another. Why just the other day, I opened the door and left it ajar! Hah! Get it? Door? Jar? Left the door ajar! Another success! AMAZ—

EDWARD: So we've heard. Amazing comedy, too. Fred, do you do anything else?

FRED: I do have some experience singing—

TED: *(Cuts FRED off.)* Only if he lip syncs! But the AMAZING TED can SING! He can DANCE! He tells JOKES! I'm an entertainment package that you won't BELIEVE!

EDWARD: You're right. Already I don't believe it. *(To FRED.)* I think I have something else for you.

TED: I KNEW it! Talent like mine is hard to find. When and where?

EDWARD: Not you, AMAZING TED. Fred, I'll contact these people for you. Here are the addresses. *(Reaches for telephone.)* Let me see if I can get you appointments right now.

FRED: Thank you. I appreciate your kindness.

TED: What about THE AMAZING TED TUNER?

EDWARD: Yes. Well, if something comes up, I'll let you know. And Ted?

TED: Yes?

EDWARD: Don't call us. We'll call you.

STANDING FIRM

SCRIPTURE: 1 Corinthians 15:58

SUGGESTED TOPICS: Holding fast to the truth; obeying God; courage

BIBLE BACKGROUND

Jeremiah's tenure as prophet in Judah seemed to have come at an auspicious time. Under the leadership of Josiah, the Temple had been restored and the Book of the Law had been found, producing a revival of worship of the one true God. Josiah's reign continued for eighteen years after God called Jeremiah. Unfortunately, all the laws in the world cannot change the hearts of people. Although changes in worship were made, they were largely superficial; the underlying sin of Judah remained unresolved. When Josiah was killed in battle, his son Jehoahaz reigned for only three months, then was forcibly replaced by the king of Egypt. The remaining kings of Judah did evil in the sight of the Lord until Judah was taken into captivity by Nebuchadnezzar, and Judah was no more.

From a worldly perspective, Jeremiah's ministry was a failure. He called a callous nation to repent, warning of the dire consequences if it refused. But his message was unpopular, so Judah turned to other prophets who would say what she wished to hear. Undaunted by beatings and imprisonment, Jeremiah still proclaimed the word of God, continuing to call the people to repentance even after the nation had fallen.

PERFORMANCE TIPS

1. Suggested props: table and chairs, stack of books to represent legal books.

2. John has no courage to match his convictions. He just wants to be liked.

3. Janet should be portrayed as sarcastic when she speaks to Jacqueline.

4. Jacqueline is polite but firm. She knows she's right.

DISCUSSION QUESTIONS

1. What do you think will happen to Jacqueline because of her stand?

2. What are some things you are asked to do to be popular? How can you resist doing those things which are wrong?

3. What are some ways to determine if an action is right or wrong?

4. What could you do if a friend asked you to do something wrong? What could you say?

STANDING FIRM

CHARACTERS

JACQUELINE

JANET

JOHN

JAKE

PRONUNCIATION GUIDE

Behemoth (buh-HEE-muth)

Megaloth (MEG-uh-loth)

JAKE: *(Stands.)* As senior partner in this law firm, I've called this meeting to discuss an unfortunate problem with one of our clients, Megaloth Industries.

JACQUELINE: *(Aside to Janet.)* That's one of our biggest clients.

JANET: *(To Jacqueline.)* Yeah. We make at least a hundred thousand dollars a year from them.

JAKE: Naturally, what concerns Megaloth concerns us.

JOHN: As well it should. The affairs of our clients are our sacred trust.

JACQUELINE: What seems to be their problem?

JAKE: At great expense, they have developed a new product. One that will revolutionize the lives of everyone in this great land...

JANET: Excuse me, sir. But you're beginning to sound like an ad executive.

JAKE: Sorry. It's just that the unfairness of the situation upsets me.

JOHN: I can understand that. You're a sensitive man.

JACQUELINE: Their problem?

JAKE: It's actually a multiple problem. Part of the problem is their largest competitor: Behemoth, Incorporated.

JANET: What's that giant trying to do? Squash the little man, again?

JAKE: Actually, Behemoth says Megaloth stole the idea from them.

JOHN: Well! The nerve of those liars!

JACQUELINE: So our job is to prove who actually developed the idea first.

JAKE: No. We DON'T want to do that.

JANET *(confused)***:** Why is that, sir?

JAKE: Because Behemoth DID develop it. Megaloth simply stole the idea and adapted it to their needs. What we need is a legal stratagem to confuse the issue until Megaloth can get their product out.

JOHN: OK. How can we do that?

JACQUELINE: We can't.

JAKE: And why do you say that?

JACQUELINE: Because it's WRONG.

JOHN: She does have a point there.

JANET: Don't be a fool, Jackie. BEHEMOTH isn't paying us. Megaloth is!

JOHN: Precisely! Just what I was going to say.

JAKE: Good. Then we're all agreed.

JACQUELINE: No, we're not all agreed. We can't do it. It's wrong.

JANET: *(Sighs.)* Miss Goody-Two-Shoes. I knew we shouldn't have taken you in.

JAKE: What seems to be your problem?

JACQUELINE: It's against the LAW. We KNOW our client stole the idea. We can't help them profit from it.

JOHN: Good point. Ethics and all that.

JANET: You want us to lose a six-figure client? They don't grow on trees, you know.

JAKE: Besides, this is nothing new to business. It's done all the time.

JACQUELINE: Not by me. It's wrong.

JANET: What's wrong with helping a client make a few bucks?

JACQUELINE: How can I make you people understand? It's a sick bird!

JAKE, JOHN and JANET: What?

JACQUELINE: It's a sick bird. Ill eagle.

JAKE and JANET: *(Groan.)*

JOHN: *(Catches on slowly.)* Ill eagle...sick bird—ha! Very good!

JAKE: Let me point out to our esteemed associate that our job is to protect our clients.

JACQUELINE: Agreed. But our job is NOT to subvert the law. If anybody respects the law, lawyers should.

JOHN: Hear, hear! *(Applauds but stops as JAKE and JANET stare at him.)*

JANET: Of COURSE we respect the law. But it's very vague on this point.

JAKE: Precisely. We simply have to ignore the portions we don't like and concentrate on those we do.

JANET: Certain considerations must bow to others.

JACQUELINE: In other words, if the fee is big enough, look the other way?

JAKE: I knew you'd see it. Janet, get right on it. Find anything that will help us.

JACQUELINE: I DON'T see it! I disagree!

JANET: No problem, sir. I've got a few tricks Behemoth has never seen.

JOHN: You said it was a multiple problem, sir?

JAKE: Yes. The government seems to be a little uncomfortable with Megaloth's version of the product. What was the term they used? "Environmentally unfriendly."

JACQUELINE: You mean, it's a POLLUTANT?

JAKE: Pollutant is such an UGLY word. *(Slowly and distinctly.)* Environmentally unfriendly.

JACQUELINE: If you call a pile of manure a bed of roses, it still stinks.

JOHN: Manure. Roses. Stinks. That's good. Very funny.

JANET: Worried about the whales again? Color Jackie green.

JAKE: It IS a point to consider.

JACQUELINE: Thank you, sir.

JAKE: But the point is, how much is too much? John, you're the best man for this. We have to prove that Megaloth's product is no more harmful than something else in common use.

JOHN: How harmful is it?

JAKE: Very. So find an analogy that will confuse people.

JACQUELINE: *(Shakes head.)* I don't believe it.

JOHN: I haven't even FOUND it yet. How can you not believe it?

JANET: Jackie Greenpeace here means she finds our callous behavior intolerable.

JACQUELINE: *(Smiles sweetly.)* Thank you. I couldn't have worded it better.

JANET: Look, little girl. Wake up and smell the coffee. Refusing to help our client will not save the humpbacks. HELPING them will save our JOBS.

JAKE: You have a way of finding the crux and stating it well.

JANET: Thank you, sir.

JACQUELINE: Don't you care about anything but money?

JANET: Of course, I do. Jewels, clothes, cars.

JOHN: *(Snaps fingers.)* That's IT! Does less harm to the environment than the exhaust from one vehicle!

JAKE: But it doesn't hurt the atmosphere. It ruins the WATER.

JOHN: That's the beauty of the argument. By comparing water pollution with air pollution, we've confused the issue. It'll take years to sort out. No politician wants to wrestle with a problem for years. They'll let it through.

JACQUELINE: But is the statement true?

JOHN: Who CARES if it's true? It'll WORK. That's the issue.

JACQUELINE: What ever happened to truth?

JANET: It disappeared with beauty. Lighten up.

JAKE: Good. Everything is settled. Back to work. Oh, Jacqueline, see me in my office. We have to reevaluate your position with the firm.

THERE'S FRUIT AND THERE'S FRUIT

SCRIPTURE: Galatians 5:22,23

SUGGESTED TOPICS: Fruit of the Spirit; wise choices; Christian life

BIBLE BACKGROUND

Paul, in writing to the Galatians, tried to warn them against trying to please God through the works of the flesh. He exhorted them to accept the "fruit of the Spirit" which is freely given from God through Christ's sacrifice on the cross. "Against such things there is no law" (Galatians 5:23).

Many people think of farming and raising crops as being some sort of easy work. You plant the seed and wait for the harvest. Nothing could be further from the truth. The land must be prepared carefully, the seed must be planted at the right depth, the correct fertilizer must be employed to achieve the greatest yield, the proper amount of moisture must be applied and the field must be weeded. Similarly, the fruit of the Spirit does not automatically grow in a person's life, but must be carefully nurtured.

PERFORMANCE TIPS

1. Suggested props: overalls and shovel for Joe.
2. If you know a farmer (or someone who used to live on a farm), ask him or her to come to your group and describe the steps in growing a crop.
3. Introduce the skit by saying, "In the book of Galatians, Paul used a word picture to describe the kinds of attitudes and actions the Holy Spirit helps a Christian to demonstrate. Paul called these attitudes and actions the fruit of the Spirit. Listen to this skit to find out what it takes to produce the fruit of the Spirit."

DISCUSSION QUESTIONS

1. Do you think Joe will harvest a large crop from his apple tree? Why or why not?
2. Paul talks about fruit of the Spirit in his letter to the Galatians. Why might he have chosen fruit as a comparison for love, joy, peace, patience, kindness, goodness, faithfulness, gentleness and self-control?
3. How can you help this fruit to grow in your life? What do you think would happen if you try to grow it alone, without God? Why?

THERE'S FRUIT AND THERE'S FRUIT

CHARACTERS

JOHN

JOE

JOHN: Hi, Joe. Hey, that's some hole you've dug. What's it for?

JOE: It's going to make me rich.

JOHN: What, you got buried treasure down there?

JOE: Better than that. If it were treasure, somebody else would want a piece of it.

JOHN: The dirt—is it some kind of special dirt? Is it full of uranium or oil or something?

JOE: Nope.

JOHN: Well if the dirt isn't special and there's no buried treasure, what's so special about this hole?

JOE: Fruit.

JOHN: Where? I don't see any fruit.

JOE: It's not there yet. But I'm going to plant an orchard, starting with one apple tree. Right here in this hole.

JOHN: That's your big money-making scheme? Planting an apple tree?

JOE: Sure. Everybody's health conscious these days. And what's healthier than apples? You know, an apple a day keeps the doctor away. So I'll grow apples, sell them, buy more trees, sell the fruit from them and become rich.

JOHN: I guess it could work. But I didn't know you could grow apples here.

JOE: Of course you can. There's no law against it.

JOHN: I was talking about the climate. Is this the right climate for apples?

JOE: Are you kidding? Apples grow anywhere.

JOHN: Are you sure?

JOE: Pretty sure. Anyway, they'll grow here for sure. Because if they wouldn't, the nursery wouldn't sell apple trees, would it?

JOHN: I guess not. How about this soil? It looks like it has a lot of sand in it. Is that good for growing apples?

JOE: Dirt is dirt. You plant the tree in dirt and it grows.

JOHN: I thought different kinds of trees grew best in different kinds of soil.

JOE: That's too much trouble. I say, just plant the trees and let them grow.

JOHN: If you say so. Where's your tree?

JOE: Over there. Leaning against the house.

JOHN: But that's just a little sapling. Should you have dug this deep of a hole for such a little tree?

JOE: Sure. Its roots need to get down real deep. That'll make it grow faster.

JOHN: I sure never knew all this before. What kind of apples are you growing?

JOE: APPLE apples. The kind you eat.

JOHN: But don't different kinds of apples need different kinds of fertilizer?

JOE: Fertilizer? Who's got money for fertilizer? That would cut into my profit. All trees need to grow is dirt and water. Man, will I be raking in the dough this year.

JOHN: This year? From that little tree? I don't think it will grow apples for a few years.

JOE: It's an apple tree. That means it will grow apples. You don't know anything about fruit, do you?

JOHN: I guess I don't know anything about the kind of fruit you're planning to grow. But I know lots about fruit of a different kind.

JOE: Oh? Is it any good?

JOHN: It's the fruit of the Spirit, the best kind of all.

JOE: Never heard of it. Where do you grow it?

JOHN: Inside yourself.

JOE: Right. This better be good.

JOHN: First you have to prepare the ground.

JOE: You mean like digging a hole.

JOHN: Well, for this kind of fruit, you start by accepting Jesus as your Savior. Then God's Spirit grows His fruit inside you.

JOE: Fruit can't grow inside of people.

JOHN: This kind can. If it's properly nurtured.

JOE: What does that mean—nurtured?

JOHN: It's like watering and fertilizing plants. But the water and plant food I use is the Bible and prayer.

JOE: Reading books and talking with your eyes closed doesn't grow fruit.

JOHN: It does with this kind of fruit. And do you know what the best part is?

JOE: I haven't a clue.

JOHN: The fruit begins to grow right away. You don't have to wait a long time for it. As long as you continue nurturing God's Spirit within you, He produces fruit.

JOE: You don't have to wait for the fruit?

JOHN: Nope.

JOE: I could make a lot of money from this. What kind of fruit are we talking about here? And how do you get it out of your body?

JOHN: The fruit of the Spirit is love, joy, peace, patience, kindness, goodness, faithfulness, gentleness and self-control. And you don't have to pick it. You give it away.

JOE: Man, I never know what you're talking about. But I don't think I could sell that any way. So you can keep it. I'll stick with apples.

JOHN: Well, if you ever need the fruit of the Spirit, you'll know where to find it. Lot's of luck with your apples. I think you'll need it.

JOE: Luck? Ha! Just old-fashioned hard work. That's all it needs. Now let's see. Which end of this thing goes up?

UNFAIR

SCRIPTURE: Philippians 4:11,13

SUGGESTED TOPICS: Response to injustice; choosing wisdom

BIBLE BACKGROUND

God never promised us a fair world. Sin has changed the perfect to the imperfect. Again and again in this lifetime we will experience disappointment, heartache and pain. The way we handle these setbacks will show the world around us our true faith.

PERFORMANCE TIPS

1. Suggested props: hat and clipboard for coach.

2. Before the skit ask, "Have you ever been judged unfairly in a competition or other situation? What happened? What did you do?" Then introduce the skit by saying, "Let's see how someone else handles an unfair situation."

DISCUSSION QUESTIONS

1. How did Julie respond when her score was lower than she and her coach believed she deserved?

2. Who could have helped her? How?

3. Why do you think unfair things happen?

4. It's easy to recognize times when we feel we are treated unfairly. It's harder to recognize the times when we may have treated someone else unfairly. When might you have been unfair to someone?

5. When you have been treated unfairly, what should you do? When you have treated someone else unfairly, what should you do?

UNFAIR

CHARACTERS

COACH

JULIE

TRAINER

COACH: Great routine, Julie! Great!

JULIE: It felt good. I think it's the best I've done.

COACH: It wasn't just good, it was great! The gold is ours for sure!

JULIE: What about the wobble on the second back flip?

COACH: Nothing to worry about. And you nailed the landing on your dismount.

JULIE: Look! They're posting the marks.

COACH: Nine-point-six-five? What are they talking about? It was worth at least a nine-point-nine!

JULIE: Nine-point-six-five isn't even good enough for bronze.

COACH: What's the matter with you judges? Are you totally blind?

JULIE: I worked so hard. For nothing.

COACH: Never mind, Julie. Don't let it bother you. Get ready for the floor exercises.

JULIE: But I was good. I did my best routine ever. It's not fair.

COACH: It sure isn't. You judges are blind! Did you know that? You can't see your noses in front of your faces!

JULIE: How can I face people back home? They all expected me to win.

COACH: You're going to have to put it behind you. Let's go over your floor routine.

JULIE: I start...I start with...oh, I can't remember!

COACH: C'mon. You can do it. Step-by-step, the first tumbling pass.

JULIE: I start on the northeast corner of the mat and...front hand spring...

(TRAINER enters.)

COACH: Joe! Can you believe those judges?

TRAINER: Unbelievable! We were robbed blind!

COACH: If you judges need new glasses, why didn't you buy them before you came?

TRAINER: Things like that shouldn't be allowed. The whole bunch should be replaced.

COACH: Learn the sport before you sit in judgment!

JULIE: Front hand spring...I can't remember!

COACH: C'mon now, Julie. You can't let one disappointment get you down.

JULIE: I know, but I can't remember.

COACH: You stupid judges! You're trying to destroy the whole competition, aren't you? Well it won't work! Do you hear me? It won't work!

JULIE: Why was I ever born? I'll make a fool out of myself. I don't want to go on. I can't remember my routine. It's not fair. It's just not fair.

WHEN I SAY JUMP

SCRIPTURE: 1 Samuel 13

SUGGESTED TOPICS: Obeying God; respecting authority

BIBLE BACKGROUND

Against Samuel's strong objections, the people of Israel demanded a king to rule over them so they could be like their neighbors. Samuel warned the people of the disasters that would befall them, but they refused to listen. So Samuel called the people together (see 1 Samuel 10:17) and had them pass before the Lord in their individual tribes, thousand by thousand. First, the tribe of Benjamin was chosen. Then, the family of Matri. Finally, Saul himself was selected to be king of Israel.

From a human standpoint, Saul was an excellent choice. Standing a full head higher than the other Israelites, he cut an impressive figure. In the beginning, he recognized his own inability to rule. Surely, he would be a man who would seek the Lord's guidance to reign over God's people. However, the reign that began so well ended in dismal failure when the Lord had to wrest the kingdom from Saul and give it to a man "after his own heart" (1 Samuel 13:14).

PERFORMANCE TIPS

1. Suggested props: army fatigues, binoculars for the captain, a radio (walkie-talkies), maps.

2. The characters in the skit are soldiers. They should speak crisply and clearly.

3. The captain should speak slowly and distinctly whenever he explains something; the sergeant should salute each time he says "Yes, sir."

DISCUSSION QUESTIONS

1. What are some times a person might be disobedient? What do you think causes someone your age to disobey?

2. What other things might cause people to disobey? What are some excuses people might give for disobeying?

3. Why is it important for soldiers to obey orders? What was wrong with the captain's leadership?

4. Have you ever thought of yourself as one of God's soldiers? (See 2 Timothy 2:3.)

5. What are some of God's orders to His soldiers? What can you do to remember these orders and to obey them?

WHEN I SAY JUMP

CHARACTERS
CAPTAIN
GUNNERY SERGEANT
RADIO OPERATOR

CAPTAIN: Sergeant, come here!

SERGEANT: Yeah?

CAPTAIN: What did you say?

SERGEANT: I said, "Yeah?"

CAPTAIN: That's no way to address a superior. Let's try it again. Sergeant!

SERGEANT: *(Salutes.)* Yes, sir!

CAPTAIN: Bring the terrain maps here and let's go over them.

SERGEANT: *(Salutes.)* Yes, sir! I have them here, sir!

CAPTAIN: *(Looks at map.)* What is this?

SERGEANT: It's the train map, sir! It shows where all the trains go. And here's the schedule that gives all their departure and arrival times.

CAPTAIN: Not the TRAIN map. *(Speaks slowly.)* The TERRAIN map. The map that shows the ground we have to go over and where the mountains and valleys and rivers are.

SERGEANT: Oh. The contour map. I have that here.

CAPTAIN: "I have that here" what?

SERGEANT *(puzzled)***:** I have that here contour map?

CAPTAIN: No! *(Speaks slowly.)* How do you address me?

SERGEANT: I have that here, sir! *(Hands map to CAPTAIN.)*

CAPTAIN: That's better. Never forget; you're in the army.

SERGEANT: *(Salutes.)* Yes, sir!

CAPTAIN: Are the men ready?

SERGEANT: Awaiting your orders, sir!

CAPTAIN: Good. Have them continue to stand by.

SERGEANT: Permission to speak, sir?

CAPTAIN: Go ahead.

SERGEANT: Thank you, sir. The men have been on alert for three days now. They're beginning to tire. Wouldn't it be better to wait until the battle is about to begin to have the troops on alert at their battle stations?

CAPTAIN: Are you questioning my orders, Sergeant?

SERGEANT: No, sir. I was just pointing out...

CAPTAIN: Well, don't! This is the army! You obey your superior officers. When I say jump, you say...

SERGEANT: How high, sir?

CAPTAIN: And don't you forget it. Dismissed!

SERGEANT: *(Salutes.)* Yes, sir. *(Exits.)*

CAPTAIN: *(Studies map.)* Now, let's see. The enemy's ammo dump is over here in the northeast. Prevailing winds from the west. Allow two degrees for drift and we should...

RADIO OPERATOR: Excuse me.

CAPTAIN: Excuse me, what?

RADIO OPERATOR: *(Salutes.)* Excuse me, sir!

CAPTAIN: That's better. What is it, soldier?

RADIO OPERATOR: New orders from HQ, sir! *(Hands CAPTAIN a piece of paper.)*

CAPTAIN: *(Mutters as he reads, then crumples paper and throws it away.)* Nonsense! What are those fools at HQ thinking anyway? Dismissed!

RADIO OPERATOR: *(Salutes.)* Yes, sir! *(Exits.)*

CAPTAIN: Sergeant!

SERGEANT: *(Salutes.)* Yes, sir!

CAPTAIN: The battle is about to start. *(Point to map.)* Now our primary target is this ammo dump. How quickly can your men take it out?

SERGEANT: As soon as you give the order, sir!

CAPTAIN: Good. Tell the men to stand by for the order to fire.

SERGEANT: *(Salutes.)* Yes, sir! *(Notices paper on ground. Picks it up and reads it.)* Permission to speak, sir?

CAPTAIN: What is it? I thought I gave you an order.

SERGEANT: *(Salutes.)* Yes, sir. But THESE orders, sir. HQ says our primary target has been changed. We're supposed to give artillery support along the southern front.

CAPTAIN: I can read, Sergeant. Those desk jockeys at HQ don't know the situation firsthand like we do. We have to take out the ammo dump so the enemy doesn't have so much fire power. Now go and obey my orders.

SERGEANT: *(Salutes.)* Yes, sir! *(Exits.)*

RADIO OPERATOR: Message from HQ, sir.

CAPTAIN *(studying map)*: I'm busy. Read it to me.

RADIO OPERATOR: It says, "Fire when ready."

CAPTAIN: Aha! The battle begins. We'll show those skunks a thing or two. Give me that radio. Sergeant! Can you hear me? Good. Fire! *(Looks through binoculars.)* Beautiful!

SERGEANT: A direct hit, sir! The ammo dump has been destroyed.

CAPTAIN: Good work, Sergeant. Commend the men on their swift obedience to orders.

SERGEANT: *(Salutes.)* Yes, sir!

RADIO OPERATOR: Message from HQ, sir.

CAPTAIN *(looking through binoculars)*: What is it? Read it to me. I'm busy.

RADIO OPERATOR: "Our commandos killed in explosion at ammo dump. Enemy breaking through on southern perimeter. Retreat from position and join with B Company at specified coordinates..."

CAPTAIN: Nonsense! We have the best defensive position we could hope for right here. Sergeant! Turn those guns around to the south.

SERGEANT: But, sir. The orders...

CAPTAIN: I'M giving the orders! We have to do everything ourselves. Those idiots at HQ have no idea what's really happening. Now go and obey my orders!

SERGEANT: *(Salutes.)* Yes, sir!

WRONG!

SCRIPTURE: 1 Samuel 28

SUGGESTED TOPICS: Listening to God; friendship; astrology

BIBLE BACKGROUND

After David spared Saul's life, Saul wept with guilt and admitted that David had no evil intent towards him. But Saul's change of heart concerning David did not last long. Soon he was chasing David again, seeking to destroy him. In spite of everything David had done, Saul still feared him as a threat. Perhaps because Saul knew the evil within himself, he was unable to trust the goodness in his most loyal ally.

Saul and David show the contrast between a person who seeks God and one who would rather do things his own way. As Saul moved further away from God, he did not repent and ask for God to forgive him. Instead, he sought out a witch, something forbidden in the Law as an abomination to God. David was not perfect, either. But when he saw his sin, he cried out to his heavenly Father for forgiveness and guidance.

PERFORMANCE TIPS

1. Suggested props: newspaper, table, Yellow Pages, Bible.
2. When April quotes the Bible, have her look up the passages. Consider having her actually read Deuteronomy 18:10-12.

DISCUSSION QUESTIONS

1. Why do people consult horoscopes, witches, fortune-tellers, etc.?
2. Read Deuteronomy 18:20. What is God's penalty for false prophets? Why do you think God would make the penalty so harsh?
3. Do friends always agree with each other? What makes a person a true friend?
4. What ways did April show her friendship to June?
5. What are some other ways friends can help you?

WRONG!

CHARACTERS
APRIL

JUNE

PRONUNCIATION GUIDE
diviners (dih-VINE-urs)

necromancers (NEK-row-man-sers)

APRIL: Hi, June. What are you doing?

JUNE: *(Looks up from newspaper.)* Hi, April. I'm trying to make a decision.

APRIL: What kind of decision?

JUNE: I'm trying to decide what to do with my life.

APRIL: Wow! Have you talked to people who could help you decide? Parents, teachers, counselors, your pastor? Not friends, I guess, because this is the first I've heard about it.

JUNE: No. I thought of something easier to help me.

APRIL: You're checking the want ads to see what's available?

JUNE: No. I'm reading my horoscope to see what the stars hold for me.

APRIL: You're not serious!

JUNE: Well, of course I'm serious. My life is serious stuff. I need the best advice I can get.

APRIL: Well, you won't find it there.

JUNE: *(Folds newspaper.)* I guess you're right.

(JUNE goes to table, picks up Yellow Pages and thumbs through them.)

APRIL: NOW what are you doing?

JUNE: Following your advice. You're right about newspaper horoscopes. I need an astrologer to make me a personal horoscope, just like you said.

APRIL: I didn't say that!

JUNE: Here's one, Mr. Armand. He sounds reliable.

APRIL: June, don't be crazy!

JUNE: You're right. I need a woman astrologer. She'll understand me better.

APRIL: What do you mean, "I'm right"? You're not listening to me! Don't consult astrologers and the stars. None of them can help you.

JUNE: There. Just like you said. Here's a better one. Madame Shasta. Sounds mystical. She'll be able to see my future.

APRIL: June! Look at me! Read my lips! DO...NOT...GO...TO...AN...ASTROLOGER! None of them can help you.

JUNE: Why not? Astrology is really catching on.

APRIL: Astrology may be popular, but it's not right.

JUNE: Sure it is. Even the Bible says so.

APRIL: Wrong! The Bible never says that.

JUNE: Sure it does. The wise men followed the star and it led them right to Jesus in Bethlehem.

APRIL: Are you sure about that?

JUNE: Sure. I see it every Christmas.

APRIL: If you read the Bible, you'll see that ONE star led the wise men to JERUSALEM. King Herod had the REAL wise men, the scribes and chief priests, consult the Scriptures to find where the Messiah was to be born. The wise men found Jesus in Bethlehem because they followed the Scriptures.

JUNE: Oh. Well. *(Thinks.)* I've got it. *(Looks into Yellow Pages again.)*

APRIL: Now what?

JUNE: Where do you think I should look for witches? I can't find any listing for them under *W*.

APRIL: Look under *E*, for evil.

JUNE: Evil? Oh, don't worry. I'd only consult a good witch.

APRIL: Don't you understand? There are no good witches.

JUNE: Oh, sure there are. They're called "white witches."

APRIL: Not according to God.

JUNE: What do you mean?

APRIL: In Deuteronomy 18:10-12, God calls ALL diviners, enchanters, witches, charmers, consulters of familiar spirits, wizards and necromancers DETESTABLE. Today, we call those people witches, astrologers, psychics, fortune-tellers.

JUNE: What does "detestable" mean?

APRIL: That's a word God uses to describe something He hates absolutely.

JUNE: Got it. I'll consult a prophet.

APRIL: No, no, no!

JUNE: But prophets are good! People always consulted them in the Bible.

APRIL: But how will you know you're consulting one of GOD'S prophets? Many times in the Bible, people consulted FALSE prophets—with awful consequences!

JUNE: I'll just find one with a good record.

APRIL: Will you find one with a perfect record?

JUNE: Of course not. Nobody's perfect.

APRIL: Then you'll be consulting a false prophet! If a prophet makes even ONE mistake, it means his information didn't come from God and that prophet is a phony!

JUNE: Then what can I do? How can I decide?

APRIL: Pray. Ask God to guide you. You don't need anyone to do that for you.

JUNE: But I don't know how to pray. I've never really done it before.

APRIL: I'll pray with you, if you'd like. We can ask God to show you what would be best for you and help you meet people who can help you make wise decisions.

JUNE: He's already doing that. Thanks, April. Friend.

WITHOUT A PREACHER

SCRIPTURE: Acts 8:26-40

SUGGESTED TOPICS: Witnessing; prejudice; salvation is for all people

BIBLE BACKGROUND

Fleeing persecution in Jerusalem and Judea, the Christians moved into Samaria and began preaching Jesus to the Samaritans. In the midst of this exciting time, Philip was called by God to leave the city and go out into the desert. There, in the middle of nowhere, Philip encountered a black man who was traveling home to Ethiopia. Using the words of the prophet, Isaiah, Philip introduced the man to Jesus. Now the Word was spread into Africa, for the black man was none other than the treasurer of the court of Candace, queen of Ethiopia. Acts 8 shows us that God intends to be God of all people—not only the Jews, not only the Samaritans, but all people.

PERFORMANCE TIPS

1. Suggested props: several books, a Bible and bookmark.
2. Either before or during the skit when the Bible passage is mentioned, read Isaiah 53:7,8.
3. The nationality of the people playing the parts of Malcolm and Phil is unimportant. If you have a mixed ethnic group, you might ask a Caucasian to play the part of Malcolm and someone of another race to play the part of Phil.

DISCUSSION QUESTIONS

1. In the skit, Malcolm is unsure about the beliefs of his religion. Why is it important to know what you believe?
2. What does 1 Peter 3:15 say you should be ready to do? How can you better prepare yourself to explain your beliefs to others?
3. Do you agree or disagree with the statement, "It's not important what you believe. It's only important that you believe something." Why or why not?
4. If you are a Christian, should you be friends with someone who isn't? Why or why not?

WITHOUT A PREACHER

CHARACTERS

PHIL

MALCOLM

SCENE ONE

PHIL: Hey, Malcolm!

MALCOLM: What? Oh. Hi, Phil.

PHIL: Where are you going?

MALCOLM: Just to the store. Errand for Mom. What about you?

PHIL: I'm off to the library. Have to return these books before the holiday. By the way, Happy Easter.

MALCOLM: What?

PHIL: Happy Easter. This Sunday. Easter. Remember?

MALCOLM: Easter! *(Sneers.)* White man's religion.

PHIL: What do you mean?

MALCOLM: Christianity! It only works for whites.

PHIL: You don't really mean that.

MALCOLM: I sure do.

PHIL: Then what do you believe?

MALCOLM: Islam. That's the belief of my people.

PHIL: We have got to talk. But I have to get these books returned and you have to get your Mom's groceries. Could I come over to your place tonight so we can talk?

MALCOLM: You mean so you can shove the Bible down my throat. No thanks. Besides, I have to baby-sit my kid sister tonight.

PHIL: I like kids. How about if I help? And we can talk, not argue.

MALCOLM: Well, I guess so. But I won't change my mind.

(Skit continues on next page.)

The Big Book of Bible Skits ©1997 Gospel Light. Permission to photocopy granted.

SCENE TWO

MALCOLM: I figured you'd bring your Bible.

PHIL: Of course. How else can I show you what I believe? And why.

MALCOLM: I suppose. But you won't get me believing white man's religion.

PHIL: Why do you call Christianity "white man's religion"?

MALCOLM: Because it is. Islam is the religion for blacks.

PHIL: But they both started in the same part of the world.

MALCOLM: What are you talking about?

PHIL: Who started Islam?

MALCOLM: Mohammed. The great prophet.

PHIL: And he was an Arab. From the Middle East. Christianity grew out of Judaism, also from the Middle East. So they're both Middle Eastern religions if that's how you judge.

MALCOLM: Well, Islam is for blacks and Christianity for whites.

PHIL: Can I show you something from this book?

MALCOLM: Why should I believe anything from it?

PHIL: Because it's from the prophet, Isaiah.

MALCOLM: So?

PHIL: Islam recognizes Isaiah as a prophet.

MALCOLM: It does?

PHIL: Yes. I thought you knew about Islam?

MALCOLM: Well, I'm kind of new. I don't know everything yet.

PHIL: Look at chapter fifty-three. What do you think it means?

MALCOLM: *(Reads chapter silently.)* I don't know. Sounds like somebody's being oppressed. Who? The prophet or somebody else?

PHIL: Somebody else asked the same question. A black man.

MALCOLM: What black man?

PHIL: Let's look at the book of Acts.

MALCOLM: White man's book.

PHIL: No, it's a book for everybody. And it shows who asked the question. Look in chapter eight, verse thirty-four.

MALCOLM: So. He asked the same question. Why do you say he was black?

PHIL: Look back a few verses. Who was he?

MALCOLM: An Ethiopian.

PHIL: Right. So let's look back at the prophet.

MALCOLM: OK. So who is the prophet talking about?

PHIL: He's talking about Jesus.

MALCOLM: No way. I may not know a lot, but I know Jesus wasn't even born then.

PHIL: But the prophet was talking about the future. Prophets do that, if they're true prophets.

MALCOLM: You expect me to believe that?

PHIL: Islam believes it.

MALCOLM: OK, then. How do you know it means Jesus?

PHIL: Because He fits the description perfectly.

MALCOLM (scornfully): Yeah? Prove it.

PHIL: You see the first part of the chapter? A man despised, rejected, someone not held in esteem.

MALCOLM: Sounds like a black man gettin' dumped on.

PHIL: Or a Galilean.

MALCOLM: Huh?

PHIL: Jesus came from Galilee. And He knew about prejudice.

MALCOLM: How? He was a Jew living in Israel.

PHIL: But Galileans were looked down on by the rest of Israel. Other Jews thought that they were second-class citizens, not very bright. See, prejudice isn't new. It's existed for centuries.

MALCOLM: So, people were prejudiced against Him. So what?

PHIL: So, when He was crucified, all His friends ran away. Left Him to face punishment alone.

MALCOLM: His friends deserted Him?

PHIL: They sure did. But read on.

MALCOLM: It says we thought He was being punished by God.

PHIL: Which is exactly why Jesus was found guilty by the Jewish court. They believed that He was a blasphemer.

MALCOLM: What's that?

PHIL: In Jesus' case, someone who claims to be God. And under Jewish law, God says that blasphemers are to be put to death.

MALCOLM: That sounds rough.

PHIL: But look at the rest of the chapter. Why was He bruised, wounded and oppressed?

MALCOLM: It says He was killed because of us?

PHIL: That's right. He was killed because people—all people—had sinned. Not just white people or black people. Not just one nation. But all people.

MALCOLM: But that's not fair.

PHIL: True. But it IS loving. Look closely at verse seven. He didn't try to defend Himself. He accepted our punishment. Not because He was guilty, but because He knew the only way to save us was to pay the price for our guilt Himself.

MALCOLM: Why would He do that?

PHIL: Because God loves ALL His people. Regardless of race or skin color or nationality. God wants people to have the best life they can. But sin blocks people from God's love. So God took the punishment Himself.

MALCOLM: Wait a minute. You're trying to trick me. Why should I believe that Jesus is God? Only Christians believe that.

PHIL: You should believe Jesus' words, because Islam recognizes Jesus as a prophet.

MALCOLM: It does?

PHIL: Yes. Are you sure you believe in Islam? You don't seem to know a lot about it.

MALCOLM: I told you I'm new at it.

PHIL: True. Tell you what. You read what Jesus said about Himself and we can talk again.

MALCOLM: You leaving?

PHIL: Yeah, you can use some time to think abut Jesus' words. We'll talk about it again. I'll leave my Bible for you to read. In the meantime, Happy Easter.

MALCOLM: Yeah. You, too. Bye.

BIBLICAL CHARACTER INDEX

Scripture Index

TOPICAL INDEX

ASTROLOGY

use of ("Wrong!" p. 426)

CHARACTER

trustworthy ("Last but Not Least," p. 89; "This Is Comfort?" p. 186)

CHOICES

making wise ("Can I?" p. 340; "Decisions," p. 129; "Emergency," p. 326; "Greeting Cards," p. 102; "Israeli Home Shopping Club," p. 106; "One Right Road," p. 381; "The Orpah Show [David's Desire]," p. 113; "The Scourge of Jerusalem, " p. 315; "There's Fruit and There's Fruit," p. 417; "Unfair," p. 420; "You Can Be King," p. 140)

showing compassion ("The Fugitive," p. 97)

CHRISTIAN LIFE

armor of God ("Knight Without Armor," p. 370)

contentment ("I Am Content," p. 362)

fruit of the Spirit ("There's Fruit and There's Fruit," p. 417)

godly vs. worldly values ("Make a Deal," p. 27)

heritage ("Remember," p. 389)

putting it into practice ("The Bully," p. 337; "Encourage One Another," p. 354; "Love, Love, Love," p. 374; "Oceanfront Property," p. 220)

CONFESSION

of sin ("Dumb, Dumb, Dumb," p. 175)

CONFLICT

handling of ("Encourage One Another," p. 354; "Standing Firm," p. 413; "Temptation in the Wilderness," p. 207)

opposition to the early church ("Crippled," p. 270; "Open Doors," p. 274; "Troublemakers," p. 305)

response to injustice ("Riot," p. 396; "Unfair," p. 420)

COURAGE

acting with ("Emergency," p. 326; "The Plot Thickens," p. 320; "Risky Business," p. 181; "Standing Firm," p. 413; "The Writing on the Wall," p. 190)

handling fear ("The Call of Gideon," p. 51)

under persecution ("The Bully," p. 337; "Free!" p. 297; "Heckling Hezekiah," p. 161; "Open Doors," p. 274)

SACRIFICE

attitude toward ("Demonstration," p. 345; "Sacrifice Until It Kind of Hurts," p. 242)

in giving ("Waste Nard, Want Nard," p. 240)

Jesus, the ultimate ("The Sacrifice," p. 406)

SALVATION

for everyone ("The Gentiles, Too?," p. 292; "Triple P Trial," p. 285; "Without a Preacher," p. 429)

God's plan fulfilled ("The Sacrifice," p. 406; "He's Alive!" p. 254)

God's plan of ("Devil's Retreat," p. 13; "Nicodemus," p. 210; "Sacrifice Until It Kind of Hurts," p. 242; "The Savior," p. 9)

Jesus' victory ("He Arose," p. 250)

SAVIOR

acts of ("It's a Miracle," p. 234)

coming of ("Christmas Quiz," p. 199

events surrounding birth ("The Birth of John," p. 195; "Herod," p. 203)

events surrounding death and resurrection ("He's Alive!" p. 254; "Remember," p. 389; "The Sacrifice," p. 406; "Trials, Trials, Trials," p. 245)

our need for ("The Savior," p. 9, "This Is Comfort?" p. 186)

role of ("Sacrifice Until It Kind of Hurts," p. 242)

SELF-CONTROL

of speech ("Silence Is Golden," p. 409)

SERVING OTHERS

Jesus washes feet ("Going Fishing," p. 259)

with talents and abilities ("Mine, Mine, Mine," p. 377)

SIN

consequences of ("Achan Brings Home the Bacon," p. 39; "Ai!" p. 43; "Count the Cost," p. 125; "Judge, Not!" p. 82; "The Orpah Show [David's Desire]," p. 113; "Trust and Obey," p. 157)

salvation from ("The Savior," p. 9)

SPREADING THE GOSPEL

disciples and early church ("Acts," p. 267; "Crippled," p. 270; "Good News," p. 263; "The Gentiles, Too?" p. 292; "Paphos by Night," p. 299; "Open Doors," p. 274; "Samaria Today," p. 280; "Troublemakers," p. 305)

need for Christ ("The Savior," p. 9)

to contemporary Islam ("Without a Preacher," p. 429)

to Gentiles ("The Gentiles, Too?" p. 292; "Triple P Trial," p. 285)

CPSIA information can be obtained at www.ICGtesting.com
Printed in the USA
LVOW09s1940201213

366165LV00002B/2/P